Trade Policy Reform

Lessons and Implications

WORLD BANK

REGIONAL AND

SECTORAL STUDIES

Trade Policy Reform

Lessons and Implications

EDITED BY

JOHN NASH

WENDY TAKACS

The World Bank
Washington, D.C.

The World Bank Regional and Sectoral Studies series provides an outlet for work that is relatively focused in its subject matter or geographic coverage and that contributes to the intellectual foundations of development operations and policy formulation. Some sources cited in this publication may be informal documents that are not readily available.

John Nash is a principal economist in the Environmentally and Socially Sustainable Development Unit, Europe and Central Asia Regional Office, the World Bank. Wendy Takacs is a professor of economics at University of Maryland, Baltimore County, and a professorial lecturer at Johns Hopkins School of Advanced International Studies.

Cover design by Sam Ferro.

Library of Congress Cataloging-in-Publication Data

Trade policy reform : lessons and implications / edited by John Nash,
  Wendy Takacs.
      p. cm. — (World Bank regional and sectoral studies)
    Based on 1995 final of the UNDP/World Bank Trade Expansion
  Program
    Includes bibliographical references and index.
    ISBN 0-8213-3983-4
    1. Developing countries—Commercial policy. 2. Economic
development. I. Nash, John D., 1953-   . II. Takacs, Wendy E.
III. UNDP/World Bank Trade Expansion Program. IV. Series.
HF1413.T733   1998
382'.091724—dc21
                                          98-10663
                                             CIP

Contents

Tables

Preface and Acknowledgments

Trade policy reform has been the cornerstone of most economic liberalization and structural adjustment programs in the developing world. But trade policy reform is a complicated matter. First, governments start out with a wide range of overlapping and interacting trade policy instruments: tariffs, surcharges, import deposit requirements, import and export prohibitions, domestic content regulations, reference prices, import and export quotas, exchange control regulations, and import and export licensing. Even that list is not exhaustive. To further complicate matters, trade policy reform interacts with other policy measures, including labor market regulations, foreign investment laws, price controls, and other regulatory restrictions, especially in the transportation and communications industries. Policymakers contemplating trade reform must also be concerned with its fiscal impacts, and with coordinating the reform program with monetary and exchange rate policies.

Given this panoply of issues, many countries have felt the need for independent technical expertise in designing and implementing reform programs. In response, the United Nations Development Programme (UNDP) and the World Bank agreed in 1987 to set up the Trade Expansion Program (TEP) to provide practical technical assistance to countries seeking to strengthen their links to the world economy.

The intention behind TEP was to provide independent advice on trade policy reform with "no strings attached"; in other words, without the the usual conditionality attached to loans from the International Monetary Fund or the World Bank. At the time TEP was initiated, the World Bank was completing a comparative study prepared by Michel Michaely, Armeane Choksi, and Demetrios Papageorgiou on the experience of trade reform in the 1960s and 1970s and was preparing to update it to include the experience of trade policy reform under adjustment lending in the 1980s based on a study carried out by Vinod Thomas, John Nash, and associates. In a broad sense the mandate of TEP was to give customized advice to those countries wanting to be included in the program, taking into account, when relevant, the experience gathered from these studies.

From the beginning an effort was made to include countries that to date had received relatively little trade policy advice, and with relatively little previous engagement with trade policy reform. The program was not intended for large countries with domestic expertise and access to other sources of external advice. Another goal was to maintain worldwide coverage but especially to attempt to include poor Sub-Saharan African countries with little experience in sustained trade policy reform. Once the movement toward reform in the previously centrally planned economies of Eastern Europe and the former Soviet republics began, it became apparent that policy advice for transitional economies would also be helpful.

Thus the core of TEP's work was a series of technical assistance projects to seventeen countries. The group included seven countries in Africa (Kenya, Madagascar, Mali, Mauritius, Morocco, Uganda, and Zimbabwe), four in Latin America (Costa Rica, Guatemala, Peru, and Uruguay), four in Eastern Europe (Czechoslovakia, Georgia, Poland, and Romania), and two in Asia (Mongolia and Vietnam). Six of the countries' economies were in transition. Each project began with a request from the government of the country to the UNDP for a TEP program. TEP staff and country officials charged with formulating trade policy met to agree on topics to be addressed by the study. The issues addressed by each country study varied depending on the technical assistance needs of each country, the particular types of trade barriers in effect, and the major issues of trade reform currently being discussed.

After identifying topics to be addressed, TEP staff identified and recruited individual consultants and World Bank staff members with expertise in those particular areas to participate on the country team. The team, which ranged from five to eleven members depending on the scope of the project, visited the country for a period of two to three weeks for intensive discussions of the selected issues with government officials and representatives from the private sector. At the end of the visit, the team drafted an *aide-mémoire*, or technical note of preliminary findings, that was discussed with key policymakers. The team finished the analysis and prepared a draft report. Certain members of the team and TEP staff representatives returned to the country to present and discuss the draft report with government officials, or in workshops attended by government officials, academics, and representatives of the private sector. Each country study was revised on the basis of these discussions, professionally edited, and published. A list of the country reports is provided in appendix A.

The comparative work across countries reveals a remarkable diversity of conditions and circumstances, which required unique strategies for design and implementation. Nonetheless, many issues were common across countries, such as the importance of macroeconomic stability and the question of what policies would best promote expansion of high value added nontraditional exports. Some questions arose repeatedly in the individual country studies, and, as experience accumulated, certain themes began to emerge that can provide guidance to other countries contemplating trade reform. TEP commissioned investigations of these issues, which appeared as a series of occasional papers or as papers presented at conferences in Kiev, New Delhi, and Washington. The program also sponsored special studies of trade policy issues in the former Soviet republics and Sub-Saharan Africa. The occasional papers, special studies, and conference volumes published by TEP are listed in appendix A.

The papers in this volume were presented at the final conference sponsored by TEP. Its premise was that policymakers, practitioners, and academics could greatly benefit from better understanding the viewpoints of the other groups. Participants in the conference included government officials responsible for trade policy in TEP project countries, practitioners involved in administering trade policy instruments, academics specializing in international trade issues, and staff members of international organizations. The two participants invited to comment formally on each paper were high-level government officials or practitioners in countries in which the topic of the paper played an important role in trade policy. Most had played a prominent role in designing and implementing trade reforms in their respective countries. Later the floor was opened for general discussion. The formal comments and subsequent discussion provided opportunities for lively interaction between conceptual and pragmatic points of view. The first chapter of this volume provides an overview of some of the "lessons" from the cumulated experience of TEP, drawing primarily on the conference papers and the discussion they provoked, and, when appropriate, on individual country reports and other literature. The papers themselves make up the rest of the volume.

Because of the diversity of backgrounds and current positions of the participants, the issues addressed in the papers range from rather abstract (what makes trade reforms politically sustainable?) to intensely pragmatic (what is the most practical design for a duty drawback system or a technical assistance program?). Readers of this volume are likely to be similarly diverse in their interests and should benefit from the cross-fertilization of ideas produced by the different perspectives of its contributors.

The editors wish to thank those who worked so hard to prepare first the conference and then this volume. They include Nen Castillo, Gabriel Castillo, Sarah Lipscomb, and Jennifer Ngaine of the International Trade Division, as well as Deirdre Teresa Ruffino of the World Bank's Office of the Publisher and Rebecca Kary of Alpha-Omega Services, Inc., who handled the copyediting and production of the volume.

Contributors

Elliot Berg is vice president for policy and research at Development Alternatives, Inc., in Bethesda, Maryland, and an adjunct professor at the University of Auvergne in France.

Shui-Chi Chuang is at the Ministry of Finance, Department of Customs and Administration, Taiwan, China.

Paul Collier is director of the Centre for Study of African Economics, Oxford University, and director of the Development Research Group of the World Bank.

Jaime de Melo is a professor at the University of Geneva and CERDI.

J. Michael Finger is lead economist at the World Bank, International Trade Division.

Rebecca Hardy was a project assistant with the World Bank, International Trade Division.

Ann Harrison is a professor at Columbia University and the National Bureau of Economic Research.

Ron Hood is an economist at R. D. Hood Economics in Vienna, Virginia.

John Nash is a principal economist at the World Bank, Europe and Central Asia Region.

Arvind Panagariya is a professor of economics at the University of Maryland and co-director of the Center for International Economics, College Park, Maryland.

Ana Revenga is the program team leader for Armenia and Georgia at the World Bank.

Wendy Takacs is a professor at the University of Maryland, Baltimore County.

Alberto Valdés is an agricultural adviser at the World Bank, Latin America and the Caribbean Region.

Chia-Sheng Wu is at the Ministry of Finance, Department of Customs and Administration, Taiwan, China.

Acronyms and Abbreviations

AD	Antidumping
AFTA	ASEAN Free Trade Area
ANCOM	Andean Common Market
ASEAN	Association of Southeast Asian Nations
BOP	Balance of payments
CACM	Central American Common Market
CAPAS	Coordinated African Program of Assistance Services
CARICOM	Caribbean Community
CAT	*Certificado de abono tributario* (tax rebate certificate)
CBI	Caribbean Basin Initiative
CEE	Central and Eastern Europe
CENPRO	Center for the Promotion of Exports and Investments
CET	Common external tariff
CFA	French franc zone
CGE	Computable general equilibrium
CIF	Cost, insurance, and freight
CIS	Commonwealth of Independent States
CMEA	Council for Mutual Economic Assistance
COMESA	Common Market for Eastern and Southern African States
CPI	Consumer price index
CSI	*Comité de Suivi des Importations*
CUFTA	Canada-U.S. Free Trade Area
CVD	Countervailing duties
EA	European Agreement
EBRD	European Bank for Reconstruction and Development
EC	European Community
ECOWAS	Economic Community of Western African States
EDS	External debt service
EEC	European Economic Community
EFTA	European Free Trade Area
EMS	European Monetary System
EPZ	Export-processing zone
EQR	Export quantitative restriction

ER	Exchange rate
ERP	Effective rate of protection
EU	European Union
FDI	Foreign direct investment
FOB	Free-on-board
FSU	Former Soviet Union
FTA	Free trade agreement
FTAA	Free Trade Area of the Americas
GATT	General Agreement on Tariffs and Trade
GDP	Gross domestic product
GNP	Gross national product
GSP	Generalized System of Preferences
IDRC	International Development Research Centre
ILO	International Labour Organisation
IMF	International Monetary Fund
INDECOPI	National Institute for the Defense of Competition and the Protection of Intellectual Property
ITA	Interim trade agreement
LAIA	Latin American Integration Association
LATAD	Advisory Group, Technical Department, Latin America and the Caribbean Region, the World Bank
MEF	Ministry of Economy and Finance
MERCOSUR	Southern Cone Common Market
MFA	Multifibre Arrangement
MFN	Most favored nation
MITINCI	Ministry of Industry, Tourism, Integration, and International Trade Negotiations
MOEA	Ministry of Economic Affairs
MTN	Multilateral Trade Negotiations
MTT	Ministry of Trade and Tourism
NAFTA	North American Free Trade Agreement
NBER	National Bureau of Economic Research
NGO	Nongovernmental organization
NRP	Nominal rate of protection
NTB	Nontariff barrier
OECD	Organisation for Economic Co-operation and Development
PSE	Producer subsidy equivalent
QR	Quantitative restriction
RER	Real exchange rate
SACU	Southern African Customs Union
SAL	Structural adjustment loan
SOE	State-owned enterprise

SSA	Sub-Saharan Africa
TEP	Trade Expansion Program
U.S.S.R.	Union of Soviet Socialist Republics
UDEAC	Customs and Economic Union of Central Africa
UN	United Nations
UNCTAD	United Nations Conference on Trade and Development
UNDP	United Nations Development Programme
VAT	Value added tax
WTO	World Trade Organization

1

Lessons from the Trade Expansion Program

John Nash and Wendy Takacs

Although each country project of the United Nations Development Program (UNDP)/World Bank Trade Expansion Program (TEP) addressed trade policy reform issues of particular concern in that country, many common issues, questions, and problems were found, with different nuances depending on particular circumstances faced by each country. Over time, as additional country reports and special issue-oriented studies were completed, certain themes began to emerge and general guidelines could be formulated to help countries design their trade reform programs.

In this introductory chapter we provide an overview of these themes, which were the focus of the final TEP Conference in Washington, D.C., in January 1995. We draw primarily on the papers and the discussion they provoked, but also on individual country reports and other literature, to summarize the lessons for trade policy reform that emerged from the experience of TEP.

Macroeconomic Stability

Lesson: Trade policy reform is facilitated by macroeconomic stability but need not wait until macroeconomic stability is fully attained. Trade policy and macroeconomic policy are linked in many ways. In the first place, many trade and foreign exchange restrictions are reactions to balance of payment problems brought on by fiscal and monetary imbalances. The corollary is that these restrictions are difficult to remove until underlying imbalances are corrected. One study of twenty-four countries receiving adjustment loans based on trade policy reforms showed that the relatively strong reformers were those that on average showed improvements in inflation rates, fiscal balances, and resource balances; those with weak reforms or that backtracked showed on average deterioration, or only small improvements, in these macroeconomic performance indicators (Thomas and others 1991). The recognition that stability contributes to the success of reforms is why the World Bank generally insists on an International Monetary Fund (IMF)–backed program as a precondition for adjustment loans. This connection is recognized by the private sector, as well. As

Arap Ng'ok of Kenya pointed out in this conference, the lack of an IMF program in Kenya after December 1991 undermined the credibility of trade liberalization in the eyes of the public, and eventually contributed to its suspension in March 1993. The reforms got back on track after a new IMF program was put in place in April 1993 and have progressed well since then.

Exchange rate policy also is crucial to trade policy reform. Most countries start out with an unsustainably appreciated real exchange rate (RER), in the sense that the value of imports far exceeds that of exports (and sustainable capital flows). This indicates that the real rate is appreciated to a level above its long-run equilibrium, given the degree of restrictiveness of trade policy, even before the reforms begin. The reforms themselves depreciate the long-run equilibrium level of the rate; thus, the need for real currency devaluation is all the more pressing. Devaluation also serves a political economic function in support of liberalization. By raising border prices in relation to domestic prices of import-restricted goods, it reduces the premium to holders of import or foreign exchange licenses, thereby reducing the incentive for them to lobby for retention of the status quo.

It is generally agreed that trade reforms are more likely to be successful if they occur under conditions of relative macroeconomic stability; but, if there is a clear need for both reforms and macroeconomic stabilization, should reforms be delayed? Many analysts have said "yes" (see, for example, Corbo and Fisher 1992) because high inflation usually results in high price variability, confusing the signals that trade reform is designed to send. Also, some reforms exacerbate the fiscal problems faced by economies in need of stabilization; and, perhaps most important, trade reforms generally require a real depreciation, which is more difficult when the nominal exchange rate is being used as an anti-inflationary anchor.

Indeed, the argument that trade reforms should await the reestablishment of a reasonable degree of stability seems to find support in the large number of countries where reforms have foundered on the shoals of macroeconomic problems (Michaely, Choksi, and Papageorgiou 1990). Yet there are many counterexamples as well. It is probably safe to say that the majority of successful (to date) cases of trade liberalization were undertaken simultaneously with stabilization programs. Clearly there are other factors at work that help determine the success or failure of trade reforms, and in general a wise policy would be to take advantage of the situation whenever a politically propitious window of opportunity opens.

Why has reform been successful even when not sequenced in accordance with the standard prescription? One clear political economic lesson emerging from the experience of the TEP countries and many others is that governments born in dire circumstances seem to have a broad mandate during a "honeymoon" period, when they can move on many fronts simultaneously (de Melo, chapter 2 in this volume; see also Haggard and Webb 1994). One reason for this is that economic crisis changes the political cost-benefit tradeoff, making the efficiency gains large in relation to the rents that reform will redistribute (Rodrik 1994). Another factor suggested by de Melo is that when reforms are "bundled," as in the "big bang" approach, many interest groups can find something they can identify as clearly benefiting them. If the main reason for opposing reform is uncertainty, this will reduce the strength of the opposition.

This helps explain why, among the TEP countries, the Eastern Europeans and Peru carried out successful stabilization programs at the same time they were lowering barriers to trade and implementing many other reforms. In these countries, the "big bang" was a success. In this conference a participant in Peru's reforms, Fritz du Bois, even expressed regret that the bang was not bigger. He feared that after the honeymoon it will take until the turn of the century to do the relatively few important things that remain on the reform agenda. To be sure, there have been minor reversals (in Poland, for example), but no wholesale backsliding. Nor has it been true that the reformist governments have been thrown out across the board. This has happened in some cases such as Poland, but in others (Peru in the TEP group, and others such as Argentina and Brazil) the governments retain considerable popularity.

But even countries that were not undergoing radical regime changes have been able to successfully undertake trade liberalization and macroeconomic stabilization simultaneously. The evidence cited above (Thomas and others 1991) showed that macroeconomic performance can be improved while trade is being liberalized. This same study and others (for example, Edwards 1989) discuss numerous examples of countries that have significantly devalued their currency while reducing high inflation rates, thereby reconciling the major putative inconsistency between reform and stabilization. It is worth noting as well that in some ways trade policy reform reinforces stabilization. For example, removal of quantitative controls on imports and eliminating exemptions—both standard components of reform packages—will generally raise revenues, helping bring the fiscal deficit under control. Lowering tariffs may reduce revenues but will lower import prices (as will removal of quantitative controls), helping fight inflation, if other means can reduce the fiscal and monetary imbalances. The main lesson here is that carrying out trade policy reform requires strong fiscal discipline; reforms have little chance of survival if stabilization is postponed. Deft exchange rate management is also required, but in most cases this ultimately rests on fiscal discipline.

Foreign Exchange Allocation

Lesson: Trade policy reform will only work when the mechanisms for allocating foreign exchange work. Discussions of trade policy reform focus much more attention on the appropriate level of the exchange rate and the mechanisms for adjusting it (fixed, clean float, dirty float, auctions, and so on) than on the mechanisms for allocating it. Yet foreign exchange is the lifeblood of a small economy; and, without an efficient way of distributing it, production, consumption, and trade will be adversely affected.

Foreign exchange restrictions not only restrict imports, they create big headaches for exporters. The main complaint of exporters is that they cannot get foreign exchange when they need it because the government allocates foreign exchange to other priorities. Regulations that force exporters to repatriate earnings at a low official rate of exchange require paperwork and red tape for enforcement.

Attempts to correct problems caused by distortions in the foreign exchange market frequently just multiply the distortions. In Mongolia, for example, state enterprises were required to surrender from 55 to 100 percent of their export earnings at the official exchange rate. Private firms were able to convert at the free market rate and received up to six times as much domestic currency per unit of foreign exchange. Under these conditions, state enterprises buying raw materials to process into products for export had trouble competing with private raw materials exporters who could outbid them in raw materials markets. This distortion in the foreign exchange market put tremendous competitive pressure on processing industries and threatened their financial solvency. The government justified quantitative export restrictions on raw materials (another distortion) as a way of assuring that the surrender requirements did not deprive domestic industries of raw materials.

Countries with highly restrictive trade regimes frequently also control access to foreign exchange as a redundant tool, on top of import licensing, to control imports. In these cases trade policy reforms have usually involved creation of or significant liberalization of exchange markets. In the 1980s and 1990s, this has been especially true in Sub-Saharan Africa (SSA) and the transitional economies. In Africa, lack of efficient foreign exchange markets has been the single most important obstacle to successful trade reform.

Most countries in SSA and the transitional economies are still in the process of making the transition to a relatively free market in foreign exchange (in other words, convertibility). Most SSA countries have made this transition slowly, passing through a number of stages involving mechanisms such as own funds import schemes, gradually expanding exporter retention of earnings, open general licensing, auctions, and, finally, an interbank market with convertible currency. So far, only a few (including Ghana, Uganda, and Zimbabwe) have made this last step. Most of the transitional economies have made faster progress, and in particular have skipped the stages using own funds schemes and open general licensing, although many do not yet have convertible currencies or well-functioning interbank markets.

For countries that are still in the process of reform of foreign exchange allocation mechanisms, there are a number of lessons worth learning from those that have gone before. A comprehensive discussion of these lessons is beyond the purview of this chapter; however, a few general lessons are worth noting here.[1]

First, transition mechanisms such as own funds schemes, gradually increasing retention rates, and open general import licensing schemes represent only very limited progress. They have significant shortcomings in relation to market allocation. There seems to be very little reason to use them; going straight to an auction may be the best way. An auction at least has the crucial advantage of incorporating an endogenous price-setting mechanism, the lack of which has been one of the biggest problems for the other schemes. Until now, even auctions have not really created market sales agents because they have been run by central banks. As Collier (chapter 3 in this volume) notes, however, there is no inherent reason why this should be true, and it may be worthwhile to set up an auction run by commercial banks, thereby better training them for their eventual role as buyers and sellers in a market system. In any case, the shortcomings of all these systems argue for a quick transition to convertibility.

Second, the success of any of these schemes is dependent on maintenance of a realistic level of the exchange rate. Reluctance to devalue when needed has resulted in shortages, queuing, and other forms of rationing in the schemes that do not endogenously determine price. Even in several countries using auctions (notably Nigeria and Zambia), governments did not want to see the currency depreciate and intervened by tampering with the auction, vitiating much of its benefit. Collier notes that this has especially been a problem in countries where the auction proceeds do not go to the federal government, implying a reduced incentive to maximize the proceeds by getting the highest possible price for the foreign exchange.[2]

Even in developing countries where foreign exchange allocation is done by a free market mechanism, the lack of forward markets is a serious deficiency. In industrial countries, by contrast, most foreign exchange transactions are in the forward market because buying exchange in the forward market allows planning without risk of unexpected exchange rate movements. In countries without a forward market, traders are exposed to large risks. As a consequence of this, in Uganda in mid-1994 some traders preferred to default on contracts and pay a 10 percent penalty rather than take the loss from the movement in the exchange rate.

---

1. La Ferrara, Castillo, and Nash (1994) discuss in a comprehensive manner the many variants of transition mechanisms. Aron and Elbedawi (1994) give a more in-depth discussion of auctions in several SSA countries.

2. Nigeria might seem to be the exception because the foreign exchange came from the sales of the government oil company. However, much of the revenue from the sale went to the state governments under a revenue-sharing formula.

One possible reason that forward markets have been slow to develop is that the private sector still lacks confidence that the government would refrain from intervention if there were a significant amount of speculative activity, which would in fact be necessary to develop a forward market. But another reason is that these markets are simply too small to support the volume of trade that would make the market thick enough to be viable. And it would be a mistake for the central banks to try to perform a speculative role, given their lack of expertise and the potential for huge losses.

One alternative strategy would be to form regional currency boards, as a number of African countries did in the past. This might create a viable size of market. Collier argues that the usual argument against a multinational currency carries little weight in African countries, where prices tend to be highly flexible *de facto* if not *de jure*. Furthermore, this approach would have the concomitant benefits of imposing greater macroeconomic restraint (it would essentially make regional exchange rate policy independent of national fiscal policy) and of avoiding the kind of exchange rate misalignments among neighboring countries that often lead to capital flight and smuggling.

Another approach would be to make currencies fully convertible on capital as well as current account. This could encourage the development of forward markets in the large international financial centers. There is, of course, no guarantee that agents in these centers would find it economical to invest in development of expertise in these currencies. But it seems more likely that this would happen than that such expertise would be developed or imported in the individual countries themselves. The likelihood of development of international forward markets would be increased if there were several such currencies of similar countries, so that there would be some economies of scale in creating a derivatives market. In any case, capital account convertibility has a number of concomitant benefits, including imposing macroeconomic restraint and encouraging risk diversification (Nash 1990).

The main lesson is that ensuring the right exchange rate is important in a trade reform program, but the right exchange rate alone is not enough. The entire foreign exchange market mechanism must be flexible, transparent, and efficient. In practice what this means is a currency that is essentially convertible, at least for current account transactions. In a transition period, a minimum requirement for export response is for exporters to have automatic, quick access to foreign currency at the best rate, and full funding for duty drawback. As long as the allocation of foreign exchange for some or all imports is discretionary, import liberalization cannot advance very far because protection remains opaque and dispersed.

Credibility of Reforms

Lesson: Trade reforms will only induce behavior that makes them self-sustaining if the reforms are credible. To have the salutary effect of which they are capable, trade policy reforms must last. Yet the history of developing countries is littered with cases of trade reforms that were planned but never carried out, or implemented only to be reversed after a short time. Two of the most significant issues in trade policy analysis are the factors that contribute to implementation of reforms in the first place and their sustainability.

Perhaps the most important factor is credibility. It is well recognized that policy reforms will only induce the response by economic agents that makes them self-sustaining if it is widely believed they will endure. Rodrik (1994) even notes that credibility may weaken the putative inconsistency between trade liberalization and stabilization.[3]

But what makes reforms credible? Several factors were identified in the conference papers and discussion. De Melo (chapter 2 in this volume) notes that the breakup of the Council for Mutual Economic Assistance (CMEA) made it clear that there could be no return to the old system of trade in the transitional economies. He also notes that the European Agreements (EAs) and the prospect of joining the European Union (EU) were very important for the credibility of trade reforms in Eastern European countries. Conversely, he argues that the absence of prospective EU membership made progress harder in Morocco.

More generally, membership in a regional arrangement, especially one linking a small reforming economy with a large liberal one, could in principle increase the credibility of reform. De Melo argues that Southern Cone Common Market (MERCOSUR) membership helped cement Uruguay's trade liberalization, and this argument is often applied to Mexico's membership in the North American Free Trade Agreement (NAFTA); however, the issue is not entirely clear, as the discussion of regional arrangements below points out.

In a similar vein, Collier argues that trade reforms in SSA have lacked credibility precisely because they were not "locked in" by some external mechanism. Regional arrangements in SSA could not perform this lock-in role because they have been generally ineffective, in the sense that members pay little attention to the rules; and, in any case, the rules themselves have been notoriously illiberal. The Lome agreement is unilaterally concessionary; that is, it does not bind the "beneficiary" countries in any way. And the

---

3. The argument goes as follows: If reforms are believed to be permanent, nominal wages may not be rigid in relation to the nominal exchange rate. Thus, it may be easier to obtain a real devaluation even with a fixed nominal exchange rate.

countries of SSA have not used the General Agreement on Tariffs and Trade (GATT), including the Uruguay Round, to signal permanence of trade reforms, as have some other countries such as Morocco and Mexico (Harrold 1995). The only external locking-in mechanism in SSA has been the conditionality of the donor community, which has been largely a "paper tiger." Although there have been exceptions (Rundheersing Bheenick noted that donor conditionality was helpful in Mauritius), Collier's argument is supported by the fact that until very recently donors continued to disburse policy-based loans even to a number of countries that continually failed to meet the trade policy conditions of the loans (Foroutan 1993). More recently, suspension of lending relationships with some of these countries (for example, Kenya and Senegal) seems to have reversed this pattern.

Internal factors have also been important in making reforms credible and sustainable. De Melo (chapter 2 in this volume) notes the importance in this respect of the "social contract" between workers and the government in the Czech Republic. (Similar arrangements have had good results in other countries, such as Mexico.) In other cases, the sheer boldness of the reform package increased its credibility. During discussion of this issue, Emmanuel Tumusiime-Mutebile noted this effect in Uganda, but the argument applies to many of the transitional economies as well, providing support for the big bang approach. Institutional changes also may either increase or decrease the credibility of trade reforms. In particular, it is important to identify up front the agencies that are likely to oppose reform and either weaken their negative impact or reform them. Ghana used the former strategy, Mexico the latter. In contrast, Zambia's ambitious trade reform program, the centerpiece of which was a foreign exchange auction, unraveled after one of the auction's most vocal critics was put in charge of administering it (Foroutan 1993).

Fiscal Impacts

Lesson: The fiscal impact of trade reform programs must be carefully considered; other taxes and expenditures may have to be adjusted for reforms to be effective and sustainable. Trade reform programs frequently fall prey to macroeconomic imbalance, so attention must be paid to the effect of trade reforms on the government budget. Many developing countries depend on import duties for a significant proportion of total government revenue, so fiscal balance is closely linked to the impact of trade reforms on tariff revenues. Trade liberalization programs usually entail some combination of removal of quantitative restrictions and lowering of tariff rates. Increases in tariff rates can be consistent with trade liberalization if quantitative restrictions are converted to tariffs, but tariff reform generally implies eventually reducing average tariff rates, reducing tariff dispersion, limiting exemptions, and ultimately moving toward a uniform rate at a level of 10 to 15 percent. The fiscal effect of trade reform is not always easy to foresee and quantify, but the important lesson is that an analysis of the fiscal impact of reform should be done up front so steps can be taken to ensure that reforms do not unduly exacerbate a budget deficit.

In his paper in this volume, Hood (chapter 5) explains the interaction of the many factors that determine the effect of trade liberalization on the government budget. Holding everything else constant, lower tariff rates would reduce tariff revenue; but, trade reform programs can either increase or decrease fiscal revenues because the impact of lower tariff rates may be more than offset by increases in import volume and value. Import volumes increase due to lower prices, elimination of quantitative trade controls, increases in international aid flows in support of the reform program, and eventually income effects, as trade liberalization spurs real economic growth. Currency devaluation that often accompanies reform programs boosts import values measured in domestic currency, which is the basis of valuation for tariff purposes. Collection rates may also improve as special exemptions from payment of duties are reduced, and lower rates reduce the incentive for smuggling and underinvoicing.

Evidence from reform experiences shows that revenue changes can go either way but increases are at least as likely as decreases, and that reform can greatly enhance revenues. In their survey of eleven countries, Greenaway and Milner (1993) found that cases in which tariff revenues expanded tended to be associated with significant changes in exemptions, exchange rate depreciation, elimination of quantitative restrictions, high initial tariff rates, and wide dispersion in the initial rate structure. Several conference participants confirmed the revenue-enhancing effects of tariff and customs reform, and emphasized the importance of improvements in customs administration. Fritz du Bois of Peru noted that customs revenue soared from $6 million in the early 1990s to nearly $2 billion in 1994 following the country's sharp tariff reduction, elimination of quantitative restrictions, and customs reform. Emmanuel Tumusiime-Mutebile attributed a large part of the increase in revenues after Uganda's trade reform program to improvements in customs administration.

Hood emphasizes the importance of reductions of average tariff rates as part of trade reform. Successful reforming countries have been characterized by lower average rates, while unsuccessful ones concentrated on the revenue-enhancing aspects of reform programs such as replacement of quotas with tariffs and removal of exemptions. Increases and decreases in tariff rates can be used to buffer fiscal swings (as in Chile), but ultimately rates must be reduced.

To ensure that tariff rates can be effectively reduced without prompting a fiscal crisis, Hood advocates substantially reforming the domestic tax system or replacing it with a value added tax or similar tax system that is fully rebatable on export goods, and then reducing the overall level of import taxation by lowering tariff rates. He notes the natural progression in the development process of initial reliance on trade taxes, with increased emphasis on domestic sources of tax revenue as domestic economic activity expands and becomes more diversified.

Benefits to Agriculture

Lesson: In most developing countries, trade policy reform that moves toward neutrality should be expected to disproportionately benefit agriculture. The final goal should be a level playing field among all sectors; but to achieve this, the most disadvantaged sector needs to receive special attention. At the beginning of the adjustment process, the agricultural sector is usually highly taxed in relation to other sectors. The most careful estimate of the degree of taxation was about 30 percent on average, with 22 percent coming from indirect taxation (protection of other sectors and exchange rate policies) and 8 percent from direct agricultural product taxes and pricing policies (Krueger, Schiff, and Valdés 1991). Consequently, reforms that shift the incentive structure toward neutrality will greatly improve incentives for agriculture in relation to other sectors. It might even be reasonably expected that in some countries manufacturing could shrink in absolute size.

Valdés (chapter 9 in this volume) examines the evidence on the sectoral effects of general trade reform in the TEP countries and finds that agriculture did indeed grow faster than the economy as a whole during and immediately following the reform period, especially in those countries that had the best records in sustaining the reforms, but even in the others as well. However, the rest of the economy would soon catch up, and in the fourth year after reform started the agricultural sector growth rate was the same as that of GDP as a whole in the sustained reformers.

But the evidence also shows that within the agricultural sector there is a high dispersion of relative incentives before adjustment begins, implying that the effects of adjustment will be uneven. Mirroring the economywide pattern, import-substituting crops are generally protected more than export crops, and even within the latter category it is the traditional exports that are most heavily taxed. Horticulture, as a nontraditional export, often benefits from preferential treatment, as in Costa Rica, Kenya, and Mauritius among TEP countries.

One economic rationale for taxing agricultural exports is that they have very low supply elasticity, so that the high taxes do not affect resource allocation very much. Another is the "adding up problem"—the hypothesis that world prices of these products would be depressed by a glut if they were not taxed. The mutual inconsistency of these two arguments notwithstanding, together they form the intellectual foundation for this policy. However, neither has withstood close empirical scrutiny. Supply elasticities have been shown to be significant. And very few empirical examples have been found of markets in which plausible production increases by a country or group of countries would cause significant reduction of world prices, once the response of other producers is taken into account. (Berg 1993b has a good survey.)

Moreover, the "adding up problem" argument misses two crucial points. First, when production increases are accompanied by productivity improvements (usually the result of investments encouraged by low taxes), they can enhance profitability and producer welfare even if the result is a decline in world prices. A comparison of the experience of the countries in Africa, which generally taxed traditional exports heavily, with those in Southeast Asia, which did not, shows that the net effect of taxation is stagnation of the sector's productivity and impoverishment of rural populations.

Second, even in those cases in which it appears that the appropriate policy would be to impose an optimal tax on exports of a traditional crop, the estimated size of the tax is far smaller than the implicit tax on exports through other trade restrictions. (For some estimates of optimal taxes, see Akiyama 1992; Coleman, Akiyama, and Varangis 1993; or Panagariya and Schiff 1992.) The implication is that direct taxes on exports should not be considered even in these cases until there is something close to free trade on the import side.

As these arguments make clear, agriculture should not be left behind in the trade reform process, and one important element in the process should be reduction of discrimination against traditional export crops. In reality, agriculture has been in many countries the most reform-resistant sector, which may help explain why its response to general trade reform is not as strong relative to that of other sectors as might be expected. Even in relatively advanced reformers, traditional crops are still burdened by the heavy hand of monopoly parastatal marketing enterprises. (See, for example, the country studies of Ghana, Tanzania, and Uganda in Foroutan and Nash 1997). And desires to be self-sufficient in food have made it politically difficult to reduce government intervention in food crops, which are usually import substitutes. Even in Chile, the paragon of reform, wheat remains a protected crop. As Devdasslall Dusoruth pointed out in his comments on Mauritius, concerns about food security are also behind the restrictions in the land market.

However, a few countries are recognizing the principle that when an economy is integrated into the world economy, it will have plenty of foreign exchange to buy food imports. To safeguard against an emergency such as drought, it is far less costly to maintain a reserve of foreign exchange than to pursue a continuous policy of import substitution. Mexico, where concerns about food security have historically been prominent in agricultural policy decisions, is carrying out a reform that may be deserving of emulation in other countries. Price supports and trade controls on food imports are being phased out. To ease the adjustment of producers of these crops, payments are being made to them, but the size of the payment is determined by past production patterns. By delinking income from price, the scheme gives farmers a predictable income while removing artificial price signals.

Valdés' examination of the experience of the TEP countries also emphasizes the complexity of interactions between agricultural trade reform and conditions and policies in other markets. Changes are often needed in the rules governing factor markets. Land markets have been especially rigid in some countries (Mauritius, for example)—a serious problem when changing incentives call for fluid movement of this and other factors across different uses within agriculture, or between this and other sectors. However, on balance, in most countries these are concerns of a lesser magnitude than the bigger issues of direct pricing, border measures, and parastatal marketing monopolies. These latter issues should therefore be given priority in designing the sequencing of reform packages. One exception is the land market in transitional economies, in which privatization deserves very high priority to encourage response to other reforms.

Avoiding Special Protection

Lesson: Measures for special protection should be avoided; if unavoidable, they should be designed to promote the national economic interest. Trade reform, if it is at all effective, will imply adjustment. A reforming country's production patterns will be rearranged as previously protected import-competing industries decline and export-oriented activities expand. These resource shifts create the gains from liberalization but will hurt and possibly spell the demise of firms in previously protected sectors. Workers in these sectors will be displaced, and it may take some time before they find employment in expanding activities. In the meantime, political pressure to slow down adjustment or even reverse reforms may become severe. Faced with this pressure, governments will be tempted to look to measures for special protection, such as "safeguard" mechanisms, temporary protection for industries faced with sudden increases in imports, antidumping duties, or countervailing duties to lessen the threat to established industries. Indeed the promise that these mechanisms will exist and will be used may be necessary to gain political support for a liberalization program. There is a delicate tradeoff between providing safeguard mechanisms to make liberalization politically acceptable and undermining the reform program through a tidal wave of ad hoc special protection measures.

The question of how developing and transitional economies should design and use antidumping duties, countervailing duties, "escape clause" actions, and other special protection measures has become more salient as more countries liberalize their trade regimes and apply for World Trade Organization (WTO) membership. Several mechanisms were legal under GATT (and remain so under WTO rules). As long as developing countries controlled trade through quantitative controls and unbound tariffs, special protection measures were not a major issue; but now, as more countries move toward tariff-only regimes and bind these tariff rates in the WTO, the protective measures allowed by WTO rules become the major instruments of trade policy.

J. Michael Finger (chapter 7 in this volume) reviews the use of provisions for special protection under GATT, and the implications for developing countries. He points out that just because certain actions are legal does not imply that it is a good idea for developing countries to use them. Moreover, the conditions under which the use of various safeguard mechanisms is legal are definitely *not* the conditions under which it makes economic sense to use them. In particular, none of the safeguard actions takes into account the interests and welfare of consumers or users of imported goods. Finger argues that instead of adopting safeguard provisions that are merely GATT-consistent, countries should do better than that and adopt safeguards that are not only consistent with GATT, but truly protect the national economic interest, including safeguarding the openness of the economy from protectionist interests.

Finger's review of the application of trade law and procedures in the United States shows that the separation of the authority to make trade law (which resides in Congress) and the administration of the procedures to determine whether a particular industry meets the prescribed conditions for special protection (which resides in the executive branch and the International Trade Commission) has served as a brake on protectionist pressures. Industries seeking protection from Congress were deflected into a set of procedures under which they had to show that their circumstances met the established criteria. Doing so involved costly studies and legal representation. Moreover, from the 1950s through the 1970s protection was in disfavor within the executive branch for a variety of reasons, including the desire to promote the postwar liberal international economic system.

His concern about the extension of similar procedures for special protection to developing countries is primarily that the circumstances that held protectionist pressures at bay for many decades in the United States are not generally present in developing countries. He reviews the trade policy regimes in a sample of countries that participated in TEP and finds that the authority to make trade policy decisions resides at a single level. This structure makes trade policy very flexible and easily changed, and it is much simpler for protectionist interests to get a decision in their favor. Also, broad discretionary power over trade policy means that there are already a number of ways in which protection can be granted. Adding antidumping will not limit the government's ability to grant special protection but may add circumstances under which the government must provide protection. To safeguard the openness of the economy the procedures must provide a basis to limit trade-restricting actions and convince protection seekers that the government's refusal is reasonable. The best method would be to bind trade liberalization through WTO negotiations. Then the threat of retaliation would be an effective bulwark against ad hoc reversals of trade liberalization.

Federico Chacon of Costa Rica pointed out that it would be very difficult for a government to explain why it does not have tools to protect against alleged unfair trade practices, when the country's exports face restrictions of this type in industrial countries every day. He also questioned whether tariff bindings alone would effectively counter protectionist pressures, because Costa Rica's tariff bindings are at levels above currently applied rates.

Gary Horlick, in commenting on Finger's paper, urged that no one underestimate the restrictive and disruptive effect of antidumping duties on trade. He pointed out that, although antidumping duties appear to be a tariff-like measure, in effect they are a minimum price regulation, and the uncertainty surrounding the possible levying of antidumping duties can restrict trade more than a high but certain tariff. He also buttressed the argument that legal requirements for antidumping actions do not coincide with economic reasons for protecting against dumping. He did so by noting that differential dumping (lower prices abroad than at home for the same product) is only sustainable if trade barriers prevent the reimportation of the good into the exporting country. Yet antidumping provisions make no mention of the existence of trade barriers in the exporting country, and thirty-eight antidumping petitions were filed against Hong Kong, which has no trade barriers. Moreover, the definition of dumping as sales below full production costs ignores the fact that business conditions frequently call for sales below full costs, but above variable cost, without any predatory intent.

Paul Collier pointed out that emerging suppliers are particularly vulnerable to antidumping actions because frequently there are limited domestic sales to compare with exports. It would be very useful for developing countries if they could negotiate arrangements with trading partners to be exempt from antidumping actions, a status that Iceland has in the EU. Although extremely beneficial, such a status may be virtually impossible to negotiate because, as Horlick noted, the United States has so far refused to exempt even Canada and Mexico from antidumping actions.

Expanding Exports

Lesson: Instruments to allow producers access to inputs at world market prices are crucial for export expansion. The best way to encourage exports is to keep barriers to imports low across the board. But there are a number of institutional policy measures that can provide further support for exporters, especially during transitional periods when not all import barriers or tariffs are at very low levels.

Export expansion frequently requires imported inputs. World markets for nontraditional exports are extremely competitive. To be competitive, exporters must be able to purchase imported inputs at world market prices. A number of alternative mechanisms can be designed to provide exporters with duty-free access to imported inputs. One way is to create special free trade or export-processing zones. Another approach is to provide administratively for return of duties paid on imported inputs when the final products are exported through duty drawback mechanisms, or simply to exempt exporters from duties on inputs to be used for export production through duty suspension provisions or a system of bonded warehouses. These various mechanisms have been examined in the context of a number of TEP country reports, and the details of the operation of duty drawback and duty suspension procedures in Taiwan (China) are the subject of the paper by Wu and Chuang (chapter 6 in this volume).

The recommendations in the country reports regarding the use of export-processing zones, duty drawback, and duty suspension vary depending on the circumstances of each country, but there are a number of common themes. One theme is that countries should carefully consider the costs and benefits of special trade zones before these zones are established. Costs include not only construction and management, but also lost revenue from tax concessions that are frequently offered to encourage firms to locate in the zones. Developing countries run the risk of giving up substantial resources to attract investment to special zones, with no permanent gain if firms move on to other locations once tax holidays expire. Moreover, special zones intrinsically disadvantage existing firms located outside the zones. Other recommendations include private construction, operation, and management of zones.

Free-trade zones or export-processing zones seem to provide the greatest gains under two circumstances. The first is in countries where trade restrictions are quantitative in nature and thus difficult to overcome through duty drawback or duty suspension. The best policy in these conditions would be to remove the quantitative restrictions to give all firms, both inside and outside the zones, access to imported inputs; but if that is not possible the free trade zone can provide these benefits to at least some firms. The second such circumstance is when weaknesses in institutional or administrative capacity limit the ability of the government to operate a duty exemption or suspension system effectively. Free trade zones, as well as bonded warehouses, offer alternatives that are not as flexible as these other mechanisms but are simpler to put into place and operate. Again, the best solution is to address the constraints directly; capacity building, however, is time-consuming and difficult, so it may be advisable to use free trade zones or warehouses at least as stopgap measures.

Wu and Chuang describe in detail the operation of the Taiwanese duty refund system and compare it with the Costa Rican "export contract" system. They point out that a system like the one implemented in Taiwan (China)—which postpones duty payment and then cancels this liability provided that firms export the finished goods within a specified time period—imposes fewer costs on firms than a true drawback system because they do not have to finance duty payments during the time between importation of the inputs and exportation of the final product. They also point out that duty drawback and suspension are compatible with GATT (and now WTO) rules; whereas other methods of encouraging exports, such as the export contract system, may provoke importing countries to impose countervailing duties.

In designing duty drawback systems and other institutional support schemes for exporters, it is important to keep in mind that many developing countries have weak institutions and limited experience with such systems. It may not be appropriate to go straight to state-of-the-art systems used in countries with stronger institutions and longer experience.

In his comments on the Wu and Chuang paper, Yung Whee Ree emphasized that the Taiwanese system evolved over several decades, and that the system that existed in the 1970s may be more appropriate for developing countries than the current system. In earlier years there was greater emphasis on duty exemption than duty drawback. He also pointed out the importance of the calculation of input-output coefficients to determine the amount of duty to be rebated, argued that these calculations should be undertaken by an agency outside customs, and suggested that a careful study of the coefficients used in the Republic of Korea and Taiwan (China) would be useful for other developing countries. He also suggested further study of the implications of using an export order–based system (in which duties are exempted based on actual export orders) as compared with an expected export order system (in which large established firms receive duty exemptions based only on expected orders). Another important administrative issue is how to provide for rebates to "indirect exporters" (firms that import inputs used to produce intermediate goods supplied to another firm, which in turn uses those goods as input into its production for export). The duty drawback of Taiwan (China) can be claimed by importers or manufacturers that are indirect exporters, or by the direct exporters.

An important point mentioned in the country studies, the Chuang and Wu paper, and the discussion of that paper is that the many possible mechanisms to provide duty-free access to imported inputs by exporters are by no means mutually exclusive. Free trade zones, duty drawback, duty exemption, and bonded warehouses can coexist, with firms choosing to use the mechanism most appropriate to their circumstances.

Another measure sometimes advocated as an alternative to duty drawbacks is the blanket exemption from duties of all imports of raw materials and intermediate products, whether used in the production of exports or not. Superficially, this seems to encourage exports by allowing exporters to import their inputs duty-free, thereby lowering production costs. It also has great political appeal because it lowers production costs for other firms as well. The problem with this reasoning is that incentives are relative: nothing can increase incentives for all economic activities simultaneously. When some domestic factors of production are limited in availability, incentives that attract these resources to one activity inevitably draw them away from another.

In the case of a blanket exemption for imported inputs, the activities which most benefit are those that use these kinds of inputs most intensively. This would not include the kind of high value added export operations based on processing of domestic raw materials, or those with extensive backward linkages to suppliers in the rest of the economy. It would mainly be assembly operations that import semimanufactured components, put them together, and sell the finished product. Some of these products might be exported; but, in most developing countries, the majority of these enterprises sell mainly import substitutes in the domestic market. Thus, while it is an empirical question whether a blanket exemption would on balance benefit mainly export or import substitute activities, there is some presumption that it would usually benefit the latter, thereby increasing antiexport bias.

Factor Markets

Lesson: Liberalization of factor markets complements trade reform, and trade reform measures themselves affect factor markets. Trade reform programs normally center on liberalization of trade barriers, specifically, removal of quantitative restrictions and reductions in the level and dispersion of tariffs. But, as pointed out above, complementary reforms in other areas such as macroeconomic policy, the domestic tax structure, and agriculture may be required to ensure successful and sustainable trade reforms. Reforms in factor markets ease the adjustment of the economy to liberalization of trade barriers by allowing resources to move out of previously protected sectors into expanding export-oriented activities. The links between trade reforms and factor markets, broadly defined to include labor, capital, and land markets, have not received sufficient attention. These links are important in both directions. One issue is how regulations in labor, land, and capital markets impinge on the success of trade reform programs. Another issue is what effect trade reform has on factor markets.

Constraints in markets for critical inputs can severely limit the supply response to trade reform. Sometimes the constraints are laws or regulations that provide benefits to certain groups but have the side effect of hampering adjustment to a new liberalized trading environment.

Even in Mauritius, perhaps the greatest economic success story in Africa, anachronistic laws need to be changed to make labor and land markets more responsive to the needs of a changing economy. The rapid

growth of employment in the export-processing zones has virtually eliminated the country's once-high unemployment. But many rules enacted
during the days of labor surplus now threaten to throttle growth in today's
labor-scarce economy. Sugar estates must keep part of their labor force in
the off season, when workers have little to do. Sugar producers cannot
reduce their labor force, even by attrition. The manufacturing sector cannot find workers to fill its needs, and wages continue to rise, making the
sugar sector less and less competitive internationally. Overly restrictive
regulations also impede the transfer of land out of sugar production into
high-value residential or commercial uses, contributing to a housing shortage. At least partially because of these inflexible factor market regulations, labor and land productivity in Mauritius is only a fraction of that of
other sugar producing countries.

In Peru, labor legislation gave workers rights not only to continued employment, but also to continue working at a particular job in a narrowly defined activity. These regulations made it more difficult for firms to adjust
their activities to the new structure of incentives brought about by trade liberalization. For example, tariff reductions and the removal of the ban on imports of assembled vehicles prompted motor vehicle producers to switch from
domestic assembly to importing. But firms could not redirect workers from
assembly lines toward servicing of imported cars, although this would have
been a rational and relatively low-cost redeployment.

Harrison and Revenga (chapter 8 in this volume) conclude that difficulty in
firing labor and distortions in the labor market caused by a large and inflexible
public sector impeded adjustment in the countries they examined. Wage adjustment can be hampered by public sector compensation as the public sector
bids employees away from the private sector. The size of the public payroll can
also hamper trade liberalization by undermining fiscal and monetary restraint
and thus macroeconomic stability. On the other hand, they did not find evidence that minimum wage legislation hampered adjustment.

In the transitional economies, uncertainty about property rights is a serious potential barrier to further growth. Without a clear title to property, banks
are reluctant to lend for investment. In Vietnam, where trade is expanding
rapidly, lack of clear title to property constrains the willingness of banks to
even issue letters of credit, a central part of modern international trade finance. Especially in countries where incomplete land privatization has resulted in a fragmented pattern of land holdings (as in Georgia among the
TEP countries), it is essential to move quickly to solidify unconditional rights
of transferability. This encourages development of a fluid land market and
consolidation of small plots into economically viable units.

The question of the impact of trade reform on factor markets is also important because widespread unemployment or rapid real wage declines can

seriously undermine support for a reform program before the long-run gains can be realized. Harrison and Revenga examine the experience of sixteen countries that participated in TEP and conclude that the unemployment and wage effects of trade reforms are generally small. They find that, in all countries other than the transitional economies, trade reforms were followed by increases in aggregate employment and a mixed pattern of increases and decreases in real wages but overall relative wage stability. Trade reform measures in the transitional economies may have been swamped by problems of transition to a market economy and the general collapse in foreign trade due to disintegration of traditional state trading arrangements. The positive impact of trade reforms on aggregate employment may have been due to devaluation that tended to accompany trade reforms, increases in productivity in response to greater import competition, labor legislation that makes firing workers expensive, and the fact that in relatively labor-abundant countries trade expansion would tend to bolster employment as labor-intensive export industries expand.

During the discussion of the Harrison and Revenga paper, Napoleon Pop of Romania pointed out that trade liberalization contributed to employment because dismantling state trading monopolies opened an entire area of economic activity to individual enterprises. In Romania international trade had been the exclusive province of 90 specialized companies employing 8,000 people. After trade reform more than 40,000 companies registered to conduct foreign trade, each employing from 2 to 40 people. In his view the serious increase in unemployment in Romania was due less to the speed of trade reform than to delays in implementation of privatization, restructuring, and sectoral development policies.

Harrison and Revenga also examine the link between trade reform and foreign investment flows. If trade reform increases the perceived profitability and decreases the perceived riskiness of investment, it can increase foreign investment flows and spur growth. In most countries, net foreign investment flows increased substantially following trade reforms, but this increase is attributed to liberalized foreign investment codes and improved macroeconomic performance rather than to trade reforms. Increased foreign investment inflows may have helped to spur employment and contribute to the observed increases in employment following trade liberalization in all but the transitional economies.

Regional Arrangements

Lesson: Regional arrangements can be costly for developing countries but can provide significant benefits; tradeoffs should be considered carefully before rushing to join. Developing countries have much to gain from participating in international markets. The challenge is to create an environment in which firms can find ways to combine relatively abundant labor supplies, climatic advantages, and available raw materials to expand high-value exports to industrial countries under multilateral most favored nation (MFN) trading arrangements. But a major question is whether preferential trading arrangements, either among developing countries or between a developing country and a group of industrial countries, will contribute significantly to expanded trade and economic growth.

The issue of regional trade arrangements has generated more dissension than any other among economists who strongly support liberal trade regimes. The reason for this is that it is seldom evident ex ante, and often not much clearer ex post, whether such agreements represent a step toward or away from a freer world trading environment. Economists have reached different conclusions on the general effects of regional arrangements by emphasizing their different facets.

One point on which there is a consensus is that from the point of view of a small country with a relatively closed trade regime, unilateral liberalization or multilateral liberalization on an MFN basis would be the preferred course of action. Regionalism is at most second best. But the real question is whether it is even second best, or whether countries are worse-off with a regional arrangement than without one.

In chapter 4 in this volume Panagariya makes the case that "the mercantilists were right when it comes to discussing regional trade agreements." He analyzes the kind of regional integration in which developing countries have traditionally participated: agreements among groups of small developing economies. For most products, an agreement to eliminate tariffs among regional partners will not result in reduction in prices within the regional market as long as marginal requirements continue to be supplied by imports from outside the region. This implies that no trade will be created in these products; rather, the only effect will be a transfer to exporters of the money that formerly was collected by importing countries as tariff revenues on intraregional trade. Thus, in each product market, regional exporters gain and governments in the importing countries lose. The net effect on each country depends on the sum of these product-specific impacts in its own import and export markets, but in general the biggest losers would be treasuries in high-tariff countries that are net importers from within the region. As Fudzai Pamacheche of Zimbabwe emphasized in his comments on Panagariya's paper, the gainers are the countries in the region with well-developed capacity to produce goods imported by the other members, which become to some extent captive markets. He points to Kenya and Zimbabwe within the Common Market for Eastern and Southern African States (COMESA) and South Africa within the Southern African Customs Union (SACU) as the big winners. This unequal distribution of gains leads to tensions within the groups and demands for compensation, and has in the past contributed to the failure of most groups to fully implement formal agreements.

The exceptions to this analysis are in product markets in which (a) the supply curve for extraregional imports is upward sloping, so there will be an improvement in the terms of trade of the region when extraregional imports are reduced; or (b) regional suppliers totally displace extraregional imports, causing regional prices to fall and creating trade. One example of this latter case is a product for which the globally most efficient producer is within the region. However, Panagariya argues that there are unlikely to be many such cases, so regional arrangements are quite unlikely to be trade-creating on balance. Consideration of nontariff barriers may make the case for regional agreements slightly more favorable, because there is an additional case in which the agreement may be trade-creating: If barriers to regional trade are eliminated while those affecting nonregional trade are not made less liberal, trade may be created. Still, the case remains uncertain at best.

It is undoubtedly true that the economic case for these "South-South" regional agreements is weak; however, it is worth noting that it is not as weak as it used to be. The reason for this is that in recent years so many developing countries have greatly reduced barriers to trade with the rest of the world. This limits the potential for trade diversion from regional agreements. Also, when countries begin with low tariff structures, the transfer of revenue among the countries is minimal when the intraregional tariffs are eliminated. In this context, some regional agreements have been useful coordinating devices for reducing regional tariffs on imports from the rest of the world. Both the Caribbean Community (CARICOM) and the Central American Common Market (CACM) have in recent years lowered their common external tariff (CET) structures on this basis. MERCOSUR has been successful so far, probably largely because its two largest members are in agreement on the desirability of converging on a low and fairly uniform CET structure. De Melo (chapter 2 in this volume) even credits MERCOSUR membership with helping keep Uruguay's trade reforms on course.

In the context of using regional groupings to encourage liberalization in relation to countries outside the group, it is noteworthy that both CARICOM and CACM, in revising their CET schedules, explicitly allowed members to move at different speeds toward this goal. The Cross-Border Initiative in Africa is also proceeding on this principle. The purpose in all these cases is to ensure that the fast reformers will not have to wait on the laggards. Of course, there is still a possibility that some members may have to a accept less liberal CET than they want. The agreements between Russia and some other Commonwealth of Independent States (CIS) republics call for a customs union with a CET based on Russia's tariff schedule, which is significantly more protectionist than those of its partners (notably Kazakhstan and the Kyrgyz Republic) and those of potential future members. This is creating tension in the union, with Kazakhstan having reversed some of its movement toward the CET when it became clear that tariffs designed to protect Russian industries would be costly for the Kazakh economy.

In recent years, developing and transitional economies have begun to participate in regional arrangements with industrial economies.[4] These include, most notably, Mexico's membership in NAFTA (with other countries also negotiating to join), and the EAs. From the viewpoint of the small economies, the analysis of the benefits and costs of joining these is basically the same as described above but with a few additional considerations and probably some difference in quantification of the effects.

One additional benefit that may come from joining an agreement with a large industrial economy is the likely substantial increase in competition in many products in the smaller market, a factor linked empirically to greater total factor productivity. Another is that such an agreement may increase the credibility of reforms. This has often been said of Mexico, and indeed, as Collier pointed out, in the recent crisis, unlike in the past, there was never any serious consideration given to using nontariff barriers to correct the current account imbalances. De Melo singles out the EAs as an important factor in sustaining trade reforms in Eastern Europe. Collier argues that a similar arrangement with the countries of SSA would be extremely helpful in bolstering the credibility of their reform programs.

But Panagariya questions this reasoning. Borrowing from Bhagwati (1993), he argues that if protectionist pressure arises in a country, foreclosure of one avenue for venting the pressure will not control the pressure but cause it to be vented in another direction. Multilateral commitments via the WTO are much more effective in locking in reforms and increasing credibility. While it is hard to disagree with this last conclusion, this is nonetheless consistent with the view that regional agreements can enhance credibility. Mexico's experience in the recent currency crisis provides some ammunition for both arguments. Faced with an unsustainable balance of trade deficit, it raised tariffs on imports from non-NAFTA countries to 35 percent on 503 tariff lines. This clearly represented some backsliding but could hardly be characterized as protectionism run amok.

Two other elements in the analysis of South-South agreements need to be given different weights in analyzing North-South agreements, and they cut in different directions. The first is the possibility that some products may be produced most efficiently globally by a member of the region. For the latter but

---

4. Here we are not including one-way preferential agreements such as the Lome Agreement or the Generalized System of Preferences.

not the former agreements, this is likely to be the case for some significant products. The United States and Canada are arguably the globally most efficient producers of wheat and corn, and the United States of telecommunications services. The benefits of NAFTA to Mexico in these products could be great. The second is the issue of tariff discrepancies between the partners. The industrial countries have very low tariffs compared to even the advanced trade reformers like Mexico; thus, there is likely to be a net financial transfer from the Mexican treasury to U.S. buyers. This discrepancy also increases the probable costs of trade diversion, a point made by Winters and Wang (1994) in the context of the EAs with the Eastern European countries, which have tariffs considerably higher than those of Mexico.

Despite all the negative aspects of membership in regional trade agreements, there seems to be a resurgence in interest among developing countries in joining them, or in reviving old agreements that had become inoperative. One question is why this should be so, and another is whether there is any practical guidance that should be offered to countries and regions contemplating or actively involved in membership. Panagariya (chapter 4 in this volume) answers the "why" with the argument that "countries are jumping on the bandwagon without fully inquiring where the wagon is headed," or possibly as insurance against being left out of super trading blocs that may form in the future. Yet both of these seem too facile, or at least incomplete.

Regional trading agreements have historically been used to try to cement regional geopolitical identities. This clearly lies at the heart of the Eastern European countries' desire to sign accords with Western Europe; they want to be part of this group, rather than part of the Soviet bloc. As Napoleon Pop of Romania put it in his comments, "The regionalism represented by the EU was one of the most important roads to democracy and the market economy..." He noted that Romania placed such a high value on these principles that it was willing to accept a rather asymmetrical design of concessions in its association agreement with the EU. For the same reason, Russia has been pushing hard to create a common economic space with the other republics of the former Soviet Union, and some of them have been resisting.

But there are good economic reasons as well. As David Tarr noted in the conference, most computable general equilibrium models show economic gains to small countries from integration with large ones, although, because of the complicated structure of these models, it is sometimes hard to figure out why. Theoretical models with differentiated products, rather than the homogeneous products on which Panagariya's model is based, can also show gains from integration. There are other good economic reasons, but they are hard to quantify in either the classical trade creation-diversion model or the computable general equilibrium models more in

vogue today. One is the putative advantage that members enjoy with respect to possible future changes in the trade rules by other members. In
the current trade environment, in which the use of nontransparent protectionist instruments is a constant threat, this can be a real advantage.
Eastern European countries that succeed in becoming full members of the
EU will enjoy freedom from antidumping actions. Membership in NAFTA
does not exempt countries from antidumping actions. However, as noted
by Hachette in his explanation of why Chile is so anxious to join, membership at least ensures some stability of the rules, because that country
will be an "insider" should the rules be changed in the future. A desire to
avoid rule changes was also clearly a motivation behind MERCOSUR,
although it is not clear how well it will perform in this regard; Brazil's
unilateral action restricting imports of Argentine cars provoked the first
serious crisis of the agreement in mid-1995.

Another potential advantage comes through the necessary harmonization of trade rules and institutions. Countries joining the EU had to upgrade
customs and bring other regulations to world standards in ways that undoubtedly facilitated trade with countries both inside and outside the region. Integration may also encourage increased foreign investment, although
the record on this is not clear.

It would probably be unwise to counsel countries not to get further involved in regional agreements without qualification because of their many
facets and the uncertainty surrounding their costs and benefits. Nonetheless,
Panagariya's advice not to jump on the bandwagon without considering
where it is headed would be well taken. But perhaps even more important is
his advice that countries joining an arrangement minimize potential costs by
reducing tariffs and barriers to trade with countries outside the arrangement
at the same time.

Trade Reform and Foreign Aid

Lesson: Industrial countries can help trade reform in developing countries. The trade
policies of developing countries have been affected by the actions of industrial countries as donors and trade partners. First, the inflow of aid as a direct
effect of stabilization and adjustment programs has several effects, some salutary and some not. One that has been well recognized is that large aid flows
maintain the RER at a more appreciated level than would otherwise be the
case. In the context of trade policy reforms, this means that the reduction of
trade restrictions is not accompanied by a depreciation as large as would
otherwise be necessary; thus, prices for import substitutes fall more. As Collier
points out (chapter 3 in this volume), this inflicts the pain on producers of
import substitutes early in the reform program, and by doing so increases

the credibility of the reforms. If they last past this initial phase, which is the most painful, they are likely to endure through succeeding phases as well.[5]

However, reducing the size of the necessary depreciation also reduces the degree by which the incentive for exporters improves through the exchange rate effect. If this defers the export supply response, it may work against the reforms. The same can be said of private capital inflows that have recently resulted from adjustment in Latin American countries, and others such as Uganda. But Fritz du Bois of Peru commented during the conference that the appreciation in Peru has not been a significant deterrent to export growth, and the same could be said of other countries, such as Argentina and Brazil.

On balance, based on the negative as well as positive experiences of reforming countries, what these two arguments seem to suggest is not that aid has had a negative effect, but rather that the reform package that accompanies the aid must significantly reduce any antiexport bias in the economy. It is important to ensure that adjustment packages have as their cornerstones trade policy reform.

Donor requirements for disbursement of aid have sometimes not been helpful to trade policy reform. To get access to foreign exchange funded through donor aid, importers have sometimes had to go through international competitive bidding procedures for large purchases and submit complicated and expensive paperwork and procedures (multiple invoices, letters of credit) even for small ones. This simply discourages use of the funds and the mechanism under which they are distributed. Louis Kasekende noted that this led to underutilization of auction resources in Uganda.

Donors and nongovernmental organizations (NGOs) have usually insisted on duty exemptions for imports purchased for their use, either directly or in investment projects. Dominique Hachette commented that this not only has the appearance of hypocrisy, given that donors (multinationals especially) generally counsel that other exemptions be reduced or abolished, but also has significant fiscal effects in some countries. Kasekende also noted that in Uganda foreign NGOs account for 50 percent of exemptions. This also has adverse effects on the local economy, and probably on allocative efficiency, because it creates an incentive to use imported inputs instead of sourcing locally.

Considerable concern has been expressed about the potential for replacing traditional barriers to imports that were removed under adjustment programs with modern barriers, such as restrictions under antidumping or safeguard actions (see chapter 7 in this volume). Clearly, much of the impetus for this in

---

5. Of course, the opposite argument could be made from the viewpoint of consumers. Deferring depreciation defers the pain of higher consumer import prices. There is some presumption, however, that the political power of import substituters dominates that of consumers, since the initial political equilibrium is characterized by significant protection for the latter.

developing countries comes from the use of antidumping actions against them by industrial countries. As Collier pointed out, small new exporters are in some ways the most vulnerable because they often try to break into markets with low-quality, low-priced products. While the Uruguay Round agreement does include some "safe harbor" provisions for small exporters, Collier argues that some kind of status for African countries that would make them exempt from antidumping actions (similar to Iceland's status in the EU) would be very helpful to them in attracting foreign investment.

Lessons for Technical Assistance

Elliot Berg concludes (chapter 10 in this volume) that the need for the kind of technical assistance provided by TEP has not diminished, recent strides in global trade liberalization notwithstanding. One might even argue that the demand is stronger than when the program began, given the huge need for advice in transitional economies that has arisen largely since that time. He points out that there is a broad consensus on what is the right advice and analytical approach to trade policy but that the capacity to design and implement reforms remains very thin in many developing countries; thus the need for outside assistance.

The basic model of the program has been very successful in bringing to bear excellent analytical skills to help policymakers resolve important trade policy issues, and in bringing together the views of the international donors and the client countries. Nonetheless, some lessons emerged that could improve the design of future programs of this kind. One is that there is a rather steep tradeoff between comprehensiveness on one hand and timeliness and flexibility of assistance on the other. In a number of countries, TEP fielded large teams in an effort to address many questions at once. This had the advantage of allowing an analysis of the interactions between all these issues, and the size of the missions created definite synergistic effects. However, the cost was that the missions were time-consuming to organize, hard to reschedule once organized, and slow to produce a final product. The latter problem should not be overstated. Much of the value came not from the final product but from advice given while the team was in the field. Nonetheless, in retrospect it might have been wiser to weigh more carefully the need and the costs in deciding on the size of the teams. It is probably also true that too much effort went into creating polished final reports, particularly given their short shelf life.

As Berg also notes, the experience of TEP and technical assistance in general shows the importance of building local capacity (see also Berg 1993a). Foreign experts are not always available when needed, and even if they were, reforms are more likely to take root if they are homegrown. But this does not necessarily devalue the role of outside advice. There is a need for both kinds of assistance. When the opportunity for reform arises, there is often a rather limited window of opportunity, as de Melo points out in chapter 2. Policymakers cannot wait for local capacity to get built; they need policy advice on an urgent basis. But at the same time, it is clear that they should not have to rely on outside advice indefinitely. Local analytical capacity is essential for sustainability of good trade policy.

This does not, however, imply that capacity building is an appropriate role for a TEP-like program. Capacity building was supposed to be one of the many roles of TEP, and, while there were some notable successes, this was probably the program's weakest area. To us this seems to have been a problem inherent to this type of program. As Berg notes, organizations good at analysis tend to be weak at capacity building. One reason for this is that to build capacity requires multi-person teams in-country for extended periods, and the personnel available for this kind of work are not necessarily the first choices to analyze specific issues in trade policy. Furthermore, the budgetary commitment for extended training activities was not available to TEP. Incorporating this task into future technical assistance would greatly raise its cost. These considerations, plus the distinct nature of short-term policy advice and long-term training, seem to argue that these would be better organized as two separate programs rather than trying to amalgamate them into one.

Bibliography

Akiyama, Takamasa. 1992. "Is There a Case for an Optimal Export Tax on Perennial Crops?" Policy Research Working Paper 854. World Bank, International Economics Department, Washington, D.C.

Aron, Janine, and Ibrahim Elbedawi. 1994. "A Typology of Foreign Exchange Auctions in Sub-Saharan Africa." Policy Research Working Paper 1395. World Bank, Policy Research Department, Washington, D.C.

Berg, Elliot. 1993a. *Rethinking Technical Cooperation: Reforms for Capacity Building in Africa.* New York: United Nations Development Programme.

_____. 1993b. "World Markets or Collective Self Reliance." Draft prepared for the Royal African Society Conference on Governance, Business, Aid, at Oxford University, March 21–23. Bethesda, MD: Development Alternatives, Inc.

Bhagwati, Jagdish. 1993. "Regionalism and Multilateralism: An Overview." In Jaime de Melo and Arvind Panagariya, eds., *New Dimensions in Regional Integration.* Cambridge, U.K.: Cambridge University Press.

Coleman, Jonathan R., Takamasa Akiyama, and Panos N. Varangis. 1993. "How Policy Affected Cocoa Sectors in Sub-Saharan African Countries." Policy Research Working Paper 1129. World Bank, International Economics Department, Washington, D.C.

Connolly, Michael, and Jaime de Melo, eds. 1994. *The Effects of Protectionism on a Small Economy: The Case of Uruguay.* World Bank Regional and Sectoral Studies. Washington, D.C.: World Bank.

Corbo, Vittorio, and Stanley Fischer. 1992. "Adjustment Programs and Bank Support: Rationale and Main Results." In Vittorio Corbo, Stanley Fischer, and Steven B. Webb, eds., *Adjustment Lending Revisited: Policies to Restore Growth: A World Bank Symposium.* Washington, D.C.: World Bank.

de Melo, Jaime, and Arvind Panagariya, eds. 1993. *New Dimensions in Regional Integration.* Cambridge, U.K.: Cambridge University Press.

Edwards, Sebastian. 1989. *Real Exchange Rates, Devaluation, and Adjustment: Exchange Rate Policy in Developing Countries.* Cambridge, MA: MIT Press.

Foroutan, Faezah. 1993. "Trade Reform in Ten Sub-Saharan Countries: Achievements and Failures." Policy Research Working Paper 1222. World Bank, International Economics Department, Washington, D.C.

Foroutan, Faezah, and John Nash, eds. 1997. *Trade Policy Reform in Sub-Saharan Africa: What Went Right? What Went Wrong? What Lessons for the Future?* Canberra: National Centre for Development Studies.

Greenaway, David, and Chris Milner. 1993. "The Fiscal Implications of Trade Policy Reform: Theory and Evidence." UNDP/World Bank Trade Expansion Program Occasional Paper 9. World Bank, International Economics Department, Washington, D.C.

Haggard, Stephen, and Steven B. Webb, eds. 1994. *Voting for Reform: Democracy, Political Liberalization, and Economic Adjustment.* New York: Oxford University Press.

Harrold, Peter. 1995. "Implications of the Uruguay Round for Sub-Saharan Africa: Much Ado About Nothing?" In Will Martin and L. Alan Winters, eds., *The Uruguay Round and the Developing Economies.* Discussion Paper 307. Washington, D.C.: World Bank.

Krueger, Anne O., Maurice Schiff, and Alberto Valdés, eds. 1991. *The Political Economy of Agricultural Pricing Policy,* five volumes. Baltimore: Johns Hopkins University Press for the World Bank.

La Ferrara, Eliana, Gabriel Castillo, and John Nash. 1994. "The Reform of Mechanisms for Foreign Exchange Allocation: Theory and Lessons from Sub-Saharan Africa." Policy Research Working Paper 1268. World Bank, Policy Research Department, Washington, D.C.

Michaely, Michael, Armeane Choksi, and Demetrios Papageorgiou. 1990. *Liberalizing Foreign Trade: Lessons of Experience in the Developing World.* Cambridge, MA: Basil Blackwell.

Nash, John. 1990. "Export Instability and Long-Term Capital Flows: Response to Asset Risk in a Small Economy." *Economic Inquiry* 28 (April): 307–16.

Panagariya, Arvind, and Maurice Schiff. 1992. "Taxes versus Quotas: The Case of Cocoa Exports." In Ian Goldin and L. Alan Winters, eds., *Open Economies, Structural Adjustment, and Agriculture.* New York: Cambridge University Press.

Rodrik, Dani. 1994. "The Rush to Free Trade in the Developing World: Why So Late? Why Now? Will It Last?" In Stephen Haggard and Steven B. Webb, eds., *Voting for Reform: Democracy, Political Liberalization, and Economic Adjustment.* New York: Oxford University Press.

Thomas, Vinod, John Nash, and associates. 1991. *Best Practices in Trade Policy Reform.* New York: Oxford University Press.

Winters, L. Alan, and Z. K. Wang. 1994. *Eastern Europe's International Trade.* Manchester, U.K.: Manchester University Press.

2

Macroeconomic Management and Trade Reform: A Political Economy Perspective

Jaime de Melo

This chapter examines the macroeconomic policies that accompanied trade liberalization episodes in fifteen countries that participated in the Trade Expansion Program (TEP), a joint United Nations Development Programme (UNDP)/World Bank technical assistance project. A third of the countries were from Sub-Saharan Africa (SSA), another third were transitional economies, and the remainder were mostly from Latin America. Emphasis is put on the conflicting roles of the exchange rate as an expenditure-switching instrument necessary under trade liberalization and as an "anchor" that influences expectations under stabilization. Rather than attempting to find common elements in the country episodes, this chapter emphasizes the political economy dimension of these episodes.

The political economy perspective suggests three lessons. Countries in distress moved on all fronts simultaneously, reducing macroeconomic imbalances while liberalizing foreign trade. From a political economy perspective, this was possible both because of a broad, if diffuse, support for change and because of relatively large short-term efficiency gains compared with the redistributive effects of the reforms. Second, the transitional economies benefited from clear signals, like the European Agreements (EAs) that enhanced the credibility of the reforms. Third, in established democracies reforms were more gradual, while in SSA countries, the lopsided development of the political system (resulting in too great a concentration of power in the hands of the political elite, for whom reforms would have high political costs) was a brake in implementing reforms.

Launched in 1987 at the initiative of the UNDP and the World Bank, TEP was intended to give independent advice on trade policy reform [without the usual conditionality that accompanies loans from the International Monetary

---

The author wishes to thank John Nash, Wendy Takacs, and conference participants for comments on an earlier draft.

Fund (IMF) and the World Bank] to countries wishing to participate in the
program. At the time TEP was initiated, the World Bank was completing a
comparative study on the experience of trade reform in the 1960s and 1970s
(Michaely, Choksi, and Papageorgiou 1990) and was preparing to update it
based on the experience of trade policy reform under adjustment lending in
the 1980s (Thomas and Nash 1991). In a broad sense, the mandate of TEP was
to give customized advice, taking into account when relevant the experience
gathered from the above-mentioned studies.

From the beginning an effort was made to look for countries that had
received relatively little advice so far and with relatively little previous engagement in trade policy reform. Another goal was to select poor SSA countries with little experience in sustained trade policy reform. Finally, large countries with domestic expertise and access to other sources of external advice
were excluded from the start. And, with the breakdown of the East-West
divide, it became apparent that policy advice would be helpful for transitional economies.

While the areas of emphasis were to be tailored to country-specific needs
identified in reconnaissance missions, it is fair to say that each one of the
fifteen country studies carried out by TEP was fairly similar in scope: recommendations for reforms based on an evaluation of the trade regime and
of the fiscal and factor market policies that affected the performance of the
trade regime. For countries facing macroeconomic difficulties, an integral
part of the technical assistance included recommendations on macroeconomic policies. And, if the primary focus was the implementation of trade
reform, it is fair to say that TEP teams were aware that macroeconomic
slippage could be fatal to otherwise sound and politically implementable
trade reforms. In some cases, it could even be said that lack of redressment
of macroeconomic disequilibria would likely prevent the implementation
of trade policy reform.

So much for the background. Not surprisingly, the sample of countries
that resulted from the intersection of country interests on the one hand, and
TEP staff objectives on the other, produced a motley group. These are listed
in the Preface and Acknowledgments. As the list suggests, it is difficult to fit
the countries into preestablished categories for evaluation of macroeconomic
and trade policies.

Countries involved in the political liberalization that swept the 1980s in
the midst of the worst economic crisis affecting the developing world since
the Great Depression were well represented in the TEP sample. Around the
time of the TEP missions, the following countries experienced deep political change, many of them sweeping regime changes: Czechoslovakia,
Mongolia, Peru, Poland, and Romania. All were characterized by highly

uncertain institutional settings and strong distributional claims from groups previously excluded from the political process.

It is increasingly recognized that the success of reform packages is as much linked to the political response to the reforms as to the economic response to them. I therefore take a somewhat broader perspective in this evaluation, bringing in political economy considerations whenever it seems relevant. Because the political response to reform packages depends also on economic design, I discuss the two jointly.

A political economy focus is also warranted for an evaluation of TEP activities. These activities were removed from the typical bargaining that takes place in adjustment programs directly supported by the IMF or World Bank. Indeed, even if it may not have always been an easy task, in the missions I participated in we always pointed out forcefully that TEP missions were not part of World Bank missions, making our advice free of conditionality. We always thought that this "independent advice" would be more easily internalized. It is in this spirit that in several countries we were able to convey joint meetings with interest groups and government bureaucrats to discuss reform proposals. While TEP missions certainly never entered into political analysis, they were somewhat less prone to the criticism often raised against international organizations that they interfere with national sovereignty or, in the case of ex-colonies, are reminiscent of past imperialism.

It is, however, with trepidation that I take on a political economy perspective in this assessment. I am only marginally informed of the political developments in many countries in the group, and categorization is difficult when it is extended to the political sphere. For example, among the "other" group, political and institutional change had in some cases been as great as in the transitional economies (as was the case in Peru). Likewise, the political and institutional setting was at times more stable and transparent in the transitional countries (such as Vietnam) than in the other countries (such as Madagascar).

This chapter is organized as follows. *Macroeconomic disequilibrium and trade restrictiveness* discusses the extent of disequilibrium and the restrictiveness of the foreign trade regime, resulting in classification into different groups, including two groups of countries combining severe macroeconomic disequilibrium and a relatively restrictive trade regime. *The economics of reform packages* reviews the literature on this subject. The section *The political economy of reforms* introduces the constraints on implementation posed by political factors (distributional, electoral, pressure group, and predatory). These remarks are used in the appraisal of country experiences in *Some political economy comparisons* after *Stabilization and reform in the TEP countries* discusses macroeconomic performance in terms of the usual indicators. Concluding comments follow.

Macroeconomic Disequilibrium and Trade Restrictiveness

Not all TEP countries faced a need to combine stabilization with trade policy reform. To give an idea of the extent of interaction between stabilization and trade reforms, table 2.1 gives a crude taxonomy of disequilibrium factors at the time of the TEP missions.[1] Although they are not analytically distinct, I distinguish countries into three categories according to the extent of their disequilibrium: (i) "bad start," (ii) "big shock," and (iii) "high antiexport bias." Falling in the category "bad start," with a (Y) entry and contributing symptoms in parentheses, are the countries with relatively large macroeconomic disequilibria.

Table 2.1. Disequilibrium Factors at Time of TEP Mission

Country and date of TEP mission	Bad start	Big shock	Antiexport bias
Costa Rica (8/91)	N(DSV)	N	M(TM)
Czechoslovakia (2/91)	N(INF,PRE)	Y(CMEA)	M(EQRs)
Kenya (9/92)	Y(DSV)	Y	H(QRs,TM)
Madagascar (2/90)	N(DSV)	N	H(QRs,ET,TM)
Mali (6/88)	N(FD)	N	M(QRs)
Mauritius (2/92)	N(DSV)	N	L(TM)
Mongolia (9/92)	Y(FD,INF,PRE)	Y(CMEA)	H(EQRs)
Morocco (10/89)	N(FD)	N	M(TM,REF)
Peru (2/91)	Y(FD,INF,PRE)	N	H(TM,QRs)
Poland (5/88)	Y(INF,PRE)	Y(CMEA)	H(LIC,EQRs)
Romania (12/92)	Y(FD,INF,PRE)	Y(CMEA)	M(EQRs)
Uganda (9/89)	Y(FD,INF,PRE)	Y	H(TM,ET,QRs)
Uruguay (12/89)	Y(INF,DSV)	N	H(TM,REF)
Vietnam (9/92)	N(FD,DSV)	Y(CMEA)	M(TM,LIC)
Zimbabwe (11/93)	N(FD,DSV)	N	M(LIC,QRs)

Note: Bad start: Yes (Y), No (N). Classification based on the following four indicators. Yes if three or more of the following criteria are satisfied: Central fiscal deficit in excess of 5% of GDP(FD); inflation >50% (INF); debt service/GDP>5% (DSV); premium on parallel market >0 (PRE).

Big shock: An external shock (fall in terms of trade) or the need to reorient the trade regime for CMEA countries.

Antiexport bias: High (H), Medium (M), or Low (L). Main instruments of protection (indicated only if judged to be pervasive or quantitatively important). Import/export licensing (LIC); export QRs (EQRs); Import quantitative restrictions (QRs); tariffs (TM), export taxes (ET), reference prices (REF).

Calculations for columns 1 and 2 based on before TEP data in table 2.2. Third column based on information in TEP reports.

Sources: TEP reports and author.

1. A "bad start"/"big shock" dichotomy is also used in Little and others (1993, table 4.4). The macroeconomic adjustments of Costa Rica and Morocco are covered in the Little and others volume up until the mid-1980s.

As indicators of disequilibrium, I take a crude measure of fiscal deficit, inflation, the servicing of the external debt, and the ratio of the parallel market exchange rate to the official exchange rate.[2] A high external debt service ratio is taken as much as an indicator of credibility as of macroeconomic imbalance.[3] Thus a "bad start" reflects as much an internal shock (imprudent macroeconomic policies) as an external shock (terms-of-trade shock). The "big shock" is to indicate whether the country recently experienced an unfavorable environment, as essentially all transitional economies did due to the collapse of the U.S.S.R. and the collapse of the Council for Mutual Economic Assistance (CMEA).[4] The "high antiexport bias" category is standard and reflects an entirely subjective judgment of the likely global distortion in the foreign exchange regime resulting from price and nonprice measures.

Table 2.1 indicates that shocks were confined to the transitional economies (the terms-of-trade and interest rate shocks of the early 1980s can be considered to have worked themselves out by the time of the TEP missions).[5] It can be argued that, in spite of their size (estimates often exceed 10 percent of GDP), the external shocks experienced by the transitional countries were different from those faced by the developing countries earlier in the decade: there was no doubt these were permanent, and this could have been a strong signal to adjust—perhaps a blessing in disguise.

The classification of countries according to the extent of protection tries to take into account the most prevalent forms of protection. In most transitional economies, because of the so-called domestic currency overhang and the lack of tariff protection under the CMEA, export quantitative restrictions (EQRs) were a frequent form of protection. In other countries (Morocco and Uruguay), reference prices (REF) played an important role. In these cases, as well as in the more common cases of licensing (LIC) (import and export) and

---

2. The central fiscal deficit taken from IMF, *International Financial Statistics* (periodical, various issues) is the only widely available measure. It has many problems: it does not include parastatals and other contributing factors to the deficit, nor does it distinguish between the various components of the deficit, such as the servicing of debt.

3. Countries with a high external debt service have to effect a "twin transfer" because the state owns the foreign debt and the private sector owns the hard currency. So the credibility of the state's policies is affected, as it typically has to extract foreign exchange from the private sector (see Rodrik 1993b).

4. The collapse of the U.S.S.R. resulted in a sharp reduction in transfer from the U.S.S.R. because subsidized energy was abruptly halted. The collapse of the CMEA implied the need to readjust the pattern of trade following the collapse of demand from the U.S.S.R. Following these collapses the average GDP growth rates for the three-year period of 1990–92 were Czechoslovakia (-8.2 percent), Mongolia (-9.8 percent), Poland (-7 percent), and Romania (-10.7 percent).

5. Vietnam is the only country that can be considered to have had a significant positive shock (along with several sizable negative shocks), as it became a substantial oil exporter starting around 1990.

import quantitative restrictions, the extent of antiexport bias that results from their joint application is hard to judge. So the high, medium, or low antiexport bias is a very approximate judgment.

It could be argued that six of the TEP countries started from severe macroeconomic imbalance and highly restrictive trade regimes. This group includes two to three transitional economies (Mongolia, Poland,[6] and Romania) and three market economies (Peru, Uganda, and Uruguay). In terms of the standard sequencing arguments (see below), these countries should have first carried out macroeconomic stabilization, then structural reforms such as the liberalization of foreign trade. Yet, this was rarely the case. Many countries were already engaged in stabilization and reform packages, and were recommended to push further ahead by TEP missions.

Once again the situation of the transitional countries deserves special consideration in the discussion of the sequencing of reforms. One of the arguments against the simultaneous pursuit of trade liberalization and macroeconomic stabilization is that trade reform will lack support in an unstable environment because of the added uncertainty (see Corbo and Fischer 1992; Fernandez and Rodrik 1991). But two of the three transitional countries benefited from the credibility that was added by the prospects of the EAs. The EAs were negotiated by three of the six transitional countries (Czechoslovakia, Poland, and Romania) at a time close to most TEP missions.[7] If the EAs did not provide much extra liberalization in goods trade, they provided less visible but very important other benefits that enhanced the credibility of the ongoing reforms.[8]

First, the EAs laid the foundation for the eventual application of the Central and Eastern Europe (CEE) countries for application to the European Union (EU) membership (officially recognized by the EU council at the August 1993 Copenhagen meeting). Second, the adoption of many institutional features of the EU (competition policy, measures to protect Foreign Direct Investment (FDI), and so on) reduced the uncertainty of inward

---

6. Poland's inflation took off in 1988, the year of the TEP visit, for three years.

7. See Panagariya (chapter 4 in this volume) for a thorough analysis of regional arrangements as a means for carrying out trade reform.

8. Much of the liberalization in goods trade between the European Union (EU) and the Central and Eastern Europe (CEE) countries was unilateral, taking place before the negotiation of the EAs. In 1989, the EU removed quantitative restrictions on the CEE countries and gave them most favored nation (MFN) status, while the CEE countries adopted low tariffs (see Messerlin 1992). Based on a comparison with the experience of Portugal and Spain after they joined the European Community, Cadot and de Melo (1994) argue that the main benefit of the EAs will come through increased Foreign Direct Investment (FDI) when macroeconomic imbalances are removed. For projections of likely trade increases between the EU and the CEE countries , see Baldwin (1994). Based on the Hungarian experience with EAs, Sapir (1994) argues that the constraints imposed by the EAs have helped trade policy formulation and implementation.

FDI and, most important, provided much added and needed credibility to the CEE countries' internal reforms. Free trade in goods outside agriculture is to be reached in ten years from signature date. And the prospect of application to EU membership was a further incentive on the part of the CEE countries not to envisage too high a protection level against third countries. It is hard to imagine a stronger incentive for preventing policy reversal, especially in countries where democracy was hardly installed and a policy reversal could well mean a return to the previous political and economic regime.

The remaining TEP countries did not face the problem of carrying out reforms under as severe macroeconomic imbalances. Among the transitional economies, Czechoslovakia, in spite of a sizable shock, did not have either a very protected trade regime or a sizable fiscal deficit, and the koruna overhang was mostly resorbed in 1991. Remarkably, Vietnam also had a stable macroeconomy in 1992 and had managed to weather the CMEA shock with positive growth. Costa Rica, Mauritius, and Morocco were close to macroeconomic equilibrium, although Costa Rica had a sizable net transfer to effect on its external debt. The remaining countries (Kenya, Madagascar, Mali, and Zimbabwe) could be qualified as being in moderate macroeconomic disequilibrium with quite restrictive trade regimes.[9]

To sum up, the TEP countries can be classified into three categories in terms of their macroeconomic disequilibrium at the time of the TEP missions: countries with both severe macroeconomic disequilibria and trade regimes with high antiexport bias (Mongolia, Poland, and Romania among the transitional countries, and Peru, Uganda, and Uruguay among the market economies); countries with sound macroeconomies (Costa Rica, Mauritius, and Morocco); and an "in-between" group (Czechoslovakia, Kenya, Madagascar, Mali, and Zimbabwe).

The Economics of Reform Packages

I will not review the TEP report recommendations. Naturally, the recommendations varied in relation to the identified main constraint (for example, land and factor markets in Mauritius, complex licensing and excessive export taxes in Uganda, hidden protection in Uruguay, EQRs in most transitional countries, and so forth). For all countries with high macroeconomic imbalance and

---

9. Mali had an average central government deficit of 6.0 percent (including grants) during 1986–88, but its external debt service was relatively low because of the high amount of concessional aid it receives. Given the size of its sustained fiscal deficit, the low inflation due to its French franc zone (CFA) membership is probably a misleading indicator of macroeconomic equilibrium. However, Mali is the only country in the TEP sample that had a fully convertible currency on both the current and capital accounts.

restrictive trade regimes the recommendation was to move on both fronts simultaneously, removing constraints in the foreign trade regime and carrying out stabilization policies. This is perhaps to be expected from TEP. After all, its main mandate was to recommend policies that would effect better integration into the world economy through export expansion and efficient import substitution. At the same time, it largely ignored the received wisdom (in World Bank circles at least) that some macroeconomic stabilization is necessary prior to structural reforms in countries with acute macroeconomic problems.[10] According to Corbo and Fischer: "In countries with acute macroeconomic problems, structural reforms designed to increase efficiency and restore growth, whose own efficiency depends on a predictable macroeconomic situation, should be initiated only when sufficient progress has been made in reducing macroeconomic imbalances"(1992, p. 7).

Yet many recent comprehensive reform packages starting from severe macroeconomic disequilibrium in both market economies (for example, Bolivia and Mexico since 1985, and Argentina since 1991) and transitional economies (such as Poland since 1990) have moved simultaneously on both fronts. To a large extent this has also been the case among the TEP countries. I therefore review arguments on the design of reform packages before taking up political economy considerations.

Because the problems of transitional economies are different, the economic arguments in the design of reform packages for transitional economies are reviewed separately. In those cases, because of the urgency of price reform, trade liberalization plays an additional role of helping de-monopolization by enhancing competition. For other economies, the debate is on the merits of sequencing the reforms. The sequencing issue is examined first.

Sequencing and the Dual Role of the Exchange Rates

The economic arguments that give broad support for sequencing in high-inflation countries are well known. First, the high relative price variability that besets high-inflation countries is not conducive to efficiency, because the price system is no longer a good conveyor of information on relative scarcities. Second, almost all stabilization episodes start from severe fiscal deficits. While it is not clear that government revenues will necessarily fall with trade liberalization (part of the reform package can involve tariffication of quantitative restrictions and

---

10. Sachs' (1987) interpretation of the success of the Republic of Korea and Taiwan (China) is that these countries sequenced their reforms, stabilizing the economy first and only much later adopting an outward-oriented development strategy. In fairness, in the case of transitional economies there has been a recognition of the desirability of moving simultaneously toward macroeconomic equilibrium and removing quantitative restrictions (see Fischer and Gelb 1991).

the tax base can expand significantly as imports increase), it is often argued that one cannot take the risk of shrinking revenues during stabilization.[11]

Third, trade liberalization will require a compensating devaluation to effect the required real exchange rate (RER) depreciation, unless, of course wages are flexible downwards. So the exchange rate is needed to maintain external balance. At the same time, the exchange rate is a helpful lid on prices, as, for instance, in several heterodox programs of the 1980s in Latin America (such as the Austral and Cruzado plans), where fixing the exchange rate was a key ingredient. There is therefore a conflict between the exchange rate as a stabilization device during a disinflation program and its use as a resource-switching device in a trade liberalization program [the "real targets" versus the "nominal anchor" approach according to Corden's (1991) terminology].

Of the objections to liberalizing trade while disinflating, the third is the most serious. Governments have countless times used the exchange rate during disinflation, even if not as explicitly as during the ill-fated TABLITA episode of the late 1970s in Argentina, Chile, and Uruguay. As the experience of the TEP countries illustrates, this tension was present in the high-inflation countries (in Czechoslovakia, Poland, and Vietnam, for example, the exchange rate was at least occasionally targeted to the price level rather than to competitiveness). On practical grounds, it is mainly because of this conflicting use of the exchange rate that sequencing is advocated with stabilization up front and trade liberalization at a later stage.

The potentially conflicting role between the two uses of the exchange rate is best shown by discussing the typical situation facing the TEP countries with a macroeconomic problem: an external deficit caused by a permanent reduction in foreign transfers or a reduction in foreign demand (the transitional economies) that resulted in a government deficit (loss-making firms were compensated by subsidies under Central Planning) or direct excessive government spending (most other cases). In either case, a reduction in government spending was called for to restore macroeconomic equilibrium. With limited access to foreign borrowing, the deficit ultimately resulted in inflation, as the governments, unable to carry out the required cuts in spending, borrowed from their central banks.[12]

Using the real targets approach, a nominal exchange rate depreciation would help switch expenditures and reduce the external deficit, provided there is sufficient real wage flexibility. Of course, unless the government also

---

11. For more on the fiscal implications of trade liberalization in the TEP countries, see Hood (chapter 5 in this volume).

12. In our sample, Mali, belonging to the CFA zone, is an exception. It had a convertible currency and access to borrowing from the French Treasury.

reduces spending, the improvement will only be temporary, as excessive government spending will work itself out in rising nontraded goods prices. Using Corden's terminology, it is reduction in the fiscal deficit that "leads." The same applies under trade liberalization: if there is no fiscal deficit initially, and the RER maintains external balance, a reduction in tariffs, export taxes, or both will require an RER depreciation if nontraded goods prices are flexible; and, a nominal exchange rate depreciation is required to bring back external balance if downward rigidity of nominal wages prevents a fall in the price of nontraded goods. Here too the exchange rate "follows" the trade liberalization. So with downward rigidity of wages, a devaluation is necessary. This is why following the trajectory of the RER during a trade liberalization is a crucial indicator of success.[13]

Chronic Inflation: A Way Out?

It is partly because of the pervasive wage indexation in chronic inflation countries (Uruguay in the TEP group) that a nominal devaluation is not favored in high-inflation countries. Here the exchange rate serves as the nominal anchor, taking the "lead" role. Of course, fixing the exchange rate implies that a coherent monetary policy must also be followed, which in turn implies a reduction in the fiscal deficit. If the monetary policy is not consistent with the exchange rate, reserves can temporarily be run down and quantitative restrictions imposed. If the government policy is credible, however, and perceived as such by the private agents, then the "prisoner's dilemma" situation that characterizes many chronic inflation countries can resolve itself fairly rapidly with relatively little output loss. The case for using the nominal anchor is, of course, its visibility; also, it is well defined. All these characteristics make it superior to an expenditure anchor or even a monetary rule. Against it is the likelihood that a nominal anchor approach will create a balance of payments problem, because it always involves at least a temporary RER appreciation.

It would thus appear that the exchange rate cannot be used in the pursuit of these two objectives. Liberalization requires a real depreciation while stabilization implies at least a temporary appreciation. Yet, as noted above, countries pursue both objectives simultaneously. Rodrik (1993a) argues that the extent of wage rigidity is itself endogenous and that, if the government can credibly commit, wages need no longer be predetermined with respect to the

---

13. In her study of liberalization episodes that failed, Krueger (1978) concludes that twelve of thirteen failures were due to the RER becoming overvalued. Similar conclusions were reached by Michaely, Choksi, and Papageorgiou in their more recent study of trade liberalization episodes. They conclude that a real exchange rate depreciation "appears to be almost a necessary condition for at least partial survival of a liberalization policy" (1990, p. 196).

nominal exchange rate. Hence a commitment to a pegged exchange rate can, if credible, resolve the potential conflict between trade liberalization and exchange rate stability because the nominal wage rigidity becomes endogenous. While this is a theoretical way out, it points to the endogenous nature of economic reactions to signals and opens the door to the discussion on political economy that follows.[14]

Reform Design in SSA Countries

For English-speaking SSA countries, where a black market for foreign exchange often prevails and the government is usually a net purchaser of U.S. dollars (Kenya and Uganda in the TEP sample), a sequencing issue arises in the unification of the foreign exchange markets. In these economies, where exporters, in principle, have to surrender foreign exchange at the official exchange rate, the black market premium serves as an implicit tax on exports, reducing the need for inflationary finance. It is therefore clear that credible fiscal reform should come first. If not, there is the risk of flight from the currency, which would lower the tax base. As pointed out by Pinto (in Classens 1993), there is likely to be a tradeoff between the inflation costs of exchange rate unification and the resource allocation benefits when unification results in the loss of a tax instrument.

In French-speaking SSA countries such as Mali, until the historic devaluation of the CFA franc in January 1994, the exchange rate was used as a nominal anchor, requiring switching to take place via adjustments in wages and the domestic price level. Typically this is a slow "automatic" adjustment process [in Mali average consumer price index inflation was only 1 percent per year during 1990–92, implying a very slow RER depreciation]. This is the main reason why the nominal anchor approach is not generally favored when large expenditure switching is required.

Transitional Economies: The Trade Liberalization Route to Price Reform

For transitional economies, the sequencing issue was somewhat different, even if the application of tight credit and fiscal policies would help reduce the current account deficit and lower inflation. First, all transitional economies in TEP had to deal with the "monetary overhang" phenomenon (money kept by consumers during the shortage of goods). The problem could be addressed either through

---

14. During the TABLITA episode, it was also believed that economic reactions would be endogenous to policy signals. Failure was partly attributable to inconsistent monetary and wage policies, and also to the design of reforms (for example, opening the capital account).

confiscation, the sale of state assets to mop up some of the overhang, a suffi-ciently sharp rise in interest rates to encourage the holding of financial assets, or, more simply, via inflation. It is this last course of action that was mostly taken in all the TEP countries (inflation operates by deception on the unsuspecting pub-lic and arouses less dissent). Some privatization also took place, helping mop up some of the overhang, but this was usually at a later stage.[15] Second, the legacy of the "soft budget constraint" from Central Planning limited considerably the use of monetary policy. Higher interest rates would not have deterred firms from refinancing growing interest charges in a giant Ponzi scheme until institutional changes made bankruptcy a credible threat.

In the transitional economies the exchange rate could also play the switch-ing and nominal anchor role that it plays in market economies. The one com-plication, however, is that firms in virtually all transitional economies were operating under price controls and, until the dissolution of the CMEA in early 1991, under a price system that was dictated by Central Planning and bore no connection to the relative scarcities suggested by a market economy. For the exchange rate to function as a switching device, it was obviously necessary to remove price controls. At the same time, for moving toward a market economy, there was no better signal of relative scarcity than world prices; hence the need to approximate closely this system as soon as possible and to adopt a liberal trade regime early on, a recommendation made by TEP teams and applied by most countries.

The trade liberalization route to price reform is even more compelling once the organizational characteristics of these economies are factored in. Central Planning had pushed monopolization to an extreme (to cite an amus-ing example, in the name of scale economy exploitation, Ulam Batar had only one bakery—and only one kind of low-quality bread, we were told!). De-monopolization, a necessary reform in all transitional countries, could be addressed in the most expeditious and efficient way in the short run by en-hancing competition through the opening of the economy to foreign trade.

At first sight the reform package outlined above would appear to any-one a tall order indeed. Considering trade reforms alone, few market econo-mies have carried out such a package rapidly and simultaneously.[16] It could be argued, however, that once again the transitional economies benefited from special circumstances that might have proven salutary in the end. In-deed, in retrospect, here too the special circumstances of the transitional

---

15. For a discussion of the alternative methods of stabilization with reference to the transitional economies, see Mundell (in Classens 1993).

16. Chile's profound reforms during 1975–79 also started from a macroeconomic cri-sis and a foreign trade regime almost as distorted as in the transitional economies. But Chile took five years to get to as close to world prices as the transitional economies did in less time.

economies probably helped them. With a weak fiscal system, using trade taxes for revenues must have been tempting, but not only had they never been used in CMEA trade (which amounted to well over three-quarters of trade) but there was no customs there to collect them. And eliminating export controls could not have met with much resistance in foreign exchange–scarce economies.

A related issue for the transitional economies is the sequencing of "systemic" legal reforms (for example, establishment of property rights and bankruptcy laws) and their relation to other economic reforms. In the TEP sample, Mongolia under a Soviet regime since 1925, is the country most subject to this sequencing issue (the CEE countries and Vietnam had such laws at least until the late 1940s). While the general advice has been to proceed simultaneously with economic and legal reforms (see Fischer and Gelb 1991), some, such as Brenner (in Classens 1993), have argued that legal reforms must come first. In Brenner's view, price deregulation cannot take place even to relieve bottlenecks until firms are subject to hard budget constraints, and the allocative benefits of price liberalization cannot be realized until there is a clear assignment of responsibility for making decisions on price policy. In practice, most of these countries' economic reforms went ahead first, with the more difficult and time-consuming legal reforms following slowly.[17] This lack of sequencing has certainly to do with the current economic woes of Russia, the new republics of the Commonwealth of Independent States, and Mongolia.

The Political Economy of Reforms

Despite the endogeneity of variables to the design of stabilization and reform programs, certainly the most important obstacles to reform in the TEP countries were not technical ones of diagnosis and information but difficulties of design associated with rendering the program politically acceptable.[18] While the issues of political feasibility were not dealt with explicitly in the TEP missions, recognition of political constraints was often reflected in report recommendations. I choose to bring them to the fore because it seems that the vast difference in reform implementation across the TEP countries had far more to do with the political situation of the countries and the distributional consequences of implementing the reform packages than the controversial nature of the recommendations. In reviewing the main political

---

17. An exception is Vietnam, which certainly followed the sequencing suggested by Brenner. Land ownership preceded deregulation of the rice market in 1986 when the doi moi policy was initiated. During the TEP visit, the Ministry of Trade was reluctant to remove licensing controls for exports prior to the adoption of a commercial code.

18. Mongolia and Vietnam probably faced large technical difficulties due to lack of expertise, information, and appropriate legal framework.

economy issues facing reform implementation, it is useful to distinguish between two broad groups of countries.

The first group of countries can be characterized by authoritarian rule
(usually by one-party dictatorships or military *juntas*) or weak democracies.
This group, which was considerably larger a decade ago, comprising most of
Latin America, is shrinking rapidly. In the case of most SSA countries in the
TEP sample (as well as in Mongolia), it can be argued that the democratic
regimes are either weakly established or do not operate as in the more ma-
ture democracies, where the polity at large participates actively in the electoral process. This group is well represented in the TEP project, and it is worth
mentioning briefly the political economy of policy formulation in this group.
Here the state is relatively autonomous, free from the pressures of interest
group lobbying and influence, although not free from the pressure of reward-
ing those who support the regime. The questions then are, the origins of this
autonomy and its effect on the formulation and implementation of policy.

The second group of countries is characterized as established democracies. In this group, which is growing in size with the political liberalization of
the late 1980s, governments face an electorate that can organize itself and
lobby effectively. The issue here is usually one of the relative role of interest
groups in influencing economic policy, and of the relative loss of autonomy
of the state in formulating policy. In the TEP group, Uruguay is an extreme
example of the state having lost all independence in policy design. But most
high-income countries belong to this category, as do the long-established
democracies in Costa Rica and Mauritius.

Pressure Groups and Reform Implementation

In a perceptive review of the origins of the "modern state," Findlay (1991)
argues that the failure of the modern state to transfer to many developing
countries is the lack of "civil society." As a result, the state is in the hands of
a minority that controls the means of administration, which usually culmi-
nates in the effective monopoly of the use of force.[19] Findlay then argues that
the size of the autonomous state depends mostly on the degree of the
legitimacy of the authoritarian regime. If the state can be viewed as both
"productive" (provision of public goods) and "predatory" (confiscation of
income for redistributive purposes or implementation of grandiose projects
producing small economic benefits), then one must consider the integration

---

19. Bauer (1987), in his discussion of marketing boards prevalent in all the SSA countries in our sample, states, "The policies of the marketing boards is a conspicuous instance of the disparity in political effectiveness between the urban political elites and the
unorganized and inarticulate rural population. The former usually control the political
and administrative machinery, the media, and usually also key elements of the military."

of both roles. In the integration of the productive and predatory elements of the state, according to Findlay, the former is likely to predominate in the well-established regimes, the latter in regimes where power is more contested and it is necessary for the elite to maximize budgetary resources to buy political support and justify its role in society.

Fascinating as it is, Findlay's discussion of the size of the state and of the extent of rent seeking is peripherally connected with our concerns with reform implementation. What is more relevant is the interest in reform of those in power under an autonomous state. In the cases of Morocco (monarchical legitimacy) and Vietnam (uncontested state), reform should be easier to implement from the top down, because there is less need to rely on the distribution of rents generated by the activities of the state.[20]

In authoritarian regimes that lack legitimacy there is no incentive for reform. On the contrary, the survival of the regime is likely to depend heavily on the rents (for example, the extraction of surplus from farmers through taxation) that would vanish under reform. Perhaps the most glaring case among TEP countries is Madagascar. It is therefore not surprising that reforms did not progress much in countries where political regimes lack legitimacy.

At the same time it must be recognized that in most SSA countries in the TEP group, predatory activities have led to a collapse of fiscal revenues. Once fiscal revenues collapse, reforms would obviously gain in political appeal, and it can be argued that the recent movement toward reform in many SSA countries occurred in countries where fiscal revenues collapsed (for example, Uganda in the TEP sample). This observation, if correct, leads to the question of whether the political elite would backtrack on reforms once the tax base gets built up again.

In sum, carrying out reforms in the autonomous state category brackets the array of possible cases in terms of ease of implementation. If convinced, an uncontested autonomous state is in the most favorable situation to carry out reform because there is little need to build coalition support [for example, the reforms under military regimes in Chile, Korea, and Taiwan (China) prior to political liberalization]. At the other extreme, if a government's power and legitimacy are contested, it is likely to resist carrying out reform.

In countries where political leaders have to contend with the electoral process, implementing reforms is more complicated, because support for the reforms must be gained. In the TEP group, all the transitional economies except Vietnam were undergoing political liberalization at the same time as economic

---

20. It is interesting to contrast the relative success of these two countries at undertaking and maintaining reforms with the failure of top-down reform in Nigeria under the military government of Babangida, where the lack of legitimacy was a major reason for the failure of reform. See the Herbst and Olukoshi chapter in Haggard and Webb (1994).

transformation, all starting from situations where the economic policies of the authoritarian regimes were discredited. Except for Czechoslovakia, they were also in the midst of macroeconomic crisis. Was this auspicious for reform?

In their summary of the experience of countries undertaking economic reforms under varying political circumstances, Haggard and Webb (1994) argue that new democracies born under dire economic circumstances have a broad, if diffuse mandate to carry out reform, and that those governments that moved most rapidly ("shock therapy" approach in Poland) were the most successful at reform implementation. New democracies enjoyed a honeymoon period during which the costs of adjustment could be traded against political gains.

Haggard and Webb also argue that rapid reforms are advocated for established political regimes on the grounds that the problem of short-term political reaction is often exaggerated. And governments are not necessarily punished for pushing reform through the system. Finally, as increasingly argued in theoretical models of the speed of reform, a government can gain credibility for moving fast as it demonstrates its commitment to reform.[21]

Haggard and Webb suggest that bundling reforms is helpful to get reforms accepted politically. The reason for this is that opposition to reforms is often driven by uncertainty. Including a large number of reforms in a package increases the probability that a larger percentage of the population will find some element beneficial to them. This in turn could help gather support for reform.

Carrying out reforms is perhaps most difficult for established democracies such as Costa Rica, Mauritius, and Uruguay. In the implementation phase, they must first build enough legislative support to push through the reform and, once it is initiated, build a supporting coalition to sustain it. In the reform initiation phases, governments must first deal with the natural shortsightedness imposed by the electoral cycle, and with the presence of parties: the larger their number the more likely that government is by coalition and the less likely that reforms can be pushed through. Second, they must deal with the bias toward the status quo, usually resulting from the creation of rents that are difficult to remove, especially once they are capitalized.[22] Third is the pressure group effect from lobbying, which is strongest when there is a large number of (small) gainers facing a small group of (large) losers. Politicians will typically respond to the demands of pressure groups engaged in intense lobbying with the result that the will of the minority can prevail in democracy.[23] Finally, in the

---

21. Alesina (in Haggard and Webb 1994) surveys these and other models of the political cycle. But see Dewatripont and Roland (1992) for a model where the gradualist approach is preferable because of the costs entailed by partial retrieval of the reforms.

22. In Poland, the outgoing military attempted to build in "authoritarian enclaves" in the new democratic order.

23. The archetypal example is Uruguay, where reform paralysis can very well be interpreted in this framework. See Connolly and de Melo (1994).

implementation phase, to avoid reversal once started, coalitions must be built in support of reform implementation typically by trading in efficiency for political support through offsetting gains, or by expanding the representation and weight of interest groups benefiting from the reforms (and minimizing access by anti-reform rent seekers by marginalizing the agencies through which they obtain special treatment).

This discussion of hurdles faced by governments initiating reforms illustrates the difficulties of carrying out and sustaining wide-ranging reforms of the type recommended in many TEP countries. How is it then that countries like Czechoslovakia, Peru, Poland, and Romania have carried out wide-ranging reforms without, so far, going back? One would be tempted to say the advice, and its independent stance! But then there are the other countries where few reforms were initiated (Kenya and Madagascar); obviously, one must look elsewhere.

First is the crisis situation faced by Peru and the transitional economies. The governments that assumed power benefited from strong electoral support, giving them a honeymoon effect (for example, Fujimori in Peru and all the transitional economies), which gave the newly elected government breathing space to initiate reforms. Second, as argued by Rodrik (in Haggard and Webb 1994), in crisis situations the political costs of carrying out trade reforms are vastly diminished. The political costs (the redistributive rectangles in relation to the efficiency triangles) are outweighed by the prospective benefits if the concurrent stabilization program is successful. Clearly, all the countries in macroeconomic crisis could hope to achieve short-term gains sufficient to compensate for the political costs of redistribution entailed by the abolishing of rents. Third, and at least equally important, the case of the CEE countries was the hope (prospect in 1993) of entering the EU. I would argue that the EAs played an important credibility role. And finally, also for the CEE countries, there was little doubt that the change of economic regime (the breakdown of CMEA and the end of subsidized energy) was for good.

Stabilization and Reform in the TEP Countries

In this section we will review the macroeconomic adjustment of the TEP countries, providing rough indicators of external and internal balance. It must be said at the outset that adjustment is still ongoing in most cases and one can only get a rough picture for the countries visited prior to 1990 (macroeconomic data are available until 1993).[24] To present the data, I have divided the countries into three groups. Group I includes countries visited between 1988 and 1990 (Madagascar, Mali, Morocco, Poland, Uganda, and Uruguay). If one counts

---

24. The use of the present tense in the description of adjustment refers to indicator values in 1993, the latest available data at the time of writing (late 1993).

the delay in report preparation and discussion this gives two to three years of postmission data for these countries. Group II includes the three countries visited in 1991 (Costa Rica, Czechoslovakia, and Peru). And group III includes the countries visited since 1992 (Kenya, Mauritius, Mongolia, Romania, Vietnam, and Zimbabwe). For this group, not enough time has elapsed for a meaningful discussion of progress in reform implementation, although these countries were engaged in reforms prior to the TEP visits.

In table 2.2, fiscal deficit, inflation, and the external debt service are used as indicators of macroeconomic balance. In table 2.3, an index of the RER is used as indicator of external balance, and the export ratio and the ratio of consumer goods in total imports as measures of "revealed" trade liberalization. The last column of table 2.2 gives average GDP growth, the usual global indicator of economic performance. Most are not particularly good indicators; the central government deficit being quite inadequate to measure the extent of fiscal pressure, and the two measures for trade reforms do not necessarily reflect the extent of trade liberalization. Their virtue is that they are

Table 2.2. *Internal Balance Indicators*

Country and date of TEP mission	Fiscal deficit		Inflation		EDS/GDP	
	Before TEP	After TEP	Before TEP	After TEP	Before TEP	After TEP
Costa Rica (8/91)	-1.6	1.4	21	16	7.2	7.8
Czechoslovakia (2/91)	-2.4	0.0	17	16	3.5	4.4
Kenya (9/92)	-4.0	—	20	46	7.0	12.3
Madagascar (2/90)	-3.8	-3.2	19	11	6.9	6.6
Mali (6/88)	-7.6	-10.0	2	-3	2.1	2.3
Mauritius (2/92)	-0.4	-0.4	6	9	5.3	4.8
Mongolia (9/92)	-15.2	-10.0	65	268	3.1	4.0
Morocco (10/89)	-5.1	-2.6	4	7	7.3	7.1
Peru (2/91)	-3.6	-1.6	2,989	61	2.0	3.2
Poland (5/88)	-1.3	—	341	192 (25)	2.7	2.1
Romania (12/92)	1.6	-1.8	112	255 (152)	2.4	2.8
Uganda (9/89)	-1.6	-3.9	155	34	2.4	2.8
Uruguay (12/89)	-1.6	0.0	71	84	7.3	7.6
Vietnam (9/92)	-6.4	—	4	6	—	—
Zimbabwe (11/93)	-7.2	—	24	—	7.9	10.5

— Not available.

Note: Figures in parentheses are forecasts for 1994. "Before TEP" is defined as average figures for three years prior to TEP. "After TEP" is defined as one to three years after TEP visit (including year of TEP visit) for missions up to 1992. For missions in 1993, "before" and "after" are 1986–89 and 1990–92 averages. EDS is external debt service.

Source: IFS and International Currency Analysis Inc.

Table 2.3. *External Balance Indicators*

Country and date of TEP mission	RER[a] Before TEP	RER[a] After TEP	I/GDP[b] Before TEP	I/GDP[b] After TEP	EXP/GDP Before TEP	EXP/GDP After TEP	CIMP/GDP Before TEP	CIMP/GDP After TEP	GDP growth Before TEP	GDP growth After TEP[c]
Costa Rica (8/91)	96	91	16.0	17.3	25.3	25.6	22.9	27.3	3.7	6.9 (6.1)
Czechoslovakia (2/91)	—	—	(29.2)	(25.2)	29.2	(98.9)	18.9	—	-3.8	-5.4 (-4.1)
Kenya (9/92)	94	82	10.6	9.1	12.6	24.1	38.5	—	2.4	1.1
Madagascar (2/90)	125	101	4.2	4.7	11.8	10.7	24.9	23.0	2.8	0.8 (2.2)
Mali (6/88)	108	95	10.4	11.9	11.0	12.7	27.9	39.1	2.1	5.7 (7.7)
Mauritius (2/92)	100	101	24.6	23.1	46.7	41.5	20.5	36.8	7.8	5.8
Mongolia (9/92)	—	—	(34.2)	(18.8)	30.3	31.9	5.0	4.4	-1.2	-1.3
Morocco (10/89)	102	96	(22.1)	(23.9)	14.9	14.7	22.2	21.9	4.7	1.5 (0.3)
Peru (2/91)	113	15	14.2	12.9	12.7	9.2	22.8	28.3	-5.2	2.1 (6.5)
Poland (5/88)	107	117	18.2	14.8	18.5	18.0	—	21.5	3.4	-2.7 (4.0)
Romania (12/92)	68	56	(29.0)	(27.0)	18.2	19.7	19.7	12.6	-9.5	1.0
Uganda (9/89)	42	49	6.7	8.6	9.7	5.8	—	—	5.6	4.3 (6.0)
Uruguay (12/89)	100	108	7.2	8.2	18.3	16.0	11.8	20.3	4.6	3.3 (1.5)
Vietnam (9/92)	104	—	(15.4)	(20.5)	24.0	22.2	—	—	6.9	7.0
Zimbabwe (11/93)	82	70	(17.6)	(17.9)	26.7	27.7	25.4	—	1.0	2.0

— Not available.

Note: "Before TEP" is defined as average figures for three years prior to TEP. "After TEP" is defined as one to three years after TEP visit (including year of TEP visit) for missions up to 1992. For missions in 1993, "before" and "after" are 1986–89 and 1990–92 averages, respectively.

a. 1989 = 100; an increase in the index indicates an appreciation.
b. Figures in parentheses refer to total investment; otherwise figures refer to private investment.
c. Figures in parentheses indicate 1993 values.

Source: IFS

widely available. In sum, apart from GDP growth, inflation is probably the more reliable measure of internal balance (no data on unemployment are available for most countries, and data are not available for low- and medium-income countries on a comparable basis), and the RER is the more reliable measure of external balance.

To control for year-to-year fluctuations, all data are expressed as period averages: "before TEP" corresponds to an average of up to three years before the TEP visit (including the year of the TEP visit) and "after TEP" corresponds to up to three years after the TEP visit.

The accumulated evidence cited in the section *The economics of reform packages* in this chapter suggests that a lasting trade liberalization requires an accompanying depreciation of the RER. On the other hand, if trade liberalization is taking place during disinflation, one would expect an appreciation of the RER in the initial phases while the program is building confidence (credibility), with wage rigidity disappearing as confidence builds up. There is no good measure of confidence, although presumably the private investment ratio (when available) is as a good an indicator as any of confidence.[25] This is why the private (total) investment ratio is entered next to the RER as an indicator of confidence. An appreciating RER with a falling private investment ratio could then suggest that the economy may be heading into trouble. But an appreciating RER coupled with a rising private investment ratio could suggest that confidence may be building up.

Group I (Madagascar, Mali, Morocco, Poland, Uganda, and Uruguay)

In this group, Poland and Uganda faced the largest visible macroeconomic imbalances. Neither country has yet eliminated inflation, but both have succeeded in bringing back inflation to manageable levels, and 1993 growth figures were encouraging (see table 2.3). In both cases, severe overvaluation was eliminated and Poland reached current account convertibility in 1990. However, the fiscal balance remains still precarious in both countries. In Poland, recovery has been driven by consumption and national savings are still declining. State-owned enterprises (SOEs) have not yet carried out the necessary adjustments, and there is risk of fiscal slippage. In Uganda, the fiscal deficit is still large, private investment has not really picked up and the economy is still extremely closed, with the lowest export ratio in the sample.

The other high-inflation country in the group, Uruguay, has not managed to reduce inflation in spite of progress in trade reform (see below). The indicators in table 2.2 still show a high external debt service that must undermine the

---

25. The premium for foreign exchange on parallel markets is also an indicator of confidence but is often quite volatile.

overall credibility of the reforms in spite of a relatively good fiscal stance. Inflation has remained stubbornly high in spite of fiscal balance. This is because of the country's long history of inflation, which has encouraged widespread indexation. The economy has also become increasingly dollarized. Because of dollarization, any increase in the money stock has a larger proportional effect, and therefore a larger inflationary effect. With a large public sector, public sector wage adjustments are the most closely watched aspect of economic policy, and the government has been so far unable to devise wage adjustments that are both consistent with stabilization and politically acceptable (backward- rather than forward-looking indexation). It is argued below that Uruguay's difficulties in carrying out reforms including macroeconomic adjustment can largely be explained in political economy terms.

Morocco appears to have been in the best macroeconomic situation in the group because inflation was low. In fact, the macroeconomic situation was not so good because of the high external debt service burden. Moreover, the well-developed finance system allowed the government to finance the deficit in a noninflationary manner by taxing an oligopolistic banking system that in turn charged high interest rates to borrowers. Given the past difficulty in containing the budget, TEP suggested a move away from pegging to a basket of currencies to a peg to the European Monetary System (EMS), as a credibility signal the government might want to consider in its stabilization effort.

Madagascar has made no progress. The macroeconomic situation has not improved and recently quantitative restrictions have been imposed on almost all imports. Traditional exports continue to be taxed, and the fiscal system is extremely complex and cumbersome in spite of several rounds of reforms.[26] Much has to do with the political uncertainty. The defeated president, Ratsirak, has not yet stepped down and is still occupying the presidential palace.

Mali's adjustment is interesting. The economy managed to depreciate its RER without using a nominal devaluation. Mali has also carried out a number of reforms, including the removal of licensing and quantitative restrictions, and the dismantling of several monopolies.[27] The data in tables 2.2 and 2.3 show an RER depreciation and a substantial increase in the ratio of consumer goods imports in total imports. It is expected that the devaluation of the CFA franc in 1994 and the expected debt relief will help sustain the high

---

26. De Melo, Roland-Holst, and Haddad (1993) show that if the tax structure prevailing in 1991 were replaced with uniform sales tax (in manufacturing only) and uniform tariffs of 6 percent, the government would have obtained the same revenue as with the prevailing tax structure.

27. See World Bank (1994, tables A.8 and A.12). Among the twenty-nine SSA countries in the study, Mali scored the highest improvement in terms of reduction in monopoly activities during the period 1987–92, compared with average levels during 1981–86.

expected growth rate for 1993 (see table 2.3). However, as noted above, the fiscal situation remains precarious, and it cannot be said that the country has reached a sustainable macroeconomic equilibrium.

Group II (Costa Rica, Czechoslovakia, and Peru)

The TEP team visited Peru at the time of the change in political regime just as the Bolona government was assuming office. In many ways, the election of Fujimori had common elements with the regime change in transitional economies although one cannot speak of a change of regime because democracy was already established. The similarity is that both governments had a strong, if diffuse, popular support for a change in policies. Peru, much like Poland, moved to carry out simultaneous stabilization and liberalization. While inflation is still high, there has been much progress on the macroeconomic front following the bold reforms in early 1991, and the external debt situation is better than for several other countries. Peru has not really turned the corner in spite of signs that the trade regime has been substantially liberalized: private investment has not picked up and the economy's openness is still very low.

Even though Costa Rica has made some progress on the fiscal front, effected a needed RER depreciation to improve its competitiveness, and liberalized its trade regime, it still has a high debt service ratio. Costa Rica faced the typical problem of economies with a high fiscal deficit: improvement in the fiscal deficit by raising taxes (surcharges on imports and sales tax). While these taxes were temporary, they conflicted with the objective of trade liberalization. If growth would help the country service its debt, Costa Rica faced the difficult tradeoff of countries carrying out trade liberalization in a situation of macroeconomic disequilibrium: compensate the loss of government revenue from trade liberalization with a reduction in public sector expenditures (including a reduction in public sector wages).

Finally, Czechoslovakia started from a much better position than the other transitional economies, in the sense that economic mismanagement had been much less under Communist rule there than in the other transitional economies. It is then understandable that time was taken prior to Czechoslovakia's engaging in reforms, although a big bang approach was taken in 1991, when at a stroke prices were liberalized, the koruna made convertible on the current account, and the exchange rate pegged. Government disengagement was remarkable, its share in GDP falling 14 percentage points between 1989 and 1992. With a fiscal surplus, unemployment at 3 percent, and inflation down to 10 percent, the Czech Republic is closer to the Maastricht criteria than several current EU members. The Slovak Republic is also making much progress, with falling inflation, apparent political stability, and GDP growth similar to that of the Czech Republic (2 percent forecast for 1994).

Group III (Kenya, Mauritius, Mongolia, Romania, Vietnam, and Zimbabwe)

For this group not enough time has elapsed to judge progress. Mauritius had no macroeconomic disequilibrium, its major problem being how to shift away from a low–labor cost development strategy and build up the necessary human capital. Vietnam comes in a close second, having established macroeconomic equilibrium and growth with no external help in spite of a large negative shock. Capitalism is mushrooming and the inflow of FDI should help smooth restructuring of the economy. Kenya and Zimbabwe are in a relatively difficult position, with large fiscal deficits and excessive reliance on foreign trade taxation to support government finances, probably adding up to highly distortionary trade regimes once all the impediments to trade are factored in. Kenya's deteriorating performance had already started in the early 1970s, but the downturn was accentuated by poor management of the coffee boom of the late 1970s and the breakup of the East African Common Market. Fiscal control was never reached, foreign exchange excess demand was met by various forms of rationing, and the incentive system became increasingly distorted. In Zimbabwe, lack of fiscal control is also the cause of the poor macroeconomic situation. In addition, a quarter of a century of self-sufficiency during the period of sanctions led to the second largest manufacturing sector in low-income countries (after China), which may not be sustainable in the context of the recent political changes in South Africa.

The worst macroeconomic disequilibria were faced by Mongolia and Romania. Mongolia probably faced the largest shock of all the countries in the TEP project. It is estimated that, prior to the collapse of the U.S.S.R., Mongolia received about 15 percent of its GDP in subsidies from the U.S.S.R. When the subsidies came to an end, this resource- and infrastructure-poor country had few means to adjust because its trade was almost entirely geared toward the CMEA. Much of the adjustment was through inflationary finance, export controls, and controlled prices for meat to cushion the decline in living standards.

Romania's situation was not as bad, although it too had developed an extremely energy-intensive economy. As in Mongolia, the fiscal deficit was driven by subsidies (5.5 percent of GDP in 1993), with foreign exchange rationing and export quotas. Inflation is forecast around 150 percent for 1994. In spite of a large adjustment in relative prices and a move toward world price anchors for all tradables, including energy, adjustment is proving difficult. However, the association agreement signed with the EU in 1993 and the prospect of eventually joining the EU has helped prevent policy reversals.

Some Political Economy Comparisons

In this section I will discuss some situations that illustrate particular reform implementation issues for three political environments: transitional economies, established democracies, and authoritarian regimes.

Transitional Economies

Following the "Velvet Divorce" of late 1992, the Czech Republic was left with a remarkably homogenous society and has managed to carry out the transition to a market economy in five years, a remarkable achievement indeed.[28] From a political economy point of view there is little doubt that the cornerstone of the success so far (much restructuring still needs to be carried out and will likely raise unemployment) is the social contract between the government and the workers whereby Czech workers accept low wages for high employment and a low cost of living. It is not clear whether this contract will continue if restructuring implies a substantial increase in unemployment. Nonetheless, the Czech Republic needs to continue to restructure its economy and maintain momentum toward increased efficiency.

In the case of Poland, one could argue that if it were not for the EAs and the prospect of membership in the EU, Poland could have resembled Uruguay, becoming a country where the exercise of democracy would have prevented the completion of the radical Balcerowitz shock therapy initiated in 1990. At the same time, much of the reform in progress in Uruguay in the last three years has benefited from the Southern Cone Common Market (MERCOSUR) agreement and improvement in economic conditions in Argentina and now in Brazil.

Reviewing the TEP recommendations discussed in November 1988 with the then-Communist government, it is interesting that the recommendations were quite close to the shock therapy program that was eventually put in place in early 1990, especially if one considers that they took into account the government's weak position.[29] The failure of the policies under the roundtable

---

28. An ingenious voucher scheme speeded up asset transfer into private hands, from less than 2 percent five years ago to 80 percent by the end of 1994.

29. The matrix of policy recommendations in the TEP report suggests immediate macroeconomic stabilization by absorbing excess liquidity through asset sales and an immediate move to what would amount to world price determination for traded goods, but gives three to five years to get to market-determined prices and allows for a "very short" list of centrally balanced goods. However, the rise in food prices in 1988 led to a 30 percent fall in real wages, Solidarity-driven strikes, and an immediate rise in wages leading into the inflationary spiral (part of the microeconomic reforms under the communist regime had handed the control of wages, but not profits, to enterprise managers).

agreements of 1989 illustrate the problems in designing reforms when power is divided. Subsidies were to be removed and goods prices decontrolled in a move toward a market economy, while wages were to be fully indexed on past inflation, and privatization would not be on the agenda (to meet the demands of the still powerful pro-Communist groups)—all this with the recognition of political freedom. The program failed but in the context was viewed as a transition toward democracy and a market economy.

The widely known Balcerowitz plan of 1990 need not be discussed. It has been discussed by Frydman and others (in Classens 1993), the Johnson and Kowalska chapter in Haggard and Webb 1994, and Rosati (1992). It is noteworthy that the shock therapy that established immediate convertibility of the zloty was faster than the World Bank's recommendation of convertibility to be reached in five years. The program also benefited from substantial external assistance in the form of debt reduction, fresh finance, and a three-year moratorium on external debt service payments. The budget deficit was to be eliminated by the removal of subsidies while providing a social safety net to cushion the expected unemployment during the transition. Inflation was somewhat slower to fall than expected, and the program was in deep trouble both economically (the unexpected 20 percent fall in output of SOEs deprived the state of its largest tax base) and politically.[30] (The social costs of adjustment were rising, the Solidarity movement disintegrated, and the political system with proportional representation that emerged was small-group, multi-party. The former Communists sought legitimacy by opposing the Bielecki government.)

By 1992, Poland had matured into a fragmented multi-party system with government by weak coalitions. The bold trade reforms of early 1990 had been partly reversed [removal of nontariff barriers (NTBs) and an average tariff of 5.8 percent had been partly reversed in 1991, with the resumption of some NTBs and an increase in the average tariff to 18 percent in 1992]; agricultural policies were moving toward European Community (EC)–style farm supports. Why then weren't the Balcerowitz policies abandoned? Above all, the signing of the association agreement with the European Community in December 1991 offered perhaps the prospect of future support and access to

---

30. This was partly because the partial wage indexation had to be augmented in the face of sharp declines in living standards and the giving in to demands from the best organized group (agriculture was always privately owned in Poland, and the farmers were the best organized political group). Frydman and others argue (in Classens 1993) that prior to the change of regime, monopolistic enterprises were not following profit-maximizing behavior, as the incentive system encourages managers to charge less-than-equilibrium prices in exchange for favors from the customers. This behavior changed in 1990, contributing to an unexpected rise in prices, and is consistent with no bankruptcies in the early months of the liberalization program.

the EU but, more important, it set limits on what policies were seen as responsible within Poland. Although the economic indicators had not turned around by 1992 (see table 2.3), there were some gainers, and the losers could not form alternative workable policies, so opposition was mainly aimed at blocking further changes.

Established Democracies

In many ways, in 1989 Uruguay was in a similar situation politically to Poland in 1992. The intervention of the state was in some sense the same as Poland's at the time of the Balcerowitz plan. Among the differences was no external shock of the magnitude felt by the transitional economies, and two economically unstable neighbors: Argentina and Brazil. Otherwise, the economy's long history of inflation was reflected in extensive indexation, and much of industry and services was in the hands of the state. The state's intervention in resource allocation was pervasive, with a relatively large welfare state mostly financed by distortionary taxation, notably of agriculture. Rent-seeking activity was rampant.

It is noteworthy that in Uruguay's recent economic history, the only period of significant rationalization of policies was under the military regime (1974–82) when the democratic process was suspended. The reforms under the military were similar in scope to those in Poland (including stabilization policies; a move toward convertibility; and deregulation of goods, foreign trade, and financial markets). The reforms also started from a situation of economic distress and were internally generated (and probably went faster and further than would have been recommended by the World Bank). If a free hand was essential to implement the reforms under the military, the crisis situation also probably contributed significantly to the acceptance of harsh policies.

Although the reforms ended with a balance of payments crisis and capital flight exacerbated by an unsuccessful attempt at using the exchange rate as a nominal anchor under the TABLITA policy, the reforms had raised the growth rate. So why weren't reforms pursued when democracy was back in 1985? Relying on Rodrik's notion of the political cost-benefit ratio and Olson's (1985) theory of collective action, Connolly and de Melo (1994) argue that the system of protection conferred very concentrated rents and diluted benefits, explaining why there was much organized opposition to reform.[31]

It is remarkable then that some progress has been made in recent years as reference prices have been progressively reduced (the 40–35–30–20–10

---

31. For a discussion of the income transfers that would result from liberalization of the automobile assembly industry, see Takacs (1994). Most recently, the attempt at privatizing the port was rejected in a national referendum.

tariff structure moved to 20–15–10–6 by 1993) and the complex restrictions in the automobile sector have been ended (see the rise in the consumer goods' share of imports in table 2.3). The authorities met with much resistance in carrying out these reforms, and it is unlikely that they would have been able to get so far had it not been for Uruguay's participation in the 1991 MERCOSUR Treaty that resulted in a customs union by 1995 with Argentina, Brazil, and Paraguay. So here too an external factor was important in getting some reforms underway.

In many respects, Uruguay's economic policy decisionmaking satisfies the conditions described in the recent wars-of-attrition political economy models: substantial distributional effects and some uncertainty about the relative strengths of the various groups. It is interesting that these models suggest that the way out of the deadlocks are adverse shocks and the granting of extraordinary powers to the government, which, ironically, are the two conditions that were met during the 1974–82 episode in Uruguay mentioned above (see Alesina in Haggard and Webb 1994).

Authoritarian Regimes

In many ways, if they are firmly established, authoritarian regimes are best poised to carry out reforms. The examples of Korea, Singapore, Taiwan (China), and more recently Chile are the most cited cases of countries where economic reforms came before political liberalization, with enough time having elapsed since the start of the reforms for the positive benefits of reform to have shown up so that a constituency for maintaining them was already in place at the time of political change. In the TEP sample, there are two traditional authoritarian regimes: Morocco and Vietnam. Both have carried out sustained reforms, perhaps not enough in the case of Morocco for a constituency to have built up in support of the reforms.

The link between macroeconomic stability and the implementation of trade reform was particularly clear in Morocco. Fiscal pressures in the public sector were shifted onto trade policy, with pervasive quantitative restrictions and a special import tax of 15 percent in place since 1980. Moroccan industrialists were opposed to the reduction of quantitative restrictions (which would have improved treasury revenue) and questioned the special import tax that raised their costs. By the time of the TEP mission, import licensing was somewhat less but there was still use of reference prices, and the average tariff on imports was 37.8 percent. Clearly the tariffication of quantitative restrictions, followed by a lowering of average protection, was the main trade recommendation. Morocco's political economy situation was not that favorable to trade reform, in spite of an authoritarian regime, because industrialists were a powerful group that would, at least temporarily, lose from the removal of quantitative restrictions.[32] Further-more, it was clear that the Mediterranean countries, unlike the CEE coun-tries, would not be taken into the EU. So there was no external pressure to liberalize on the part of Morocco because the preferential trade treatment had not been reciprocal. However, Morocco used its application to General Agreement on Tariffs and Trade (GATT) membership in 1987 to bind tar-iffs, although in some cases at relatively high levels.

Vietnam seems to have gone further than Morocco in terms of controlling its fiscal budget. Like Morocco, Vietnam has followed the more traditional sequencing path to reform: stabilization before trade liberalization. In terms of the political economy perspective taken here, it could be argued that Vietnam's impressive economic performance in recent years has laid the re-quired foundation for political support that will be needed to maintain and continue the reforms underway.

Conclusion

In many ways the diversity of the economies that participated in TEP render comparisons difficult. Not only were initial economic conditions very differ-ent across the group; so were the institutions and political regimes. It is there-fore not surprising that countries followed different paths to reform. Com-parison suggests perhaps three lessons.

First, the countries in distress (Peru and transitional economies except Czechoslovakia and Vietnam) were able to move on all fronts simultaneously, reducing macroeconomic imbalances and liberalizing foreign trade. While there are good economic reasons for such a move, two political economy reasons must have also contributed to this strategy: a broad, if diffuse, support for change; and relatively large short-term efficiency gains compared with the redistributive effects of the reforms.

Second, the transitional countries benefited from clear signals that en-hanced the credibility of reforms. The shocks were certainly viewed as per-manent, which must have been a contributing factor to implement reforms. Certainly the collapse of CMEA could not have been a clearer signal that the trade regime needed to be overhauled. Moreover, the CEE countries ben-efited from the EAs, which helped implement the reforms and made them more irreversible in the eyes of the public. Indeed it was argued that, in the case of Poland at least, the benefits of reforms were slow in coming, and if it had not been for the EAs and the prospect of membership in the EU, reforms would probably have been reversed.

---

32. Industrialists in textiles have duty-free access to inputs. They would probably only gain marginally from the removal of quantitative restrictions.

Third, transitional economies that were in a better macroeconomic situation opted for gradual reform without, so far, any reversal. It can be argued that in Czechoslovakia and Vietnam reforms proceeded more gradually, to the benefit of both countries. Vietnam has had strong growth, and Czechoslovakia avoided the high unemployment experienced in other transitional economies. In political economy terms, Vietnam's authoritarian regime did not have to contend with the organized political opposition that is encountered in established democracies. In Czechoslovakia, good initial conditions and a social contract between the government and workers helped implementation.

Most other TEP countries also made progress, although not benefiting from the external pressure to adjust that faced the CEE countries. In established democracies, reforms were more gradual, largely because of the redistributive conflicts entailed by the reforms. These were also present in the SSA countries, although in these countries difficulties in carrying out reforms was compounded by technical difficulties (lack of expertise). Also the lopsided development of the political system resulting in too great a concentration of power in the hands of the political elite, for whom reforms would have had high political costs, was a brake on implementing reforms.

Bibliography

Baldwin, Robert. 1994. *Toward an Integrated Europe.* London: Cambridge University Press.

Bauer, P. T. 1987. "Marketing Boards." In J. Eatwell, M. Milgate, and J. Newman, eds., *The New Palgrave: Economic Development.* London: Macmillan Press.

Cadot, Olivier, and Jaime de Melo. 1994. "France and the CEECs: Adjusting to Another Enlargement." Centre for Economic Policy Research Discussion Paper 1049. London.

Classens, Emil-Maria, ed. 1993. *Exchange Rate Policies in Developing and Post-Socialist Economies.* San Francisco: ICS Press.

Connolly, Michael, and Jaime de Melo, eds. 1994. *The Effects of Protectionism on a Small Country: The Case of Uruguay.* Regional and Sectoral Studies. Washington, D.C.: World Bank.

Corbo, Vittorio, M. Goldstein, and M. Khan, eds. 1987. *Growth-Oriented Adjustment Programs..* Washington, D.C.: IMF and World Bank.

Corbo, Vittorio, and Stanley Fischer. 1992. "Adjustment Programs and Bank Support: Rationale and Main Results." In Vittorio Corbo, Stanley Fischer, and Steven B. Webb, eds., *Adjustment Lending Revisited: Policies to Restore Growth: A World Bank Symposium.* Washington, D.C.: World Bank.

Corden, W. Max. 1991. "Exchange Rate Policy in the Developing World." In Jaime de Melo and A. Sapir, eds., *Trade Theory and Economic Reform: North, South, and East.* Oxford, U.K.: Basil Blackwell.

de Melo, Jaime, D. Roland-Holst, and M. Haddad. 1993. "Fraude et réforme de la fiscalité dans une économie à faible revenu: analyse à travers un modèle CGE appliqué à Madagascar." *Revue d'économie du développement* 1(93):63–89.

Dewatripont, M., and G. Roland. 1992. "The Virtues of Gradualism and Legitimacy in the Transition to a Market Economy." *Economic Journal:* 291–300.

Fernandez, R., and Dani Rodrik. 1991. "Resistance to Reform: Status Quo Bias in the Presence of Individual-Specific Uncertainty." *American Economic Review* 81 (December): 1146–55.

Findlay, Ronald. 1991. "Is the New Political Economy Relevant to Developing Countries?" In G. M. Meier, ed., *Policy and Policy Making in Developing Countries.* San Francisco: ICS Press.

Fischer, Stanley, and Alan Gelb. 1991. "The Process of Socialist Economic Transformation." *Journal of Economic Perspectives:* 91–105.

Guillaumont, Patrick, and Sylviane Guillaumont, eds. 1994. *Ajustement et développement: l'expérience des pays ACP.* Paris: Economica.

Haggard, Stephen, and Steven B. Webb, eds. 1994. *Voting for Reform: Democracy, Political Liberalization and Economic Adjustment.* New York: Oxford University Press.

Krueger, Anne O. 1978. *Liberalization Attempts and Consequences.* Cambridge, MA: Ballinger.

Little, Ian M. D., Richard N. Cooper, W. Max Corden, Sarath Rajapatirana. 1993. *Boom, Crisis and Adjustment: The Macroeconomic Experience of Developing Countries.* New York: Oxford University Press.

Messerlin, Patrick. 1992. "The Association Agreements Between the EC and Central Europe: Trade Liberalization vs. Constitutional Failure." In J. Flemming and J. M. C. Rollo, eds., *Trade, Payments, and Adjustment in Central and Eastern Europe.* London: Royal Institute for International Affairs.

Michaely, Michael, Armeane Choksi, and Demetrios Papageorgiou. 1990. *Liberalizing Foreign Trade: Lessons of Experience in the Developing World.* Cambridge, MA: Basil Blackwell.

Olson, Mancur. 1985. *The Logic of Collective Action.* Cambridge, MA: Harvard University Press.

Rodrik, Dani. 1993a. "Trade Liberalization during Disinflation." Discussion Paper 832. Centre for Economic Policy Research, London.

_____. 1993b. "The Transfer Problem in Small Open Economies: Exchange Rate and Debt Fiscal Policies for Debt Service." In Jaime de Melo and R. Faini, eds., *Fiscal Issues in Adjustment in Developing Countries.* London: Macmillan.

Rosati, Dariuscz. 1992. "The Politics of Economic Reform in Central and Eastern Europe." Occasional Paper 6. Centre for Economic Policy Research, London.

Sachs, Jeffrey. 1987. "Trade and Exchange Rate Policies in Growth-Oriented Adjustment Program." In Vittorio Corbo, M. Goldstein, and M. Khan, eds., *Growth-Oriented Adjustment Programs.* Washington, D.C.: IMF and World Bank.

Sapir, Andre. 1994. "The Europe Agreements: Implications for Trade Laws and Institutions: Lessons from Hungary." Discussion Paper 1024. Centre for Economic Policy Research, London.

Takacs, Wendy. 1993. "Libéralisation du Commerce au Mali: le jumelage entre achats intérieurs et licenses d'importation." *Revue d'économie du développement* 3: 81–100.

_____. 1994. "Domestic Content Restrictions and Compensatory Export Requirements in the Automobile Sector." In Michael Connolly and Jaime de Melo, eds., *The Effects of Protectionism on a Small Country: The Case of Uruguay*. Regional and Sectoral Studies. Washington, D.C.: World Bank.

Thomas, Vinod, and John Nash, eds. 1991. *Best Practices in Trade Policy Reform*. New York: Oxford University Press.

World Bank. 1994. *Adjustment in Africa: Reforms, Results and the Road Ahead*. New York: Oxford University Press.

3

Exchange Rate Arrangements during Trade Liberalization

Paul Collier

There are two distinct senses in which the depreciation of the exchange rate is integral to trade liberalization. First, to maintain payments compatibility, the exchange rate will normally have to be depreciated when trade restrictions are reduced, although the extent of depreciation will depend in part on the resort to program aid. Second, in most cases of severe trade restrictions, the process of foreign exchange allocation is itself central to the mechanisms of restriction. In this latter case it is not just that the exchange rate needs to be depreciated, but that the mechanism for determining the exchange rate and allocating foreign exchange must be changed. With respect to the former, I argue that there is a role for program aid in avoiding what is otherwise liable to be exchange rate overshooting, but that the resort to such aid is itself conditional on the extent of the government's credibility problem, which differs substantially between countries at the start of liberalizations. With respect to the latter, I argue that the transition from foreign exchange rationing to market allocation is more a matter of introducing an appropriate agent than an appropriate mechanism.

Exchange rate policy during trade liberalization with a preexisting foreign exchange market discusses the evolution of the exchange rate and the use of aid. *Reform of exchange rate mechanisms* discusses the transition from rationing to market institutions. *Designing better foreign exchange markets* examines approaches to the introduction of appropriate agents. This is followed by concluding remarks and a summary of some pertinent country experiences.

Exchange Rate Policy during Trade Liberalization with a Preexisting Foreign Exchange Market

Some governments, such as Uruguay, were fortunate enough to have liberalized the exchange rate ahead of trade liberalization. In this case the exchange rate will still need to change in response to trade liberalization but the mechanism by which it can do so is already in place. A very common phenomenon when the exchange rate is freely determined during trade liberalization is that it sharply depreciates in the early phases and then has a phase of very strong real appreciation. Neither of these phases is very appealing to governments. When possible, they may be tempted to avoid the exchange rate adjustment by using reserves. The recent experience of Mexico is an example of this. The trade liberalization in the context of the North American Free Trade Agreement (NAFTA) unusually gave the government a massive capacity to borrow. By choosing to borrow, the Mexican government achieved a temporary reduction in inflation at the price of a large payments deficit.

Trade liberalization requires a large initial depreciation in order to maintain current account balance; otherwise the reduction in protection lowers the price of importables, lowering the demand for money and generating a currency outflow. The rationale for depreciation in this context is to offset this incipient fall in the price level. Trade liberalizing devaluation is not inflationary; rather it prevents a falling price level (in relation to the counterfactual). Governments that are locked in to fixed exchange rates are unable to use depreciation to offset the reduction in the demand for money caused by lower trade restrictions. They face precisely the same problem as other governments but without the exchange rate instrument. The remaining policy menu divides into those strategies which, like depreciation, induce an offsetting increase in the demand for money, and those which work by reducing the money supply. An increase in the demand for money can be increased by raising indirect taxation. A reduction in the supply of money can be achieved either by a tightening of fiscal policy or by increasing the required cash or liquidity ratio of the banking system. Fiscal policy, however, only reduces the money supply gradually, and an increase in the cash ratio in effect achieves trade liberalization at the cost of financial repression. In the absence of any of these measures a large trade liberalization will be "payments incompatible": there will be a deterioration in the balance of payments.

The government may choose to finance a payments deficit caused by trade liberalization through borrowing. This has some rationale, although not to the extent adopted by the Mexican government. In the absence of any capital flows the exchange rate will overshoot: depreciating more initially than eventually as a result of the trade liberalization. There are three reasons to expect this. First, lags in resource reallocation imply that there will be a gradual increase in exports and, consequently, a gradual appreciation in the exchange rate for current account balance. Second, as resources reallocate there is a gain in real income, which raises the demand for money.

These two effects are shown in figure 3.1. The figure depicts price space. The vertical axis shows the price of nontradables (such as many services) and the horizontal axis the domestic price of importable goods. The domestic price is determined by the world price, the exchange rate, and trade restrictions. The upward-sloped schedule shows equilibrium in the

Figure 3.1. *Exchange Rate Overshooting in Trade Liberalization*

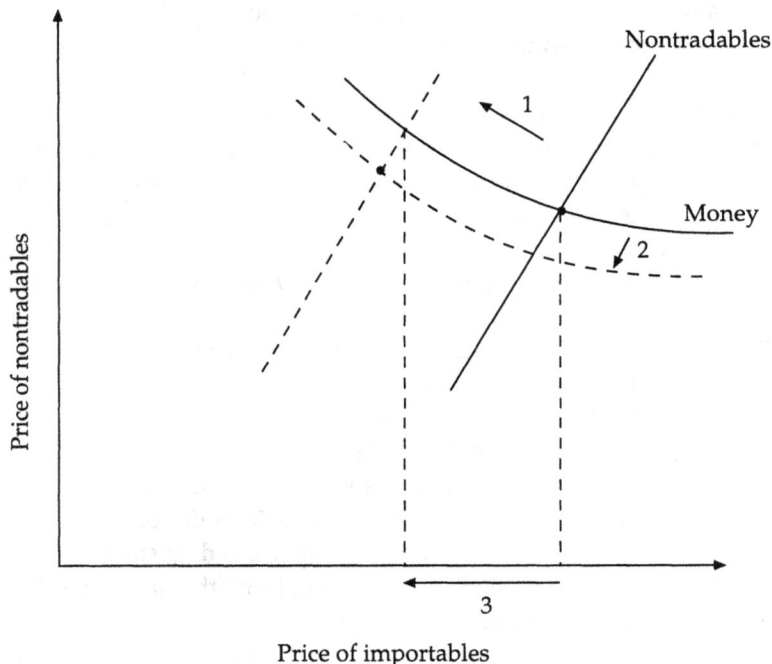

Note: 1, gradual shift of resources into x; 2, gradual gain in real income; 3, gradual e appreciation.

nontradables market. To see why a trade liberalization combined with devaluation shifts the schedule upwards (effect 1), consider the following thought experiment. Suppose that a policy package of trade liberalization and devaluation initially left the domestic price of importables unaltered: the exchange rate depreciation precisely offsetting the reduction in tariffs. The domestic price of exports would rise; the devaluation would benefit exporters. Take any initial point on the nontradables equilibrium schedule. The rise in the price of exports induces labor and capital to shift out of nontradables into exports. The resulting reduced supply of nontradables tends to drive up their prices in relation to importables; that is, the schedule shifts upwards. The downward-sloped schedule depicts equilibrium with respect to money. To simplify, suppose that exportable goods (such as copper or coffee) are not consumed domestically in significant quantities. The schedule then plots the combinations of prices that yield a demand for money, which equals a given money supply and so gives monetary equilibrium. As the price of either good increases, this tends to raise the transactions' demand for money, and so needs an offsetting reduction in the price of the other good to maintain money demand constant. As the trade liberalization package gradually leads to resource reallocation into exports, real income gradually rises, and so, in real terms, people are able to spend more. Were prices to remain unchanged, this increase in the real value of spending would increase the demand for money and so, for a given money supply, cause monetary disequilibrium. For a given supply of money the higher real spending is only compatible with monetary equilibrium if the price level gradually falls, and this is shown by the shift downwards in the money schedule (effect 2). Both of these shifts in the schedules shift the overall price equilibrium to the left (effect 3); that is, the domestic price of importables gradually falls after the reform package. The fall in the domestic price is brought about by a gradual *appreciation* of the exchange rate. Thus, the initial depreciation needed to accommodate the tariff cut is subsequently at least partially offset.

Third, and probably more important, private capital movements are liable to switch from negative in the early stages of liberalization to positive thereafter. A capital outflow in the early stages is possible either because there has been pent-up portfolio demand for foreign assets (as in Zimbabwe, where controls were fairly effective) or because firms wish to build up stocks of imported inputs. Both of these are reinforced to the extent that the liberalization is less than fully credible for whatever reason. This switches to an inflow in response to either greater credibility as a result of the persistence of the reforms, or due to financial liberalization and very high real interest rates. The resulting swing in the exchange rate (at least in real terms) creates a countersignal for the export sector, and also may give the impression of volatility. There may be a role for temporary public borrowing, with the objective of avoiding the overshoot, while leaving the long-term path of the exchange rate unaffected. Suppose that, rather than suffer the political costs of the overshoot, the government chooses to have a nominal depreciation of x percent per month, as in Kenya, until the exchange rate should reach its long-run sustainable level. This policy will require temporary aid, which the government will repay.

This is shown in figure 3.2. The top panel depicts the path of the exchange rate, e, defined as the domestic currency price of a dollar.[1] Without aid the exchange rate is first abruptly devalued (e jumps) to compensate for the abrupt reduction in tariffs, and thereafter gradually appreciates (e reduces), as discussed above. With aid the initial devaluation is avoided and there is a gradual depreciation (e increases along the dotted line). In the first phase the price level falls because aid avoids abrupt devaluation; the trade liberalization lowers the price of importables. In turn this lowers the demand for money, causing an excess supply of money. This monetary disequilibrium manifests itself as a

---

1. *Dollar(s)* is used throughout to mean foreign exchange.

Figure 3.2. *Aided and Unaided Adjustment Paths*

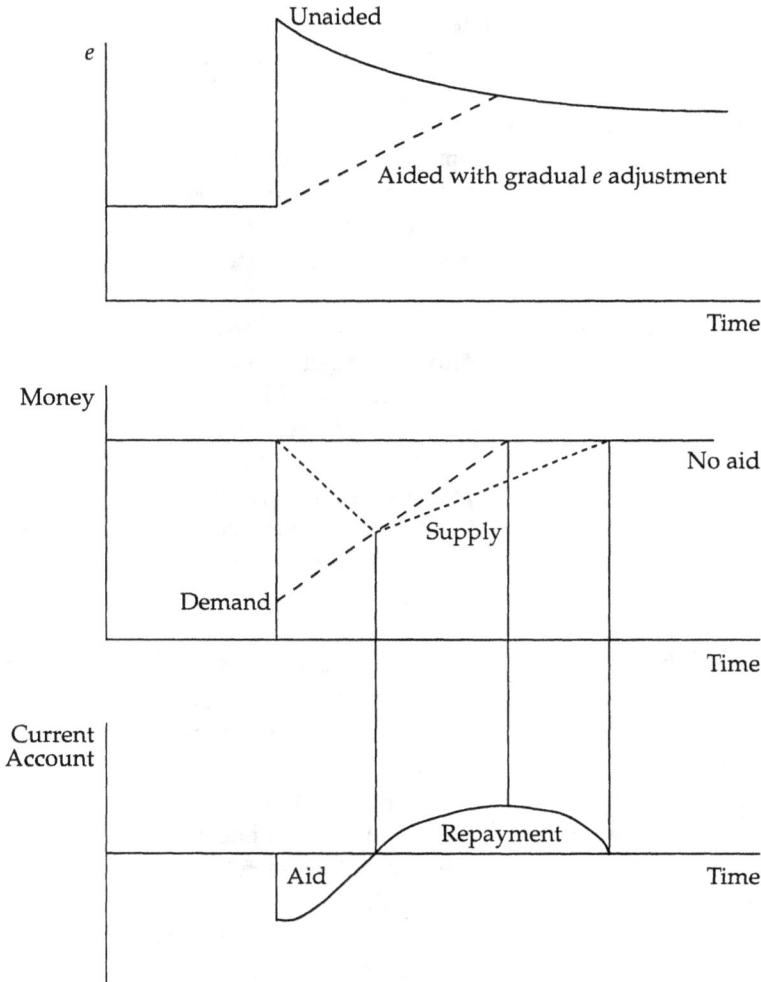

current account deficit (financed by the foreign aid). Gradually, the excess money supply is depleted by the payments deficit. Hence, this phase is characterized by a falling money supply. Simultaneously, the exchange rate is gradually being depreciated by policymakers, and this is driving the price level back up, and with it the demand for money. This phase ends with the attainment of a brief monetary equilibrium at which the money supply has fallen to equal the rising demand so there is current account balance. Were the government not to repay the borrowing this position would be sustainable, but the consequence would be that, in addition to avoiding the overshooting, the exchange rate would be permanently more appreciated than without aid. To avoid such long-run effects, the government must repay the aid. In the second phase it gradually depreciates the exchange rate beyond the payments equilibrium level, causing a rise in the price level, a consequent increase in the demand for money, and thereby a current account surplus, which is used to repay the aid. However, the surplus in turn causes an increase in the money supply. Once the exchange rate has reached the long-run level, the depreciation is stopped, so there is no further increase in money demand. Money supply will continue to increase as long as there is a surplus, but this is, of course, self-correcting; so at some stage the money supply grows to equal money demand, and long-run equilibrium is attained.

The advantage of an aid-assisted strategy is that it avoids the phase of postliberalization real appreciation (as in Kenya, Uganda, Zambia, and Zimbabwe), which can be a source of confusion for both the government and the private sector. By having a phase during which the exchange rate is anchored to a rate of depreciation, the government might inject a greater degree of certainty into the macroeconomic system. Once the exchange rate has reached its long-run equilibrium rate, which occurs when the debt has been repaid and the current account is in balance (in our stylized example with no other capital flows), the exchange rate can be left to float because the temporary rationale for intervention has expired. One disadvantage of the temporary borrowing strategy is that there is temporary Dutch disease. Whereas without borrowing the export sector initially enjoys unsustainably favorable incentives; with borrowing sufficient to finance the gradual adjustment of the exchange rate, it initially gets no direct benefit from the liberalization (because the exchange rate only gradually adjusts). Indirectly the sector benefits because the fall in the price of importables induces a contraction in that sector, which shifts resources into both nontradables and exportables.

An intermediate position would be to devalue the exchange rate at the outset of trade liberalization to the long-run level but to borrow to avoid the overshoot. This has the advantage that the incentives for the export and import substitute sectors are constant postliberalization. This has the effect that the distributional consequences of trade liberalization are not postponed. Governments thereby reduce their credibility problem: if it is politically feasible to initiate such a liberalization, it is more likely to be sustainable. By contrast, unaided liberalization due to overshooting initially cushions the import substitute sector. Compatible unaided trade liberalization does not initially cheapen imports, because the price reduction effect of trade policy must be precisely offset by devaluation. Hence, in one sense aid may, paradoxically, increase the credibility of trade liberalization, not by meeting the "costs of adjustment," as is popularly imagined, but rather the opposite: by inflicting the full costs of adjustment on the import substitute sector from the outset instead of letting them build up gradually. The reform then either collapses very early on, or is sustainable. This credibility effect, however, is only correct if the risk of reform collapse is determined by the degree of opposition to liberalization from the import substitute sector. A variant of the political economy of reform would be that the government can, in effect, be bribed to put up with opposition. Aid may then undermine credibility because it signals that the government is being temporarily bought but the opposition to reform will be able to reassert itself once the aid ceases. However, even if the aid is itself only capable of temporarily making the liberalization politically desirable, during this period new proliberalization lobbies might emerge so that the liberalization becomes sustainable. There may indeed be a coordination problem. If sufficient numbers of agents to commit resources to the export sector, the reform would become politically sustainable.

Underlying the credibility problem is the need to account for why the government is changing its policy. The previous trade policy presumably reflected some sort of political equilibrium. Temporary aid provides the most obvious explanation for policy change, but it implies that the reform will itself only be temporary. Therefore, aid inevitably contaminates to an extent the analysis of why the government has changed its policy. The two sustainable reasons for policy change are, first, that the balance of political power has shifted between groups, and second, that the government has decided that its previous policy was wrong. The first, a discrete shift in the balance of political forces, is probably only convincing in the context of a change of government. This provides the more obvious difference between the liberalizations of Eastern Europe and much of Africa. The only remotely analogous economic reforming change of government in Africa to those in Eastern Europe was that in Zambia. Failing a change of government, there must be reasonable grounds for believing that there has been a change of mind. Here East Asian and Latin American governments are better placed than African governments. In Vietnam, although there has been no change of government, the collapse of communism elsewhere, the abandonment of the control economy in China, and the huge success of market-orientated neighboring economies are all credible reasons for a change of mind. In Latin America there has been an intellectual revolution (partly based on the contrasting performances of the rival role models constituted by Chile and Cuba), reflected in the remarkable volte-face of the Economic Commission for Latin America. In Africa there have been no equivalent intellectual changes. Africa was never communist, so the collapse of communism has not had a major intellectual impact. There are no proximate role models of successful market economies. There is no equivalent to the core of technocratic Latin American economists in Africa, and this is reflected in the failure of the Economic Commission for Africa to do other than mimic the populist political sentiments of African politicians. Hence African governments wishing to reform their trade policies start from a much more severe credibility problem than those in East Asia or Latin America (although possibly no more severe than India). Consequently, the acceptance of aid as part of a liberalization package is much more problematic for African governments than for other governments, because it immediately becomes the most plausible explanation for why the government is undertaking the reform, whereas elsewhere the reform is otherwise more readily explicable.

Reform of Exchange Rate Mechanisms

Now suppose that a government starts trade liberalization from intense trade restrictions achieved primarily through rationed access to foreign exchange. This was, indeed, the case with most of the liberalizations discussed in the previous section, *Exchange rate policy during trade liberalization with a preexisting foreign exchange market*. The only information as to the market clearing rate is the illegal parallel rate, but this is a poor guide precisely because of the illegality of transactions.

The agent that really matters in the evolution to a proper market in foreign exchange is the government. Institutional transitions through "own funds" schemes and auctions may be necessary to educate the government, but they may equally be a distraction.[2] They are not in themselves a proper market for foreign exchange. Furthermore, they share a feature that, although seemingly attractive, is quite damaging; namely, they give rise to unsustainable increases in the supply of imports. The damage arises partly through temporary Dutch disease taxing the export sector, and partly through the signaling difficulty that arises in interpreting the motivation of the government. Own funds schemes are sold to governments on the basis that private capital flight can be harnessed to finance imports. Auctions are sold to them on the basis that extra aid will be provided for sale through the auction. In each case there is a confusion of liberalization for liberality. Liberalization is the process whereby domestic relative prices of tradables are brought into line with world relative prices. By liberality I mean increased consumption of imports. Under conditions quite common in the least developed countries, a compatible trade liberalization will not in the short term significantly increase imports; rather it will alter the allocation of an existing value of imports and redistribute rents to exporters.

One condition for this is that there should be no short-run supply response of exports. By taking a sufficiently short period, this must necessarily be the case. A very low supply elasticity in the short run is quite consistent with large

---

2. An own funds scheme is one in which importers are permitted to bring in goods for which they have not purchased foreign exchange through official channels.

supply responses once resources have had time to move, this depending on the planning period for production. A second condition is that exportables are not consumed domestically. This is approximated in several economies in which trade is initially highly restricted. Restrictions give rise to export concentration, as all but core export activities become unprofitable. Where these core activities are mineral extraction such as copper, or nonfood agriculture such as coffee, very little output will be consumed domestically. Given these conditions, the impact of a trade liberalization follows directly from how it changes the domestic demand for money, which in turn follows from how liberalization affects the price level. The reduction in tariffs or other restrictions directly cheapens importables and so reduces the price level. Because real income is given in the short term by the assumption that there is no supply response, the demand for money falls. With a given money supply there is now an excess supply of money. Imports rise and there is a payments deficit. Exchange rate depreciation avoids this by creating an offsetting rise in the price level. However, given that exportables are not consumed domestically, the depreciation only raises the price level through increasing the price of importables. Hence, the fall in the price level brought about by trade liberalization and the increase in the price level brought about by exchange rate depreciation work on precisely the same base, namely the price of importables. To prevent a deterioration in the balance of payments, the price level must be unaltered by the net effect of the liberalization and the depreciation. Imports are therefore no cheaper as a result of the package and the demand for them does not increase. There is liberalization without liberality.

The redistributions to exporters and among importers that are generated by such a compatible liberalization are both intensely political changes. The composition of imports will alter away from the developmentalist concentration on capital goods and essential intermediates to incentive goods. Existing exporters, invariably a politically weak group, will be hugely rewarded. These are the political changes intrinsic to genuine trade liberalization. If governments are unprepared to make these changes then liberality is both wasteful and reputation-destroying.

Own Funds Versus Export Retention Schemes

Both own funds and export retention schemes are common in the early stages of liberalization, and indeed sometimes both are used together. They each provide a loophole in the control regime. While they are both steps toward liberalization, their political economy is rather different.

A major difference between African and socialist liberalizations is that African governments had a powerful and arguably dominant political interest in antiexport bias, whereas for socialist governments the equivalent was antiprivate bias. Own funds schemes are intrinsically proprivate, and export retention schemes are intrinsically proexport. Thus, in African trade liberalizations a useful touchstone is whether the liberalization is driven by an own funds scheme, because the essential step in most African foreign exchange liberalizations is that exporters should be free to sell their dollars to other private agents at a market-determined rate. Until this is done the government is not facing the political consequences of liberalization. Therefore export retention schemes with marketable rights are a more viable approach to liberalization than auctions. In retrospect, this can be seen as the successful gradualist policy in Poland during the 1980s, and in Zimbabwe during the early 1990s. Unusually in Africa, the government of Zimbabwe was a substantial potential net purchaser of foreign exchange. It did not own any part of the export sector and was not a major recipient of aid since per capita income was too high. The export sector was taxed through exchange rate overvaluation, partly to subsidize the import substitute sector (which was a heavy user of intermediate imported inputs) and partly to subsidize government imports. The government proceeded by the introduction and gradual expansion of an export retention scheme. This had the opposite effect on the parallel market to that of an own funds import scheme. As is well understood, an own funds scheme tends to depreciate the parallel exchange rate by raising the demand for foreign exchange without any equivalent effect on the supply. The dynamic version of this is that as the range of goods that can be imported through an own funds scheme is widened, so the premium on the official exchange rate increases. By contrast, an export retention scheme in which the rights are marketable increases the supply of foreign exchange on the parallel market without any corresponding increase in demand. As the rate of retention is increased, the premium falls. Because governments tend to measure the progress of liberalization in part by the closing of the premium, working from the export side is more encouraging than working from the import side. Furthermore, working from the export side tends to emphasize that the rationale for trade liberalization is to increase the incentives for, and hence the supply of, exports. Working from the import side tends to produce the confusion between liberalization and liberality. Success of the reform tends then to be measured not in terms of export response but directly in volumes of imports. A successful compatible trade liberalization will not, in the short run, increase imports. It will do so in the long run through export expansion. Own funds schemes feed the psychology of quick and easy returns to reform coming from capital flows rather than resource reallocation. Hence, on the whole, foreign exchange rationing has been a significant part of the trade control regime, but liberalizing through the export side (export retention) is probably more conducive to sustainability than liberalizing through the import side (own funds). Nevertheless, own funds schemes have greater popularity with governments than export retention schemes. The latter reward the flow of export activity; the former reward also, and perhaps in Africa predominantly, the accumulated stock of previous capital flight. Because in Africa much of this will be held by the political elite, an own funds scheme is consistent with the political status quo that generated the trade control regime. At some point, as its external wealth accumulates, the interest of the elite turns in favor of legal repatriation of goods, although this may reduce the profitability of import substitution production.

Auctions

The Nigerian, Romanian, and, for a period, Zambian auctions had in common that they were not proper auctions and that the degree of misalignment varied: the government held constant neither the exchange rate nor the premium for any length of time. Exchange rate policy was at its maximum degree of confusion, both for private agents and for the government itself. When the government officially fixes the exchange rate and rations foreign exchange, it can at least focus on developing criteria for rationing, forlorn as this task might be. With a clean floating, the government can hope to influence the rate indirectly by focusing on interest rates, money supply, and trade policies. With an explicitly dirty float, the central bank can develop criteria for its intervention policy, which itself takes the form of the use of reserves; however, with a dirty auction, intervention takes the form of illicit rationing. The central bank comes up with devices week-by-week that it hopes will eliminate some bids. As private agents come to learn of them and meet the requirements, the criteria are in constant flux. This produces an environment of even greater uncertainty than with official rationing. The illicit behavior has shifted from the private sector to the public sector.

Some important questions are, therefore, what are the incentives for a government to wreck an auction in this way, and are there devices that can prevent it?

An auction in which the foreign exchange is supplied entirely or predominantly by donors is in the interest of the political elite, because it controls, at least to an extent, the government expenditure financed by the foreign exchange sales. Thus, an essential issue in an auction is the source of the money. When the source is entirely donor funds, the government has the least incentive to frustrate the proper operation of the auction. After all, it is getting revenue from the sales of dollars, and the foreign exchange has, in effect, no opportunity cost. Even in these circumstances governments sometimes have interfered with the auction. Because the proceeds of the auction accrue to the government, the government might be thought to have an interest in maximizing these proceeds. Sometimes there are indeed signs of this, as in the prevalence of Dutch auctions, which ostensibly seek to raise the average price paid for foreign exchange. However, even with Dutch auctions part of the impetus is not so that the government can get as high a price as possible per dollar, but rather the opposite: a desire to discourage high bids so as to appreciate the rate. For example, in the Zambian auction the bids were published in newspapers, with the objective of shaming firms that bid high as unpatriotic.

Nigeria, Romania, and Zambia had in common that all or a substantial part of the dollars coming onto the auction were from the domestic export sector rather than from donors. By contrast, the auctions in Uganda were fed by aid. In the first three the government had less interest in maximizing the yield from the auction, as opposed to benefiting elites by favored foreign exchange allocation. It might seem that Nigeria is an exception to this because the export, oil, was publicly owned; however, under the revenue-sharing formula with the regions, the central government in fact received little of the oil receipts, most accruing either to debt service or to the regional governments. The elites controlling the central government therefore had an interest in generating rents through foreign exchange rationing rather than through maximizing regional public expenditure.

This does not, of course, lead to a policy implication that auctions are improved by confining the source of the funds to donors rather than domestic exporters. Rather it tells us that the nearer an auction gets to being a proper market, matching domestic buyers with domestic sellers, the less attractive it becomes for a government that does not favor trade liberalization. The collapse of an auction or interbank market during a liberalization sequence may arise, not because the sequence is intrinsically ill judged, but because the initial incentives for the government to comply with the arrangements have been removed as the reforms move from liberality to liberalization. Program collapse is itself a highly damaging event, both costly in itself and making future reform more problematic, so this would imply that when there is substantial doubt as to the government's commitment to trade liberalization, a desirable attribute of a liberalization sequence is that pain for the government is not deferred.

An alternative strategy to sequencing liberalization would depend on the rationale that the government can cumulatively be coaxed and maneuvered into policies that it would not initially have chosen but, as a result of their delivery of good economic performance, finds it wise to maintain. Such a strategy may well be successful sometimes, but it will have a fairly high failure rate. The gains from liberalization, as opposed to liberality, are usually not rapid in coming. Even when the gains do accrue unusually rapidly because they do not depend on export supply response (as in Nigeria during 1986–91 or Venezuela during the early 1990s), governments have shown themselves well able to repudiate the liberalization. The abandonment of this method by the World Bank and the International Monetary Fund is implicit in the new emphasis on program "ownership" by the government.

Turning from the incentives for intervention to possible restraints, a design option that might appear to matter is the range of agents which are permitted to participate in the auction. In Nigeria and Uganda, it is only banks; in Zambia, firms bid directly. However, this distinction appears not to be very important. In Uganda, banks have chosen only to make bids on behalf of firms, in effect making the system equivalent to that in Zambia. It is not whether banks bid that is important, but whether they are free to hold onto foreign exchange and choose to do so.

Auctions have invariably been run by central banks. There seems to be no intrinsic reason for this other than that if foreign exchange controls are sufficiently tight no other agent in the economy can legally undertake the auction. Many of the problems with auctions come from the fact that a government agency is the organizer. The process does not create new market agents or permit old ones to return. Rather, it is a small administrative step from central bank–rationed allocation. This is one reason why auctions so easily degenerate back into rationing systems. Insidiously, when this happens, because they continue to be called auctions, parts of the domestic elite actually think there is a market process at work. Potentially, auctions could be run by commercial banks. One advantage of such an arrangement would be that the government or the central bank could draw up a contract in which its objectives were set out explicitly, and design an incentive system that would induce behavior by the commercial bank consistent with those objectives. The government then has less scope for day-to-day interference, because the commercial bank managers are not public employees and must focus on meeting the terms of the contract. Aid disbursements could then be handled in one of two ways. Donors could sell their aid through the auction just like any other agent, with the domestic currency proceeds being credited to the government's account at the central bank. Or, donors could deposit the aid with the central bank, which would then sell it through the auction, proceeds again being credited to the government's account. A central bank is no more suited to run a currency auction than is any government agency to undertake an activity normally in the commercial sector of the economy.

Bureaux de Change

The history of foreign exchange transitions is more that of a search for an agent than for a mechanism. Both auctions and the interbank market *de facto* leave the central bank as the agent. Bureaux de change, by contrast, genuinely permit new and fairly competitive agents into the market. Bureaux have to make a market, purchasing from exporters and selling to importers. However, bureaux de change have difficulty evolving into proper intertemporal functions because, not being banks, they cannot finance large portfolio positions. There is some evidence in Uganda of stabilizing bureau de change speculation, but the scale is modest. Essentially, bureaux de change trade foreign exchange as if it were a perishable rather than an asset. For elementary commodity trade this may be sufficient, and it is certainly an improvement on illegality; however, the formal economy needs banking transactions rather than bureaux for much the same reasons that most of the economy is formal rather than informal. Cash transactions have their own quite high costs, and most formal sector transactions are contracted forward. The informalization of the currency market, which is what a spot cash–based set of transactions amounts to, is a reflection of a wider weakness in such economies: the lack of agents with sufficient reputations to be able to undertake substantial forward transactions, so that too many transactions get driven inappropriately into the spot market. The government itself is in such a position, unable to sell debt domestically except at penal interest rates, due to suspicion of its liabilities. Currency, being a liability of the government, suffers from this same uncertainty, and it may be this high degree of uncertainty which is limiting the emergence of a forward market. But the high risk does not go away; rather, the absence of a forward market accentuates it and makes it inseparable from international transactions. The impediments to international trade are thus shifted from quantitative restrictions and tariffs to risk. In countries where risks are lower, the absence of a forward market is less important. In the newly liberalized economies, the risks largely stem from government behavior. No private agent is willing to insure other private agents against this risk.

Emergence of an Interbank Market

An interbank market becomes a reality only as the nationally held reserves become privatized, and the banks and other private agents perform the speculative function of smoothing fluctuations in the demand and supply of foreign exchange. Initially no domestic agents are experienced in foreign exchange trading or management. Firms have been accustomed to simply attempting to get foreign exchange by whatever means are feasible. Banks have been in the habit of handling foreign exchange transactions as a piece of administration rather than as an asset transaction. This is a major obstacle to the rapid emergence of an interbank market. Although there are typically very few banks, each is secretive and has in the past dealt only directly with the central bank. There may be few or no foreign exchange dealers in the country, in the sense of agents willing and given the responsibility to take positions in the foreign exchange market. In the absence of the banks taking positions, there is no interbank market. The banks merely administer transactions that could equivalently be administered by the central bank. The market maker is the central bank. It is difficult to evolve from this position to a proper interbank market because it implies that for a while the main player in the market will be the central bank, with the commercial banks, once they start to take positions, playing against it. The central bank has no more experience in this than have the local branches of the commercial banks; but the latter are in a much better position to bring in such experience. First, they can bring in staff from the foreign exchange departments of their branches in other countries. Second, they are in a position to pay their dealers the very high salaries that experienced traders command and that central banks, subject to public sector salary scales, cannot hope to match. There is a dangerous likelihood that the central bank will find itself playing against much more competent traders. Furthermore, the central bank is likely to be under some political pressure to deliver a "desired" exchange rate. Even in industrial countries, central bank traders have faced the problem that their intentions are quite easy to read during certain periods. Commercial banks have made very large amounts of money successfully speculating against these intentions. In newly liberalized foreign exchange markets this is much more likely to be the case.

Furthermore, because there is a sense in which nobody knows what they are doing, the banks may be very cautious in taking positions, widening spreads dramatically in periods of uncertainty. This was the experience in Uganda in mid-1994, when the commercial banks became unsure whether the central bank would allow the rate to appreciate. Spreads briefly widened considerably as banks became extremely reluctant to purchase dollars. Supposing that the commercial banks are unwilling to take positions in the market (as in Uganda) or are limited to very small positions (as in Zimbabwe), the central bank has the task of setting the exchange rate or, equivalently, of determining its reserve policy. This is undesirable in that a government agency is still determining the exchange rate as prior to the liberalization. Although foreign exchange is no longer rationed, the institution of the market has not really emerged, and so there is no institutional defense against a gradual erosion back into rationing. The extreme alternative to this is for the central bank to stay out of the market altogether, as it does with the bureaux de change. However, until some agents come in as stabilizing speculators, the market is liable to be volatile. Even simple matters such as the seasonal pattern of export earnings may not be well understood. Nor may a central bank commitment to stand aside from the market be credible, given a history of total central bank control.

As an illustration of this, the move from auction to interbank was initially perceived by the private sector in Uganda as a retrogression and its announcement met by panic buying in the auction. This was partly because the old foreign exchange control apparatus, Form E, was extended to bureaux de change in order to generate the documentation that donors required, but mainly because the interbank market was seen as less transparent than the auction. The latter involved a known amount of donor funds that had to be sold to private agents, with banks merely acting as administering intermediaries. The interbank market was perceived as reintroducing the scope for central bank discretion. To date, in Uganda there have been virtually no interbank transactions; banks deal with the central bank. The central bank has intervened heavily in the market, to curb appreciation resulting from capital inflows and the coffee boom. What would happen were market forces leading to depreciation, as in Nigeria, is yet to be tested. Because the central bank remains the source of foreign exchange, it is still in a position to start disallowing purchases.

The suspicion generated by the transition to a so-called interbank market is symptomatic of the dilemma in which a central bank that has been entirely under the thumb of the government is promoted, in the absence of private agents willing to take the risk, into the role of market maker. As a result, the market is not trusted. The problem becomes most acute if the government is unable to follow a fiscally prudent course, so that the market-clearing nominal exchange rate must depreciate. For example, in Ghana in early 1994, the government became sufficiently disillusioned with the depreciation of the exchange rate that it came very close to reverting to a fixed and therefore rationed rate, only withdrawing from this action when the market rate started to appreciate just in time. That the government of Ghana, after seven years of a market exchange rate and with large donor funding, could come this close to reversion is an indication of the fragility of market-determined exchange rates in Africa and thereby of trade liberalization.

Designing Better Foreign Exchange Markets

The dismantling of foreign exchange rationing is a necessary and indeed a central step in the liberalization of trade; however, it is not synonymous with the creation of a well-functioning foreign exchange market. To date, in many trade-liberalizing economies the most popular way in which foreign exchange transactions are undertaken is through cash spot exchange. This essentially informal bartering of currencies would in more normal circumstances be considered a hopelessly high-cost, risky way of doing international business. Its prevalence reflects the underlying uncertainty which now inhibits trade by adding to its cost. Intrinsic to the liberalization of foreign exchange markets is then the reduction in the risk of government mismanagement of its liabilities. In part this is the creation of effective agencies of restraint. In part it is a matter of putting the government in a position where its true type can be revealed. The latter makes aid problematic, particularly in cases in which there is no change in government, and therefore no otherwise obvious reason why the government has changed its policy. An aid inflow also induces special mechanisms for its disbursement, notably an auction, which may distract from the real business of liberalization.

Some of the economies of Africa are so small, certainly in terms of international private trade, that the fixed costs of operating a well-informed domestic speculative market may be prohibitive. English-speaking Africa is attempting to run market-determined exchange rates with currencies which have radically smaller usage than any previously experienced floating currency. One indication of the inadequate scale of these foreign exchange markets is the absence of a forward market—with the possible exception of Kenya, which has an atypically large financial sector—or any of the derivatives markets, despite considerable uncertainty. Although banks will make forward transactions, they are based simply on the spot rate plus the relevant interest rate. An importer may buy foreign exchange forward at the spot rate, plus the borrower's rate of interest in the domestic market, less the lending rate of interest in dollars. An exporter may sell forward at the spot rate plus the lenders rate of interest in the domestic market, less the borrowers' rate of interest in dollars. Because of very wide spreads between the domestic borrowing and lending interest rates facing firms, the spread in the implicit forward market is very large in relation to that in the spot market. This is quite unlike the transactions in a developed foreign exchange market, where the bulk of transactions are in the forward market, with the spot market essentially derived from the forward rate, and with a narrow spread around a directly quoted price. Most business transactions involving international trade are forward transactions, so risk is reduced by entering into forward foreign exchange transactions. The lack of a forward market periodically exposes the international trading sector to massive losses. For example, in Uganda during mid-1994, some traders found it more advantageous to default on contracts, suffering a 10 percent penalty, rather than complete contracts and take uncovered foreign exchange losses.

Yet the central bank itself would be most unwise to enter into forward transactions. This was inadvertently done by the Zambian central bank during the failed auction of 1985–87 as a consequence of the "pipeline," whereby the bank undertook to deliver foreign exchange at an agreed price but lacked the foreign exchange to meet its sales on the spot market. The scope for losing very large sums on the forward market exists because there is no natural limit to the amount of business that a central bank can contract. To summarize, many of these economies may simply be too small to have a well-functioning private domestic market for their national currencies.

One alternative is to amalgamate currencies back into the multinational currency boards that existed when African trade was much larger in relation to world trade than it is now. Optimal currency areas are usually discussed in terms of the characteristics of the economy; however, that discussion pertained to countries with differing and substantial institutions setting nominal variables, notably labor unions. By contrast, in much of Africa prices are highly flexible, so that arguments in favor of small currency areas carry little weight. Regional currencies might provide the scale that would permit derivative markets to operate. Arguably the gains from regional cooperation in merging currencies would be much greater than regional cooperation in reducing trade barriers. Such cooperation would have two important additional benefits. First, it would reduce the powerful shocks that have been suffered by the failure to coordinate exchange rate policy. For example, during 1992–93 the Uganda shilling appreciated strongly because of capital flight out of Kenya. Second, regional currency boards can operate as a macroeconomic agency of restraint, possessing a degree of independence from government influence, which is lacking in national central banks. Setting a currency area larger than a fiscal area thus permits a mechanism of restraint on fiscal policy that is otherwise very hard to create.

If regional amalgamation of national currencies is not acceptable, then a radical alternative would be to introduce full convertibility and shift the weight of trading to London or New York. In effect, a market complete with derivatives might be made by traders dealing in, and being prepared to take positions in, several small currencies. Whether London or New York firms would find it profitable to invest in the specialist knowledge required for such trades is uncertain, but it is probably much easier than importing such a foreign exchange–trading culture into each small developing country. For example, some bureaux de change in the United Kingdom now accept Kenyan shillings; and, given the recent move to full convertibility, some of London's banks might start to hold more significant balances.

The remaining alternative is for national central banks to continue to set the exchange rate, in the sense of being the dominant player in the market. The latter involves not only the possibility of an easy reversion to overvaluation, but the possibility that the central bank will incur heavy losses through mistaken intervention, such as the recent attempt by the central bank of Kenya to resist appreciation. It is not clear that the central bank should acquire these essentially new functions of being the leading market maker in foreign exchange. It might be better to subcontract this role to a foreign bank, which would be given a management contract and required to operate both spot and derivative markets at agreed spreads, leaving the central bank with bank supervision and government debt functions.

Conclusion

To summarize, as the rest of the world learns to shift risk entirely from trade transactions, using the innovative products of the large financial centers, African trade has become more risky but in some respects more feasible. Africa needs to buy the services of the big financial centers, which could operate the markets in their currencies. For this it is essential that African currencies be convertible. The combination of being freely convertible for trade transactions but inconvertible for capital transactions is peculiarly damaging given the lack of domestic financial agents in a position to perform the speculative role. Inconvertibility does not matter if the central bank can be trusted to perform the stabilizing role of the speculator, or if trade flows are sufficiently even that the role for stabilization is limited. African currencies are *de facto* usually convertible, in that capital flight has proved feasible. But this is not the same as *de jure* convertibility, because it shuts out the very agents, namely international banks, which might otherwise be given the stabilizing role.

Convertibility also functions as a restraining device on government. By increasing the responsiveness to macroeconomic mismanagement, the government is punished by depreciation more severely, and so is less likely to behave in a shortsighted manner. This is an important function because governments have usually stumbled into trade restrictions because there were not enough agencies of restraint. Budget deficits have produced inflation and payments deficits. By inhibiting the resulting needed depreciation of the exchange rate through currency rationing, governments solved the immediate problem of depleting reserves and at the same time hoped, wrongly, that inflation would be restrained. To prevent the import substitute sector from taking advantage of the shortage of imports, price controls on its output were often imposed. Although these were unsuccessful in restraining prices to consumers, they often contaminated the consumer price index by overweighing goods bought at official prices.

The dismantling of the control regime, even if done in a way that preserves macroeconomic compatibility, may, however, be unsustainable unless the underlying political problem is resolved. This stems from the twin phenomena that there is too little restraint on expenditure in relation to taxation and that, faced with the resulting emerging excess demand for foreign exchange, the government gets more advantage from rationing foreign exchange than from allowing the exchange rate to depreciate. The sustainability of exchange rate reform thus depends on either a strengthening of fiscal agencies of restraint, which is achieved by the increased capital mobility consequent on convertibility, or a strengthening of trade policy agencies of restraint. A current example of the success of the latter strategy is the recent crisis in Mexico. During 1993–94 the Mexican exchange rate became seriously overvalued, financed by heavy public borrowing. It was inevitable that this would result in a foreign exchange crisis. However, during this period Mexico committed itself to a liberal trade policy both by signing the Uruguay Round and, probably more important, establishing NAFTA. Remarkably, during the Mexican foreign exchange crisis, which was substantial, at no stage did the government resort to foreign exchange rationing or other devices for trade restriction. NAFTA and the General Agreement on Tariffs and Trade (GATT) had succeeded in restraining government policy in a way that the domestic agencies designed to restrain fiscal policy, notably the independent central bank, had proved too weak to do. Mexico has thus passed from being a high-inflation and therefore trade-restricted economy, to a high-inflation but nevertheless trade-liberalized economy.

Even a compatible liberalization may not be sustained, or be seen as likely to be sustained, unless agencies of restraint are strengthened. These can either be by way of formal institutions, or by the change in the political power of the export sector. It is no surprise that Nigeria, which has in effect no export sector, has had the most difficulty establishing a foreign exchange market.

Foreign exchange is an asset. In regimes that preclude convertibility it is denied this role. Hence, the focus of liberalization is intratemporal allocative efficiency. However, once liberalized, the asset role reasserts itself. Fiscal imbalances that were made payments-compatible by trade restrictions may now be made compatible by high interest rates. The intratemporal gain in allocative efficiency may be achieved at the cost of an intertemporal loss. Much hinges on private expectations of future government policy. In this respect the Eastern European transitions have been easier than those in Africa because the bedrock of policy change was popular revolution rather than donor pressure.

A Brief Summary of Experiences in Selected Countries

Costa Rica

Trade liberalizations in the late 1980s and early 1990s were not adequately matched by exchange rate adjustment. Although the official exchange rate was devalued, the current account deficit grew to an unsustainable 7 percent of gross domestic product (GDP), financed by short-term borrowing.

Kenya

During the 1980s Kenya had an administered official exchange rate well below the free market equilibrium. Foreign exchange rationing was a major component of the trade regime. In an attempt to depoliticize changes in the rate while keeping it administered, the central bank adopted a crawling depreciation by, in effect, pegging to whichever currencies happened to be depreciating most rapidly. This technique did not enable significant real depreciation, so that episodes of attempted substantial trade liberalization, notably at the beginning and end of the decade, both failed due to balance of payments deterioration. During the 1990s policy has become more volatile. A period of substantial liberalization of the exchange rate was followed by revaluation and severe rationing. This in turn was abandoned in 1993, when an interbank market was created. In 1994 the currency was made partially convertible and in January 1995 virtually fully convertible. During 1994 a forward market emerged and the both the nominal and real exchange rates appreciated strongly.

Nigeria

The government established an auction for foreign exchange. Initially this was properly conducted, but gradually the government manipulated the rate. Only banks were permitted to bid in the auction, and the central bank imposed both the rate and the amount which commercial banks were permitted to bid. Bids beyond this were disallowed. The banks were able to capture the resulting rents, for example, by requiring firms to hold deposits at heavily negative real interest rates before they could purchase at the auction rate. For a while this coexisted with a legal bureau de change market.

Peru

During the 1980s Peru had multiple exchange rates but all official rates were heavily overvalued in relation to the parallel rate. In August 1990 the new government unified the exchange rate through a large devaluation and thereafter maintained a managed float. After the first few months the central bank announced that it would only intervene as a purchaser of dollars needed to finance foreign debt. While there may have been some intervention, the managed rate stayed very close to the parallel rate. After an initial large depreciation, private capital inflows gave rise to real and even nominal appreciation.

Poland

Poland had the curiosity of a virtually open capital account for individuals, and a highly restricted and segmented market for the current account. As a result of the open capital account it was very heavily dollarized (that is, many transactions were carried out using foreign exchange, particularly dollars, instead of zlotys). However, a large part of this dollarization was in the form of dollar-denominated claims on the government. The market for current account transactions was highly complex but had four principle components: (a) The official rationed allocation of foreign exchange at a highly overvalued exchange rate, set with a view to maintaining 80 percent of exports as profitable; (b) an export retention scheme that gradually expanded during the 1980s and that increasingly permitted firms to hold or resell their retained export earnings (retention rates were firm-specific and so constituted a form of commercial policy); (c) an auction that was so restricted as to entry and use that the auction rate was the same as the official rate; and (d) an own funds scheme whereby individuals could purchase imports in government shops for dollars.

Romania

The government established an interbank auction for foreign exchange but maintained exchange controls on capital transactions. The auction was supposed to be run by a computer program. In fact it was manipulated by the government to the extent that at times only 5 percent of bids were accepted and a 30 percent premium emerged between the auction rate and the black market rate. Banks were able, *de facto*, to capture the resulting rents.

Uganda

The Museveni government, which came to power in 1986, revalued the exchange rate and rationed foreign exchange. In an environment of rapid inflation, the real exchange rate rapidly appreciated. By this time most financial assets were probably held in banks abroad. The subsequent liberalization was achieved by a conjunction of devaluations and the reestablishment of fiscal control. The government shifted from being a net purchaser to a net seller of foreign exchange, due to the increase in net aid receipts, so that devaluation assisted the fiscal improvement. The government introduced an auction restricted to banks and then legalized bureaux de change. The unification of the two rates proved problematic: only the differential had been reduced to around 10 percent, probably due to the greater likelihood of import taxation arising from auction-purchased dollars. In 1993 the auction was replaced by an interbank market. From early 1993 the nominal and real exchange rates appreciated strongly, probably fueled by private capital inflows, although the capital account was not fully liberalized. Real and nominal interest rates persisted very high until mid-1994.

Uruguay

Since 1974 Uruguay has had a fully convertible currency and the authorities have followed a crawling peg rule ostensibly aimed at maintaining the real value of the peso against a basket of currencies. There were two major episodes of departure from this rule. During 1977–81 the real exchange rate continuously appreciated, and during 1979–81 a trade deficit emerged. The 1982 Latin American debt crisis forced a large and rapid depreciation in 1983.

Vietnam

During the 1980s the official exchange rate was very heavily overvalued and foreign currency was rationed. In 1988 export retention was expanded and the capital account was liberalized. Enterprises could borrow from abroad and both enterprises and individuals could hold foreign exchange. In 1989 the dong was devalued by 80 percent and the official rate unified with the parallel rate, subsequently tracking it within 1 or 2 percent. The economy was heavily dollarized, and about 47 percent of financial assets were dollar-denominated. More than half were liabilities of the domestic banking system. However, the currency was not freely convertible: dollars could not be held in foreign banks. The exchange rate was quite volatile, and this imposed risk costs on international trade that could not be covered because of the absence of a forward market. Private capital inflows were leading to real appreciation.

Zimbabwe

Foreign exchange controls were established in 1965 and were continued by the Mugabe government. Unusually, the controls were largely effective. Liberalization came in stages. In 1991 there was a large devaluation, but it was insufficient to close the gap with the small parallel market. An export retention scheme was introduced, initially at a very small rate, and this foreign exchange was made tradable. Gradually, the proportion retained was increased so that the rate on this market fell, despite quite rapid inflation and a further devaluation. In January 1994 an interbank market was created without abandoning an official exchange rate; however, the interbank rate appreciated to the official rate and the latter was abandoned by mid-1994. In real terms the exchange rate appreciated considerably during 1994, due in part to private capital inflows. Capital account controls were relaxed for foreigners but remained for Zimbabwean enterprises and individuals. Real interest rates were volatile but usually very high.

4

Rethinking the New Regionalism

Arvind Panagariya

It is now well understood that, at a minimum, the implications of a regional arrangement must be assessed at two levels: the trading system as a whole and the countries contemplating the arrangement. We may also be concerned about the effect of several independent regional arrangements on each other and on outside countries.

The systemic implications of regional arrangements, discussed eloquently by Bhagwati (1993), are both complex and controversial. On the one hand, regional blocs enhance the member countries' monopoly power in trade and increase the temptation for protection. On the other, if the leadership within blocs is farsighted, regional arrangements can, through expansion of membership and interbloc negotiations, speed up the move toward global free trade.

In the present discussion, I do not pretend to shed light on this hotly debated subject.[1] Instead, I look at regional arrangements from the viewpoint of individual developing countries. It is perhaps fair to say that the exercise of the regional option by individual developing countries will not have a determining influence on the global trading system. Indeed, it is no accident that the debate on whether regional and multilateral processes are complementary or competitive did not heat up until the United States, the largest and richest economy in the world, began its journey to the North American Free Trade Agreement (NAFTA). Therefore, the main issue confronting developing countries is how best to respond to the challenges posed by the spread of regionalism around the world and whether, as a part of that response, to enter into regional arrangements of their own.

Today there is no continent on earth that does not have a regional arrangement of its own. A simple count of the regional agreements on the list in Harmsen and Leidy (1994) yields fourteen in Africa, seven in Asia, seventeen involving Europe, five in the Middle East, and twenty-four in the Western Hemisphere. It

The author wishes to thank John Nash, Fudzai Pamacheche, Napoleon Pop, Wendy Takacs, and conference participants for their thoughtful comments, and Gabriel Castillo for invaluable research assistance.

1. The debate is summarized in de Melo and Panagariya (1992). The author's own position is stated clearly in Panagariya (1994).

is tempting to think of the continent of Australia, a single country, as an exception; but Australia, too, has a regional arrangement with New Zealand.

Of course, many of these agreements are inconsequential in the sense that they have minimal effect, positive or negative, on the world trading system and even on the participating countries themselves. Agreements such as the East Asian Economic Caucus or Enterprise of the Americas Initiative, included in the Harmsen and Leidy list, have no operational significance. Others such as the South Asian Association for Regional Cooperation and the Black Sea Economic Cooperation have had virtually no economic impact to date. At the other extreme, agreements that have been or are potentially important include the European Union (EU) in Europe; NAFTA in North America; the ASEAN[2] Free Trade Area (AFTA) in Asia, the Southern Cone Common Market (MERCOSUR), the Andean Common Market (ANCOM), and the Central American Common Market (CACM) in Latin America; and the Economic Community of Western African States (ECOWAS), the Customs and Economic Union of Central Africa (UDEAC), the Common Market for Eastern and Southern African States (COMESA), and the Southern African Customs Union (SACU) in Africa.

It is perhaps counterproductive to attempt yet another survey of various regional arrangements in existence. These are now available aplenty. Contributions by Brada on Eastern Europe, Winters on the European Community (EC), Whalley on North America, Saxonhouse on Asia, Foroutan on Africa, and Nogues and Quintanilla on Latin America in the de Melo and Panagariya (1993) volume offer a detailed account of the most important regional arrangements in various parts of the world. A compact survey of various regional arrangements around the world has been provided by de la Torre and Kelly (1992) and updated by Harmsen and Leidy (1994). For Latin America, which has served as the most fertile ground for the growth of regional arrangements in the 1990s, Lustig and Braga (1994) provide a list of more than twenty regional arrangements. The European Agreements (EAs) signed between the European Community and its trading partners in Eastern Europe and Africa have been examined by Winters and Wang (1994) and Kaminski (1994).[3]

Rather than look at each scheme microscopically, in this chapter I analyze various regional options countries have, and the pros and cons of such options from *their* viewpoint. I draw from the experiences of the countries to date, including a subset of those studied by the Trade Expansion Program (TEP). Schemes involving industrial and developing countries (North-South), as well as those between two or more developing countries (South-South),

---

2. ASEAN refers to the Association of Southeast Asian Nations.
3. Needless to say, this list is extremely partial. More references can be found in these contributions.

are considered. I also discuss how the countries outside regional arrangements are affected by such arrangements and whether they should themselves seek entry into those arrangements.

Traditionally, the analysis of regional arrangements has focused almost exclusively on trade. In practice, the scope of regional arrangements has been wider than that and is continuing to grow. Cooperation between two or more countries in projects of mutual interest—for example, building of dams and roads—can be part of a regional arrangement. More recently, issues relating to harmonization of policies in areas such as taxation, environmental standards, labor laws, and policies toward direct foreign investment have been discussed in the context of regional arrangements. This expansion of scope makes the assessment of regional arrangements a complex task. Although the emphasis of this chapter is trade issues, I also touch briefly on the possible role of regional arrangements in promoting harmonization.

In this chapter I first review briefly the basic Vinerian analysis. My main message in this first section, which plays a central role in the rest of the chapter, is that the mercantilist approach to trade policy is essentially right when it comes to trade liberalization on a preferential basis. When two countries form a free trade area, the gains to each come largely from preferential access to the other's market, rather than from liberalization of its own market. In *The generalized system of preferences: one-way preferences*, I look at one-way trade preferences by industrial countries to developing countries, and conclude that these preferences, although trade-diverting, have been beneficial to developing countries. The section *North-South integration: two-way preferences* pays particular attention to NAFTA and the EAs involving the EU on the one hand and Central and Eastern Europe (CEE) countries on the other. My main message on NAFTA is that, because the United States already has nondiscriminatory free trade, on balance, Mexico gave the former far more preferential access than it received. At least in Vinerian terms, the gains went largely to the United States. In *Outsiders: to join or not to join*, I discuss the impact of NAFTA on outsiders and whether they stand to gain from entry into NAFTA or the EU. The section *Renewed South-South integration* gives an overview of this topic with special emphasis on MERCOSUR. This is followed by a section on the role of harmonization within regional arrangements.

Discriminatory Liberalization: Mercantilists Were Right

In a small open economy and, to a point, even in a large open economy, the primary source of gains from trade liberalization is the reduction in home tariffs. Reduced protection at home leads to a more efficient allocation of resources and of consumer expenditures. Yet, in trade negotiations, the reduction in home tariffs is viewed as a cost and a reduction in the partner country's tariffs as the benefit. Because of this mercantilist bias, it is commonly suggested that the negotiations under the General Agreement on Tariffs and Trade (GATT) lead to the right outcome for the wrong reason.

Surprisingly, when it comes to regional integration, at least within the Vinerian framework, the mercantilist approach is right: gains from regional integration come primarily from a reduction in the partner country's tariffs. Although this point is implicit in the standard Vinerian analysis, to my knowledge it has not been recognized explicitly. I will explain the point first in the case of a tariff and then in the presence of a quota.

Free Trade Agreements under Tariffs

Let A and B be the potential partners and C the rest of the world. In figure 4.1, $M_A M_A$ represents the import demand for a product by A. The height of this curve represents the marginal benefit from imports and, hence, the area under it the total (gross) gains from trade. The most realistic case is the one in which imports come from both B and C, before and after the change in trade policy.

Figure 4.1. *Welfare Effects of FTA with Tariffs and No Quotas*

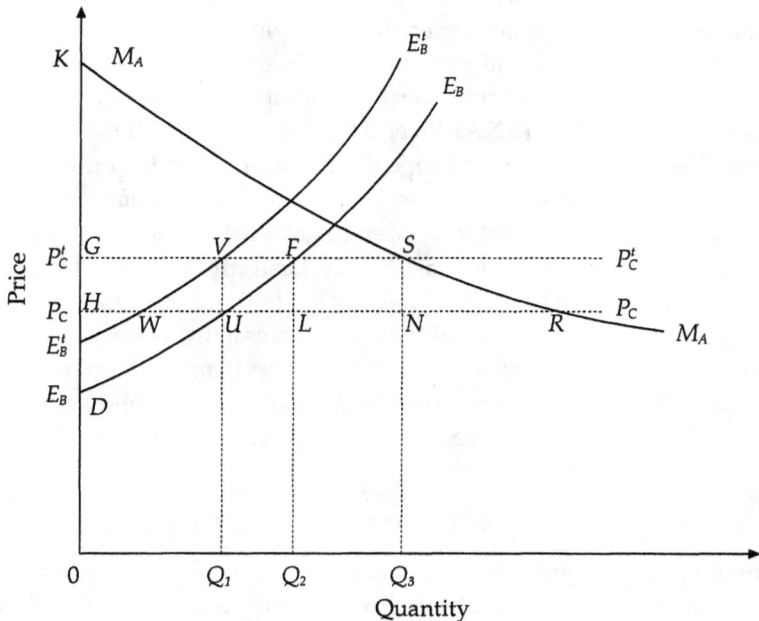

Note: NSR, gains to *A* from unilateral liberalization; *GFLH*, loss to *A* from *FTA*; *HUFG*, gain to *B* from *FTA*; *UFL*, net loss from *FTA*.

This case is captured most simply under the assumption that the export supply of the product is less than perfectly elastic for B, and is perfectly elastic for C. Therefore, in figure 4.1 the export supply of B is represented by the upward-sloped curve $E_B E_B$ and that of C by the horizontal line $P_C P_C$. Other cases are taken up later.

Under a nondiscriminatory tariff at rate t per unit, supplies from B and C, as perceived by buyers in A, are given by $E_B{}' E_B{}^t$ and $P_C{}' P_C{}^t$, respectively. Total imports into A equal OQ_3, of which OQ_1 comes from B and $Q_1 Q_3$ from C. A collects tariff revenue in the amount represented by rectangle *GHNS*. The gains from trade are represented by the area under the import demand curve and above the domestic price plus the tariff revenue, in other words, triangle *KSG* plus rectangle *GHNS*. For country B, the gains from trade equal the area above $E_B E_B$ and below the net price received, P_C, and equals *HDU*. Table 4.1 summarizes this information in column 1.

Suppose now that A decides unilaterally to adopt a policy of nondiscriminatory free trade. The price in A declines to P_C, imports from B do not change, and imports from C rise by *NR*. Tariff revenue disappears, but the gains from trade rise to *KGS+GHNS+RSN*. There is a net welfare gain of *RSN*. The extra gain comes from increased benefits to consumers. The gains to country B remain unchanged at *HDU*. Because of the perfectly elastic supply, country C neither gains nor loses from trade before or after trade liberalization by A. Therefore, the world as a whole benefits by area *RSN*. These changes are summarized in column 2 of table 4.1.

Next, assume that, instead of adopting nondiscriminatory free trade, A forms a free trade agreement (FTA) with B, retaining the original tariff on C. Imports from B rise to OQ_2, and those from C decline to $Q_2 Q_3$. Although there is trade diversion, B gains from discriminatory liberalization by A due to an improvement in its terms of trade. The net price received by the exporters of B increases

Table 4.1. *Gains from Trade under Unilateral Liberalization and Free Trade Agreement*

Policy country	Nondiscriminatory tariff at rate t (1)	Complete free trade (2)	FTA with B (3)
Country A	KGS+GHNS	KGS+GHNS+RSN	KGS+GHNS- GFLH
Country B	HDU	HDU	HDU+GFLH-UFL
Country C	0	0	0
World	KGS+GHNS+HDU	KGS+GHNS+HDU +RSN	KGS+GHNS+HDU -FLU

Note: Variables relate to figure 4.1.

from P_C to $P_C{}^t$ and the gains from trade to B rise to *HDU+HUFG*. Because imports continue to come from C before and after the FTA, the price in A is unchanged. But now that there is no tariff revenue on goods coming from B, A's gains from trade decline by *GFLH*. A loses from its own discriminatory liberalization. Because the FTA diverts imports Q_1Q_2 from the more efficient C to less efficient B, A's loss exceeds B's gain by area *UFL*. The world as a whole loses by area *UFL*. The last column in table 4.1 shows these changes.[4]

An important point to note is that the loss to A from the discriminatory liberalization is substantially larger than the welfare cost of trade diversion. The latter is limited to triangle *UFL*, whereas the total loss to A is rectangle *GFLH*. The change brings about a large redistribution of tariff revenue from A's government to B's firms. Because redistribution effects generate rectangular areas while efficiency effects give rise to triangular areas, the former are crucial.

Figure 4.1 is drawn on the assumption that the supply from C is perfectly elastic and that imports from C do not disappear entirely after the formation of the FTA. These conditions are sufficient to ensure that the FTA leaves A's internal price ratio unchanged, and hence its allocation of resources and consumer expenditure unaffected. The FTA leads to no trade creation whatsoever.

To generate trade creation in the presence of a tariff, we must assume one of the following two conditions: (i) Country C's supply is less than perfectly elastic, or (ii) after the formation of the FTA, imports from C cease altogether. In case (i), an FTA improves A's terms of trade with respect to C, and thus lowers the internal price in A. Domestic consumption rises and production falls. In case (ii), after the formation of the FTA, C's tariff-inclusive price is higher than the price at which B is able to supply the entire demand in A. Once again the domestic price in A falls and there is trade creation.

Realism of both of these cases can be questioned. As we will see, in most cases of interest, the union partner in question (country A) imports too small a proportion of the rest of the world's output to have a significant influence on the external terms of trade. Similarly, FTAs are not known to eliminate altogether the imports from the rest of the world.

Even if we assume one of these unrealistic possibilities, the presence of trade creation is far from sufficient to yield a net improvement in the welfare of country A. The decline in the domestic price generates a triangular welfare gain but a rectangular tariff loss on imports coming from B. Conditions for the latter to be smaller than the former are strong. Presumption is that, on balance, discriminatory liberalization by A still hurts A and benefits B.

---

4. Note that throughout this section it is assumed that, from a social standpoint, a dollar is a dollar whether in the hands of producers, consumers, or the government; but this is a standard assumption in welfare analysis.

Sufficient conditions for discriminatory tariff liberalization by A to improve its own welfare are indeed quite stringent and more unrealistic than (i) and (ii). One such condition is that the good be supplied entirely by the partner before and after the FTA at fixed terms of trade and that no close substitutes be available from the rest of the world. In this case an FTA becomes equivalent to nondiscriminatory free trade and is necessarily welfare-improving.[5]

Free Trade Agreements under Quotas

Let us now briefly turn to the case of a quota. The first point to note is that under a quota the wedge between the domestic and the border price, the so-called quota rent, is captured by the recipient of the license. For example, if import licenses are issued free of charge to domestic importers, license holders get the quota rent. If the government auctions the licenses freely, it captures the quota rent in the same way as it gets the tariff revenue in the case considered above in *Free trade agreements under tariffs*. Either way, the quota rent, represented by $GHNS$ in figure 4.1 (assuming the quota to be set at GS on a nondiscriminatory basis) remains a part of A's gains from trade.

Consider now the formation of an FTA that frees B but not C from the quota restriction. It should be obvious that the results depend critically on how the quota on C is fixed. If the quota on C is fixed such that total imports from all sources do not change after the union is formed, our previous analysis remains unchanged. In terms of figure 4.1, the import quota on C is fixed at FS. Country B, although freed of the quota restriction, continues to export GF. No quota rent is generated on imports from B, which now receives the full price, P_C^t. The results in column 3 of table 4.1 are entirely unchanged.

A more plausible assumption, however, is that the quota on C is fixed at the pre-FTA level of imports from that country. In this case, total imports into A will rise after the formation of the union; the price in A will fall and trade creation will take place. In figure 4.2, under a nondiscriminatory quota equal to GS, the price in A is P_A^{Quota}. The border price is determined by C's supply price and equals P_C. Imports from B equal HU ($= GV$) and those from C are VS. The difference between the domestic and border prices is the quota rent per unit of imports. Quota holders, all of them A's residents, collect rectangle $GSNH$ as quota rent.

Under an FTA, A removes the quota on B but retains it on C at the latter's original level of exports. The demand-for-imports curve facing B shifts to the left by the amount of quota on C as represented by $M'_A M'_A$. The price in A falls to P_A^{FTA}, with imports from B expanding from GV to RJ. The consumers'

---

5. If close substitutes from C are available, trade diversion will reappear. We are then back to weighing this trade diversion against trade creation.

Figure 4.2. *Welfare Effects of FTA with Quota on Country C*

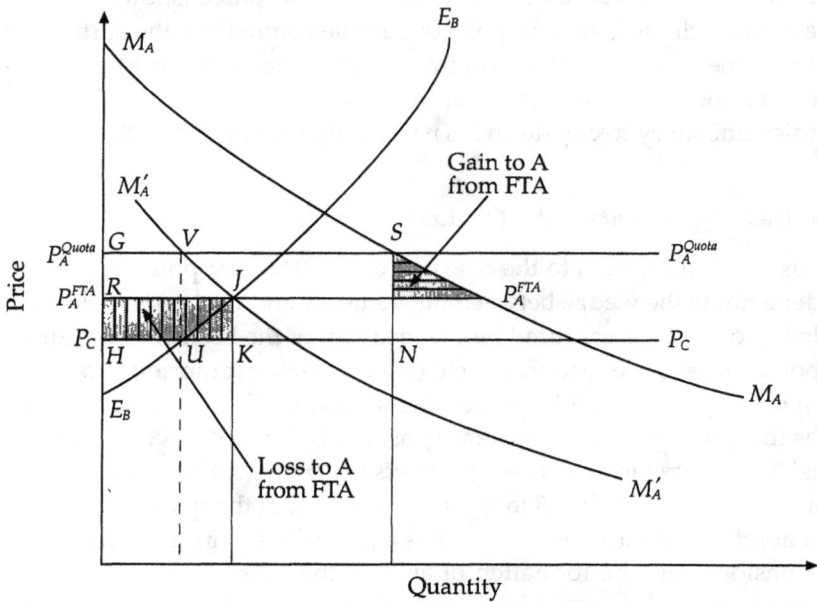

surplus rises but the quota rent declines. The rent on imports from B disappears altogether while that on C declines to $P_A^{FTA}P_C$ per unit. It is easily verified that the shaded rectangle represents a net loss to A and the shaded triangle a net gain. Although the logical possibility of the gain being larger than the loss cannot be ruled out, the loss being given by a rectangle and gain by a triangle, the likelihood of it is small. All else being equal, the smaller the imports from the rest of the world in the pre-FTA equilibrium, the tighter the quota on it and the larger the rectangle in relation to the triangle. As in the tariff case, A's losses come largely from the redistribution of the quota rent from its residents to B's exporters.

Implications and Limitations

A central point that emerges from the above analysis is that, in an FTA, a country is likely to lose from a discriminatory liberalization of its imports and gain from similar liberalization by its partner country. Precisely as mercantilists would have argued, the gains come from obtaining a higher price on exports to the union partner and losses accrue from having to give a higher price on imports from the latter. This conclusion has two important implications. First, because each country is an exporter of some products and an importer of others within the union, it wins in some markets and loses in others. But countries need not, and usually do not, have balanced trade with their union partners. If the initial tariff levels are similar between union partners, net exporters gain and net importers lose. This disparity in outcomes can very well be one source of friction among union partners and may explain why the arrangements in Africa and Latin America during the 1960s and 1970s fell apart.[6]

A second implication of the mercantilist bias is that if the initial tariffs in one country are much higher initially and that country has either a deficit or balanced trade with the union partner, it is likely to be a net loser from the FTA. In such a situation its tariff reduction will be larger than that of the partner and it will experience a net deterioration in its terms of trade. This fact will play a crucial role in the development of my argument that the static welfare gains to Mexico from NAFTA will be tiny and may even be negative.

Before we turn to a discussion of actual experience, we must raise an important possibility left out of consideration so far. In *Free trade agreements under tariffs* and *Free trade agreements under quotas*, I have assumed that A's union partner is not the most efficient supplier of the product under consideration. For example, in figure 4.1, what if the supply curves of B and C are interchanged? With the partner's supply given by $P_C P_C$ and the rest of the world's by $E_B E_B$, the FTA lowers the price in A to P_C and is necessarily beneficial to that country. This possibility seriously undercuts the argument made so far.

There are at least three limitations of this possibility. First, with more than 150 countries in the world, a single potential partner is unlikely to be the most efficient producer of all or even most of the country's imports. For example, with Japan, the Republic of Korea, Hong Kong, China, and the EU in the rest of the world, the most efficient suppliers of a majority of Mexico's products cannot be in the United States. Constant demands by U.S. firms for antidumping and other protectionist actions is *prima facie* evidence that efficient suppliers are in the rest of the world. Second, if supply curves of both B and C are upward sloped, the most efficient producer cannot be identified uniquely. The marginal cost now depends on the level of output, and we cannot say that, at the margin, a given country is the lowest cost supplier. It can be shown that in this case the likelihood of gains to A from a preferential liberalization of trade with either B or C is small. Finally, and most important, if the union partner is the most efficient producer of most of A's imports, it has no incentive to form an FTA with the latter. In figure 4.1, there are no gains to C from forming an FTA with A.[7]

I conclude that the mercantilist bias is likely to dominate in preferential trading. In this background, let me analyze a variety of regional arrangements around the world.

---

6. I am grateful to John Nash for suggesting this point.

7. It is assumed here that C has complete free trade and, as such, cannot offer any tariff reductions to A. Of course, if C does have tariffs and offers to lower them as a part of the FTA deal, it will actually lose from the FTA.

The Generalized System of Preferences: One-Way Preferences

During 1971–72, Japan and the West European countries introduced tariff preferences for developing countries under the Generalized System of Preferences (GSP), sponsored by the United Nations Conference on Trade and Development (UNCTAD). In the United States and Canada, similar preferences were introduced on January 1, 1976. The provision for these preferences in the United States was introduced in the Trade Reforms Act of 1974. Because the original idea was that all industrial countries would offer the same preferences to all other countries, the scheme was titled the "Generalized" System of Preferences; but, as it turned out, different countries adopted schemes with different product coverage, lists of beneficiary countries, and safeguard measures. Following the Tokyo Round in 1979, the GSP was given legal status under GATT.

Even before the GSP was introduced, trade preferences had existed between former colonial powers and their ex-colonies. Until its entry into the EC, the United Kingdom granted trade preference to the Commonwealth countries. Similarly, the EC has had a long history of tariff preferences to the former French and Belgian colonies. Originally, these preferences were two-way; thus, the United Kingdom and France were also *recipients* of tariff preferences from their former colonies. The prevailing wisdom was that such "reverse preferences" were detrimental to the interests of developing countries. Therefore, when the GSP was brought into the GATT framework in 1979 following the Tokyo Round, the reverse preferences were made GATT-illegal and had to be gradually phased out. The GSP as it exists now is very likely trade-diverting but nevertheless beneficial to the recipient developing countries.[8]

A good example that brings out various issues of interest related to one-way preferences is that of EC preferences to many of its developing-country partners. At the top of the "privilege pyramid" created by these preferences were twelve Mediterranean nations: Algeria, Cyprus, Egypt, Israel, Jordan, Lebanon, Malta, Morocco, Syria, Tunisia, Turkey, and the former Yugoslavia. The agreements offered these countries (a) duty-free access for all manufactured products, with limits on certain products, and (b) duty reduction on a large number of agricultural, livestock, and fish products.

Table 4.2 shows the share of exports from five of the above twelve countries to EC9.[9] For comparison, shares of exports from Greece, Portugal, and Spain (which entered the EC in 1986) going to EC are also shown. The share of Morocco's exports going to EC9 has been steady at about 50 percent while

---

8. Many analysts have viewed the GSP as an instrument of aid.
9. Table 4.1 is an updated version of the table 4.7 in the TEP report on Morocco (TEP 1990).

Table 4.2. *Morocco and Competitors' Exports*
(percentage of global exports)

Country	1973	1980	1985	1986	1987	1988	1989	1990	1991	1992	1993
Fish and preparations											
Morocco	57.3	55.8	25.6	31.5	31.0	27.5	29.7	33.4	26.8	25.6	22.3
Egypt	66.6	73.3	46.8	84.9	71.5	63.5	89.3	91.5	69.0	71.2	37.3
Israel	81.6	68.8	70.9	76.7	78.4	79.0	84.4	86.5	78.1	70.2	73.1
Tunisia	95.0	74.0	78.5	72.2	64.0	69.9	57.7	65.9	59.2	48.9	61.4
Turkey	65.1	61.7	55.8	51.6	67.6	66.3	53.9	63.6	56.3	59.5	58.5
Yugoslavia	48.1	25.0	23.3	27.3	34.7	54.8	58.6	61.5	n.a.	n.a.	n.a.
Spain	28.9	29.2	29.3	32.8	40.0	44.4	57.1	43.8	39.0	41.5	46.1
Greece	69.4	76.8	77.0	77.3	72.2	75.2	76.5	85.1	86.4	84.7	0.0
Portugal	56.5	52.0	46.1	44.5	42.3	41.1	51.0	57.3	51.4	46.3	0.0
Fruit and vegetables											
Morocco	82.4	69.6	76.4	76.3	77.7	80.2	80.5	80.8	67.1	64.6	65.7
Egypt	28.5	40.9	18.8	24.7	17.5	30.6	23.6	28.1	26.0	25.3	27.2
Israel	72.3	75.9	75.2	73.0	77.1	77.3	75.1	74.9	63.1	67.2	66.2
Tunisia	77.3	76.5	85.4	76.2	72.3	74.4	77.1	79.0	65.7	66.8	74.9
Turkey	59.6	54.0	43.6	47.2	52.1	43.3	46.0	51.6	26.3	28.9	30.4
Yugoslavia	62.7	52.2	17.4	54.9	57.2	63.8	70.7	72.7	n.a.	n.a.	n.a.
Spain	71.4	76.0	71.6	76.2	78.0	77.9	77.6	79.5	55.5	55.8	55.6
Greece	65.8	50.6	65.5	71.0	73.1	75.4	71.7	72.4	41.0	41.6	0.0
Portugal	46.6	36.5	29.0	24.2	37.9	32.6	34.1	54.4	53.2	54.4	0.0

(table continues on following page)

(Table 4.2 continued)

Country	1973	1980	1985	1986	1987	1988	1989	1990	1991	1992	1993
Crude fertilizer and minerals											
Morocco	46.7	42.0	38.1	33.4	31.1	28.8	28.6	29.9	27.6	20.9	15.0
Egypt	1.2	24.4	26.8	9.7	30.1	21.5	62.9	47.9	47.4	75.3	40.0
Israel	54.8	34.1	74.4	75.2	74.4	72.1	69.1	69.3	55.2	49.6	49.0
Tunisia	39.9	38.8	36.8	25.8	30.3	28.0	27.9	43.5	32.1	23.8	17.6
Turkey	43.9	50.5	40.6	44.7	47.9	40.8	44.2	43.1	34.6	29.6	33.3
Yugoslavia	32.6	28.1	35.7	34.9	41.5	57.6	49.0	60.0	n.a.	n.a.	n.a.
Spain	55.7	67.7	51.7	57.8	63.6	60.1	43.7	63.9	56.0	53.2	55.1
Greece	63.0	49.9	48.5	50.9	56.3	56.6	51.5	54.6	34.5	41.7	0.0
Portugal	72.2	57.5	39.6	48.8	37.4	28.5	34.3	41.4	35.3	42.6	0.0
Textile yarn, fabric											
Morocco	60.3	74.5	61.7	71.9	71.4	63.6	60.9	53.1	27.3	32.0	31.3
Egypt	14.6	26.6	32.1	33.0	33.6	30.1	40.5	42.8	28.5	36.2	35.1
Israel	25.1	76.0	57.3	63.8	61.6	57.9	53.7	57.6	45.5	45.9	42.6
Tunisia	88.4	86.2	74.8	72.6	67.7	72.7	73.8	60.9	51.7	56.1	57.5
Turkey	69.4	69.2	50.4	56.4	59.4	60.8	62.2	65.0	43.0	38.9	34.7
Yugoslavia	36.1	19.8	36.7	35.6	45.5	39.5	37.5	53.2	n.a.	n.a.	n.a.
Spain	37.9	42.2	48.9	50.0	49.6	48.5	51.1	56.2	41.7	40.6	41.0
Greece	80.5	79.2	84.5	85.3	83.6	81.2	78.3	77.1	52.9	53.7	0.0
Portugal	45.4	61.2	64.6	67.4	65.6	63.1	59.8	60.7	46.3	45.3	0.0

(table continues on following page)

(Table 4.2 continued)

Country	1973	1980	1985	1986	1987	1988	1989	1990	1991	1992	1993
Clothing											
Morocco	92.6	94.2	80.7	83.6	85.4	85.5	68.6	89.3	82.6	82.6	82.1
Egypt	0.3	22.6	14.3	20.5	17.0	25.5	35.2	35.8	18.2	24.5	25.7
Israel	43.6	84.0	73.4	70.8	70.4	67.9	61.8	62.5	44.4	44.7	40.1
Tunisia	56.5	99.0	98.0	96.3	97.9	97.0	96.6	97.5	68.5	70.6	69.0
Turkey	67.5	71.7	77.4	77.4	77.5	78.7	71.9	78.1	25.8	27.5	25.0
Yugoslavia	24.6	16.3	18.3	20.7	31.4	31.9	40.0	54.0	n.a.	n.a.	n.a.
Spain	48.5	61.3	48.5	56.5	58.7	57.1	49.7	52.8	46.2	45.5	41.0
Greece	82.0	89.7	81.6	81.9	80.4	78.8	72.5	74.8	20.0	21.9	0.0
Portugal	50.1	63.1	64.5	65.1	65.1	65.7	65.5	65.9	42.6	42.4	0.0
All products											
Morocco	64.6	54.6	48.5	49.7	52.5	48.0	54.6	54.7	47.3	49.1	48.2
Egypt	16.0	42.7	37.9	29.7	35.3	33.6	38.3	34.7	28.6	29.9	28.0
Israel	37.2	38.8	29.8	28.9	29.9	30.3	28.8	32.6	26.1	25.7	21.9
Tunisia	55.4	53.5	64.3	64.2	68.9	69.8	67.1	74.5	55.7	56.1	59.0
Turkey	46.4	42.7	38.4	41.7	46.4	41.8	44.1	50.2	23.6	23.5	21.3
Yugoslavia	35.8	24.6	23.2	23.9	32.7	34.9	35.0	43.5	n.a.	n.a.	n.a.
Spain	47.8	49.0	49.5	56.1	58.6	59.3	59.8	62.5	47.7	47.1	45.0
Greece	55.0	47.6	53.3	62.5	65.5	62.4	63.4	62.1	37.7	38.9	0.0
Portugal	48.6	54.6	58.1	61.1	61.6	60.1	58.6	59.9	40.7	40.5	0.0

n.a. Not applicable.
Source: COMTRADE database.

that of Tunisia hovers around the 60 percent mark. For some specific products, EC9 share is even larger. For example, more than 80 percent of Morocco's and 70 percent of Tunisia's clothing exports go to EC9. Duty-free or low-duty access on this very large proportion of exports must amount to a considerable gain in the form of better terms of trade for these countries.

In 1986, the EC granted entry to three of its southern neighbors, Greece, Portugal, and Spain (EC3). This decision generated two types of effects on the recipients of EC preferences, one negative and the other positive. First, to the extent that the new entrants were competitors of products sold by nations enjoying preferences in the EC market, the entry was harmful. The entry meant a reduction in the market share and a deterioration in the terms of trade of the countries enjoying preferences.[10] Second, insofar as the exports of beneficiaries of preferences were sold in Greece, Portugal, and Spain, their preferences expanded. Tariffs in the new member countries fell not merely against the other EC members but also against countries enjoying EC preferences under the GSP or other provisions.

The extent of the negative effect of the southern expansion on recipients of preferences can be judged by examining the shares of the new members in the EC market for products of greatest importance to the former. For example, Morocco's five principal exports to the EC in the 1980s were clothing, fruits and vegetables, phosphate ore, textiles, and fish. In 1987, these products accounted for 70 percent of Morocco's exports. Table 4.3 shows the shares of Greece, Portugal, and Spain in total exports to the EC in aggregate and for the five products just listed for several years. According to this table, in 1985, at the aggregate level, the EC3 account for only 3.1 percent of total EC12 imports. Among the five products of interest to Morocco, the EC3's share was the largest in fruits and vegetables: 14.4 percent in 1985 and 18 percent in 1993. There is a clear possibility of an adverse effect on Morocco of increased competition from the EC3 in this sector. The next sector of importance was clothing, in which the EC3's share was 8.4 percent in 1985 but did not rise significantly in subsequent years. For the remaining three commodities, the share of the EC3 was between 5 and 6 percent and has not risen significantly in subsequent years. In sum, the negative effect of the entry could have been significant in fruits and vegetables only.

(Text continues on page 107)

10. Note that I do not address here the issue of whether the expansion was trade-creating or trade-diverting from a global perspective. Resolution of this issue requires more information than we have. As is very likely, the new entrants will expand their market share by displacing sales by local EC producers, sales from countries enjoying preferences, and the outside world. Displacement of the first two sources is trade diversion while that of the last one is trade creation. We cannot say whether, on balance, there is trade creation or trade diversion.

Table 4.3. *Exports of Partner Country to EC12 by Commodity Group*
(percent)

Partner	1973	1980	1985	1986	1987	1988	1989	1990	1991	1992	1993
Fish and preparations											
Morocco	2.0	1.8	2.0	2.1	2.2	2.0	2.1	2.2	2.2	2.3	2.7
Spain	4.8	2.1	3.5	2.9	3.0	2.8	2.9	3.0	3.0	2.8	2.9
Greece	0.5	0.4	0.7	0.7	0.8	0.6	0.6	0.5	0.6	0.7	0.9
Portugal	2.3	1.4	1.1	1.2	1.0	1.1	1.5	1.6	1.6	1.3	1.3
EC3	7.6	3.9	5.3	4.9	4.8	4.5	5.0	5.1	5.1	4.9	5.1
EC9	37.1	38.4	37.7	37.7	36.3	35.9	36.2	36.3	33.1	33.1	32.2
EC12	44.7	42.3	43.1	42.6	41.2	40.5	41.2	41.4	38.2	38.0	37.4
World	100.0	100.0	100.0	100.0	100.0	100.0	100.0	100.0	100.0	100.0	100.0
Fruit and vegetables											
Morocco	4.8	2.9	2.3	2.2	1.7	1.8	2.0	2.0	2.1	1.7	1.9
Spain	12.5	11.5	10.9	12.1	13.3	12.9	12.8	12.8	13.6	13.9	14.9
Greece	2.9	2.7	3.3	3.3	2.9	2.8	3.0	3.1	2.7	2.4	2.6
Portugal	0.8	0.2	0.2	0.2	0.2	0.3	0.3	0.3	0.4	0.5	0.4
EC3	16.1	14.5	14.4	15.6	16.4	16.0	16.1	16.3	16.7	16.7	17.9
EC9	37.8	39.6	41.7	43.2	43.1	42.3	43.8	44.0	40.1	39.6	35.0
EC12	53.9	54.0	56.1	58.8	59.5	58.3	59.9	60.3	56.8	56.3	52.9
World	100.0	100.0	100.0	100.0	100.0	100.0	100.0	100.0	100.0	100.0	100.0

(table continues on following page)

(Table 4.3 continued)

Partner	1973	1980	1985	1986	1987	1988	1989	1990	1991	1992	1993
Crude fertilizer and minerals											
Morocco	9.4	11.4	10.2	8.7	6.3	5.8	5.2	4.5	3.9	3.3	2.4
Spain	1.6	2.4	3.0	3.3	3.6	3.6	3.4	3.8	3.9	4.0	3.2
Greece	2.1	2.0	1.6	1.8	1.8	1.6	1.7	1.7	1.6	1.5	1.3
Portugal	0.7	0.4	0.4	0.6	0.7	0.7	0.8	0.9	1.0	1.0	0.9
EC3	4.4	4.9	5.0	5.6	6.1	5.9	5.8	6.4	6.5	6.5	5.4
EC9	39.0	34.4	36.3	40.1	43.5	42.4	41.7	45.4	33.8	35.4	27.1
EC12	43.4	39.3	41.3	45.7	49.6	48.3	47.5	51.8	40.3	41.9	32.5
World	100.0	100.0	100.0	100.0	100.0	100.0	100.0	100.0	100.0	100.0	100.0
Textile yarn, fabric											
Morocco	0.3	0.4	4.0	0.4	0.4	0.3	0.3	0.3	0.2	0.2	0.3
Spain	0.8	1.3	1.8	1.7	1.7	1.8	1.9	2.2	2.3	2.3	2.1
Greece	1.2	1.7	1.7	1.7	1.6	1.2	1.1	0.9	0.8	0.7	0.7
Portugal	1.7	1.7	2.3	2.1	2.1	2.1	2.1	2.1	2.1	2.2	2.3
EC3	3.6	4.7	5.8	5.4	5.3	5.1	5.1	5.2	5.2	5.2	5.1
EC9	69.6	61.4	62.5	63.1	62.0	62.2	62.5	62.6	46.4	47.1	42.0
EC12	73.1	66.1	68.3	68.5	67.3	67.3	67.6	67.8	51.6	52.3	47.1
World	100.0	100.0	100.0	100.0	100.0	100.0	100.0	100.0	100.0	100.0	100.0

(table continues on following page)

(Table 4.3 continued)

Partner	1973	1980	1985	1986	1987	1988	1989	1990	1991	1992	1993
Clothing											
Morocco	0.3	0.7	1.4	1.6	1.9	2.0	2.4	2.7	2.5	2.6	3.2
Spain	1.2	1.0	1.0	1.0	1.0	0.9	0.8	0.8	0.8	0.9	0.6
Greece	2.0	4.8	3.5	4.0	3.9	3.4	3.3	2.9	2.7	2.7	2.4
Portugal	1.8	2.0	3.9	3.9	4.2	4.3	4.9	5.2	5.0	5.1	4.3
EC3	5.0	7.9	8.4	8.9	9.1	8.6	9.0	8.9	8.5	8.6	7.3
EC9	56.8	45.5	44.5	43.7	40.7	38.7	37.7	37.7	28.9	28.9	21.3
EC12	61.8	53.3	52.9	52.6	49.8	47.3	46.7	46.6	37.3	37.4	28.6
World	100.0	100.0	100.0	100.0	100.0	100.0	100.0	100.0	100.0	100.0	100.0
All five products											
Morocco	2.3	2.0	1.9	1.7	1.6	1.6	1.8	1.8	1.8	1.8	2.1
Spain	4.3	3.7	3.9	3.9	4.2	4.1	4.0	4.1	4.3	4.3	4.3
Greece	1.8	2.7	2.5	2.7	2.6	2.2	2.2	2.1	1.9	1.8	1.8
Portugal	1.4	1.3	2.0	2.1	2.2	2.3	2.5	2.7	2.7	2.8	2.6
EC3	7.5	7.7	8.4	8.7	8.9	8.6	8.7	8.8	8.9	8.9	8.7
EC9	53.9	48.1	48.8	49.2	47.6	46.8	46.9	46.9	36.8	36.8	30.7
EC12	61.4	55.9	57.2	57.9	56.6	55.4	55.6	55.7	45.8	45.8	39.4
World	100.0	100.0	100.0	100.0	100.0	100.0	100.0	100.0	100.0	100.0	100.0

(table continues on following page)

(*Table 4.3 continued*)

Partner	1973	1980	1985	1986	1987	1988	1989	1990	1991	1992	1993
Total trade											
Morocco	0.3	0.2	0.2	0.2	0.2	0.2	0.2	0.3	0.3	0.3	0.3
Spain	1.4	1.6	2.0	2.2	2.4	2.5	2.5	2.7	2.9	3.0	2.8
Greece	0.4	0.4	0.5	0.5	0.5	0.5	0.5	0.4	0.4	0.4	0.4
Portugal	0.4	0.4	0.6	0.7	0.7	0.8	0.8	0.9	0.9	0.9	0.9
EC3	2.2	2.4	3.1	3.4	3.6	3.7	3.8	4.0	4.2	4.3	4.1
EC9	51.0	47.0	49.8	53.9	54.6	54.3	53.7	54.2	39.6	39.8	35.6
EC12	53.2	49.4	52.9	57.3	58.2	58.0	57.5	58.2	43.8	44.2	39.8
World	100.0	100.0	100.0	100.0	100.0	100.0	100.0	100.0	100.0	100.0	100.0

Source: COMTRADE database.

104

Table 4.4. Morocco's Principal Exports to Partners for Five Products
(percentage of global exports)

Partner	1973	1980	1985	1986	1987	1988	1989	1990	1991	1992	1993
Fish and preparations											
EC12	61.0	63.1	47.8	52.5	56.3	49.3	54.1	59.2	54.7	55.5	50.2
EC9	57.3	55.8	25.6	31.5	31.0	27.5	29.7	33.4	26.8	25.6	22.3
EC3	3.7	7.3	22.2	21.0	25.3	21.7	24.4	25.8	28.0	29.9	27.9
Spain	1.2	6.3	14.9	15.4	18.8	16.7	18.5	22.7	20.4	22.8	22.2
Greece	2.4	1.0	1.7	1.2	2.0	1.6	1.8	1.2	1.4	1.5	1.1
Portugal	0.0	0.0	5.6	4.4	4.5	3.4	4.1	1.9	2.2	2.0	1.8
Fruit and vegetables											
EC12	84.4	70.3	78.2	77.4	78.8	81.2	82.7	84.4	81.4	80.9	81.0
EC9	82.4	69.6	76.4	76.3	77.7	80.2	80.5	80.8	67.1	64.6	65.7
EC3	2.0	0.8	1.8	1.1	1.0	1.0	2.2	3.6	14.3	16.2	15.3
Spain	1.8	0.2	0.6	0.6	1.0	0.8	2.0	3.2	5.0	6.6	4.8
Greece	0.1	0.2	0.0	0.3	0.0	0.2	0.1	0.1	0.1	0.2	0.1
Portugal	0.1	0.3	1.2	0.2	0.0	0.1	0.2	0.3	0.4	0.2	0.0
Crude fertilizer and minerals											
EC12	59.6	59.0	58.1	53.2	49.4	46.7	44.7	45.7	49.8	41.4	36.2
EC9	46.7	42.0	58.1	33.4	31.1	28.8	28.6	29.9	27.6	20.9	15.0
EC3	12.9	17.1	20.0	19.8	18.3	17.9	16.1	15.8	22.3	20.5	21.2
Spain	10.3	13.5	16.1	17.1	15.3	15.3	13.1	13.2	16.6	16.7	17.3
Greece	1.0	1.1	2.2	0.9	1.3	1.5	1.9	1.8	2.1	0.7	1.2
Portugal	1.6	2.4	1.6	1.8	1.8	1.1	1.1	0.9	0.8	0.3	0.6

(table continues on following page)

(Table 4.4 continued)

Partner	1973	1980	1985	1986	1987	1988	1989	1990	1991	1992	1993
Textile yarn, fabric											
EC12	62.1	74.9	61.9	72.4	73.2	65.3	63.2	57.9	53.4	54.6	53.9
EC9	60.3	74.5	61.7	71.9	71.4	63.6	60.9	53.1	27.3	32.0	31.3
EC3	1.8	0.4	0.2	0.5	1.8	1.7	2.3	4.7	26.1	22.6	22.6
Spain	1.8	0.4	0.2	0.4	1.3	1.4	2.1	4.3	5.2	4.7	3.5
Greece	0.0	0.0	0.0	0.1	0.5	0.3	0.0	0.0	0.1	0.2	0.0
Portugal	0.0	0.0	0.0	0.0	0.0	0.0	0.2	0.5	0.9	1.2	1.5
Clothing											
EC12	94.1	94.7	81.3	84.7	87.9	90.4	93.6	94.4	93.9	93.8	92.4
EC9	92.6	94.2	80.7	83.6	85.4	85.5	88.6	89.3	82.6	82.6	82.1
EC3	1.5	0.4	0.6	1.1	2.5	4.9	5.0	5.0	11.3	11.2	10.3
Spain	1.5	0.4	0.6	1.1	2.4	4.9	5.0	5.0	5.6	5.9	5.3
Greece	0.0	0.0	0.0	0.0	0.0	0.0	0.0	0.0	0.0	0.0	0.1
Portugal	0.0	0.0	0.0	0.0	0.0	0.0	0.0	0.1	0.1	0.1	0.1
All products											
EC12	70.8	62.7	58.6	58.2	61.3	56.6	64.6	65.0	62.4	64.0	62.4
EC9	64.6	54.6	48.5	49.7	52.5	48.0	54.6	54.7	47.3	49.1	48.2
EC3	6.3	8.1	10.1	8.5	8.8	8.6	10.0	10.4	15.0	15.0	14.3
Spain	5.0	5.9	7.4	6.6	6.8	7.2	8.3	9.2	8.8	9.0	8.8
Greece	0.8	1.1	1.0	0.8	0.9	0.6	0.6	0.4	0.4	0.3	0.3
Portugal	0.5	1.0	1.7	1.0	1.1	0.8	1.1	0.8	1.0	0.9	0.7

Source: COMTRADE database.

The likely gains from acquiring preferential access to the markets of the new members can be judged by examining the volume of exports from Morocco to the latter. This is done in table 4.4. In 1985, the year before the three countries entered the EC, 10 percent of Morocco's exports went to EC3. In some products such as fish and minerals, the share was more than 20 percent. This is a significant amount on which Morocco acquired additional preferences. Even more important, Morocco acquired more or less free access to EC3 markets in textiles and clothing. The effect of this change is reflected in the sharp rise in the proportion of Morocco's exports of textiles and clothing going to EC3. Between 1985 and 1993, the proportion of textiles exports to EC3 rose from 0.2 percent to 22.6 percent and that of clothing from 0.6 percent to 10.3 percent.[11] The change in the share of total exports during the same period was from 10.1 percent to 14.3 percent.

Recently, there have been exploratory discussions between Morocco and the EU about an association agreement that would create an FTA between the two entities. In this context, it may be asked whether countries enjoying trade preferences should form an FTA with a country giving the preferences. If the preferences are extensive, as is true in the case of Morocco, at least the Vinerian analysis argues against such an FTA from that country's viewpoint. The FTA will not create any new preferences for Morocco but will, through the back door, resurrect the reverse preferences eliminated after the incorporation of the GSP into GATT. It is not clear why if the reverse preferences were harmful before they could be beneficial now.

To summarize, from a global perspective trade preferences to developing countries have been very likely trade-diverting, but from the viewpoint of the recipients the preferences have been beneficial. They have offered a guaranteed access to a large market. Moreover, because the access has been duty free or at a preferential tariff, the recipients have also benefited from better terms of trade. Entry of new members has led to a dilution of the preference but, at least in the case of Morocco, only marginally. Finally, association agreements intended to create an FTA between recipients of extensive preferences and the country giving those preferences is likely to hurt the former. The FTA will essentially amount to a reintroduction of reverse preferences banished in the 1980s to protect developing-country interests.

North-South Integration: Two-Way Preferences

The first regional movement that flourished in the 1950s and 1960s consisted of regional arrangements that were either North-North or South-South type.

---

11. For reasons not known to the author, the share of Morocco's exports of textiles to the EC9 declined sharply over this period.

The original members of the EC and of the European Free Trade Area (EFTA) were all industrial countries. Members of other regional schemes such as the CACM, the Andean Pact, the Association of Southeast Asian Nations (ASEAN), UDEAC, and ECOWAS were all developing countries.[12]

The second regional movement, also referred to as the New Regionalism, can be traced to the beginning of negotiations for the Canada-U.S. Free Trade Area (CUFTA) in the mid-1980s. This movement began with the conversion of the United States to regionalism, and has been characterized by several regional agreements between industrial and developing countries.[13] The most prominent of these is, of course, NAFTA, which supersedes CUFTA and is designed to create a free trade area among Canada, Mexico, and the United States. The second enlargement of the European Community in 1986, which gave Greece, Portugal, and Spain entry into the European Community, also had elements of North-South integration. Finally, a large number of association agreements between the EC on the one hand and East European countries on the other represent examples of North-South agreements.

In principle, developing-country participants of North-South arrangements can expect three advantages that are not available in South-South arrangements. First, such arrangements guarantee access to a large market. So far, North-South arrangements have involved either the United States or the EC as the northern participant. Both of these entities can offer large markets to their partners. Second, free trade with an industrial country is likely to enhance competition in the domestic market and give rise to faster technical progress. Finally, a regional arrangement with a large, rich trading partner can be an effective instrument of imparting credibility to reforms. An international treaty can ensure that protectionist future governments cannot reverse trade reforms enacted by their predecessors.

These benefits are not without qualification, however. First, to the extent that the southern country has higher initial tariffs, the FTA is likely to worsen its terms of trade. In the limit, if the northern country already has free trade, there is no change in the southern country's access to the former's market as a result of the FTA. On the contrary, it is the northern country that succeeds in acquiring access to the southern country on a *preferential* basis. For example, in the case of NAFTA, tariffs in Mexico were close to 20

---

12. The only arguable exception was the Southern African Customs Union (SACU), membership of which included South Africa and four developing countries. Defining South Africa as an industrial country, we can think of SACU as a North-South arrangement.

13. Though the United States supported the EC for geopolitical reasons, it remained otherwise committed to multilateralism during the first regional movement. According to Bhagwati (in de Melo and Panagariya 1993), the conversion to regionalism was a major turning point in the history of regionalism.

percent while those in the United States and Canada were 5 percent. Moreover, Mexico already enjoyed preferential access to the U.S. market under the GSP. Hence, NAFTA is virtually certain to improve U.S. access to Mexico without a major change in Mexico's access to the U.S. market. Put differently, NAFTA will worsen Mexico's terms of trade.

Second, as was amply demonstrated during NAFTA debate, integration with a southern country generates fears of adverse income distribution effects on unskilled labor in the North. These fears, in turn, lead to adoption of provisions (such as restrictive rules of origin) that partially undo the FTA in precisely those areas in which it is likely to generate trade creation.

Third, the benefits in terms of enhancing the credibility of reforms can be easily overstated. As far as tariffs are concerned, a country can attain the same objective on a *nondiscriminatory* basis through the GATT bindings. Regarding other instruments such as antidumping, an FTA does not offer any more restraint than GATT. At most it precludes such actions against the union partner (although not quite). But that is likely to precisely enhance the possibility of such action against countries outside the union. This is the point made forcefully by Bhagwati (in de Melo and Panagariya 1993):

> Imagine that the United States begins to eliminate (by outcompeting) an inefficient Mexican industry once the FTA goes into effect. Even though the most efficient producer is Taiwan, if the next efficient United States outcompetes the least efficient Mexico, that would be desirable trade creation.... But what would the Mexicans be likely to do? They would probably start AD [antidumping] actions against Taiwan.

In the light of these benefits and costs of North-South regional arrangements, let us look closely at their evolution in the two major regions: North America and Europe.

NAFTA

In the Western Hemisphere, the North-South integration began with NAFTA. To assess the future desirability of similar FTAs, it is best to review briefly the main achievements of NAFTA. What follows are the major items.

- Liberalization of imports of fresh fruits and vegetables from Mexico into the United States, and that of corn (and other grains) in the opposite direction.
- Liberalization of tariffs and quotas on North American trade in textiles and apparel.

- Removal of most tariffs and nontariff barriers (NTBs) on cars by Mexico within five to ten years.
- Mexico agreed to a rapid access for U.S. and Canadian firms to Mexico's telecommunications market. Mexico is to eliminate the majority of tariff and NTBs to its telecommunications equipment market on implementation of NAFTA.
- In the government procurement area, during a period of ten years, Mexico will open up to North American companies.
- NAFTA commits Mexico to follow the GATT intellectual property rights.
- Member countries agreed to provide national treatment to investors of another NAFTA member.
- The North American Agreement on Environmental Cooperation commits NAFTA members to improve environmental protection laws and enforce existing laws. Persistent failures are subject to a dispute settlement procedure that can assess monetary fines up to US$20 million.
- The North American Agreement on Labor Cooperation does the same in the area of labor laws and labor standards.

Let us first identify the areas of gains for Mexico. There are two important sectors in which Mexico stands to benefit from its own liberalization although it is preferential: telecommunications and corn. In both of these sectors, the United States is a highly efficient producer and will lower prices. In telecommunications, the local company, a monopoly, is notoriously inefficient. Therefore, the entry of U.S. firms will confer gains on Mexico through increased competition and improved technology. Mexican consumers and businesses are likely to benefit from reduced prices and improved service. Mexico also stands to benefit from preferential access to the U.S. market in two areas: fruits and vegetables, and textiles and clothing. The United States is highly protective of its agriculture, so entry into that sector may turn into a major gain.

At least in the area of textiles and clothing, the likely gains are often overstated. There are four factors that limit possible gains in this area. First, during the 1980s, Mexico consistently underutilized its Multifibre Arrangement (MFA) quotas with the United States. Erzan and Yeats (1992) place Mexico's average quota utilization rate during 1985–89 in the United States at 51.5 percent.[14] Therefore, there will be no major gain from liberalization of quotas on clothing and textiles. Second, under NAFTA, imports are subject to strict rules of origin based on "triple transformation." There are 200 pages on the rules of origin in the NAFTA document. These rules can become an easy

---

14. Of course, this is an average figure, which can mask the differences across various MFA categories. According to Erzan and Yeats, for at least 70 percent of the categories, Mexico did not use up its quota during 1985–89.

instrument of protection. Third, the dismantling of the MFA under the Uruguay Round will erode Mexico's preferential access to the U.S. market to a considerable extent. Finally, the gains from tariff liberalization are limited due to a tiny share of textiles and clothing in total Mexican exports to the United States. The average tariff on Mexico's clothing and textiles exports in the United States in 1987 was 17.3 percent (Erzan and Yeats 1992). The eventual removal of this tariff is a significant gain. But given that clothing and textiles account for less than 2 percent of its total exports to the United States, the associated gain, even if such exports double, cannot be very large.

From the viewpoint of market access, it is difficult to argue that the effect on Mexico's terms of trade compared with that of the United States will be favorable. In terms of trade restrictions subject to negotiations within NAFTA, the United States had rather limited restrictions applicable to Mexico. Not only were the tariffs low to begin with, the United States also gave extensive preferences to Mexico under the GSP. According to Erzan and Yeats (1992), for the year 1986, Mexican exports to the United States, which faced a tariff of 5 percent or more and also had one or more significant NTBs, accounted for only 8.5 percent of total exports.

By comparison, concessions granted by Mexico—all of them on a preferential basis—are many and more substantial. Given the relatively high restrictions on outside countries (the highest tariff rate is 20 percent), NAFTA is bound to lead to trade diversion. The liberalization in the automobile sector is likely to benefit mostly the United States. In addition, under plausible assumptions, a stricter enforcement of environmental and labor laws, without similar changes in other developing countries that compete against Mexico in the United States and elsewhere, is likely to make Mexico worse-off. Above all, at least in the short run, tighter intellectual property rights will make technology imports more expensive. In particular, reduced access to or increased prices of medicines are almost sure to hurt the poor.

Can we claim that for most products imported by Mexico, the United States is the lowest-cost producer over the relevant range? Acknowledging the U.S. efficiency in telecommunications and corn sectors, for a broad class of products this is debatable on at least two grounds. First, if the United States were the lowest-cost source, there would be no need for an FTA; Mexico could liberalize trade on a nondiscriminatory basis and all additional imports would still come from the United States. There would be no cost of such liberalization to anyone and the world efficiency would improve unambiguously. Second, with a large number of U.S. industries constantly complaining about competition from East Asia and seeking protection through antidumping duties and other means, *prima facie*, it is difficult to believe that the United States is the most efficient supplier of Mexican goods.

An important gain claimed for Mexico from NAFTA is the increased credibility of its economic reforms. In Panagariya (1995), I subject this view to a detailed examination and conclude that the advocates of NAFTA have greatly exaggerated this gain. Here let me note that NAFTA says nothing about member countries' domestic polices beyond intellectual property rights and side agreements on labor and environmental standards. In all other areas of domestic policy, the only international discipline remains that provided by GATT or the World Trade Organization (WTO). As for macroeconomic stability, the recent crisis has demonstrated that NAFTA does not contribute positively to it. The only area in which the credibility argument can have potential relevance is tariff reform.[15]

In assessing NAFTA's contribution to the credibility of trade reform, we must recognize that GATT bindings provide an alternative instrument in this area. In principle, GATT bindings are superior in that they are nondiscriminatory and make tariff reductions irreversible against more than 120 countries. NAFTA accomplishes that objective against only two trading partners.

But advocates of NAFTA point out that GATT discipline is weak. Countries bind tariffs well above their actual levels, and that is true of Mexico. This leaves room for tariff escalation when protectionist pressures rise. NAFTA leaves no such flexibility. The Salinas government has tied the hands of future governments permanently.

There are two problems with this argument. First, the fact that countries choose to bind tariffs above actual tariff levels is not a weakness of the instrument. It simply reflects a lack of seriousness for reforms on the part of the country. If the present government itself does not want its hands tied, it cannot tie the hands of future governments. Second, suppose we accept that this is a weakness in GATT and we complement it by NAFTA. But what will happen if protectionist pressures rise in this case? Mexico will have to raise tariffs on outside countries. Because the bulk of Mexico's imports come from the United States, the necessary increase in tariffs on outside countries will have to be very substantial. The margin of preference for the United States and the level of discrimination against outside countries will become very large. By contrast, in the absence of NAFTA, Mexico will need only a small nondiscriminatory tariff increase.

Perhaps the most balanced evaluation of NAFTA prior to its approval is offered by Nash (1993, p. 48) in his review of the volume edited by Lustig, Bosworth, and Lawrence (1992):

---

15. Contrary to popular belief, NAFTA does not protect member countries from antidumping actions by each other. Nor does it impose any discipline on the use of quantitative restrictions on outside countries. That discipline is provided by GATT.

Well, there is good news and bad news about the North American Free Trade Agreement (NAFTA). The good news is that the costs of adjusting to it will be insignificant.... The bad news is that the benefits are not anything to get excited about.

Expressing skepticism toward the large effects generated by some studies in the volume based on computable general equilibrium (CGE) models, Nash (1993, p. 49) concludes the review thus:

The authors treat these models with more seriousness than they deserve, mainly because so few offer anything better. But therein lies my source of unease. If the only way to show significant impact is through dynamic effects, which are not (or cannot be) well modeled, we seem to be left with *Hamlet* without the Prince. The authors never reach this conclusion, but the overall corpus of evidence shows as yet little basis for optimism, pessimism, or even neutrality about the effects of NAFTA—only agnosticism.

My analysis lends support to this minority view and, indeed, raises a good deal of skepticism, even pessimism, with respect to NAFTA. The CGE models of NAFTA I have seen do not incorporate the mercantilist element of FTAs I have pointed out and sometimes even fail to make a distinction between free trade and free trade areas.[16] Once we correct for these two factors, it will not be surprising if the small gains generated by CGE models turn into losses. In addition, the gains from increased credibility fail to stand up to a careful scrutiny.

What should Mexico do to minimize the losses resulting from the transfer of tariff revenue to U.S. firms? The answer is intellectually simple but may be politically difficult to implement: it should gradually extend the concessions granted to NAFTA members to the rest of the world. Such a change will bring the tariff revenue back to Mexican consumers by subjecting U.S. exporters to competition with the rest of the world. This simple remedy is likely to be resisted by not merely the import-competing industries in Mexico, but also manufacturers in the United States, which now has preferential access to Mexican markets. It may even be opposed by those that view NAFTA and an eventual Free Trade Area of the Americas (FTAA) as a bargaining device to force concessions from the EU.[17]

---

16. Astonishingly, the book edited by Lustig, Bosworth, and Lawrence is titled *North American Free Trade*, as if free trade and free trade areas are one and the same thing.

17. During a recent panel discussion at the IMF's Economic Forum, Jeffrey Schott of the Institute for International Economics conceded that nondiscriminatory liberalization is a superior strategy for countries in Latin America but went on to argue that the Western Hemispheric FTA was needed to force the EU to open its markets. Effectively, this argument puts all the burden of opening the EU markets on countries in Latin America while the United States reaps benefits twice: first through a preferential access to markets in Latin America and then through the opening of the EU markets.

Table 4.5. The EC–Romania Association Agreement: Main Provisions on Trade in Goods, 1993–2003

Item	Nontariff barriers	1993	1994	1995	1996	1997	1998	1999	2000	2001	2002	2003
Industrial goods (except textiles and apparel, iron and steel)												
Romania												
General	T	100	n.c.	n.c.	80	n.c.	60	50	35	20	0	n.c.
	Q	Elimination of all quantitative restrictions at the entry into force										
	EXP	Elimination of all restrictions at the entry into force										
Annex IV	T	0	n.c.	n.c.	n.c.	n.c.	n.c.	n.c.	n.c.	n.c.	n.c.	n.c.
Annex V	T	80	n.c.	n.c.	40	n.c.	0	n.c.	n.c.	n.c.	n.c.	n.c.
Annex VI	T	80	n.c.	n.c.	70	n.c.	60	n.c.	40	20	0	n.c.
Annex VII	T[a]	100	n.c.	n.c.	80	n.c.	60	n.c.	40	20	0	n.c.
	Q	Reduction of tariffs (as for General) for imports above the quotas										
Annex VIII	Q	Annual increase (10 percent) of the initial (1993) quotas of 20,000 units										
Annex IX	Q	Elimination of all restrictions on second-hand (8 years old) cars in 2000										
	EXP	Elimination of all these restrictions between 1993 and 1998										
European Community												
General	T	0	n.c.	n.c.	n.c.	n.c.	n.c.	n.c.	n.c.	n.c.	n.c.	n.c.
	Q	Elimination of all quantitative restrictions at the entry into force										
	EXP	Elimination of all restrictions at the entry into force										
Annex IIa	T	50	0	n.c.	n.c.	n.c.	n.c.	n.c.	n.c.	n.c.	n.c.	n.c.
Annex IIb	T	80	60	40	20	0	n.c.	n.c.	n.c.	n.c.	n.c.	n.c.
Annex III	T[a]	85	70	55	40	25	0	n.c.	n.c.	n.c.	n.c.	n.c.
	Q	Annual increase (20 percent) of the initial quotas or ceilings										

(table continues on following page)

(Table 4.5 continued)

Item	Nontariff barriers	1993	1994	1995	1996	1997	1998	1999	2000	2001	2002	2003
Agricultural products (nonprocessed) and fisheries												
Romania												
General	Q	Elimination of all quantitative restrictions at the entry into force										
Annex XIII	T	Reduction of tariffs between 1993 and 1997										
Annex XV	T[b]	Reduction of tariffs in 1993										
European Community												
General	Q	Elimination of all quantitative restrictions still subject to EC Reg. 3420/83										
Annex XIa	T	Reduction of levies by 50 percent										
Annex XIb	Q	Annual increase (10 percent) of the quotas										
	T	Reduction of tariffs										
Annex XIIa	T	Reduction of tariffs and levies (20 percent in 1993; 40 percent in 1994; 60 percent after 1994)										
Annex XIIb	Q	Annual increase of the quotas										
Annex XIV	T	Reduction of tariffs in 1993										
Special protocol 1: textiles and apparel												
Romania	T	Tariff reduction in accordance to above-mentioned provisions on industrial goods										
European Community	T[c]	71	n.c.	57	43	29	14	0	n.c.	n.c.	n.c.	n.c.
	T	Elimination of tariffs on Romanian exports under "outward processing" rules										
	Q	Increase of the quotas (to be negotiated)										

(table continues on following page)

(Table 4.5 continued)

Item	Nontariff barriers	1993	1994	1995	1996	1997	1998	1999	2000	2001	2002	2003
Special protocol 1: textiles and apparel												
Romania	T	Tariff reduction in accordance to above-mentioned provisions on industrial goods										
European Community	Tᶜ	71	n.c.	57	43	29	14	0	n.c.	n.c.	n.c.	n.c.
	T	Elimination of tariffs on Romanian exports under "outward processing" rules										
	Q	Increase of the quotas (to be negotiated)										
Special protocol 2: iron and steel												
Romania General	T	100	n.c.	n.c.	80	n.c.	60	50	35	20	0	n.c.
	Q	Elimination of all quantitative restrictions										
Annex IIa	T	0	n.c.	n.c.	n.c.	n.c.	n.c.	n.c.	n.c.	n.c.	n.c.	n.c.
Annex IIb	T	80	n.c.	40	40	n.c.	0	n.c.	n.c.	n.c.	n.c.	n.c.
European Community	T	80	60	40	20	10	0	n.c.	n.c.	n.c.	n.c.	n.c.
	Q	Elimination of all quantitative restrictions										

n.c. No change.
T = Tariff quotas; Q = Quotas; EXP = Export restrictions
a. Suspension of tariffs for imports within the quotas.
b. Products subject to quantitative restrictions.
c. Products subject to minimum prices.
Source: EC–Romania Association Agreement (1993).

The European Agreements

Following the demise of the Council for Mutual Economic Assistance (CMEA), the CEE countries have entered into the so-called European Agreements (EAs) with the EU. The objective of the EAs is to create FTAs between the EU and each of the CEE countries.[18] To the extent that the CEE countries are much poorer than their western counterparts and are less stable macroeconomically, these agreements have the flavor of North-South regional integration.

A lucid discussion of the EAs can be found in Winters and Wang (1994), from whom I draw unabashedly in this section (see also Kaminsky 1994). The first EAs were signed in early 1992 by the EU with Czechoslovakia, Hungary, and Poland. They were subsequently supplemented by additional agreements with Bulgaria, the Czech Republic, Romania, and the Slovak Republic. The EAs define the relations between the EU and the CEE countries in the areas of international trade, financial cooperation, and political contact. Although full agreements come into force only after ratification by EC member governments—a long process—the trade components have been brought into operation through interim trade agreements (ITAs), which require only discussions in European Parliament.

The ITAs are intended to create FTAs (excluding agriculture) between the signatories within a period not to exceed ten years. Table 4.5, taken from TEP (1994), provides detailed information on the extent and timing of liberalization under the EU-Romania FTA. As far as access to EC markets is concerned, various ITAs are virtually identical. On the date the ITA comes into force, the EU removes quantitative restrictions on all industrial products except textiles and clothing. Quotas on textiles and clothing, subject to the MFA, are to be relaxed gradually until they are abolished in less than five years and no more than half the time agreed in the Uruguay Round for the removal of the MFA. Tariff duties on the "standard industrial" products will be eliminated at the starting date of the agreement. Duty elimination will take four years on certain metal products, five years on iron and steel, and six years on textiles, clothing, and certain sensitive products such as steel products, furniture, leather goods, footwear, glass, vehicles, and some chemicals. These changes will amount to duty- and quantitative restriction-free entry for the CEE industrial products within six years (see Winters and Wang 1994). There is also some liberalization in agriculture but it is very limited. Tariff concessions are to be granted in some categories of agricultural goods inside quota limits. The quota limits are rigidly related to historical trade levels and will grow by 10 percent per year from 1990.

---

18. The EAs were preceded by the accession of Greece, Portugal, and Spain to the European Community. This expansion of the European Community also had the flavor of North-South integration but will not be covered due to the focus of this chapter on developing and transitional economies.

There are two possible sets of instruments that may have a restrictive effect on market access for CEE countries in the EU: antidumping and safeguards, and rules of origin. In view of the heavy bias in implementing antidumping against exporters (Messerlin 1989), fears have been expressed that EU markets may not be as open to CEE countries as appears from the EAs. Indeed, there have been reports of EU iron and steel industries threatening antidumping suits even before the agreement came into force (Hindley 1993). Messerlin (1992) and Winters and Wang (1994) also warn against some of the safeguards clauses in the EAs that can be invoked to protect EU producers from CEE imports.

The "rules of origin" may constitute yet another restriction on CEE countries' access to the EU. The agreements require that 60 percent of the gross value added be sourced locally (including EU and possibly all CEE countries) to qualify for preferential treatment. This means that the CEE countries will not be able to take advantage of preferences in the case of light processing tasks applied to non-EU materials.

On the CEE side, agreements differ in details. For the former Czechoslovakia and Poland, complete liberalization is to take seven years; for Bulgaria, Hungary, and Romania, it is to take ten years. Table 4.5, taken from TEP (1993), provides details on the agreement with Romania. According to this table, quantitative restrictions on many industrial products are to be abolished at the beginning of the agreement. Quantitative restrictions on other products (for example, those in Annexes IV, V, and VI in the European Agreements) are to be relaxed through a 10 percent per year expansion of the quota. Complete liberalization in industrial products is envisaged by the year 2002.

The ITAs also aim at upgrading the economic legislation in the CEE countries. The regulatory measures relate to unfair competition and monopolistic practices and are to be brought to EU level within three years; legislation regulating state assistance and subsidies is to be brought to EU level within five years; and intellectual property protection in the CEE countries is to be brought to EU level within five years.

Winters and Wang (1994) point out that there is a real possibility of trade diversion as a result of the EAs. The unweighted average tariff was 9 percent in Bulgaria , 6 percent in what was then Czechoslovakia, 15 percent in Hungary, 12 percent in Poland, and 18 percent in Romania. The highest rates of duties were 260 percent in Bulgaria, 150 percent in Poland, and 60 percent in Romania. Unless the countries also liberalize further with respect to outside countries, the potential for trade diversion is great. To make matters worse, EU residents have an incentive not to press for multilateral liberalization. Thus, according to Winters and Wang, EU-based advisors have been prominent in persuading Romanian authorities to favor their current tariffs over lower ones.

Despite these criticisms, it is perhaps fair to say that, under the EAs, the EU offers the CEE countries, purely in terms of preferential market access, at least as much as it receives from the latter. On balance, then, the CEE countries do not experience a deterioration in within-union terms of trade. Kaminski (1994) looks at the increased market access to CEE countries due to EAs in detail and concludes that the likely impact is quite substantial. Remembering that the EU is less open to outsiders than the United States, entry into that market through EAs is worth more than into the latter through NAFTA.

This is not the only, or even the major, difference between the EAs and NAFTA. The essential difference is the political context. After decades of domination by the U.S.S.R., CEE countries are now integrating themselves back into the world economy. The natural starting point for them, at least politically, is the EU. And, if the EAs serve as the stepping stone to full membership in the EU in the future, there will be little ambiguity about their economic desirability. As argued in Bhagwati (1995) and Panagariya (1995), the EU is a scheme superior to NAFTA. For one thing, it is a customs union that eliminates the need for the rules of origin. It also outlaws anti-dumping actions by members on each other. Finally, with full capital mobility and a commitment to labor mobility, the EU has a much stronger commitment to integration than NAFTA.

Outsiders: To Join or Not to Join?

An important issue facing many countries today is how they will be affected by developments such as NAFTA and whether they too should seek entry into such an arrangement. This issue can be illustrated with the help of Costa Rica, a country studied in detail by TEP (1992). According to the study, fears have been expressed that NAFTA will lead to a displacement by Mexico of Costa Rica's exports to the United States, and that it will also divert investments to Mexico. Because the United States alone accounts for more than 50 percent of Costa Rica's exports, and an equally high proportion of its imports, at first glance such fears seem justified. But, as the TEP report points out, a serious injury can happen only in the case of products that are currently subject to high barriers in the United States and are important to Costa Rica. There are few products that satisfy both of these conditions. For a large number of exports into North America common to Mexico and Costa Rica, both countries enjoy duty-free access. For example, this is true of *maquilla* assembly industries like garments and electronics, as well as Costa Rica's major traditional exports. Sugar is the major exception; but, in that case, Mexico's access has itself been limited by special agreements. The only area in which NAFTA can have some adverse effect is in nontraditional agricultural exports, which is not particularly large for Costa Rica. Not surprisingly, the TEP report concludes, "Overall then, a Mexico-U.S. agreement offers little reason for pessimism."

What applies to Costa Rica perhaps applies to a large number of other countries. As argued above, within NAFTA there was limited room for discriminatory liberalization in the United States and Canada. Discriminatory liberalization by Mexico was more extensive, but its market is relatively tiny. Not surprisingly, estimates of the effects of free trade within North America on developing country exports are generally small. Laird (1990) estimates that complete removal of tariffs within North America reduces the exports of other countries in the Western Hemisphere to the United States by less than .8 percent. Erzan and Yeats (1992) estimate that the total trade diversion from tariff elimination in North America will amount to 0.5 percent of U.S. imports from nonmembers. Of this, only 6 percent will fall on countries in the Western Hemisphere!

Turning to the issue of entry, I do not share the enthusiasm of many for a rush to sign an FTA with NAFTA and eventually create an FTAA. For reasons that must be clear by now, it is highly doubtful that Latin American countries stand to gain much from entering into an arrangement that gives their rich counterparts, the United States and Canada, a much greater preferential market access than they are able to offer. Table 4.6, taken from Lustig and Braga (1994), provides the information on trade barriers in Latin America. Unilateral trade reforms have virtually eliminated quantitative restrictions in the countries shown, and have lowered the average tariff rates considerably; yet, the top tariff rates remain high at 20 percent or more. Discriminatory liberalization with the United States under these circumstances is unlikely to confer major gains and will, very likely, lower welfare. Indeed, in the end, if the FTAA does come into being, gains to developing countries in the region will come more from improved access to each other's market than from any additional access to U.S. and Canadian markets.

A different twist is added to the issue if we bring in the possibility of the EU forming FTAs with countries in Latin America. Recalling that EU markets are less accessible to outsiders than North American markets, an argument can be made that Latin American countries may be better-off seeking FTAs with the former. Not surprisingly, possibilities have been raised of an FTA between MERCOSUR and the EU. Whether such an arrangement would be favored by the United States, and whether it could go ahead even if the latter were opposed, remains to be seen.

Although this is not compelling if one goes by the intensity of trade, for a large number of countries in Latin America, EC12 is a larger trading partner

Table 4.6. *Tariffs and Liberalizing Reforms in Latin America and the Caribbean*

Country (prereform year and postreform year, as applicable)	Average unweighted legal tariff rate (percent)		Tariff range (percent)		Coverage of QRs on imports (percentage of tariff, unless otherwise noted) [a]	
	Prereform	Postreform [b]	Prereform	Postreform [b]	Prereform	Postreform [b]
Argentina (1987, 1991)	42(p)	10	15–115(p)	0–22	62 of domestic production	8
Belize, 1992	n.a.	—	n.a.	5–45	n.a.	—
Bolivia (1985, 1994)	35	7.5	0–100	5–10	n.a.	Minimal
Brazil (1987, 1993)	51	14.2	0–105	0–35	39	Minimal
Chile (1984, 1992)	35	11	35	11	Minimal	0
Colombia (1984, 1993)	61	12	0–220	5–20	99	1.4
Costa Rica (1985, 1992)	53(p)	15(p)	0–1,400(p)	5–20	—	0
Dominican Republic (1990, 1994)	—	—	—	3–35	—	Significant
Ecuador (1989, 1994)	53	9.3	0–290	5–37	100	0
El Salvador, 1992	—	—	—	7–30	—	Minimal
Guatemala (1985, 1993)	50(p)	15(p)	5–90	5–20	6 of domestic production	0(1)

(table continues on following page)

(Table 4.6 continued)

Country (prereform year and postreform year, as applicable)	Average unweighted legal tariff rate (percent)		Tariff range (percent)		Coverage of QRs on import (percent of tariff, unless otherwise noted) a	
	Prereform	Postreform b	Prereform	Postreform b	Prereform	Postreform b
Honduras (1985, 1992)	41(p)	15(w,p)	5–90	5–20	—	0
Jamaica (1981, 1993)	—	20	—	5–30	—	0(1)
Mexico (1985, 1994)	22.6	12.5(w)	0–100	0–20	28	1.6
Nicaragua, 1992	—	—	—	0–20	—	—
Panama, 1991	88.2	59.8	—	0–90	—	n.a.
Paraguay (1988, 1991)	—	16	—	0–20(y)	—	Significant
Peru (1990, 1994)	66	16	0–120	15–25	100	0(1)
Uruguay (1987, 1993)	32	18(y)	10–55	6–20	0	0
Venezuela (1989, 1992)	37	10(m)	0–135	0–20	40	10

— Not available.

n.a. Not applicable.

Note: p, including tariff surcharges; w, production-weighted average tariff; m, import-weighted average tariff; y, for 1992; QR = quantitative restrictions.

a. Some QRs exist for health and safety reasons.

b. In practice, several countries have higher actual tariffs than those that appear in the table. These are tariffs that have been applied to some specific goods or temporarily to control sudden import surges. See text for details.

Source: Lustig and Primo Braga (1994). Sources for the original were Alam and Rajapatirana (1993); ECLAC (1992); Edwards (1993); GATT, various issues; IMF (1993); World Bank data.

than the United States. Tables 4.7–4.12 show the direction of exports and imports, respectively, of Mexico and ten other Latin American countries. Based on exports for six of these countries (Argentina, Brazil, Chile, Paraguay, Peru, and Uruguay), EC12 was a larger trading partner in 1990 and 1993 than the United States. Particularly striking is the relationship between MERCOSUR countries and the United States. U.S. exports to and imports from MERCOSUR have been 2.5 percent or less of its total exports and imports. Proportions of exports from Argentina, Brazil, and Uruguay to the United States show a persistent decline during the three years shown. Only Paraguay shows a slight increase in 1993 from the corresponding proportion in 1990. Another interesting case is Chile. The United States and EC12 accounted for roughly equal proportion of Chile's exports in 1985 (28 percent), but by 1993 their importance had declined. In 1993, EC12 accounted for 25 percent and the United States for 16 percent of Chile's exports. On the import side, the United States is more important for Chile than EC12. On balance, these data, combined with more substantial restrictions in the European Community, lend some support to the view that many Latin American countries may be better-off forming an FTA with the EC than with NAFTA.

If countries do rush to join NAFTA or the EU, as they certainly will, it is critical that they minimize the margin of preference to the potential partner. The inescapable implication of this prescription is that they must liberalize externally as they liberalize within an FTA framework. For instance, a country such as India will eventually be tempted to seek entry into the EU. But before doing so, it is important that its unilateral trade liberalization be carried much further. At the current tariffs, which go up to 65 percent and average more than 35 percent, the potential trade diversion from joining the EU is substantial.

One final point remains. If the analysis here is correct, why is there such a rush on the part of Latin American countries to get into regional arrangements with each other and with the United States? Unfortunately this is a question we have been unable to answer satisfactorily, even in the context of the first regional movement of the 1960s and 1970s, when innumerable South-South regional arrangements mushroomed. The consensus among economists today is that those schemes were harmful to the member countries.[19] Yet there is no better explanation of the spread of regionalism at that time than the fact that its pursuit by the EC led to false expectations in developing countries. "What is good for Europe," went the argument, "must be good for Africa and Latin America." The same explanation can be applied to the new regionalism. The pursuit of CUFTA and NAFTA by the United States has given

(Text continues page 136)

---

19. See Foroutan (1993) on Africa and Nogues and Quintanilla (1993) on Latin America.

Table 4.7. Exports from Country to Partner Region, 1985

Country	World (millions of dollars)	Share (percent)	Percentage of world total to:				Percentage of world total to:	
			All industrial countries	United States	European Community	Other industrial countries	All developing countries	Latin America and the Caribbean
Argentina	9,648	0.5	49.1	12.1	26.4	10.6	50.9	18.1
Brazil	28,182	1.5	70.0	28.9	28.2	12.8	30.0	8.6
Chile	4,139	0.2	70.8	20.7	32.2	17.9	29.2	14.5
Colombia	3,844	0.2	84.2	37.9	32.1	14.2	15.8	12.1
Costa Rica	1,220	0.1	79.1	46.7	17.3	15.1	20.9	16.9
Ecuador	3,493	0.2	66.7	56.5	6.1	4.1	33.3	8.7
Mexico	28,968	1.5	92.5	66.9	14.6	10.9	7.5	5.8
Paraguay	466	0.0	63.0	5.5	51.8	5.8	37.0	31.6
Peru	3,297	0.2	71.0	34.9	22.4	13.7	29.0	14.0
Uruguay	1,353	0.1	63.1	42.2	15.2	5.7	36.9	18.1
Venezuela	13,914	0.7	84.1	49.1	20.9	14.1	15.9	14.3
United States	227,541	11.7	65.1	n.a.	23.3	n.a.	34.9	11.5
World	1,943,220	100.0	70.9	18.6	34.2	18.1	29.1	3.8

(table continues on following page)

(Table 4.7 continued)

Country	Percentage of world total to:		Percentage of world total to:				
	Asia	Other developing countries	MERCOSUR	Argentina	Brazil	Paraguay	Uruguay
Argentina	5.8	27.0	6.9	n.a.	5.1	0.9	0.9
Brazil	7.8	13.6	3.2	2.2	n.a.	0.6	0.4
Chile	10.5	4.1	7.9	2.1	5.5	0.1	0.2
Colombia	0.8	2.8	0.8	0.6	0.1	0.0	0.0
Costa Rica	0.3	3.6	0.2	0.2	0.0	0.0	0.0
Ecuador	23.0	1.7	0.5	0.3	0.2	0.0	0.0
Mexico	1.3	0.4	1.7	0.2	1.4	0.0	0.1
Paraguay	4.7	0.7	22.4	4.3	16.3	n.a.	1.8
Peru	7.3	7.7	3.0	1.1	1.8	0.0	0.1
Uruguay	6.4	12.4	15.8	4.9	10.5	0.5	n.a.
Venezuela	1.3	0.3	2.0	0.0	2.0	0.0	0.0
United States	14.3	9.0	1.6	0.3	1.2	0.0	0.0
World	11.3	14.0	1.0	0.2	0.7	0.0	0.0

n.a. Not applicable.
Source: COMTRADE database.

Table 4.8. *Exports from Country to Partner Region, 1990*

Country	World (millions of dollars)	Share (percent)	Percentage of world total to: All industrial countries	Percentage of world total to: United States	Percentage of world total to: European Community	Percentage of world total to: Other industrial countries	Percentage of world total to: All developing countries	Percentage of world total to: Latin America and the Caribbean
Argentina	13,844	0.4	52.6	12.0	31.9	8.7	47.4	25.0
Brazil	36,023	1.0	71.0	23.8	32.7	14.4	29.0	9.7
Chile	9,366	0.3	73.1	16.8	34.7	21.7	26.9	11.7
Colombia	6,995	0.2	85.4	48.7	26.0	10.6	14.6	11.1
Costa Rica	2,156	0.1	87.6	51.3	25.3	11.0	12.4	10.5
Ecuador	3,003	0.1	76.2	51.5	14.4	10.3	23.8	19.1
Mexico	41,032	1.2	93.5	75.1	9.2	9.2	6.5	3.8
Paraguay	1,156	0.0	53.3	4.8	46.6	1.9	46.7	38.8
Peru	3,764	0.1	70.3	22.6	27.4	20.2	29.7	13.6
Uruguay	2,169	0.1	44.0	15.5	22.4	6.1	56.0	38.6
Venezuela	17,895	0.5	77.2	55.5	11.5	10.1	22.8	20.3
United States	402,017	11.5	65.1	n.a.	26.1	n.a.	34.9	10.7
World	3,498,250	100.0	73.4	14.8	40.4	18.2	26.6	3.2

(table continues on following page)

(Table 4.8 continued)

Country	Percentage of world total to:		Percentage of world total to:				
	Asia	Other developing countries	MERCOSUR	Argentina	Brazil	Paraguay	Uruguay
Argentina	7.7	14.7	13.7	n.a.	10.9	1.2	1.6
Brazil	10.5	8.8	3.5	2.0	n.a.	0.6	0.8
Chile	12.2	2.9	7.3	1.2	5.6	0.3	0.2
Colombia	1.4	2.2	1.6	0.4	0.5	0.0	0.7
Costa Rica	0.8	1.1	0.3	0.0	0.3	0.0	0.0
Ecuador	2.2	2.6	0.8	0.6	0.2	0.0	0.0
Mexico	2.1	0.6	0.9	0.3	0.5	0.0	0.1
Paraguay	6.0	1.9	33.8	3.6	29.0	n.a.	1.3
Peru	8.6	7.5	4.1	0.3	3.8	0.0	0.0
Uruguay	5.3	12.1	33.2	5.4	27.4	0.4	n.a.
Venezuela	2.0	0.6	2.3	0.0	2.2	0.0	0.0
United States	17.6	6.6	1.4	0.2	1.1	0.0	0.0
World	13.3	10.0	0.8	0.1	0.6	0.0	0.0

n.a. Not applicable.
Source: COMTRADE database.

Table 4.9. *Exports from Country to Partner Region, 1993*

Country	World (millions of dollars)	Share (percent)	Percentage of world total to: All industrial countries	United States	European Community	Other industrial countries	Percentage of world total to: All developing countries	Latin America and the Caribbean
Argentina	14,059	0.4	42.9	9.2	27.2	6.4	57.1	37.4
Brazil	38,983	1.0	57.8	20.6	25.6	11.6	42.2	22.5
Chile	10,501	0.3	62.4	16.2	24.9	21.3	37.6	17.7
Colombia	7,824	0.2	73.1	41.8	22.3	9.0	26.9	24.2
Costa Rica	2,954	0.1	84.3	56.6	19.1	8.6	15.7	14.2
Ecuador	3,303	0.1	74.6	47.3	18.9	8.4	25.4	22.7
Mexico	51,274	1.3	93.5	79.5	5.8	8.2	6.5	4.8
Paraguay	843	0.0	45.9	6.4	34.6	4.9	54.1	52.2
Peru	3,372	0.1	63.5	23.7	26.1	13.7	36.5	18.7
Uruguay	1,940	0.1	38.3	14.3	20.1	3.8	61.7	49.7
Venezuela	14,253	0.4	77.7	61.1	10.2	6.3	22.3	20.9
United States	487,491	12.8	56.4	n.a.	21.4	n.a.	43.6	16.4
World	3,804,550	100.0	66.5	15.8	34.2	16.5	33.5	5.0

(table continues on following page)

(Table 4.9 continued)

Country	Percentage of world total to:		Percentage of world total to:				
	Asia	Other developing countries	MERCOSUR	Argentina	Brazil	Paraguay	Uruguay
Argentina	6.7	13.1	23.9	n.a.	18.7	1.8	3.4
Brazil	11.5	8.3	12.3	10.3	n.a.	0.3	1.6
Chile	18.0	1.9	11.0	6.2	4.2	0.3	0.4
Colombia	0.8	1.9	1.7	0.9	0.8	0.0	0.0
Costa Rica	0.3	1.2	0.2	0.2	0.0	0.0	0.0
Ecuador	1.1	1.6	2.2	1.4	0.8	0.0	0.0
Mexico	1.5	0.1	1.1	0.5	0.6	0.0	0.1
Paraguay	1.7	0.2	40.2	7.1	32.3	n.a.	0.8
Peru	14.8	2.9	4.6	0.7	3.7	0.1	0.1
Uruguay	7.2	4.9	41.1	17.9	22.2	0.9	n.a.
Venezuela	1.2	0.2	2.8	0.2	2.6	0.0	0.0
United States	19.3	7.9	2.2	0.9	1.2	0.1	0.0
World	18.0	10.5	1.3	0.5	0.7	0.0	0.1

n.a. Not applicable.
Source: COMTRADE database.

129

Table 4.10. Imports to Country from Partner Region, 1985

Country	World (millions of dollars)	Share (percent)	Percentage of world total to:				Percentage of world total to:	
			All industrial countries	United States	European Community	Other industrial countries	All developing countries	Latin America and the Caribbean
Argentina	3,813	0.2	64.2	18.9	31.2	14.0	35.8	31.8
Brazil	14,035	0.8	48.8	22.4	14.6	11.9	51.2	11.2
Chile	2,641	0.1	62.0	25.8	22.8	13.4	38.0	29.3
Colombia	3,895	0.2	76.1	37.7	20.4	18.1	23.9	21.6
Costa Rica	1,059	0.1	66.1	39.8	15.1	11.2	33.9	30.3
Ecuador	1,765	0.1	71.7	33.5	21.5	16.6	28.3	20.4
Mexico	18,432	1.0	95.0	74.0	11.4	9.6	5.0	3.4
Paraguay	660	0.0	35.8	15.0	14.3	6.5	64.2	58.7
Peru	1,625	0.1	72.0	30.5	23.7	17.8	28.0	24.4
Uruguay	760	0.0	33.8	8.5	19.0	6.4	66.2	38.2
Venezuela	6,902	0.4	86.8	49.3	25.4	12.1	13.2	9.8
United States	327,540	17.7	65.0	n.a.	20.0	n.a.	35.0	12.3
World	1,854,620	100.0	68.4	11.5	35.0	21.9	31.6	5.4

(table continues on following page)

(Table 4.10 continued)

Country	Percentage of world total to:		Percentage of world total to:				
	Asia	Other developing countries	MERCOSUR	Argentina	Brazil	Paraguay	Uruguay
Argentina	1.5	2.5	16.4	n.a.	14.4	0.4	1.7
Brazil	4.6	35.4	5.0	3.5	n.a.	0.4	1.0
Chile	5.6	3.1	13.9	4.2	9.0	0.5	0.2
Colombia	0.8	1.5	6.3	3.4	2.6	0.0	0.2
Costa Rica	2.9	0.7	2.0	0.3	1.7	0.0	0.0
Ecuador	4.8	3.1	7.7	0.8	6.8	0.0	0.1
Mexico	0.9	0.8	2.6	1.4	1.2	0.0	0.0
Paraguay	4.5	1.0	57.6	11.0	45.7	n.a.	0.9
Peru	1.6	2.0	15.8	10.0	5.6	0.0	0.1
Uruguay	1.6	26.3	32.4	13.0	18.5	0.8	n.a.
Venezuela	2.1	1.3	5.4	1.1	4.3	0.0	0.1
United States	16.5	6.2	2.5	0.3	2.1	0.0	0.0
World	11.2	15.1	1.9	0.5	1.4	0.0	0.0

n.a. Not applicable.
Source: COMTRADE database.

131

Table 4.11. Imports to Country from Partner Region, 1990

Country	World (millions of dollars)	Share (percent)	Percentage of world total to:				Percentage of world total to:	
			All industrial countries	United States	European Community	Other industrial countries	All developing countries	Latin America and the Caribbean
Argentina	4,971	0.1	67.6	23.7	31.7	12.3	32.4	26.6
Brazil	28,945	0.8	43.0	17.5	16.2	9.3	57.0	12.5
Chile	6,670	0.2	63.0	25.1	22.4	15.6	37.0	24.4
Colombia	5,158	0.1	76.0	39.5	20.3	16.2	24.0	19.7
Costa Rica	2,019	0.1	68.2	49.1	10.0	9.0	31.8	25.6
Ecuador	1,923	0.1	69.8	35.4	21.5	12.9	30.2	25.0
Mexico	40,141	1.1	92.3	70.7	12.0	9.7	7.7	3.3
Paraguay	1,676	0.0	40.2	18.3	13.3	8.6	59.8	39.3
Peru	2,430	0.1	61.3	32.0	17.1	12.2	38.7	33.3
Uruguay	1,368	0.0	39.9	10.6	21.0	8.3	60.1	48.5
Venezuela	7,435	0.2	82.2	41.8	29.1	11.3	17.8	13.5
United States	494,128	13.9	61.5	n.a.	19.5	n.a.	38.5	10.1
World	3,556,480	100.0	68.8	11.1	38.4	19.3	31.2	3.6

(table continues on following page)

(Table 4.11 continued)

Country	Percentage of world total to:		Percentage of world total to:				
	Asia	Other developing countries	MERCOSUR	Argentina	Brazil	Paraguay	Uruguay
Argentina	3.9	1.9	15.7	n.a.	13.0	1.1	1.7
Brazil	1.9	42.6	7.7	4.9	n.a.	1.1	1.7
Chile	7.7	4.8	14.9	6.9	7.3	0.4	0.2
Colombia	2.3	2.0	4.8	1.4	3.2	0.0	0.2
Costa Rica	5.7	0.6	3.2	0.6	2.6	0.0	0.0
Ecuador	2.7	2.5	8.8	2.2	6.6	0.0	0.0
Mexico	4.0	0.4	2.1	0.8	1.3	0.0	0.1
Paraguay	17.2	3.2	31.9	8.8	22.7	n.a.	0.4
Peru	2.8	2.5	14.2	7.7	6.0	0.2	0.4
Uruguay	4.0	7.7	41.6	19.2	21.5	0.8	n.a.
Venezuela	2.5	1.8	5.6	1.9	3.6	0.1	0.0
United States	20.1	8.2	2.0	0.3	1.6	0.0	0.0
World	12.7	14.9	1.3	0.3	0.9	0.0	0.0

n.a. Not applicable.
Source: COMTRADE database.

Table 4.12. Imports to Country from Partner Region, 1993

Country	World (millions of dollars)	Share (percent)	Percentage of world total to:				Percentage of world total to:	
			All industrial countries	United States	European Community	Other industrial countries	All developing countries	Latin America and the Caribbean
Argentina	16,191	0.4	56.3	23.3	24.4	8.6	43.7	31.5
Brazil	24,959	0.7	62.2	24.3	24.4	13.5	37.8	17.3
Chile	10,463	0.3	56.9	24.9	18.9	13.1	43.1	22.7
Colombia	8,680	0.2	71.0	37.2	17.6	16.2	29.0	24.6
Costa Rica	2,818	0.1	77.4	54.9	15.0	7.5	22.6	18.5
Ecuador	2,956	0.1	69.5	37.1	19.5	12.9	30.5	23.9
Mexico	59,868	1.6	91.5	69.5	11.6	10.4	8.5	3.4
Paraguay	2,605	0.1	36.4	20.0	7.9	8.5	63.6	50.9
Peru	3,649	0.1	54.1	29.3	13.4	11.3	45.9	39.7
Uruguay	2,683	0.1	43.3	9.4	27.5	6.3	56.7	49.4
Venezuela	11,108	0.3	75.6	41.4	21.2	13.0	24.4	16.0
United States	581,848	15.5	58.4	n.a.	16.9	n.a.	41.6	11.7
World	3,745,780	100.0	67.6	12.4	34.8	20.4	32.4	4.3

(table continues on following page)

(Table 4.12 continued)

Country	Percentage of world total to:		Percentage of world total to:				
	Asia	Other developing countries	MERCOSUR	Argentina	Brazil	Paraguay	Uruguay
Argentina	10.4	1.8	24.9	n.a.	22.6	0.3	2.0
Brazil	7.3	13.3	11.4	9.6	n.a.	0.4	1.5
Chile	12.7	7.7	16.5	5.0	10.6	0.3	0.5
Colombia	2.4	2.0	6.7	2.2	4.3	0.0	0.2
Costa Rica	3.6	0.5	3.7	0.2	3.5	0.0	0.0
Ecuador	4.7	1.9	8.3	2.5	5.8	0.0	0.1
Mexico	4.8	0.2	2.1	0.4	1.7	0.0	0.1
Paraguay	11.6	1.2	48.2	10.8	36.9	n.a.	0.6
Peru	4.9	1.4	15.4	6.7	7.5	0.2	1.0
Uruguay	5.0	2.3	45.5	16.4	28.9	0.3	n.a.
Venezuela	7.4	1.0	5.5	2.0	3.5	0.0	0.0
United States	24.0	5.9	1.6	0.2	1.4	0.0	0.0
World	17.2	10.9	1.4	0.3	1.0	0.0	0.0

n.a. Not applicable.
Source: COMTRADE database.

regionalism renewed respectability. And countries are jumping on the bandwagon without fully inquiring where the wagon is headed.[20]

Renewed South-South Integration

Although the "new game" in the South is to seek entry into NAFTA or the EU, the old game of South-South integration is not finished. This is particularly true of Latin America, where, during the 1990s alone, seven free trade area or common market agreements have been signed and another six are in progress.[21] In addition to these agreements, the Andean Pact and the CACM have been revived. In Africa and Asia, the level of activity has been lower. According to the Harmsen and Leidy (1994) list, there are four new arrangements in Africa. In Asia, the ASEAN countries have reached an agreement to create AFTA.

In this chapter, I will restrict my discussion to Latin America.[22] I will give an overview of the region and analyze in detail the most significant arrangement: MERCOSUR.

New Regionalism and Latin America: An Overview

Latin America has 8.5 percent of the world's population. In 1990, the region's share in world trade at 3.5 percent was at its lowest in one hundred years. There has been some recovery since then, the share climbing to 4.2 percent in 1994. Mexico accounts for approximately a quarter of all of Latin America's trade. If Mexico is included into North America instead of South America, the latter's share in world trade declines considerably.

As noted before, tables 4.7–4.12 present the direction of exports and imports, respectively, of the major countries in Latin America for 1985, 1990, and 1993. For every country shown, except the relatively closed Argentina and relatively small Uruguay and Paraguay, the largest trading partner is the United States or EC12, not Latin America.

Although there is no clear basis in economic theory for a preference for regional integration between countries that trade more with each other than

---

20. This explanation of the popularity of regionalism is obviously inconsistent with rational behavior. If countries wish to maximize their own welfare, why should they do something which is harmful, even if Europe and the United States do it? Unfortunately, an alternative explanation that does not sacrifice rationality is less plausible. According to this explanation, today countries are rushing to regionalism because of the fear that the world may turn into closed blocs in the future. In that event, it would be catastrophic to be left out of a bloc. A preferential access to a large country such as the United States may then be a reasonable insurance premium to pay.

21. See Lustig and Primo Braga (1994).

22. For a detailed discussion of the new regionalism and East Asia, see Panagariya (1994).

those that do not, this criterion is employed frequently in discussions.[23] Although the observed intraregional trade shares in Latin America are lower than if they had been as open as industrial countries, it is difficult to imagine that they will be larger than the shares of the United States or the EU. Therefore, if we judge the desirability of regional integration by intraregional trade shares, whether actual or potential, the case for South-South integration within Latin America is weak.

For some countries the share of Latin America in their exports and imports is substantial. Not surprisingly, these are also the countries most actively engaged in negotiating regional arrangements presently. One of the countries that has traditionally gone the unilateral route but is negotiating several FTAs currently is Chile. Chile already has FTA agreements with Colombia, Mexico, and Venezuela, and may sign one with MERCOSUR. In 1993 Latin America accounted for 23 percent of Chile's exports and 18 percent of its imports. Similarly, Colombia and Venezuela have FTAs signed or under negotiations with a large number of trading partners in Latin America. In 1993, Latin America accounted for 24 percent of Colombia's exports and imports. For Venezuela, the figures are 21 percent for exports and 16 percent for imports.

It is not possible to address each of these arrangements in detail. Instead, I look at MERCOSUR to derive lessons for other countries.

MERCOSUR

Today, the most significant regional arrangement in Latin America is the Southern Cone Common Market, or MERCOSUR. Although Paraguay and Uruguay are also members, initially only Argentina and Brazil were involved. During the first stage (1986–90), Argentina and Brazil began by exchanging trade preferences on a sectoral basis. Increased access for Argentina to the Brazilian market led to a more than doubling of its exports to the latter between 1988 and 1990. Because liberalization received greatest attention in the capital goods sector in the first stage, trade expanded most in that sector. Very likely this expansion was the result of import substitution on a regionwide basis.

In 1989, Argentina and Brazil abandoned the sectoral approach and signed an accord to create a common market between themselves by the year 1998. Within a few months, in July 1990, the two countries signed the Acta de Buenos Aires, which moved up the timetable and set the date for a common market by the end of 1994. The two countries agreed to lower their tariffs by 40 percent on January 1, 1991. After that date they were to lower tariffs by 7 percent

---

23. See Panagariya (1995) for details. In terms of figures 4.1 and 4.2, the larger the share of the potential partner in total imports the greater the transfer of tariff revenue to the latter's exporters.

every six months until, on July 1, 1994, tariffs were reduced by 89 percent of the initial level prevailing on December 31, 1990. The remaining 11 percent reduction took place on January 1, 1995. In 1991, Paraguay and Uruguay also signed a treaty with Argentina and Brazil to create MERCOSUR. They began in June 1991 by lowering their tariffs by 47 percent and, thus, caught up with the Argentina-Brazil schedule.

The 1991 treaty aimed at a single market with free flow of goods, capital, and people. It is now clear that this far-reaching objective will not be reached in the near future, although an approximate customs union was expected by January 1, 1995. A common external tariff (CET), with eleven tariff positions between 0 and 20 percent, has been agreed on by the member countries. But there are some exceptions to the CET, as well as to the free trade area within MERCOSUR.

Establishment of the CET will be delayed in capital goods, information and telecommunications equipment, and some additional items. On capital goods, a CET of 14 percent is to be achieved by January 1, 2001, by Argentina and Brazil, and by January 1, 2006, by Paraguay and Uruguay. Information and telecommunications equipment is to have a CET of 16 percent by January 1, 2006. Finally, until January 1, 2001, each country is allowed to deviate from the CET in 300 (399 for Paraguay) tariff items of the Common Nomenclature, which has 8,000 items.

Internal free trade will also be delayed in 384 out of the 8,000 items of the Common Nomenclature until January 1, 1999, in the case of Argentina and Brazil, and January 1, 2000, in the case of Paraguay and Uruguay. An automatic liberalization schedule is in place to achieve this remaining liberalization.

There is little doubt that MERCOSUR promises to be one of the most effective regional arrangements in Latin America. For example, Brazil's exports to MERCOSUR as a percentage of its total exports rose from a paltry 3.2 percent in 1985 to 12.3 percent in 1993. For Argentina, during the same period intra-MERCOSUR exports climbed from 6.9 percent to 23.9 percent. In 1993, Argentina alone accounted for 10.3 percent of Brazil's exports. In the same year Brazil accounted for 18.7 percent of Argentina's exports. These figures indicate the dominant position of Brazil and Argentina within MERCOSUR.[24]

MERCOSUR has at least three advantages over past regional integration efforts in Latin America. First, with the exception of CACM in its first incarnation, it is the only scheme in the region that has adopted across-the-board liberalization. With some exceptions noted below, all four countries have eliminated barriers to intraunion trade. This means that internal liberalization cannot remain limited to products likely to lead to trade diversion. Under a

---

24. These figures have been taken from Nofal (1994). Data for 1993 relate to the first nine months.

sectoral strategy pursued in the past, inefficient industries often survived by ensuring that imports of their products were not liberalized. Liberalization takes place in products not produced at home so that increased imports generally displace imports from the less efficient outside countries. This type of sheltering is precluded in an across-the-board approach.

Second, as tariffs have been reduced internally they have also been reduced externally. Argentina's external tariffs ranged 15–115 percent in 1987 and fell to the 0–22 percent range by 1991 (table 4.5). Brazil's external tariffs ranged 0–105 percent in 1987 and fell to the 0–35 percent range in 1993. In Paraguay and Uruguay also, the top external tariff had come down to 20 percent in 1993. These tariff reductions minimize to a considerable extent the chances of trade diversion.

Finally, MERCOSUR has chosen to be a customs union rather than an FTA. A customs union has the major advantage that it does not require complicated rules of origin, which become a powerful instrument of resurrecting protection through the back door in an FTA. A customs union can also more effectively contain pressures from lobbies to raise tariffs on outside countries. Under an FTA the external tariff is determined at the national level, at which lobbies can be more successful. Under a customs union, the decisionmaking power is shifted to a supranational entity which is likely to be less responsive to a single member's lobby.[25]

Despite these positive features, it is difficult to be enthusiastic about MERCOSUR. There are many reasons. First, when all is said and done, the union offers only a tiny market in relation to the world. As noted before, all of Latin America including Mexico accounts for only 4.2 percent of world trade at present. This is a major drawback. Discussing South-South integration, Corden (1993) writes:

> The plain fact is that such FTAs (or preferential areas) would not make a great deal of difference, and have not in the past…. It is far better for Argentina to go for the world market—i.e., to liberalize unilaterally and in a nondiscriminatory fashion as she has been doing—than just to go for the Brazilian market. Brazil has the largest economy in the Third World and yet it is smaller than Canada's (as measured by the dollar value GDP). And this applies even more to Brazil.

Second, despite what has been called an "across-the-board" approach, MERCOSUR has not been immune to protectionist pressures. Some major industries did manage to escape complete liberalization within MERCOSUR. For example, Argentina's steel, paper, textile, sugar, and petrochemicals industries will continue to be protected from Brazilian imports until January 1, 1999. Similarly, Brazil, Paraguay, and Uruguay have chosen not to establish

---

25. For a formal analysis of this issue, see Panagariya and Findlay (1993).

complete internal free trade in some major products. Given the substantial liberalization that has been undertaken, the exclusion of these sectors by itself is not particularly disturbing. What is disturbing is the signal it sends to lobbying interests. When competition intensifies and liberalized industries begin to feel the competitive pressure, governments will very likely be willing to invoke some protection mechanism.

Finally, there is a real danger that the establishment of a customs union will lower the pace of nondiscriminatory external liberalization. The smaller members, Paraguay and Uruguay, are now entirely at the mercy of Argentina and Brazil for further external liberalization. Although, on balance, a customs union is superior to an FTA, as far as further external liberalization is concerned, it leaves smaller members at the mercy of larger members. And if the larger members are protectionist, the process of liberalization is sure to be hampered in smaller countries.

What should be MERCOSUR's future strategy? Rather than venturing into many different aspects of the issue, let me address two. First, given the past history of regional integration in Latin America, member countries will have to be on a constant guard to ensure that MERCOSUR does not become an instrument of import substitution on a regionwide basis. The lessons learned from the CACM should not be forgotten. The member countries must not only resist demands for resurrection of trade barriers within the union but also keep up the momentum in external liberalization. Pressures to resort to antidumping measures against outside countries should also be resisted.

Second, in considering entry into NAFTA or the EU, a careful analysis of costs and benefits should be done. In the case of NAFTA, it should not be forgotten that while MERCOSUR will be giving preferential access to the former it will not be receiving the same in return. On the benefit side, at present, the credibility of MERCOSUR is in question and entry into NAFTA will help counter fears of a reversal. But if the United States offers entry only after MERCOSUR has established credibility on its own, desirability of joining NAFTA will be questionable. By contrast, there is likely to be a greater benefit from joining the EU. That market is far less open than the U.S. market, and an FTA with it will improve MERCOSUR's access.

Regionalism and Harmonization

Let me now turn briefly to the possible role of regionalism in promoting harmonization of domestic policies in the member countries of a union. Interest in this area has been sparked primarily by the pursuit of harmonization in areas of environmental standards, labor legislation, tax policy, exchange rates, monetary policy, product standards, competition policy, and intellectual property rights among countries within the EU, and between the EU and countries with which it has association agreements. The side agreements concluded by NAFTA members on environmental and labor standards have also given rise to an interest in harmonization issues.

Although space constraints do not permit a detailed analysis, it is worth-while to make a simple but important point here. Areas in which harmonization is desirable through regional arrangements involving developing countries are very limited. As an example, consider environmental issues. To the extent that a negative environmental externality is national in scope, the matter must be dealt with at the national level. If auto emissions in Mexico City affect residents of Mexico City only, the problem must be handled by Mexico, not NAFTA. If the externality is global in scope, it requires global, not regional, cooperation. Carbon emissions that contribute to global warming must be handled through mechanisms such as the Montreal Convention. A regional approach makes sense only when the issue is regional in character as, for example, in the case of acid rain.

The issue of harmonization becomes particularly tricky in the context of North-South regional arrangements. The pressure in such schemes is on the southern country to bring its standards up to those of the northern country. Because the optimal standard for the southern country is likely to be differ-ent than for the northern country, such harmonization ends up becoming an instrument of protection for the northern country. In addition, even when the southern country's standard is below the optimum, it is likely to conform to that in other southern countries. If it adopts the standards of the northern country, it will be placed at a disadvantage in relation to its southern com-petitors. The inevitable conclusion is that if the actual standards in southern countries are below whatever is viewed as "optimal," the right institution for raising them is a multilateral, not bilateral, forum. Specifically, intellec-tual property rights and higher labor standards should be promoted through the WTO, not NAFTA.

The implication of this discussion is that, in considering harmonization at a regional level, countries must satisfy themselves that the issue is primarily regional in nature. Once this is done, it is difficult to think of cases in which developing countries can use the regional mechanism for harmonization. Most of the examples I can think of are those of cooperation in infrastructure build-ing, including roads, dams, and sharing of river water. Occasionally there may be environmental issues when a river flows through two or more countries.

To think of examples of policy harmonization on a regional basis, one must stretch his imagination. One example I can imagine is the export tax on cocoa. When Ghana taxes cocoa at a higher rate than Côte d'Ivoire, it runs the risk of having a large proportion of exports being channeled illegally through the latter. In principle, each country has an incentive to tax at a rate lower than the other. This can lead to a "race to the bottom," such that both countries tax cocoa at an infinitesimally small rate. Given a less than perfectly elastic world demand, this is suboptimal. Harmonization on a regional basis can restore the tax rate to the optimal level.

Conclusion

This discussion takes a pessimistic view of regionalism. The main conclusions may be summarized as follows:

- When trade is liberalized on a discriminatory basis as in regional arrangements, the mercantilist conclusion is essentially valid: A country gains from liberalization by the partner and loses from its own liberalization.
- One-way preferences from industrial to developing countries under the GSP were beneficial to the latter. Enlargement of the EU is likely to benefit developing countries subject to preferences through an extension of the preferences to markets of the new members. To the extent that new members can be developing countries' competitors within the EU, the latter may lose from a worsening of their terms of trade. But this effect is likely to be small. Creation of an FTA between developing countries subject to the GSP (for example, Morocco) and the EU will amount to a reintroduction of "reverse preferences" and is likely to hurt the former and benefit the latter.
- Because the United States had little tariff preferences to grant to Mexico, while the reverse was not true, static welfare effects of NAFTA are likely to be positive on the former and either mildly positive or negative on the latter. Potential benefits to Mexico from increased credibility to its reforms are limited. In any case, Mexico's future strategy should be to continue its nondiscriminatory liberalization, thereby reversing the trade diversion likely to result from NAFTA.
- The effects of NAFTA on other Latin American countries are minimal. This is because NAFTA has little effect on the openness of the U.S. and Canadian markets. Access of other Latin American countries to the Mexican market declined slightly, but that market is a tiny part of the North American market.
- Static welfare effects of the proposed FTAA will be very likely negative on Latin America and positive on the United States. The FTAA will do little to give Latin America a preferential access to the U.S. market, while the reverse is not true. Because the most efficient producers of many products are in East Asia, not North America, trade diversion will dominate the FTAA.
- Potential benefits to CEE countries from FTAs with the EU are larger than those to Latin America from an FTAA. Such agreements do offer

the CEE countries preferential access to the EU, which is less open than the United States.

- The achievements of MERCOSUR to date are impressive. In a very short period it has created a customs union among four countries, including Brazil, which enjoys the highest GDP (measured at exchange rate) in the South. Alongside internal liberalization, it has helped lower tariffs on outside countries. Despite these achievements, we cannot be enthusiastic about MERCOSUR. All of Latin America taken together accounts for only 4.2 percent of the world trade. Moreover, less than 20 percent of Argentina and Brazil's trade is within MERCOSUR.

- MERCOSUR has more to gain by joining the EU than NAFTA in an FTA. The member countries already have free access to the North American market. An FTA with the EU can help improve access to that market.

- Great caution should be exercised in using regional arrangements to promote harmonization of domestic policies. Most areas requiring harmonization are global in nature and harmonization at a regional level can be counterproductive. This is particularly true of North-South arrangements. Optimal standards in many areas (for example, environment and labor practices) are likely to be lower for a southern than northern country. In cases in which optimal standards are uniformly below the "optimum" due to a race to the bottom, harmonization must be done on a global basis.

Bibliography

Bhagwati, Jagdish. 1993. "Regionalism and Multilateralism: An Overview." In Jaime de Melo and Arvind Panagariya, eds., *New Dimensions in Regional Integration*. Cambridge, U.K.: Cambridge University Press.

_____. 1995. "President Clinton's Trade Policy: Is It Really a Triumph?" Department of Economics. Columbia University. Processed.

Brada, Josef C. 1993. "Regional Integration in Eastern Europe: Prospects for Integration within the Region and with the European Community." In Jaime de Melo and Arvind Panagariya, eds., *New Dimensions in Regional Integration*. Cambridge, U.K.: Cambridge University Press.

Corden, Max. 1993. "Round Table Discussion." In Jaime de Melo and Arvind Panagariya, eds., *New Dimensions in Regional Integration*. Cambridge, U.K.: Cambridge University Press.

de la Torre, Augusto, and Margaret R. Kelly. 1992. *Regional Trade Arrangements*, IMF Occasional Paper 93. International Monetary Fund, Washington, D.C.

de Melo, Jaime, and Arvind Panagariya. 1992. *The New Regionalism in Trade Policy*. World Bank. Washington, D.C.: Center for Economic Policy Research and World Bank.

_____. 1993. *New Dimensions in Regional Integration*. Cambridge, U.K.: Cambridge University Press.

Erzan, Refik, and Alexander Yeats. 1992. "Free Trade Agreements with the United States. What's In It For Latin America?" Working Paper 827. World Bank, Washington, D.C.

Foroutan, Faizeh. 1993. "Regional Integration in Sub-Saharan Africa: Past Experience and Future Prospects." In Jaime de Melo and Arvind Panagariya, eds., *New Dimensions in Regional Integration*. Cambridge, U.K.: Cambridge University Press.

Harmsen, Richard, and Michael Leidy. 1994. "Regional Trading Arrangements." In *International Trade Policies. The Uruguay Round and Beyond. Volume II*. Washington, D.C.: International Monetary Fund.

Hindley, Brian. 1993. "Helping Transition Through Trade? EC and U.S. Policy Towards Exports from Eastern and Central Europe." Working Paper 4. European Bank for Reconstruction and Development, London.

Kaminski, Bartlomiej. 1994. "The Significance of the 'Europe Agreements' for Central European Industries." Working Paper 314. World Bank, Washington, D.C.

Laird, Sam. 1990. "U.S. Trade Policy and Mexico: Simulations of Possible Trade Regime Changes." International Trade Division, World Bank, Washington, D.C. Processed.

Lustig, Nora, and Carlos Primo Braga. 1994. "The Future of Trade Policy in Latin America." Paper presented at the Future of Western Hemisphere Economic Integration conference, Center for Strategic and International Studies and the Inter-American Dialogue, Washington, D.C., March 2–4.

Lustig, Nora, B., P. Bosworth, and R. Lawrence. 1992. *North American Free Trade*. Washington, D.C.: Brookings Institution.

Messerlin, Patrick. 1989. "EC Anti-Dumping Regulations: A First Economic Appraisal 1980–85." *Weltwirtschäftliches Archiv* 125(7): 563–87.

_____. 1992. "The Association Agreements Between the EC and Central Europe: Trade Liberalization vs. Constitutional Failure?" In J. Flemming and J. M. C. Rollo, eds., *Trade, Payments and Adjustment in Central and Eastern Europe*. London: Royal Institute of International Affairs.

Nash, John. 1993. "NAFTA: The Good, the Bad, and the Unknown." *Finance and Development* 30(2, June): 48–49.

Nofal, Maria Beatriz. 1994. "MERCOSUR and Free Trade in the Americas." Paper presented at the Future of Western Hemisphere Economic Integration conference, Center for Strategic and International Studies and the Inter-American Dialogue, Washington, D.C., March 2–4.

Nogues, Julio, and Rosalinda Quintanilla. 1993. "Latin America's Integration and the Multilateral Trading System." In Jaime de Melo and Arvind Panagariya, eds., *New Dimensions in Regional Integration*. Cambridge, U.K.: Cambridge University Press.

Panagariya, Arvind. 1994. "East Asia and the New Regionalism in World Trade." *World Economy* 17 (November):817–39.

_____. 1994. "Let Us Uphold the MFN Principle." Presented at the Economic Forum on Regional Trading Arrangements and the Prospects of Global Free Trade, International Monetary Fund, Washington, D.C., November 29.

_____. 1995. "Free Trade Area of the Americas: Good for Latin America?" Department of Economics, University of Maryland, College Park.

Panagariya, Arvind, and Ronald Findlay. 1993. "A Political Economy Analysis of Free Trade Areas and Customs Unions." Working Paper 61. World Bank, Washington, D.C.

Saxenhouse, Gary A. 1993. "Trading Blocks and East Asia." In Jaime de Melo and Arvind Panagariya, eds., *New Dimensions in Regional Integration*. Cambridge, U.K.: Cambridge University Press.

Whalley, John. 1993. "Regional Trade Arrangements in North America: CUFTA and NAFTA." In Jaime de Melo and Arvind Panagariya, eds., *New Dimensions in Regional Integration*. Cambridge, U.K.: Cambridge University Press.

Winters, L. Alan. 1993. "The European Community: A Case of Successful Integration?" In Jaime de Melo and Arvind Panagariya, eds., *New Dimensions in Regional Integration*. Cambridge, U.K.: Cambridge University Press.

Winters, L. Alan, and Z. K. Wang. 1994. *Eastern Europe's International Trade*, Manchester, U.K.: Manchester University Press.

World Bank. 1990. *Morocco 2000. An Open and Competitive Economy*. UNDP/World Bank Trade Expansion Program Country Report 7. World Bank, Trade Policy Division, Washington, D.C.

_____.1992. *Costa Rica. Strengthening Trade Links to the World Economy*. UNDP/World Bank Trade Expansion Program Country Report 9. World Bank, Trade Policy Division, Washington, D.C.

_____. 1994. *Romania. Restructuring to Face the World Economy*. UNDP/World Bank Trade Expansion Program Country Report 14. World Bank, Trade Policy Division, Washington, D.C.

5

Fiscal Implications of Trade Reform

Ron Hood

Trade Expansion Program (TEP) studies on various aspects of trade reform have in most cases been forward looking in the sense that an agenda of reform was proposed and the likely consequences anticipated. In general it is fair to say that the fiscal effect of trade reforms has not been the centerpiece of the studies. As is appropriate, the emphases were improving incentive regimes, eliminating distortions, pursuing comparative advantage, and increasing exports, investment, and growth. It was generally recognized, however, that the achievement of these objectives can be compromised if proper attention is not paid to the maintenance of macroeconomic balance—particularly the fiscal balance—while adjusting taxes and incentives. Accordingly, most of the studies undertook some analysis of the probable fiscal consequences of adopting the proposed reforms. These ranged from simple exercises, such as applying proposed tariff rate and exemption structures to the existing (or a simply extrapolated) import base, as was done in Peru and Uganda; to more complicated general equilibrium estimates, as were done in Kenya and Morocco. In several countries, including Mauritius, Peru, Uganda, and Vietnam, the trade tax changes were only part of a broader package of tax changes involving sales taxes, value added taxes (VATs), land taxes, and excise taxes. In these cases attempts were made to calculate the collective impact of all the changes on government revenue. These latter estimates were all made using simple partial equilibrium methods usually covering only one immediate postreform period.

Recognizing the importance of revenue considerations to the success of trade reform programs, TEP conducted a study (Greenaway and Milner 1993) that examined the fiscal implications of trade policy reform. This study had a theoretical and empirical component and was conducted retrospectively looking at the experiences of several countries that had gone through trade reform programs.

This chapter reviews the fiscal implications of trade reform. In the first section, *Trade policy and the fiscal deficit*, the various mechanisms linking trade reforms to the size of the deficit are traced out, including the impact of tariff rate adjustments, the elimination of quantitative restrictions and exemptions, exchange rate adjustments (as they affect both revenues and expenditure), changes in donor support, and, ultimately, the emergence of higher real growth.

In the next section various country experiences are reviewed, drawing on the work of Greenaway and Milner but modifying some of the analytical methods and extending them to other countries. The results suggest that, while most countries eventually see an increase in the real value of import duties after reforms, there is volatility of revenues in the short term as well as significant intercountry differences. In particular, the successful reformers tend to reduce their average collection rates. For them the increases in real revenue are attributable to even greater adjustments in the real exchange rate (RER) and to the volume of trade. Moreover, there frequently are fiscal difficulties that lead to temporary reversals of the initial cuts in tariff rates. The successful reformers are the ones that are able to weather the transitional crises, in large part because they had had a measure of success in taming fiscal deficits prior to embarking on the trade reform. Unsuccessful reformers concentrate on some of the tax-increasing aspects of reform such as replacing quotas with higher tariffs and eliminating exemptions, while failing to make adequate cuts in nominal tariff rates. In addition, they are unable or unwilling to make the necessary exchange rate adjustments.

The third part of the chapter concentrates on the complementary reforms in domestic indirect taxation that should accompany, or preferably precede, trade reform and that help to preserve fiscal stability through the period of reform. The role of VATs is assessed and a case is made that a VAT may not always be necessary or even desirable. Depending on individual country circumstances other types of tax reform may be preferable.

The chapter concludes with a brief section, *Exemptions*, suggesting opportunities for future research on tariff exemption schemes in trade reform.

Trade Policy and the Fiscal Deficit

Tariff reform programs generally involve reductions in tariff rates and the consolidation of multiple rates into a smaller set. There is a variety of approaches to rate adjustments including uniform rates, proportionate reductions, proportionate movements toward some positive level, minimum rates, and imposition of progressively lower maximum rates (the concertina method). In addition, quantitative restrictions administered through import-licensing systems or regulations governing access to foreign exchange are relaxed or are replaced with temporarily higher tariff rates. There is frequently an effort to reduce the scope of exemptions extended to favored firms or industries. With some variations the general objective is to move toward a system with a basic customs duty at a uniform rate of no more than 10 to 15 percent with few exemptions.

These policies have an impact on government revenue. Where there is a heavy emphasis on replacing quantitative restrictions with tariffs there tends to be an increase in revenues. But in general tariff rate cuts mean that the average import tax rate falls and the import tax base rises, so the overall effect on revenues is not certain. Several key elasticities condition the outcome. The smaller the price elasticity of demand for importables and the smaller the price elasticity of supply of importables by domestic industry, the sharper the contraction of tariff revenue will be when tariff rates are cut. If these elasticities are such that the net import demand elasticity is greater than unity, tariff revenue will rise. Elasticities of substitution between imports also matter, especially when tariff rates are highly dispersed. Relative price changes can be such that people demand more of the high rate goods and less of the lower-rate goods when rates change, with the result that revenues increase although import volumes contract. There are also income elasticity effects. The tariff cuts increase disposable income, which tends to increase demand for all goods, including imports. Offsetting this to some degree is the income-reducing impact of the contraction in the import-competing sector.

Short- and long-term effects may be different, since supply responses take time to emerge. The volume of imports may zigzag, possibly ballooning with a relaxation of restraints and subsiding in time, or contracting sharply in response to conservative fiscal and monetary polices and then building as more sustained growth is established. Macroeconomics play an important role in the evolution of revenues. But it is useful to recognize that in an accounting sense changes in import tax revenues can only come from three sources: changes in the foreign currency value of imports, changes in the exchange rate, and changes in the average collection rates. Greenaway and Milner (1993) separate the changes in import tax revenues into these components for several countries during the period of adjustment. A modified version of the Greenaway and Milner formulation is presented below:

Let:

D = import duty collections in local currency.

M = value of imports in U.S. dollars.

E = the exchange rate in local currency per U.S. dollar (increase implies devaluation of local currency).

T = the average import duty collection rate [import duties collected or cost, insurance, and freight (CIF) value of imports].

Then:

(5.1) $D = M - E - T$

Dividing through by the local price level (the local GDP deflator) gives constant U.S. dollar values. (subscript $_L$ denotes local)

(5.2) $\dfrac{D}{P_L} = E\dfrac{P_{us}}{P_L}T\dfrac{M}{P_{us}}$

If we let lower case denote one plus the rate of change of corresponding upper case variable, in other words:

$$x = 1 + \frac{X_1 - X_0}{X_0}$$

then from (5.1):

(5.3) $d = etm$

which simply says that the value of import duties moves in direct proportion to changes in the U.S. dollar value of imports, to changes in the exchange rate and to changes in the duty collection rate. However, when there is heavy inflation the whole formula tends to be swamped by changes in the exchange rate and the nominal value of duties.

From (5.2) it follows that

(5.4) $\dfrac{d}{p_L} = e\dfrac{p_{us}}{p_L}t\dfrac{m}{p_{us}}$

This can be interpreted as saying that changes in the real value of import duties (d/p_L) are proportional to changes in the RER (e [p_{us} / p_L]), changes in the average collection rate (t), and changes in the real value of imports (m/p_{us}).[1]

---

1. The real value of imports should also reflect changes in the unit price of imports in U.S. dollars. The unit (U.S. dollars) price of imports by all developing countries as reported in United Nations (UN) trade data change very little beyond 1979. However, there were some significant movements in the index between 1974 and 1975, and again between 1977 and 1980. A refinement of the analysis presented here might be attempted by constructing unit price indexes for the individual countries and thereby obtaining more accurate measures of real and nominal changes. The effect of omitting this adjustment is to overstate the effect of movements in the real exchange rate.

Tables 5.1 through 5.5 give data on the evolution of import duty collections and its three components during the course of trade reforms for Chile, Ghana, Jamaica, Morocco, and Turkey. The first group of data shows basic information on duties collected, imports, exchange rates, GDP, and so forth. The second group shows the four elements of equations (5.2) and (5.4) expressed in percentage change form. The last two groups show the same information expressed in index form. The index form is the easiest to interpret. The index is set to one in the prereform period. In each period the index for import duties is equal to the product of the other three indices.

Behind the accounting identity, the relative magnitudes of the three factors contributing to changes in real import duties are determined by policies and behavioral characteristics that can be quite different across countries. The forces at play in determining the fiscal position in the wake of trade reforms are itemized in more detail below in an effort to provide insight into the types and timing of complementary measures that may be needed to ensure fiscal stability during the course of reforms.

Rate Adjustments

There are various reasons why tariff rate reductions may actually increase tariff revenues. Greenaway and Milner argue that countries starting from a position of high initial tariffs are more likely to see revenues rise as tariff rates are cut since these high rates are more likely to be above the revenue-maximizing levels.[2] In the extreme, rates may be reduced from prohibitive levels to ranges where some positive imports occur. In addition, the returns to smuggling and underdeclaration are greater at high rates. Accordingly, concertina type rate adjustments are more likely to enhance revenues, as are adjustments that involve imposition of a low minimum rate. This suggests that countries with high dispersion in rates are more likely to experience revenue increases under tariff reform.

Expenditure Switching

Rate adjustments can reduce the relative price of imports, shifting demand toward imports and increasing the import tax base. This effect is

(Text continues on page 172)

2. Greenaway and Milner point out, however, that for a small open economy, the revenue-maximizing tariff depends only on the elasticity of demand; and, if this is conservatively assumed to be -2, the revenue-maximizing tariff would be 100 percent, which is well above average statutory tariff rates for most developing countries, and is certainly above average collection rates.

Table 5.1. *Import Duties and Trade, Chile, 1972–93*

Year	1972	1973	1974	1975	1976	1977	1978	1979	1980	1981	1982
Import duties (pesos b)	0.007	0.041	0.178	1	29	88	96	11	15	21	13
Export taxes (pesos b)	0	0	0	0	0	0	0	0	0	0	0
Total tax revenue (pesos b)	0.058	0.269	1.84	8.8	26	67	118	166	275	323	286
Imports (US$ m)	941	1,098	1,911	1,338	1,843	2,259	3,002	4,218	5,124	8,364	3,528
Exports (US$ m)	858	1,231	2,481	1,552	2,083	2,190	2,478	3,894	4,671	3,906	3,710
GDP (current pesos b)	0.2	1.2	9.2	38	120	287	486	772	1,075	1,273	1,238
Exchange rate (pesos/US$)	0.025	0.36	1.9	8.5	17	28	34	39	39	39	73
Deficit (pesos b, surplus negative)	0.006	0.003	0.099	0.713	-17	31	0	-37	-58	-33	12
GDP deflator	0.8035	0.8849	1.23552	1.2	88	138	217	317	409	458	52
Import duties/GDP (percent)	3.5	3.4	1.9	2.5	2.2	2.4	2.0	1.4	1.4	1.6	1.0
Import duties/total tax revenue (percent)	12.1	15.2	9.6	11.4	10.0	10.1	8.6	5.9	5.5	6.5	4.5
Average collection rate import duties/imports (percent)	28.8	10.4	4.6	8.8	10.4	10.6	9.4	6.7	7.5	2.5	5.0
Total tax revenue/GDP (percent)	28.0	22.4	20.0	24.4	22.3	23.3	23.0	24.1	25.6	25.4	23.1
Deficit/GDP (percent)	3.0	0.3	1.0	2.0	-1.3	1.1	0.0	-4.6	-5.4	-2.6	1.0
Nominal import duties (m current pesos)	7	41	176	1,000	2,900	6,800	9,800	11,000	15,000	21,000	13,000
Percentage increase in import duties as accounted for by:		486	328	468	190	134	41	15	36	40	-36
Percentage depreciation of nominal exchange rate		1,340	428	347	100	65	21	15	0	0	88
Percentage increase in average collection rate		-65	-53	81	18	4	-13	-29	12	13	-41
Percentage increase in U.S. dollar value of imports		17	74	-30	23	37	33	41	21	24	-45

(table continues on following page)

152

(Table 5.1 continued)

Year	1972	1973	1974	1975	1976	1977	1978	1979	1980	1981	1982
Real import duties (nominal/ GDP deflator)	9	46	142	526	426	493	442	347	367	450	250
Percentage increase in real import duties as accounted for by:		432	207	269	-19	15	-10	-22	6	25	-45
Percentage depreciation of real exchange rate		1,292	312	220	-41	-13	-17	-15	-15	-2	77
Percentage increase in average collection rate		-65	-53	81	18	4	-13	-29	12	13	-41
Percentage increase in real value of imports		10	60	-36	16	29	24	28	11	13	-48
Nominal import duty		1	4.29	24.39	70.73	185.65	234.15	266.29	365.85	512.20	317.07
Nominal exchange rate		1	5.26	23.61	47.22	77.73	94.44	108.33	108.33	108.33	203.89
Average collection rate		1	0.47	0.65	1.00	1.04	0.91	0.64	0.72	0.82	0.48
Value of imports (US$)		1	1.74	1.22	1.50	2.06	2.73	3.84	4.67	5.80	3.21
Real import duty		1	3.07	11.36	9.20	10.64	9.35	7.49	7.92	9.87	5.40
Real exchange rate		1	4.12	13.19	7.83	8.78	5.82	4.80	4.06	3.97	7.01
Average collection rate		1	0.47	0.85	1.00	1.04	0.91	0.64	0.72	0.82	0.48
Real value of imports		1	1.60	1.02	1.17	1.51	1.87	2.42	2.69	3.05	1.59
Memo item U.S. GDP deflator	41.9	44.6	48.6	53.5	56.6	60.6	65.1	70.8	77.3	84.7	90.1

(table continues on following page)

153

(Table 5.1 continued)

Year	1983	1984	1985	1986	1987	1988	1989	1990	1991	1992	1993
Import duties (pesos b)	30	83	81	81	119	150	164	222	278	335	
Export taxes (pesos b)	0	0	0	0	0	0	0	0	0	0	
Total tax revenue (pesos b)	338	433	571	724	943	1,189	1,240	1,803	2,200	2,870	
Imports (US$ m)	2,754	3,191	2,743	3,436	4,386	5,292	7,144	7,678	8,094	10,128	11,125
Exports (US$ m)	3,836	3,857	3,823	4,191	5,224	7,052	8,080	8,310	6,929	9,965	9,202
GDP (current pesos b)	1,556	1,893	2,577	3,246	4,540	5,918	7,502	9,202	11,870	14,958	17,664
Exchange rate (pesos/US$)	88	128	184	205	236	247	297	337	375	362	458
Deficit (pesos b, surplus negative)	41	88	61	31	-20	12	-135	-77	-184	-341	
GDP deflator	65.9	75.3	100	119	145	175	202	240	292	334	372
Import duties/GDP (percent)	1.9	2.8	3.1	2.5	2.6	2.5	2.2	2.4	2.3	2.2	
Import duties/total tax revenue (percent)	6.8	12.2	14.2	11.2	12.6	12.9	13.8	14.8	12.5	11.7	
Average collection rate import duties/imports (percent)	12.4	13.0	16.0	11.5	11.4	11.5	7.7	8.6	9.1	8.7	
Total tax revenue/GDP (percent)	21.7	22.9	22.2	22.3	20.8	19.7	16.5	18.3	18.5	19.2	
Deficit/GDP (percent)	2.6	3.0	2.4	1.0	-0.4	0.2	-1.5	-0.8	-1.6	-2.3	
Nominal import duties (m current pesos)	30,000	53,000	81,000	81,000	119,000	150,000	164,000	222,000	276,000	335,000	
Percentage increase in import duties	131	77	53	0	47	26	9	35	24	21	
as accounted for by:											
Percentage depreciation of nominal exchange rate	20	45	44	11	16	4	20	13	11	2	20
Percentage increase in average collection rate	147	5	24	-28	-1	1	-33	11	8	-5	
Percentage increase in U.S. dollar value of imports	-22	16	-14	25	28	20	35	7	5	25	10

(table continues on following page)

(Table 5.1 continued)

Year	1983	1984	1985	1986	1987	1988	1989	1990	1991	1992	1993
Real import duties (nominal/ GDP deflator)	455	704	810	680	824	857	814	925	945	1,004	0
Percentage increase in real import duties as accounted for by:	82	55	15	-16	21	4	-5	14	2	6	
Percentage depreciation of real exchange rate	-2	32	11	-4	-1	-12	9	-1	-4	-9	
Percentage increase in average collection rate	147	5	24	-28	-1	1	-33	11	6	-5	
Percentage increase in real value of imports	-25	11	-16	22	24	17	30	3	1	23	
Nominal import duty											
Nominal import duty	731.71	1,292.66	1,975.61	1,975.61	2,902.44	3,658.54	4,000.00	5,414.63			
Nominal exchange rate	244.44	355.56	511.11	569.44	661.11	686.11	825.00	936.11			
Average collection rate	1.19	1.25	1.55	1.11	1.10	1.11	0.75	0.83			
Value of imports (US$)	2.51	2.91	2.50	3.13	4.00	4.82	6.51	6.99			
Real import duty											
Real import duty	9.83	15.19	17.48	14.67	17.77	18.49	17.57	19.96			
Real exchange rate	6.89	9.12	10.14	9.73	9.63	8.50	9.24	9.16			
Average collection rate	1.19	1.25	1.55	1.11	1.10	1.11	0.75	0.83			
Real value of imports	1.20	1.33	1.11	1.36	1.68	1.97	2.55	2.63			
Memo item											
U.S. GDP deflator	93.6	97.3	100	102.7	106.1	109.3	113.6	118.719	124.483	127.005	

Source: International Financial Statistics and Country Customs Data. Some figures derived from these sources via authors' calculations.

Table 5.2. Import Duties and Trade, Ghana, 1976–92

Year	1976	1977	1978	1979	1980	1981	1982	1983	1984
Import duties (cedis m)	131	177	241	355	361	472	570	1,782	3,156
Export taxes (cedis m)	187	276	296	1,250	928	201	0	2,000	4,974
Total tax revenue	765	1,041	1,251	2,411	2,747	2,970	4,182	8,459	17,931
Imports (US$ m)	663	1,037	612	652	1,128	1,106	705	367	417
Exports (US$ m)	827	1,014	575	595	1,257	1,063	873	340	403
GDP (current cedis b)	0.5	11.2	21.0	28.2	42.9	72.5	86.5	184.0	270.6
Exchange rate (US$/cedis)	1.15	1.15	2.78	2.75	2.75	2.75	2.79	30.03	50.00
Deficit (cedis b, surplus negative)									
GDP deflator	2	3.4	5.9	5.8	12.4	21.3	27.4	57.7	82.8
Import duties/total tax revenue (percent)	17.1	17.0	19.3	19.3	13.1	15.9	13.8	21.2	17.6
Average collection rate import duties/imports (percent)	13.2	14.8	14.3	14.3	11.8	15.5	29.4	16.3	15.1
Total tax revenue/GDP (percent)	11.7	9.3	6.0	6.0	6.4	4.1	4.8	4.8	6.6
Deficit/GDP (percent)									
Nominal import duties (cedis m)	131	177	241	355	361	472	570	1,792	3,159
Percent increase in import duties		35	36	47	2	31	21	214	76
as accounted for by:									
Percent increase in exchange rate		0	139	0	0	0	0	992	67
Percent increase in average collection rate		12	-3	6	-23	33	39	-45	-7
Percent increase in U.S. dollar value of imports		20	-41	39	32	-2	-36	-48	14

(table continues on following page)

(Table 5.2 continued)

Year	1976	1977	1978	1979	1980	1981	1982	1983	1984
Real import duties (nominal/GDP deflator)		52	41	44	29	22	21	31	38
Percentage increase in real import duties			-22	7	-34	-24	-6	49	23
as accounted for by:									
Percentage depreciation of real exchange rate		-37	48	-21	-29	-36	-17	439	20
Percentage increase in average collection rate		12	-3	6	-23	33	89	-45	-7
Percentage increase in real value of imports		13	-45	28	21	-11	-40	-50	9
Nominal import duty		1	1.36	2.01	2.04	2.67	3.22	10.12	17.85
Nominal exchange rate		1	2.39	2.39	2.39	2.39	2.39	26.11	43.48
Average collection rate		1	0.97	1.02	0.78	1.05	1.98	1.10	1.02
Value of imports (US$)		1	0.59	0.82	1.09	1.07	0.66	0.35	0.40
Real import duty		1	0.78	0.84	0.56	0.43	0.40	0.60	0.73
Real exchange rate		1	1.48	1.17	0.84	0.53	0.44	2.38	2.86
Average collection rate		1	0.97	1.02	0.78	1.05	1.96	1.10	1.02
Real value of imports		1	0.55	0.70	0.85	0.76	0.46	0.23	0.25

(table continues on following page)

(Table 5.2 continued)

Year	1985	1986	1987	1988	1989	1990	1991	1992
Import duties (cedis m)	6,581	14,236	17,784	25,561				
Export taxes (cedis m)	9,172	14,321	26,660	24,464				
Total tax revenue	31,916	61,923	93,317	131,193				
Imports (US$ m)	885	776	851	807	1,142			
Exports (US$ m)	554	654	838	884	908			
GDP (current cedis b)	343.0	511.4	746.0	1,051.0	1,417.0	2,031.0	2,574.6	3,009.0
Exchange rate (US$/cedis)	59.88	90.09	175.44	230.00	303.00	345.00	3.91	521.00
Deficit (cedis b, surplus negative)								
GDP deflator	100	141.7	197.3	263.3	337.666	468.728	584.006	634.460
Import duties/total tax revenue (percent)	20.6	23.0	19.1	19.5				
Average column rate import duties/imports (percent)	16.5	20.4	11.9	13.6				
Total tax revenue/GDP (percent)	8.3	12.1	12.5	12.5				
Deficit/GDP (percent)								
Nominal import duties (cedis m)	8,591	14,236	17,784	25,561				
Percent increase in import duties as accounted for by:	109	118	25	44				
Percent increase in exchange rate	20	50	95	31	32	14		
Percent increase in average collection rate	9	23	-42	16				
Percent increase in U.S. dollar value of imports	59	17	10	-5	42	-100		

(table continues on following page)

(Table 5.2 continued)

Year	1985	1986	1987	1988	1989	1990	1991	1992
Real import duties (nominal/GDP deflator)	66	100	90	97				
Percentage increase in real import duties	73	52	-10	8				
as accounted for by:								
Percentage depreciation of real exchange rate	2	9	44	1	7	-14		
Percentage increase in average collection rate	9	23	-42	16	36	-100		
Percentage increase in real value of imports	55	14	6	-8				
Nominal import duty	37.24	80.43	100.47	144.41				
Nominal exchange rate	52.07	78.34	152.56	200.01	263.49	300.01		
Average collection rate	1.12	1.37	0.80	0.93				
Value of imports (US$)	0.64	0.75	0.82	0.78	1.10			
Real import duty	1.27	1.93	1.73	1.86				
Real exchange rate	2.92	3.19	4.60	4.66	4.98	4.26		
Average collection rate	1.12	1.37	0.80	0.93				
Real value of imports	0.39	0.44	0.47	0.43	0.59			

Source: International Financial Statistics and Country Customs Data. Some figures derived from these sources via authors' calculations.

Table 5.3. *Import Duties and Trade, Jamaica, 1976–93*

Year	1976	1977	1978	1979	1980	1981	1982	1983	1984
Import duties (J$ m)	39	30	50	64	43	91	158	175	277
Export taxes (J$ m)									
Total tax revenue (J$ m)	863	947	1,068	1,107	1,327	1,566			
Imports (US$ m)	913	960	741	997	1,172	1,474	1,382	868	915
Exports (US$ m)	630	768	872	812	963	975	768	424	588
GDP (J$ m)	2,701	2,990	3,749	4,203	4,773	5,307	5,847	8,883	9,355
Exchange rate (US$/J$)	0.91	0.91	1.70	1.78	1.78	1.78	1.78	3.28	4.03
Deficit (J$ m., surplus negative)									
GDP deflator	22.1	24.8	31.2	36.4	43.0	46.6	50.9	59.3	80.0
Import duties/total tax revenue (percent)	5.0	4.5	4.7	5.8	3.2	5.7			
Average collection rate import duties/imports (percent)	4.7	3.8	4.0	3.6	2.0	3.5	6.5	6.2	6.1
Total tax revenue/GDP (percent)	24.5	22.5	26.5	25.8	27.6	29.9			
Deficit/GDP (percent)									
Nominal import duties (J$ m)	39	30	50	64	43	91	159	175	277
Percentage increase in import duties		-23	65	29	-34	114	75	10	58
as accounted for by:									
Percentage increase in exchange rate		0	87	5	0	0	0	84	50
Percentage increase in average collection rate		-16	2	-9	-44	70	86	-5	0
Percentage increase in U.S. dollar value of imports		-6	-14	35	18	26	-6	-37	6

(table continues on following page)

(Table 5.3 continued)

Year	1976	1977	1978	1979	1980	1981	1982	1983	1984
Real import duties (nominal/GDP deflator)	1		2	2	1	2	3	3	3
Percentage increase in real import duties			31	10	-44	98	60	-6	17
as accounted for by:									
Percentage depreciation of real exchange rate		-5	80	-2	-6	1	-3	64	16
Percentage increase in average collection rate		-18	2	-9	-44	70	86	-5	0
Percentage increase in real value of imports		-12	-20	24	8	15	-12	-40	2
Nominal import duty		1	1.65	2.13	1.40	3.00	5.25	5.78	9.14
Nominal exchange rate		1	1.87	1.96	1.96	1.96	1.96	3.61	5.42
Average collection rate		1	1.02	0.94	0.53	0.90	1.67	1.59	1.59
Value of imports (US$)		1	0.86	1.16	1.36	1.71	1.61	1.01	1.06
Real import duty		1	1.31	1.45	0.81	1.60	2.56	2.42	2.83
Real exchange rate		1	1.60	1.58	1.44	1.46	1.42	2.33	2.70
Average collection rate		1	1.02	0.94	0.53	0.90	1.67	1.59	1.59
Real value of imports		1	0.80	0.99	1.07	1.23	1.08	0.65	0.66

(table continues on following page)

(*Table 5.3 continued*)

Year	1985	1986	1987	1988	1989	1990	1991	1992	1993
Import duties (J$ m)	498	601							
Export taxes (J$ m)									
Total tax revenue (J$ m)									
Imports (US$ m)	1,122	971	1,235	1,457	1,846	1,732	969	1,725	
Exports (US$ m)	571	588	704	861	887	1,033	609	1,082	
GDP (J$ m)	11,151	13,310	16,628	19,456	23,354	30,513	44,128	72,903	
Exchange rate (US$/J$)	5.48	5.48	5.50	5.48	6.48	8.04	21.49	22.19	32.48
Deficit (J$ m., surplus negative)									
GDP deflator	100.0	117.1	131.5	145.4	167.1	210.3			
Import duties/total tax revenue (percent)									
Average collection rate import duties/imports (percent)	8.1	11.3							
Total tax revenue/GDP (percent)									
Deficit/GDP (percent)									
Nominal import duties (J$ m)	496	601							
Percentage increase in import duties	60	21							
as accounted for by:									
Percentage increase in exchange rate	11	0	0	0	18	24			
Percentage increase in average collection rate	32	39		18	13				
Percentage increase in U.S. dollar value of imports	23	-13	27	18	13	5			

(*table continues on following page*)

162

(Table 5.3 continued)

Year	1985	1986	1987	1988	1989	1990	1991	1992	1993
Real import duties (nominal/GDP deflator)	5	5							
Percentage increase in real import duties	44	3							
as accounted for by:									
Percentage depreciation of real exchange rate	-9	-12	-8	-7	7				
Percentage increase in average collection rate	32	39							
Percentage increase in real value of imports	19	-16	23	15	9				
Nominal import duty	16.44	19.83							
Nominal exchange rate	6.03	6.03	6.05	6.03	7.13	8.84			
Average collection rate	2.09	2.91							
Value of imports (US$)	1.30	1.13	1.44	1.69	1.91				
Real import duty	4.08	4.20							
Real exchange rate	2.47	2.16	2.00	1.85	1.99				
Average collection rate	2.09	2.91							
Real value of imports	0.79	0.67	0.82	0.94	1.02				

Source: International Financial Statistics and Country Customs Data. Some figures derived from these sources via authors' calculations.

Table 5.4. *Import Duties and Trade, Morocco, 1980–93*

Year	1980	1981	1982	1983	1984	1985	1986
Import duties (dirham m)		3,851	4,697	4,228	4,416	4,466	4,408
Export taxes (dirham m)							
Total tax revenue (dirham m)		19,715	19,545	20,502	22,933	25,478	30,074
Imports (US$ m)	3,878	4,257	4,144	3,169	3,802	4,020	3,973
Exports (US$ m)	2,227	2,319	1,967	1,777	2,001	2,260	2,558
GDP (current dirham b)	74	79	93	99	112	130	154
Exchange rate (dirham/US$)	4.33	5.33	0.27	8.06	9.55	9.62	8.71
Deficit (dirham m, surplus negative)	7,184	10,557	10,630	7,680	6,762	9,424	11,872
GDP deflator	58.3	67.3	73.8	79.1	84.9	92.2	100.0
Import duties/total tax revenue (percent)		23.6	24.0	20.6	19.3	17.5	14.7
Average collection rate import duties/imports (percent)		17.4	18.1	16.8	12.8	11.5	12.7
Total tax revenue/GDP (percent)		21.2	21.0	20.8	20.5	19.6	19.5
Deficit/GDP (percent)	9.7	13.4	11.4	7.8	6.0	7.2	7.7
Nominal import duties (dirham m)		3,951	4,697	4,229	4,418	4,466	4,406
Percentage increase in import duties			19	-10	4	1	-1
as accounted for by:							
Percentage depreciation of nominal exchange rate		23	18	29	18	1	-9
Percentage increase in average collection rate			4	-8	-22	-10	10
Percentage increase in U.S. dollar value of imports		10	-3	-24	14	12	-1

(table continues on following page)

(Table 5.4 continued)

Year	1980	1981	1982	1983	1984	1985	1986
Real import duties (nominal/GDP deflator)		59	64	53	52	48	44
Percentage increase in real import duties			8	-16	-3	-7	-9
as accounted for by:							
Percentage depreciation of real exchange rate		17	14	25	15	-5	-14
Percentage increase in average collection rate			4	-8	-22	-10	10
Percentage increase in real value of imports		0	-8	-26	9	9	-4
Nominal import duty		1	1.19	1.07	1.12	1.13	1.12
Nominal exchange rate		1	1.18	1.51	1.79	1.60	1.63
Average collection rate		1	1.04	0.95	0.74	0.66	0.73
Value of imports (US$)		1	0.97	0.74	0.85	0.94	0.93
Real import duty		1	1.08	0.91	0.89	0.83	0.75
Real exchange rate		1	1.14	1.42	1.63	1.56	1.33
Average collection rate		1	1.04	0.95	0.74	0.66	0.73
Real value of imports		1	0.92	0.67	0.74	0.80	0.77

(table continues on following page)

(Table 5.4 continued)

Year	1987	1988	1989	1990	1991	1992	1993
Import duties (dirham m)	4,461	7,126	9,319	9,863			
Export taxes (dirham m)							
Total tax revenue (dirham m)	33,114	39,454	43,001	48,891			
Imports (US$ m)	4,522	4,767	5,738	5,848	7,328	6,940	6,899
Exports (US$ m)	2,099	3,624	3,492	4,370	4,575	3,752	3,300
GDP (current dirham b)	157	182	184	214	241	248	
Exchange rate (dirham/US$)	7.80	8.21	8.12	8.04	8.15	9.05	9.85
Deficit (dirham m, surplus negative)	7,025	5,841	9,951	4,700			
GDP deflator	110	116	169	202			
Import duties/total tax revenue (percent)	13.5	18.1	19.3	20.3			
Average collection rate import duties/imports (percent)	12.6	18.2	17.5	21.0			
Total tax revenue/GDP (percent)	21.1	21.7	22.2	22.8			
Deficit/GDP (percent)	4.5	3.2	5.1	2.2			
Nominal import duties (dirham m)	4,461	7,126	8,319	9,883			
Percentage increase in import duties as accounted for by:	1	60	17	19			
Percentage depreciation of nominal exchange rate	-10	5	-1	-1			
Percentage increase in average collection rate	-1	44	-2	17			
Percentage increase in U.S. dollar value of imports	14	5	20	2			

(table continues on following page)

(Table 5.4 continued)

Year	1987	1988	1989	1990	1991	1992	1993
Real import duties (nominal/GDP deflator)	41	62	44	34			
Percentage increase in real import duties	-8	52	-28	-23			
as accounted for by:							
Percentage depreciation of real exchange rate	-16	3	-37	-33			
Percentage increase in average collection rate	-1	44	-2	17			
Percentage increase in real value of imports	10	2	16	-2			
Nominal import duty	1.13	1.80	2.11	2.50			
Nominal exchange rate	1.46	1.54	1.52	1.51			
Average collection rate	0.73	1.05	1.03	1.20			
Value of imports (US$)	1.06	1.12	1.35	1.37			
Real import duty	0.69	1.05	0.75	0.58			
Real exchange rate	1.12	1.16	0.73	0.49			
Average collection rate	0.73	1.05	1.03	1.20			
Real value of imports	0.65	0.87	1.00	0.98			

Source: International Financial Statistics and Country Customs Data. Some figures derived from these sources via authors' calculations.

Table 5.5. Import Duties and Trade, Turkey, 1976–92

Year	1976	1977	1978	1979	1980	1981	1982	1983	1984
Import duties (lira b)	24	30	47	54	56	77		166	247
Export taxes									
Total tax revenue	134	176	261	406	750	1,206		1,936	2,375
Imports (US$ m)	5,129	5,798	4,595	5,069	7,815	8,864	8,794	9,179	10,663
Exports (US$ m)	1,960	1,753	2,283	2,261	2,910	4,703	5,746	5,728	7,134
GDP (current lira m)	629	860	1,273	2,182	4,328	6,414	9,620	11,532	18,212
Exchange rate (lira/US$)	17	13	25	35	90	134	187	283	445
Deficit (lira b, surplus negative)	13	53	55	137	161	117		483	1,816
GDP deflator	3.2	3.9	5.9	9.6	20.0	28.4	36.1	46.3	69.5
Import duties/total tax revenue (percent)	17.9	17.0	16.0	13.3	7.5	6.4		8.6	10.4
Average collection rate import duties/imports (percent)	28.0	26.7	40.4	30.1	7.9	6.5	0.0	6.4	5.2
Total tax revenue/GDP (percent)	20.3	20.5	20.5	18.6	17.3	18.8	0.0	16.8	13.0
Deficit/GDP (percent)	2.0	6.2	4.3	6.3	3.7	1.8	0.0	4.2	10.0
Nominal import duties (lira b)	24	30	47	54	56	77		166	247
Percentage increase in import duties as accounted for by:		25	57	15	4	38		116	49
Percentage increase in exchange rate		16	30	40	155	49	40	51	57
Percentage increase in average collection rate		-5	51	-26	-74	-18		-1	-19
Percentage increase in U.S. dollar value of imports		13	-21	10	54	13	-1	4	16

(table continues on following page)

(Table 5.5 continued)

Year	1976	1977	1978	1979	1980	1981	1982	1983	1984
Real import duties (nominal/GDP deflator)	7,500	7,692	7,966	5,510	2,600	2,711		3,585	3,554
Percentage increase in real import duties		3	4	-31	-49	-3		32	-1
as accounted for by:									
Percentage depreciation of real exchange rate		2	-7	-8	36	15	17	23	9
Percentage increase in average collection rate		-5	51	-26	-74	-18		-1	-19
Percentage increase in real value of imports		6	-20	1	41	4	-7	0	12
Nominal import duty	1.00	1.25	1.96	2.25	2.33	3.21	3.21	6.92	10.29
Nominal exchange rate	1.00	1.15	1.51	2.12	5.40	8.02	11.20	16.95	26.65
Average collection rate	1.00	0.95	1.44	1.07	0.28	0.23	0.23	0.23	0.19
Value of imports (US$)	1.00	1.13	0.90	0.99	1.52	1.73	1.71	1.79	2.08
Real import duty	1.00	1.03	1.05	0.73	0.37	0.36	0.36	0.45	0.47
Real exchange rate	1.00	1.02	0.94	0.86	1.16	1.35	1.57	1.93	2.10
Average collection rate	1.00	0.95	1.44	1.07	0.28	0.23	0.23	0.23	0.19
Real value of imports	1.00	1.06	0.78	0.79	1.12	1.16	1.08	1.09	1.21

(table continues on following page)

(Table 5.5 continued)

Year	1985	1986	1987	1988	1989	1990	1991	1992
Import duties (lira b)	382	465	774	1,155	1,961	3,338	4,574	7,813
Export taxes								
Total tax revenue	3,982	5,001	9,072	14,250	25,572	45,431	78,734	141,797
Imports (US$ m)	11,275	11,020	14,158	14,955	15,702	22,502	21,047	22,072
Exports (US$ m)	7,958	7,466	10,190	11,862	11,625	12,950	13,594	14,716
GDP (current lira m)	27,552	30,288	58,288	100,820	167,770	203,187		
Exchange rate (lira/US$)	577	756	1,020	1,815	2,313	2,030	5,060	8,564
Deficit (lira b, surplus negative)	2,050	1,259	2,346	3,859	7,503	11,782	33,317	47,328
GDP deflator	100	131	161	300	312	331	355	374
Import duties/total tax revenue (percent)	9.1	7.8	8.5	8.1	7.7	7.3	5.8	5.5
Average collection rate import duties/imports (percent)	5.6	5.6	5.4	4.4	5.4	5.1	4.3	4.0
Total tax revenue/GDP (percent)	14.5	15.2	15.6	14.1	15.2	16.0		
Deficit/GDP (percent)	7.4	3.2	4.0	3.8	4.5	4.2		
Nominal import duties (lira b)	362	485	774	1,155	1,961	3,336		
Percentage increase in import duties as accounted for by:	47	28	66	49	70	70		
Percentage increase in exchange rate	30	31	35	76	27	27		
Percentage increase in average collection rate	7	0	-4	-17	21	-5		
Percentage increase in U.S. dollar value of imports	6	-2	28	1	10	41		

(table continues on following page)

(Table 5.5 continued)

Year	1985	1986	1987	1988	1989	1990	1991	1992
Real import duties (nominal/GDP deflator)	3,620	3,550	4,276	3,850	8,285	10,069		
Percentage increase in real import duties	2	-2	20	-10	83	80		
as accounted for by:								
Percentage depreciation of real exchange rate	-7	3	1	11	28	24		
Percentage increase in average collection rate	7	0	-4	-17	21	-5		
Percentage increase in real value of imports	3	-5	24	-2	6	35		
Nominal import duty	15.08	13.38	32.25	48.13	81.71	139.00		
Nominal exchange rate	34.55	45.39	61.08	108.66	138.50	175.45		
Average collection rate	0.20	0.20	0.19	0.16	0.19	0.18		
Value of imports (US$)	2.20	2.15	2.76	2.80	3.08	4.35		
Real import duty	0.48	0.47	0.57	0.51	0.84	1.34		
Real exchange rate	1.95	2.00	2.02	2.23	2.85	3.54		
Average collection rate	0.20	0.20	0.19	0.16	0.19	0.18		
Real value of imports	1.25	1.19	1.48	1.45	1.54	2.08		

Source: International Financial Statistics and Country Customs Data. Some figures derived from these sources via authors' calculations.

limited by the availability of foreign exchange. However, there can also be redistribution of expenditure from lower tariff rate items toward higher (but reduced) tariff items, raising the average collection rates with no additional demand on foreign exchange.

Stock Adjustment

Where there is a tendency toward temporary postreform ballooning of import volumes it may partly be the result of a stock adjustment process. Tariff rate adjustments cause changes in relative prices that induce consumers to stock up on imported durables and semidurables when their relative prices fall. To the extent that these are manufactured consumer goods bearing higher-than-average tariffs, the overall average collection rate will tend to increase.

Removal of Quantitative Restrictions

The removal of quantitative restrictions will result in a permanent change in the flow demand for imports. In addition, a transitional increase may be observed, as pent-up demand for goods previously subject to quantitative restrictions swells imports when restrictions are removed. This may be heightened by fears that the liberalizations will prove temporary and that quantitative restrictions might be reimposed (or tariff reductions reversed) if the reform effort fails. Again the substitutions can be between domestic and quantitative restriction goods, in which case the foreign exchange constraint comes into play, or between quantitative restriction goods and other imports, in which case there is no net effect on the demand for foreign exchange.

Elimination of Exemptions

Exemptions from tariffs and other border taxes are frequently extended to "priority" industries, pioneer industries, or public entities. These exemptions form part of the system of protection of domestic industry that can significantly undermine revenue collections (by 50 percent in the case of Zimbabwe). Withdrawal of the exemptions can enhance revenues (although in the case of public entities there is little effect on the fiscal deficit). This suggests that reforms will tend to increase revenues more in countries that make extensive use of exemptions. The tendency for the import base to swell, thereby offsetting the revenue-reducing effects of the tariff rate reductions, is limited by the availability of foreign exchange. There are four further mechanisms to consider in this regard.

Increased Balance of Payments Support

Agreements with the World Bank and the International Monetary Fund (IMF) under which reform programs are launched involve the commitment of additional balance of payments support from multilaterals, which can trigger further resource flows from bilateral donors. These additional foreign exchange inflows allow a higher volume of imports than would otherwise be possible. These increases, however, are not necessarily permanent. IMF loans in particular are very short-term.

Exchange Rate Adjustments

Often structural adjustment programs call for an immediate devaluation to restore external balance. In the absence of increased external resources, further depreciation will be necessary if the program calls for tariff reductions and the elimination of quantitative restrictions, since these will fuel import demand. Depreciation of the currency increases the domestic currency value of imports, which automatically increases tariff revenues. The government's fiscal position is also affected by the impact of exchange rate changes on public expenditures. In the general equilibrium response to a trade and foreign exchange liberalization, one should expect to see the relative price of tradables fall and that of wages and nontradables rise. The exchange rate will adjust, but, other things being equal, the change in the exchange rate will be less than proportional to the change in the tariff rate.[3] For private agents nontradable goods prices will rise relative to tradables; however, the government is either exempted from tariffs or pays the tariff to itself. Either way the tariff adjustment by itself has no net effect on the government's cost of tradables or on the deficit. The exchange rate adjustment, however, has the effect of making the relative cost of tradables to the government rise. The overall effect will tend to be to worsen the deficit when the share of tradables in government spending is high and when elasticities are such that a large depreciation is needed to offset the tariff reduction. (Further evidence on the traded-good intensity of government spending is found in Matin 1992). Nontraded items of government expenditure would include public sector wages, current transfers, and domestic debt service. These will typically account for something on the order of 50 percent of total spending. These tariff and

---

3. A 10 percent import tax plus a 10 percent export subsidy would result in a 10 percent appreciation. A 10 percent import tax alone will result in a less than 10 percent appreciation. Only if there were no substitution in production or consumption of tradables and nontradables would the import tariff translate into a fully offsetting change in the exchange rate.

exchange rate effects on the deficit may be worth additional study. In most instances, however, they will be combined with sharp shifts in the composition of expenditure that reflect the need to cut spending overall. Such efforts usually involve major reductions in capital spending.

Foreign Exchange Management

If tariff rate adjustments take place in the context of a fixed exchange rate and exchange control, then the pattern of imports will not shift to reflect changes in the tariff rates if the exchange allocation mechanism continues to determine the composition of imports. The overall level of imports will not be able to expand much either. If exchange controls are relaxed, there may be a shift in the composition of imports, quite possibly toward the higher rated categories that may have been less favored under controls. Still, if the exchange rate is fixed, imports can only expand to the extent that exports rise due to lower input costs, exchange reserves are run down, or financing can be obtained through capital inflows or official lending. With a floating rate, lowering tariffs will depreciate the currency (unless export or capital flows increase), but the depreciation will automatically increase revenues.

Shift toward More Open Economy

Over time, reductions in trade barriers should stimulate increased trade as domestic industries take advantage of their comparative advantages and specialize. The increased volume of trade should increase tariff revenues. There should be an increase in growth rates, particularly of exports.

With all these various forces at work, almost any pattern of import tariff revenue changes can emerge in the wake of reform. In addition, countries often find it difficult to follow through with the full set of intended reforms. Much depends on the initial conditions at the time trade reforms are implemented, the level of political commitment to reforms, and the timing and sequencing of the whole package of reforms—trade, exchange rate, financial, monetary, and fiscal.

The credibility and consistency of reform policies are critical. The authorities must adopt monetary, fiscal, and commercial policies consistent with the exchange rates that they envisage. Moreover, the public must be convinced of the authorities' commitment to their declared course of action. When the policies are inconsistent or incredible, speculative pressures build up and force resolution of the issue. Repegging of exchange rates or abandonment of fixed rates altogether may afford temporary relief; but, generally it is necessary to make adjustments to underlying monetary, fiscal, and commercial polices to prevent a continuing series of crises. Rodrik (1989) points out many examples. For instance, a trade reform in the context of a pegged exchange rate and sticky prices will not prove viable. Similarly, shifts in the terms of trade or international interest rates will require adjustments in exchange rate targets or domestic monetary and fiscal policies, or a combination of these changes. A common consistency or credibility problem is a growing anticipation of devaluation that can precipitate a large swell in imports. This is most likely when the overvaluation is associated with an increase in real wages, when the unemployment effects of high wages come with a lag, and when the level of protection to local tradables producers has been reduced. When these events take place in the context of political instability, fully liberalized capital markets, and more modest levels of trade reform, speculation may take the form of capital flight. Gross borrowings may increase sharply, but if these are returned in the form of speculative outflows there may be very little effect on the trade account. In the context of relative political stability there may be a more pronounced import boom that may even have significant capital good and consumer durable good component. The impact on trade tax revenues is, of course, very different in these two cases.

Country Experiences

Studies of trade reform efforts across countries have produced very different results in different countries. A 1992 study by the World Bank, *Trade Policy Reforms Under Adjustment Programs*, compared the experience of five "intensive adjusters" (Ghana, Indonesia, Mexico, Morocco, and Turkey) with that of four less successful adjusters (Colombia, Côte d'Ivoire, Jamaica, and Pakistan) (World Bank 1992b). The study pointed out that, while all countries were able to reduce quantitative restrictions, only the intensive adjusters lowered import tariff collection rates. Part of the reason is that the less intensive adjusters were much more dependent on import tariffs as a revenue source to begin with, and tariff rate reductions therefore represented a greater threat to macroeconomic stabilization. Moreover, the intensive adjusters pursued a more active exchange rate policy, which gave them greater scope for tariff rate reductions without sacrificing fiscal balance.

The experiences of Chile and Argentina illustrate the importance of expectations and the commitment to reform. The Allende government that came to power in Chile in 1970 ran a huge public sector deficit financed virtually entirely by monetary expansion. Attempts to control the resulting inflation and balance of payments deficit included the imposition of price controls, trade restrictions, and a system of highly differentiated multiple exchange rates.

Inflationary pressures that developed as a result of these policies became deep rooted, and proved difficult to tame. A substantial monetary overhang had developed. Despite the controls, there had been significant increases in black market prices, fueling expectations of further price increases. In October 1973 the new regime that overthrew Allende liberalized most prices, instituted a large devaluation, and held public sector wage increases below the rate of inflation. Trade was liberalized in steps, which culminated in a uniform 10 percent tariff by 1979. Fiscal policy was tightened sharply by major tax reforms in 1974 and 1975, and by asset sales and large reductions in public expenditure in 1975. Analysis of the excess demand for money suggests that monetary policy was tightened as well in 1975 and the first half of 1976 (Corbo and Solimano 1990).

Despite these steps, inflation proved difficult to root out. There were two likely reasons for this. First, the planned tariff reductions and a 45 percent drop in the price of copper exports necessitated a major devaluation, which had inflationary consequences. Second, the public wage indexation rule, instituted in 1974 and extended to the private sector in 1979, was implemented with a lag. This worked as a brake on wage movements while inflation was accelerating, but it kept wage increases ahead of inflation on the way down. Inflation remained at three-digit levels into 1977. In 1978 the government decided to switch policy. The reasoning was that the fiscal deficit was under control and the trade regime was liberalized. In a more open economy, inflation was largely imported and could be brought to heel by slowing the rate of devaluation. A devaluation schedule was announced at rates below the difference between foreign and domestic inflation, and in 1979 the rate was fixed. The government regarded the policy as credible but domestic inflation remained above international inflation for two years, resulting in a 30 percent real appreciation of the peso by the end of 1981. Gradually, exports became uncompetitive and the trade deficit rose. In view of the widening trade deficit and a deteriorating fiscal position, the government raised the uniform tariff rate from 10 percent to 35 percent in 1984, but brought it back down to 20 percent in 1985.

In fact, throughout the adjustment period, import taxes had the effect of softening swings in the budget deficit. Between 1981 and 1983 the budget moved from a surplus of 2.6 percent of GDP to a deficit of the same amount. The deficit persisted for two more years. Import tax collections increased from 8.5 percent of imports in 1981 to 16 percent in 1985. Import taxes as a share of total revenues also rose sharply during this period, settling back when the deficit shrank thereafter. Despite the crisis and the moderate reversal of trade liberalization policies in the first half of the 1980s, Chile was able to preserve the core of its reform program. There has been a very substantial increase in the volume of trade and in the level of real economic activity. At the same time, import taxes have fallen somewhat and, while there has been some backtracking, the rates are now much more uniform than they were prior to 1973.

These changes are reflected in table 5.1. Despite sustained increases in the real volume of imports, real import duties fell from 1976 through 1979 because of steady real appreciation of the currency and lower tariff rates. Between 1979 and 1981 real import duties rose by 32 percent despite continued appreciation because of a reversal of tariff rate reductions and further increases in import volumes. Then in 1982 the large devaluation resulted in a sharp reduction in import volumes. Average tariff rates also fell substantially, resulting in a contraction of revenues. This was the lowest real tariff revenue had been since 1974 and was about half that of 1976. From this point on real tariff revenues increased sharply. The index rose from 5.4 in 1982, to 17.8 by 1988. The largest contributor to increased revenues from 1981 on is the depreciation of the peso. It is worth noting the changes during the whole period of reforms. Comparing 1973 to the average for 1987–90, the average tariff rate is just slightly higher. Virtually all the substantial hike in revenue is attributable to devaluation and increased trade volume.

In Argentina, political and economic chaos reigned in the wake of the death of President Peron in 1974. Wages were allowed to rise despite worsening terms of trade. Inflationary pressures built up behind price controls. The public sector deficit rose sharply and by 1976 inflation was running at greater than 900 percent a year. A plan to deal with the crisis was adopted in early 1976. It was to rely on orthodox wage and fiscal policies to rein in hyperinflation, followed by financial and labor market restructuring. It was also envisaged that inflation would be moderated by the effects of import competition stemming from trade liberalization, tariff reductions, and slowing the rate of devaluation of the currency. However, the plan was not implemented as intended. Tax revenues were increased; but, after an initial contraction, public expenditures rose because of large hikes in military spending, civil service wages, and public investment. Monetary policy was largely accommodative. For a short period after financial liberalization real interest rates rose, but then they settled back to less than 1 percent for a year and a half due to the opening up of the capital account and the slow rate of devaluation. The effects of trade liberalization began to be felt in late 1979. Import volumes began to build rapidly. This and the announcement of a depreciation schedule helped to bring about a sharp decrease in inflation. Nominal interest rates reacted with a lag and real rates went up sharply. The banking system was weak because of overly rapid expansion, induced partly by a 100 percent deposit guarantee, and there was a series of major bank failures in the wake of interest rate gyrations.

In essence the government was trying to manage expectations. But in trying to ensure continuous full employment through the transition period, it was not setting the underlying policies in a manner consistent with its own price and exchange rate targets. A flaw in the program was the fact that the slow rate at which the peso was allowed to devalue meant that there was a 40 percent real appreciation between 1977 and 1980. This hurt all traded goods producers, although exporters got some relief in the form of expanded fiscal and credit incentives, while import substitute producers suffered reductions in tariff protection. These developments, combined with the effects of natural disasters on agriculture, produced a rapid deterioration in the trade balance in 1980. The trade balance improved in 1981, but the service balance was already suffering from the accumulation of large capital inflows. Capital flight grew to disastrous proportions because the public lost all confidence in the economic plan. By this point it was recognized that the plan had failed, and the new administration that took office in March 1981 departed from one of the central planks of the reform program by introducing a series of substantial devaluations in an effort to reduce accelerating capital flight.

In addition to inappropriate management of the exchange rate, the financial sector policies contributed to failure of the program. The rapid expansion of loans in an environment of poor supervision and blanket guarantees meant that when interest rates rose shaky industries were unable to cope. Large bailouts of banks and firms contributed to excessive monetary expansion.

Argentina was not as aggressive in lowering tariffs as Chile. The slow and uneven cuts meant that the burden of adjustment was not felt as strongly by import-substituting firms as it was by export industries, which were affected by both real appreciation and continued high cost local inputs. Overall there was a shift in demand from locally produced tradables (particularly exports) toward nontradables. This was reflected in high growth rates for services, particularly financial services and construction, and low rates in manufacturing. Despite the tepid tariff reform, the result of the overvaluation of the exchange rate was a marked, if temporary, dampening effect on inflation.

The main differences between the Argentinean and Chilean cases include the fact that Chile made sustained early efforts to control the public sector deficit as the reforms were initiated. Chile maintained relatively conservative monetary and fiscal policy throughout the reform period. The fiscal position moved between deficit and surplus, but at no time did the deficit exceed 3 percent of GDP. Unemployment was 10 percent in 1974 and stayed in the range of 13 to 17 percent to the end of the decade. By contrast, Argentina made an initial attack on the deficit but was never able to get it below 6 percent of GDP. There is a general principle here as stated in Thomas, Matin, and Nash (1990):

> In the absence of any reduction in the fiscal deficit or depreciation of the exchange rate, the removal of trade controls would worsen the current account deficit. However, as long as the fiscal deficit and money supply growth are sufficiently reduced before or simultaneously with liberalization, the excess demand for imports can be lowered and the current account deficit kept in check.

Several messages can be taken from the Chile-Argentina comparison:

- Fiscal deficits need to be corrected early in the trade reform process.
- Trade taxes can be used in a limited way to buffer fiscal swings during the reform period, but ultimately rates must be reduced.
- A real devaluation is a central part of the process of trade reform. Exchange rates should not be used for controlling the inflationary effect of import prices. This should be done through monetary and fiscal polices, which are the only effective means of ensuring that a nominal devaluation retains a real component. Overvaluation may help to keep import volumes and therefore tariff revenue up, but not in a sustainable fashion.
- A credibility and consistency problem can feed an import boom, which tends to sustain import tariff revenue (Chile). But in the context of extreme political and financial market instability, mobile capital, and weak tariff reform, it may result primarily in large scale capital flight (Argentina).

Jamaica and Turkey illustrate differences in approaches to trade reform along a different dimension. Jamaica is what the World Bank refers to as a "quantitative restriction adjuster." Others in this category include Colombia, Côte d'Ivoire, and Pakistan. Turkey is termed a "tariff adjuster" (World Bank 1992b). Other tariff adjusters are Ghana, Indonesia, Mexico, and Morocco. The quantitative restriction adjusters experienced increases in import tax collection rates during adjustment, while the tariff adjusters experienced decreases. These differences are quite marked.

The Jamaican reforms that took place during the early 1980s included the removal of licensing and a wide variety of quantitative restrictions, as well as the elimination of a pervasive system of exemptions. The resulting sharp increase in revenue collections was reinforced by the expansion of stamp duties and surcharges. In 1980 import taxes were only 3.5 percent of imports but rose to 58.3 percent in 1986. The import tax base shrank but import taxes as a share of total taxes still rose dramatically. This contrasts with the experience of Turkey, which undertook massive reductions in tariffs.

The Jamaican adjustment program is regarded as at best a limited success. Part of the problem is that Jamaica made no serious attempt to control the public sector deficit in the early stages of its program. When it did finally act it did so by using trade reform to increase average tariff rates. Jamaica was also slow to implement exchange rate adjustments and kept the nominal rate fixed from 1979 through 1982. In 1983 it finally allowed a large devaluation, which, combined with the tariff rate hikes, caused a sharp contraction in imports. Nonetheless the trade taxes increased overall. In the summary table, real import values slumped from an index value of 1.23 in 1981, to 0.65 in 1983. During the same period the average tariff rate index rose from 0.90 to 1.59 and then to 2.91 by 1986. The RER index moved from 1.46 to 2.33. The combined effect of these movements was a 51 percent increase in real tariff revenue by 1983. Tariffs rose by a further 74 percent by 1986. This was due entirely to increases in the average tariff rate because the real import volume was unchanged and the exchange rate actually appreciated slightly.

The tariff adjusters' import taxes all fell as a share of imports—substantially in the case of Turkey. The tariff adjusters were all classified as successful or very successful adjusters by the World Bank (1992a). By contrast, the programs of the quantitative restriction adjusters, for which average import tax collection rates all rose, were classified as failed or only moderately successful adjusters. The basis of classification was changes in before-and-after growth rates and industrial and manufacturing value added.

The data for Jamaica stand in sharp contrast to those of the other countries. The index for the average collection rate fell in all the other countries except for Morocco. In Turkey the average collection index fell very substantially, to 0.18. It is significant that even among the successful adjusters there appears to be a pattern of sharp cuts in average rates, then a reversal triggered by fiscal problems. Collection rates are then raised temporarily and gradually cut back. This is readily apparent in the data for Chile, where sharp cuts in 1979 and 1982 were reversed in 1983, and in Ghana, where the cuts in 1980 were reversed in 1982.

It is also significant that in all countries the real value of import duties increased during the reform period. The most significant contributor to the real growth of import duties is the real depreciation of the local currency. It is also clear from the data that the depreciations negatively affect real imports. Particularly in the early stages of the programs, real imports contract, and only with time is growth reestablished; and increases in the volume of imports contribute to increased real duty collections. In Chile, one of the earliest and most successful adjusters, the real import effect was negative after 1981 and bottomed out only in 1985 after a second round of depreciations. The volume of imports has grown steadily since then and has made the largest contribution to real import duty collections of all the countries reviewed here. In Turkey the effects of the depreciation on the volume of imports were offset by massive cuts in tariff rates. The volume of imports actually increased between 1979 and 1981 as the RER rose (the currency depreciated) by 56 percent. The relatively smooth growth of the volume of imports in Turkey through the reform period was probably less disruptive to the local economy but, maintained as it was by huge collection rate cuts, the real value of collections contracted to only 37 percent of what it had been four years before. Yet the deficit was only 3.7 percent of GDP in the year of the biggest rate cuts, and it averaged less than this for the following three years despite the maintenance of the low tariff rates.

Turkey was able to do this because, like Chile, it had taken important steps toward fiscal stabilization before the trade reforms were initiated.

Increases in average collection rates do not appear to be one of the hallmarks of success in trade reform programs. However, policies for the elimination of licensing, quantitative restrictions, and exemptions and adjustments, which lessen the dispersion in import tax collection rates across goods, are also necessary for successful reform. These initiatives by themselves will increase the amount of import tax revenue. While deficit control is a recurring problem in adjusting countries, reliance on increased trade taxes to fill a deficit gap is a poor strategy, except perhaps in the very short term. One cannot liberalize trade by increasing trade tax rates, and one cannot have a success- ful adjustment in terms of growth without trade liberalization.

The theory of optimal taxation further supports this view. Uniform import taxes eliminate differences in effective protection rates across import-substituting firms. This is the rationale behind striving for reductions in tariff rate dispersion. But tariffs discriminate against exports unless there is a uniform export subsidy, which under balanced trade would absorb all the tariff revenue. Export-led growth will be hampered by an increase in import taxes, particularly if the higher import taxes hinder RER adjustments. Less distortionary methods of raising revenue include income taxes, lump sum taxes, or consumption taxes such as a VAT applied uniformly across domestically produced and imported goods. Trade taxes may, however, be necessary in some developing countries because the costs of collection of domestic taxes are high relative to trade taxes.

Complementary Tax Reforms

In 1985, in the industrial countries as a whole, import taxes provided only 2 percent of government revenue. This compares with 26 percent for Sub-Saharan Africa (SSA). Average import collection rates in the United States are 3.7 percent of the CIF value of imports, which is high for an industrial country. Most industrial countries have rates of less than 1 percent. Developing countries typically have collection rates that are in the range of 10 to 25 percent, and some much higher. Moreover, some developing countries have significant export taxes. These are virtually nonexistent in the industrial world.

But, while trade taxes are a large, if not the largest, source of revenue in many developing countries, the distortions and efficiency consequences may not always be that serious. The range of local products may be narrow, especially in the smaller countries, and is often concentrated in primary agriculture, forestry, and extractive industries. Consequently, a high proportion of local demand for goods other than primary food is met through imports. Under these circumstances the relatively high tariffs and stamp taxes on imports are not that different in effect from a consumption tax system in which food is exempted, and the distortions are not that damaging.

But as the developing economy matures, its capacity to produce finished goods (and services) increases. A greater portion of local consumption is met from domestic rather than foreign sources. These domestically produced goods do not bear the "consumption tax." The tax base becomes relatively narrow and the burden of taxation across goods becomes more skewed. This tendency is reinforced by the creation of special incentives within the system of import tariff and exemptions designed to assist new finished goods–producing industries.

Failure of the revenue base to expand along with the economy induces the authorities to take new tax measures. Stamp taxes or surcharges or surtaxes on imports are usually the first line of defense. This temporarily plugs the revenue hole but it worsens the unequal treatment of goods. It creates greater incentives for smuggling and for the (inefficient) production of import substitutes. These influences eventually reduce the revenue base even further.

The second course of action is to capture some of the escaped consumption tax base. One method is to introduce or increase sales taxes that apply to domestic production as well as imports. Another is to bring in service taxes on operations such as hotels and restaurants. Collection of service taxes on a wider basis is often difficult because the sector has such a large number of small-scale operations, especially in retail trade.

These actions can create several problems. First, the owners of new firms, established under the various incentive plans and largely exempted from the old taxes, feel they have been misled when the government introduces new taxes from which their firms are not exempt. Second, problems of cascading emerge, in which the producers of intermediate and final goods pay taxes on their inputs and then have further taxes charged on their outputs. Depending on how broad the service tax is, firms can end up paying tax on legal, accounting, design, engineering, advertising, and transportation services. With sales taxes on material inputs, capital goods, and outputs, there can be a high degree of cascading. Large firms that have greater potential for performing these services in-house are better able to insulate themselves from double taxation than are smaller firms that may even do their photocopying at the (taxable) local copy shop.

The greatest difficulty arises, however, with respect to export firms. Unless they are in a free trade zone they must pay tariffs on imports, and this puts them at a disadvantage in international markets. Many exporters feel the need to sell locally to supplement export revenues, especially in the startup years. But it is awkward to accommodate these firms in the context of a free trade zone and still give fair treatment to other local producers. Duty drawback systems operate fully and effectively in very few countries. In addition, it is virtually impossible to compensate exporters for the cascading service and sales taxes. The underlying problems are that (a) at the typically high level of tariff rates, insulating exporters from taxes is difficult, and (b) the patchwork system of domestic indirect taxes that emerges as the authorities try to reconstruct their eroded "consumption tax" base becomes unwieldy, unfair, and inefficient.

Thomas, Matin, and Nash (1990) point out that a number of countries undergoing trade reform programs also undertook tax reform programs to improve tax administration and collection (Ghana, Pakistan, and Thailand), to increase rates and coverage of sales and excise taxes (Malawi, Mauritius, Mexico, and the Philippines), or to introduce a VAT (Jamaica, Morocco, and Turkey). The World Bank made specific recommendations for enhancement of domestic revenue sources to complement trade reform programs in Bangladesh (1987), Malawi (1987), and India (1990), and has generally been actively involved in providing advice on tax administration.

There have been a few instances of failure to predict accurately the revenue consequences of tariff reforms. As indicated in *Lessons of Tax Reform*:

> A number of studies (such as for Kenya in 1986 and the Philippines in 1980) projected that revenue losses due to tariff reform would be negligible because items formerly subject to quantitative restrictions would move to the tariff list, imports through legal channels would increase, and gains in productivity would increase output. But the projections did not fully materialize. (World Bank 1991)

In Morocco and Thailand domestic tax reforms intended to enhance revenues performed poorly, resulting in a reversal of some of the tariff reductions.

In principle, what countries have to do is to substantially reform the domestic indirect tax system or replace it with a more comprehensive rebatable VAT, and then reduce the overall level of import taxation by lowering tariff rates. At this point the burden of raising revenue can be switched to the new or reformed domestic tax system. Adoption of VATs has been an important recommendation in several of the countries studies under TEP, including Mali, Uganda, Vietnam, and Zimbabwe. Among the other TEP countries, Madagascar and Morocco already have a VAT, and Mauritius has a sales tax and ring system, described below, that is similar in effect to a VAT. The appropriate nature and timing of reforms need careful consideration.

VAT systems typically take up to eighteen to twenty-four months to implement, starting from the time a political decision is made. But even before this a good deal of public relations work must be done to ensure public understanding and support for the system. Another consideration is that of administrative capacity. TEP studies in Uganda and Vietnam recommended a transitional stage during which a modified sales tax would continue until administrative capacities could be enhanced. Responsibility for VAT administration can be placed with the customs and excise department, the sales tax department, the income tax department, or a separate department. Existing staff and systems may be useful in launching the VAT. For instance, the sales and service tax systems may already have computerized registration lists covering most of the entities that would be liable for a VAT.

A third issue is that of how serious the defects of the existing indirect tax system are and whether temporary fixes can sufficiently improve the system, giving the country more time to prepare for an eventual VAT. This is particularly relevant when the tax administration is weak. There are some misconceptions in this area that can lead to starting a VAT too soon. Adoption of a VAT is often urged when existing domestic indirect taxes are levied at the factory gate (as a manufacturers' sales tax is). It is asserted that all the value added in wholesale and retail trade escapes the tax net and that a VAT, by including these activities, would broaden the tax base, would be more fair, and would make it easier to preserve revenue while reducing distorting trade taxes. This argument is not entirely valid. Assume for a moment that 50 percent of value added is in manufacturing and 50 percent is in distribution and retailing. From the revenue perspective, it makes no difference whether there is a 10 percent manufacturers' tax, a 5 percent VAT, or a 5 percent sales tax. The total tax take will be the same. In fact, the sharing of the burden of taxation between the manufacturer, the distributor or retailer, and the consumer is unaffected by the choice of tax mechanism. This is true regardless of what the elasticities of supply and demand are at the various levels. So, for instance, if the burden of a VAT falls most heavily on the retailer, the burden of the other two taxes would fall most heavily on him as well. There is a slight difference in incentives under the different taxes. Investment in product improvement will be taxed differently under the three systems depending on whether the investment is focused on manufacturing or distributing and retailing; but, the choice of tax is unlikely to shift very much the shares of value added between the levels. (One exception here involves vertically integrated firms that can use transfer pricing to avoid tax.)

The more relevant issue in this area concerns the variations in the shares of value added at each stage as one looks across industries. What stands out is the low proportion of manufactured content in service industries other than retail trade and distribution. These services should fare better under a manufacturers' tax than under the other forms of tax. But what are these industries? They are hotels, restaurants, professionals (doctors, lawyers, engineers), and a large number of small enterprises such as repair shops and barbers. The central problem with small enterprises is registration, and this is just as true for a VAT as for any other type of tax. Most countries have separate taxes for hotels and restaurants so there is an independent mechanism for determining the tax burden on this group. Similarly, some countries have recognized that professionals are "undertaxed" in a manufacturers' tax system and have adopted separate service taxes to complement the manufacturers' tax. This is appropriate, but one needs to be careful of double taxation when introducing more types of taxes.

There is a mechanism for handling the problem called the ring system. In the ring system certain firms are designated as ring members. They can import without having to pay sales or other domestic indirect taxes on their purchases, and they can buy and sell among themselves without tax. But when a ring member sells to a non–ring member, taxes must be paid. Exports are not taxed. The system is usually set up to avoid double taxation in the context of a manufacturers' tax; but, it can be extended to deal with professionals and other service industries that have relatively little manufactured content. These service firms are required to register as ring members along with the manufacturers. Then, for example, when a lawyer sells his services to a firm manufacturing lamps, no tax is charged, but the cost of the lawyer is embodied in the price of the lamps, which are taxed when they are sold to consumers. Lawyers' services to private individuals (who are not ring members) would be taxed. This kind of system is not equivalent to a VAT, but it has a tax incidence that is fairer and more VAT-like than a manufacturers' tax alone. It is an appropriate intermediate step for countries wanting to undertake tariff reductions but unable to set up a full-fledged VAT, to generate the extra revenue that will be needed when the tariff revenues decline. Unfortunately what often happens is that either method of capturing services are not set up or they are set up as separate systems that create double taxation.

Exemptions

The role of exemptions in determining tariff revenue collections is frequently overlooked. In part the reason is that detailed data on exemptions has been difficult to obtain. Pritchett and Sethi (1994) offer some empirical analysis of exemption patterns in Jamaica, Kenya, and Pakistan. Their study indicates that, because exemptions collected and official tariff rates are almost completely unrelated, the variance of collected rates becomes greater the higher the statutory rate. The collected rate increases much less than one-for-one with increases in the statutory rate; and, above a certain level of the official rate, further increases in the official rate produce no increase in the collected rate.

Because of data limitations, the effect of tariff rate adjustments on total revenues has required some guesswork and rough approximation in most adjusting countries. The World Bank's own SINTIA model, which is used for these estimates, looks at the change in potential revenue (in other words, the revenue that would be collected if there were no exemptions) resulting from rate adjustments. It is then assumed that changes in actual revenues will be proportional to changes in potential revenue. Without line item data on exemptions, this is the best that can be done.

Recently much better data have become available in many countries because of new automated customs administration systems. This offers an important opportunity for policy-oriented research. The new data will make it possible not only to predict more accurately the revenue consequences of rate adjustments but, also, to look at the relative importance of various exemptions and to build revenue enhancement measures into the trade reform in a more informed manner. For example, the detailed disaggregation will allow analysis of exemptions that derive from fiscal incentive programs for pioneer industries, many of which are temporary. It will be possible to isolate revenue-reducing exemptions to private agents from those granted to public bodies, which offer little opportunity for deficit reduction since the government will simply have to pay itself if the exemptions are withdrawn. This may also have important implications for the budget in the event that there is a privatization component to the reform program.

Conclusion

A number of conclusions can be drawn from this discussion:

- Fiscal deficits need to be corrected early in the trade reform process.
- Real devaluation of the local currency is a central part of the process of trade reform. Exchange rates should not be used for controlling the inflationary impact of import prices. This should be done through monetary and fiscal polices, which are the only effective means of ensuring that a nominal devaluation retains a real component. Overvaluation may help to keep import volumes and therefore tariff revenue up but not in a sustainable fashion. By contrast, devaluation gives an immediate increase in revenues.
- A credibility or consistency problem can feed an import boom, which tends to sustain import tariff revenue. But in the context of extreme political and financial market instability, mobile capital, and weak tariff reform, it may result primarily in large-scale capital flight.
- Countries that do not tackle the problem of reducing nominal tariff rates and instead limit their reforms to the elimination of quantitative restrictions are less likely to succeed in the longer term.

Since trade taxes are a major revenue source for most developing countries, careful planning is needed to ensure that revenue-reducing effects of rate reductions do not upset the fiscal balance. The elimination of quantitative restrictions can help make up the revenue shortfall, but it is also necessary to look at ways of shifting away from trade taxes to less distortionary forms of taxation, such as a VAT. Otherwise it will not be possible to make adequate reductions in average collection rates and reduce the burden on exporters, which ultimately provide the greatest opportunity for enhanced growth.

Bibliography

Corbo, Vittorio, and Andrés Solimano. 1990. "Chile's Experience with Stabilization Revisited." Policy Research Working Paper 579. World Bank, Country Economics Department, Washington, D.C.

Dornbusch, Rudiger. 1986. "External Debt, Budget Deficits, and Disequilibrium Exchange Rates." In Gordon W. Smith and John T. Cuddington, eds., *International Debt and the Developing Countries*. Washington, D.C.: World Bank.

Greenaway, David, and Chris Milner. 1993. *The Fiscal Implications of Trade Policy Reform: Theory and Evidence*. UNDP/World Bank Trade Expansion Program Occasional Paper 9. World Bank, Washington, D.C.

Matin, Kazi M. 1992. "Fiscal Adjustment and the Real Exchange Rate: The Case of Bangladesh." Policy Research Working Paper 850. World Bank, Country Economics Department, Washington, D.C.

Mitra, Pradeep. 1992. "The Coordinated Reform of Tariffs and Indirect Taxes." *World Bank Research Observer* 7: 195–218.

Pritchett, Lant, and Geeta Sethi. 1994. "Tariff Rates, Tariff Revenues, and Tariff Reform: Some New Facts." *The World Bank Economic Review* 8: 1–16.

Rodrik, Dani. 1989. "Promises, Promises: Credible Policy Reform via Signaling." *Economic Journal* 99 (September): 756–72.

Thomas, Vinod, Kazi Matin, and John Nash. 1990. *Lessons in Trade Policy Reform*. Policy Research Series Paper 10. Washington, D.C.: World Bank.

World Bank. 1991. *Lessons of Tax Reform*. Washington, D.C.: World Bank.

_____. 1992a. "Structural and Sectoral Adjustment Operations: The Second OED Overview." Operations Evaluation Department. Washington, D.C.

_____. 1992b. "Trade Policy Reforms under Adjustment Programs." A World Bank Operations Evaluation Study. Washington, D.C.

6

Duty Drawback Mechanisms:
The System in Taiwan (China) and
Recommendations for Costa Rica

Chia-Sheng Wu and Shui-Chi Chuang

The rapid growth achieved by export-oriented Asian economies has led many developing countries, previously focused on import substitution industrialization as a development strategy, to shift their development efforts toward export expansion. But the policies often chosen to promote export expansion, such as direct export subsidies or lucrative tax benefits as rewards for export performance, create distortions, represent a fiscal drain on deficit-plagued governments, and tempt retaliation on the part of importing countries.

Governments can adopt policies to facilitate export expansion without creating costly distortions or prompting retaliation by trading partners. To compete in highly competitive world markets, firms must have free access to the imported raw materials and intermediate inputs needed to produce their export products. But high tariffs on imports in many developing countries, for revenue as well as protective purposes, increase production costs and hinder potential export industries. Policy measures that provide duty-free access to imported raw materials and semifinished products when these are used to produce export goods can contribute significantly to export expansion. Duty-free access can be provided in a number of ways, including exemptions from import duties on inputs for exporting firms (provided they export their finished goods); refunds of duties on inputs once firms export the finished product, bonded factories under the supervision of customs authorities into which firms can bring imported inputs and from which they can ship (but only for export); and free trade zones. (See box 6.1 for an example of duty refund criteria.) While all of these measures are simple in principle, implementing them can be complicated. This chapter explains in detail one mechanism that has been used successfully to provide exporters with duty-free access to imported inputs for exports: the duty drawback system used in Taiwan (China). It compares the operation of the Taiwanese duty drawback system with the Costa Rican "export contract" system of export promotion, examines the advantages and disadvantages of each, and discusses how the Costa Rican system might be converted into a duty drawback system similar to the Taiwanese system.

Box 6.1. *Example of Raw Material Duty Refund Criteria*

Refund of duty/taxes on "artificial flower" export.

When imported or locally made silk fabric is used to make artificial flowers (leaves), the cutting attrition rate is determined to be 30 percent.

The following formula is used in computing the raw material consumption:

$$C = A \div (1 - B)$$

Where: A = The weight of export artificial flowers (leaves) made of silk fabric

B = Cutting attrition rate

C = The weight of silk fabric used as raw material

Duty Refunds in Taiwan (China)

Taiwan (China) is an island economy, with scarce natural resources and limited market capacity. Economic growth, employment, and national income are heavily dependent on international trade and foreign investment. In the early years of the duty drawback system, duty refunds were only given on a few selected items, such as wheat for exported wheat flour and cotton yarns and linen for handkerchiefs. In 1955, eligibility was expanded to cover all exported items. At the time, the duty drawbacks were potentially very important because import tariffs were quite high: in 1956 the average tariff rate was more than 40 percent.

The duty/tax drawback system lowered production costs for exporters who used imported inputs and encouraged exportation to the world market. Taiwan's success at expanding foreign trade has been remarkable. Taiwan's trade, measured as the sum of imports and exports, increased from $500 million (U.S. dollars) in 1960 to $159 billion in 1993, when it ranked as the thirteenth largest trading nation in the world (table 6.1). Taiwan's remarkable trade growth has prompted interest in the design and operation of their duty refund system, and how such a system might be adapted to other economies seeking growth through export expansion.

The Duty/Tax Drawback System in Taiwan (China)

The purpose of the duty/tax drawback system is to encourage exports by lowering production costs and enhancing competitiveness in the world market. Raw materials or semifinished products are usually subject to duties and taxes upon importation. When these inputs are imported for the manufacture of products that will be exported, the duties and taxes levied on the imported inputs are returned to the producer or exporter. The system has proved particularly beneficial for exporters of labor-intensive light industry products such as small motors, electric fans, thermos bottles, toys, calculators, sewing machines, bicycles, tennis and badminton rackets, shoes, textiles, and plastics.

Table 6.1. *Trade Development of Taiwan (China)*
(thousands of U.S. dollars)

Calendar year	Exports	Imports	Balance
1961	195,158	322,116	126,958
1966	536,270	622,361	89,091
1971	2,060,393	1,843,038	216,456
1976	8,166,340	7,598,931	567,409
1981	22,611,197	21,199,551	1,411,646
1982	22,204,270	18,888,375	3,315,895
1983	25,122,747	20,287,078	4,835,669
1984	30,456,309	21,959,086	8,497,304
1985	30,725,662	20,102,049	10,623,613
1986	39,861,504	24,181,460	15,680,044
1987	53,678,748	34,983,380	18,695,368
1988	60,667,362	49,672,800	10,994,562
1989	66,303,952 ·	52,265,326	14,038,626
1990	67,214,446	54,716,004	12,498,442
1991	76,178,309	62,806,545	13,317,764
1992	81,470,250	72,006,794	9,463,456
1993	85,091,458	77,061,203	8,030,255

Source: Ministry of Finance, Monthly Statistics of Exports and Imports.

These industries benefited a great deal from the drawback system in the 1980s. Table 6.2 shows the distribution of duty refunds across industry categories.

The number of firms using the system has grown steadily, from 27,437 in 1966, to 81,685 by 1993. The number of duty refund applications processed rose from 15,554 in 1966, to a peak of 646,753 in 1987, but declined to 153,005 by 1993 (table 6.3). In 1984, processing nearly 600,000 refund applications submitted by almost 60,000 firms (more than half of all manufacturers for export) required about 230 customs employees.

The duty drawback system provided significant relief from import duties for exporters, especially during the 1970s and early 1980s. In 1971, more than 77 percent of import duties were refunded, but duty refunds declined during the late 1980s both in absolute terms and as a percentage of duties collected (table 6.3).

The legal basis for the duty drawback system resides in Article 36 of the Customs Law, which provides that the customs duty paid on imported raw

Table 6.2. *Refund Cases: Number, Amount Refunded, and Industry Distribution, 1981–93*
(refund amounts in millions of NT dollars)

Year	Applications		Textiles		Electrical equipment		Plastics		Machinery equipment		Others		Total	
	Number	Index	Refund	Percent	Refund	Percent	Refund	Percent	Refund	Percent	Refund	Percent	Refund	Percent
1981	683,527	100	4,371	18	3,895	16	4,705	19	7,553	31	3,663	16	24,192	100
1982	686,257	100	4,443	17	3,752	15	4,673	18	8,798	34	4,122	16	25,788	100
1983	745,087	109	3,724	17	2,483	11	3,765	17	7,341	33	4,666	22	21,979	100
1984	592,249	87	3,304	12	2,899	10	5,353	19	8,653	30	8,426	29	28,635	100
1985	540,411	79	2,218	9	3,012	11	4,058	15	10,026	38	7,000	27	26,314	100
1986	543,921	80	1,322	7	2,657	18	2,213	11	9,058	44	5,138	25	20,388	100
1987	646,758	95	1,081	5	3,304	16	1,589	8	9,111	44	5,622	27	20,657	100
1988	555,323	81	391	3	2,318	16	854	6	7,467	51	3,546	24	14,576	100
1989	306,696	45	135	2	1,886	26	168	2	3,218	44	1,877	26	7,284	100
1990	209,022	31	117	2	1,121	22	46	1	2,449	49	1,257	25	5,000	100
1991	173,833	25	118	8	744	18	41	1	2,320	56	941	22	4,164	100
1992	183,049	26	121	3	626	15	32	1	2,474	60	859	21	4,112	100
1993	153,005	22	90	2	490	13	17	1	2,354	63	800	21	3,751	100

Source: Department of Customs Administration, Ministry of Finance, Annual Customs Report.

Table 6.3. *Duty Drawback System in Taiwan (China): Trade Volumes, Duty Collections and Refunds, and Frequency of Use*

Year	Export value (millions of NT dollars)	Import value (millions of NT dollars)	Import duties/taxes (millions of NT dollars)	Refund amount (millions of NT dollars)	Percentage of duties refunded	Average import duty rate (percent)	Number of firms	Number of cases
1966	21,450	21,379	4,776	1,365	28.6	19.2	27,437	15,554
1971	82,415	64,035	12,036	9,356	77.7	14.2	20,247	200,589
1976	309,912	256,731	39,234	18,541	47.3	11.3	43,809	429,888
1986	1,507,044	832,412	93,340	20,388	21.8	7.7	68,265	543,921
1987	1,707,608	1,021,940	103,957	20,657	19.9	7.5	72,181	646,753
1988	1,731,804	1,282,656	133,988	14,756	12.8	6.1	74,268	555,921
1989	1,747,800	1,418,631	126,832	7,283	5.7	6.3	77,870	306,696
1990	1,802,783	1,395,244	118,622	5,000	4.2	5.9	76,945	209,022
1991	2,040,350	1,599,859	120,058	4,163	3.5	5.0	79,360	173,833
1992	2,047,962	1,725,748	144,184	4,112	2.6	5.1	79,631	183,049
1993	2,235,140	1,942,448	101,587	3,751	3.7	5.1	81,685	153,005

Sources: Ministry of Finance, Monthy Reports of Exports and Imports. Ministry of Finance, Yearbook of Tax Statistics. Department of Customs Administration, Ministry of Finance, Annual Customs Report.

materials for use in manufacturing export products may be refunded after exportation of the finished products made from the said raw materials. Article 4 stipulates that imported goods that are exported or used to make products that are later exported are also eligible for refund of commodity taxes. Specific practices, such as which department is in charge of administration, items eligible for refund, deadline for refund application, standards for refund, conditions for charging account, processing of export declaration document, are set out in Regulations Governing the Offsetting or Refund of Duties and Taxes on the Raw Materials of Export Products.

Generally, importers of raw materials or semifinished goods, or producers or exporters of the finished goods, are eligible to apply for return of duties and taxes paid when the inputs were imported. If the duties were paid in cash upon importation, they are returned in cash and called a refund. Refunds are now remitted directly to the recipient's bank account rather than paid by check. Importers of raw materials can use a system in which the duty liability is added to their account when materials are imported, and when the finished products are exported the account is credited in what is termed an offsetting transaction. This method helps alleviate the financial burden of duty payment for manufacturers when they import raw materials. This system of charges and offsetting transactions is available only when the applicant for the return of duties is the importer of the inputs and when a guarantee is provided by a financial institutional or through a self-executed affidavit by the export manufacturer.

Applicants for refund must submit a refund application form, provide a copy of the import application to show that import duty on raw materials was paid in cash or charged to their account, and submit the export application to demonstrate that the finished goods have been exported overseas or to bonded areas.

The time limit for filing an application for duty/tax refund depends upon whether the imported inputs require import licenses. For imports requiring licenses, the application for refund must be made within eighteen months from the date the imported raw materials or semifinished goods are released from Customs. Two extensions of six months each are allowed if the request is made to the Ministry of Finance in due time. For imports requiring no license, application for refund should be made within six months from the date of the release of the exported goods. If the application is not filed on time, importers are required to pay the duty plus a penalty. An application fee of 0.5 percent of the refund is charged when duty is paid, by charging the importer's account. This fee must be paid upon importation. If the account cannot be credited within the required period of time, the fee is refunded.

There are also deadlines within which applications for refunds must be processed by Customs. The export declaration document must be approved and issued to exporters within fourteen days of exportation. The refund application procedure must be completed within fifty days of filing; although, in fact, the average for refund applications is currently fifteen days.

The administrative agency in charge of policymaking for duty and tax refunds for exports is the Department of Customs Administration, Ministry of Finance; administrative responsibilities fall to the Refund Department, Taipei Customs Office.

As the system evolved, a number of changes were implemented to streamline administrative work. A minimum base threshold for refunds was adopted. The refund is not granted if the refundable amount is less than 1 percent of the free-on-board (FOB) value of exported goods. The process of examining and approving duty refund applications was centralized in one department of the Customs office and was computerized.

Duty/Tax Refund Criteria

To speed up administrative operations, standard duty rebate rates have been established by product as the basis for calculating refunds. This section describes the four different methods or criteria used to calculate duty drawback rates and how the rates are calculated under each method. The four methods are raw material duty refund criteria, fixed amount or specific duty refund criteria, fixed percentage (*ad valorem*) duty refund criteria, and special provisions for certain components.

Raw material criteria. Raw material duty refund criteria are determined by the Industrial Development Bureau of the Ministry of Economic Affairs (MOEA) based on raw materials needed for manufacture of various export products under normal conditions. A general raw material duty refund rate applies to all manufacturers or firms exporting the same kind of product.

The refund is calculated in the following way:

Total weight (quantity) of raw material used = weight (quantity) of export products x weight (quantity) raw material per unit of export.

Total weight (quantity) of raw material used x import duty/taxes paid per unit of raw material = amount of refundable duty/taxes.

A firm also can apply to the Industrial Development Bureau of MOEA for special raw material duty refund rates. MOEA must determine and publish the criteria, or notify the applicant of the reason why the criteria cannot be determined, within sixty days of receipt of the application. The application must be filed by the manufacturer when production of the product to be exported begins. The firm must submit with the application a list of raw materials used in the finished product, relevant export documents, and raw material consumption data. During the investigation the firm must submit daily reports, monthly reports, warehouse in-and-out records, and other relevant information. The proposed criteria for refund of duty/taxes on raw materials will not be approved if there is no way to investigate and approve the quantity of the raw materials used because the exportation of the products has taken place before the filing of the application; if the raw material used is minimal or of insignificant value; if the price of raw material used is higher than the price of the finished product; if the consumption rate of the raw material used is unreasonable; or, if manufacture of the export product at issue is not included in the scope of business as indicated in the "Profit-seeking Enterprise Registration Certificate" of the applicant.

Fixed amount (specific duty) criteria. The fixed amount refund system provides for a predetermined refund per unit of the product exported, either by weight or by quantity. The fixed amount (specific duty) duty and tax refund rules are established by the Ministry of Finance, consistent with the standards for refunding the cost of materials as promulgated by MOEA. This system applies primarily to export products such as hardware, steel, iron, rubber, chemical engineering products, canned food, wood products, leather and fur products, shoes, paper products, stationery, glass products, and transportation equipment that incorporate a small number of raw materials and are made using simple manufacturing processes. Examples can be found in table 6.4. These specific refund rates are based on export quantity and so will not automatically adjust as prices of finished products change.

Fixed percentage (ad valorem duty) criteria. The fixed percentage (ad valorem duty) duty/tax refund criteria also are established by the Ministry of Finance. The fixed percentage duty refund system is based on a table of percentage refund rates that are applied to the FOB value of export shipments. The table of percentage rates is based on information on average refunds relative to value of exports in a base period for each product category.

Compared with the specific or fixed amount criteria, the fixed percentage refund system applies primarily to export products that incorporate a greater variety of inputs and use more complicated manufacturing processes, such as televisions, refrigerators, air conditioners, telephones, bicycles, lathes, tennis rackets, umbrellas, and shoes. Examples can be found in table 6.5. Because it is based on *ad valorem* percentages, the rebate amount depends on the export price of the finished product, so the refund will vary proportionately with any change in export (FOB) price.

Table 6.4. *Examples of Fixed Amount Duty Refund Rates*

Product number	Export product			Name and specification of raw material(s) to be used (basic export price)	Import duty refund rate
	Name	Specification	Unit of quantity		
9601 99 90 04	Toothbrush	Standard	1 kg	Nylon filament	101.00
				Cellulose acetate plastic	18.00
7313 05 01 01	Galvanized steel sheet	BWG 35–43 (0.156–0.169m/m)	1 ton	Cold-reduced steel sheet	1,814.00
				Zinc ingot	369.00
7313 05 01 02	Galvanized steel sheet	BWG 30–34 (0.17–0.305m/m)	1 ton	Cold-reduced steel sheet	1,849.00
				Zinc ingot	295.00
7313 05 01 03	Galvanized steel sheet	BWG 26–29 (0.33–0.457m/m)	1 ton	Cold-reduced steel sheet	1,845.00
				Zinc ingot	224.00

Source: Department of Customs Administration, Ministry of finance.

Table 6.5. *Examples of Fixed Percentage Duty Refund Rates*

Tariff number	Product number			Export product			Basic export price		Import duty refund rate
	Class	Item	Subitem	Name	Specification	Unit of quantity	Specification	FOB price (yen)	
9211	02	90	01	Cassette memory	Standard	FOB 100		1,300	6.53
9211	99	00	02	Stereo cassette recorder	Standard	FOB 100		2,400	12.10
9211	99	00	03	Double cassette stereo	Standard	FOB 100		2,800	14.50
8710	01	01	01	12"–28" bicycle	Standard	FOB 100	12"–16" 16"–20" (16")	1,100 1,400	3.22

Source: Department of Customs Administration, Ministry of Finance.

198

The advantage of the fixed amount and fixed percentage refund system lies in the simplification of calculations of duty refunds both for the refund authorities and for manufacturers who can easily calculate duty refunds when quoting prices to prospective customers. The system also simplifies administrative operations and expedites duty/tax refund procedures.

Special provisions. If imported components are directly incorporated into an export product, and there is therefore no need to calculate any wastage or attrition of inputs in the production process, the duty/tax refund may be based on the quantity of imported inputs used in an export shipment.

Order of precedence. When fixed amount or fixed percentage duty/tax refund criteria have already been established, these criteria are the preferred method of calculating the refund. If not, the relevant raw material refund criteria are applied. If the refund criteria are amended or rescinded, the date of exportation of the products involved is taken as the reference date to determine the applicability of the new criteria or the old criteria. Application for refund should be filed on a "first import, first refund" basis. Manufacturers may adjust the sequence of their applications, but they are then responsible for any failure to get the duty/tax offset or refunded.

Comparison between the Systems in Taiwan (China) and Costa Rica

In Costa Rica, a system of export contracts is the government's principal instrument for promoting exports to extraregional markets. To qualify for an export contract a firm must make a commitment to export a given percentage of its output to extraregional markets. In return the firm is eligible for exemption (in proportion to its extraregional exports) from import duties on raw materials, components, capital goods, consumption and sales taxes, and profit taxes. Qualifying firms are also exempt from taxes on exports to extraregional markets. Extraregional exports with more than 35 percent national content qualify for direct subsidies in the form of tax rebate certificates (*certificados de abono tributario* or CATs). These can be used at face value (after a delay of about a year) to pay tax liabilities, or can be sold in a secondary market, normally at a discount.

The export contract system implemented in Costa Rica reduces firms' production costs and enhances international market competitiveness. Manufacturers of export products are exempted from import duties on the raw materials and manufacturing machinery and equipment they import. Payment of import duties is not required upon importation of raw materials and machinery and equipment, but instead is paid pro rata if any of the products manufactured using the imported raw materials or machinery and equipment are sold on the domestic market.

The system, however, has several disadvantages. Implementation of the system puts an enormous burden on the national budget, causing financial difficulties that could affect economic stability and growth. Allocating CAT export duty credit coupons to export manufacturers constitutes a governmental subsidy contrary to international regulations and therefore may provoke international retaliation. From an administrative standpoint, case-by-case examination and approval of duty exemption applications under the export contract system involves complicated and administratively costly operational procedures in various government agencies, including the Center for the Promotion of Exports and Investments (CENPRO), the Ministry of Finance, and customs offices. Moreover, it is difficult for the government to enforce proper control over the use of imported duty-free raw materials because it is hard to investigate whether the products made of such raw materials are exported or not.

Since implementation of the export contract system in 1984, Costa Rica has laid an appropriate foundation of operational organization and procedures and has gained experience in cooperation among the Ministry of Finance, customs authorities, the central bank, and CENPRO. A critical factor for implementing a duty drawback system is effective cooperation among the authorities in charge of financial, trading, monetary, and foreign exchange affairs. Implementing a duty drawback system should be feasible provided that a computerized management and operation system can be established and close coordination with manufacturers can be maintained.

A major difference between the export contract system and a duty drawback system is that manufacturers under the export contract system are exempted from paying import duties, whereas under the duty drawback system they must first make full payment of the import duties and are entitled to apply for refund after exportation of their products. Import duties on machinery and equipment are also not refundable in the duty-drawback system. Manufacturers will have a heavier financial burden because they have to raise sufficient capital to pay import duties upon importation of raw materials. Therefore, the most important issue to be resolved is how to lighten the financial burden of manufacturers and expedite duty-refunding operations.

Under the export contract system, the import application examination and approval process is completed before the follow-up control of imported raw materials. The government and manufacturers both will incur considerable management costs in maintaining good control of imported raw materials, resulting in a waste of manpower and material resources. Under the export products duty drawback system, the operational procedures are simpler, management costs are lower, and undesirable effects are fewer.

A duty drawback system of the type currently being implemented in Taiwan (China) is quite suitable to satisfy the actual requirement of Costa Rica. The duty drawback system does not conflict with the internationally applicable regulations established by the General Agreement on Tariffs and Trade (GATT), will not give rise to international retaliation, and will maintain the competitive power of export products by providing an export incentive in terms of drawback of indirect tax. Table 6.6 compares the major features of the export contract system with the duty drawback system of Taiwan (China). Because of the practical experience gained and the operating structure founded through years of implementation of the export contract system, Costa Rica would not in principle have significant difficulties adopting an export products duty drawback system provided that the policy is fully supported by all sectors concerned. Costa Rica will set an example for Central American countries if it is the first to adopt this system.

To substitute the export products duty drawback system for the export contract system, new laws governing enforcement of the new system must first be enacted. It is important to make preimplementation preparations by setting up the mechanisms for proper communication and coordination between the government and manufacturers, as well as for training of operational personnel involved. An "Export Products Duty Drawback Commission" could be formed jointly by various ministries and commissions concerned, to take charge of necessary training. In the technical aspect of operation, Ministry of Finance, customs authorities, and CENPRO should improve their respective administration efficiency by establishing computerized operation and management systems so as to speed up the duty-refunding operation.

Conversion to a Duty Drawback System

The export contract system could be replaced by a duty drawback system similar to that used in Taiwan (China). Successful implementation of a duty drawback system would require a highly effective administrative management mechanism based on close cooperation and coordination among financial, trade, banking and foreign exchange agencies, and customs offices, and on the completion of computerized operations. In addition, manufacturers and firms applying for duty drawback must be given necessary assistance, guidance, and training in the operation of duty drawback procedures so as to expedite the process of duty drawback application cases.

CENPRO could be the primary executing authority, working in association with the Ministry of Finance, customs offices, and financial institutions. The flow chart in figure 6.1 indicates the agencies that could be responsible for the various stages of the procedures.

Table 6.6. *Comparison between the Export Contract System in Costa Rica and the Export Products Duty Drawback System in Taiwan (China)*

Item	Export contract system in Costa Rica	Export products duty drawback system in Taiwan (China)	Remarks
Applicable stage of economic development.	Suitable to an industrial structure that performs simple processing/assembling of export products.	Suitable to an industrial structure processing export products.	1. High duty rates. 2. Export of products are encouraged by means of import duty exemption or export products duty drawback.
Comparison of system functions.	1. Import duty exemption may be applied for only by manufacturers producing export products. Numerous restrictions result in great manpower and material costs. 2. Import duty must be paid on raw materials used in products for domestic sales. Tax evasion is easier.	1. Duty drawback system is simpler than the export contract system. Importers/exporters and manufacturers will have the discretion to apply for duty drawback in a rapid and direct manner. 2. Follow-up tracking and control of the use of imported raw materials is no longer necessary. Tax evasion is difficult.	
Comparison of financial burden of manufacturers.	Exemption of import duties on raw materials and machinery and equipment will relieve the financial burden of paying import duties.	Manufacturers must pay import duties on imported raw materials and machinery and equipment therefore will have a heavier financial burden.	
Compliance with international regulations (against government subsidy).	CAT subsidy provided under this system conflicts with international regulations and therefore is subject to retaliatory measures.	This system conforms to the international regulations and therefore will not cause retaliatory measures.	

(table continues on following page)

(Table 6.6 continued)

Item	Export contract system in Costa Rica	Export products duty drawback system in Taiwan (China)	Remarks
Comparison of the government financial burden.	Exemption of import duty plus the CAT export subsidy creates a financial burden on the national budget.	Manufacturers must pay import duty leviable on imported raw materials before they are eligible for applying for duty drawback; therefore, it will help to reduce government financial burden.	In Taiwan (China), imported machinery and equipment that are "not manufactured by local manufacturers" are exempted from import duties.
Scope of duty exemption (or duty drawback).	Raw materials, machinery, and equipment.	Raw materials.	
Items of taxes to be exempted (or to be refunded).	Customs duties/business tax/special commodity tax/1 percent.	Customs duties/commodity tax.	
Is payment of duties and taxes required at the time of customs clearance of imported goods?	No payment of duties/taxes is required at the time of customs clearance of imported goods.	Duties/taxes must be paid at the time of customs clearance of imported goods.	
Manufacturers/ firms eligible for exemption of duties/taxes (or for duty drawback).	Manufacturers importing raw materials.	Importers/processing manufacturers/exporters.	

(table continues on following page)

(*Table 6.6 continued*)

	Export contract system in Costa Rica	*Export products duty drawback system in Taiwan (China)*	*Remarks*
Duration for exemption of duties and taxes.	No limitation	One year and six months	
Payments of duties/ taxes on products for domestic sale.	Duties/taxes leviable on the raw materials used in the products for domestic sale must be paid.	No additional payment of duty/tax is required on raw materials used in the products for domestic sale since duty/ tax has been paid at the time of importation.	
Benefited manufacturers.	1,596 manufacturers.	80,000 manufacturers and firms.	
Executive authority.	CENPRO.	Customs (centralized into one unit).	In Taiwan (China), duty drawback application and refunding operations are centralized into one unit.
Manpower used in duty exemption (or duty drawback) operation.	Technical department of CENPRO/18 persons.	The unit handling duty drawback cases/200 persons.	

Figure 6.1. *Suggested Flow Chart of Duty Drawback Operations*

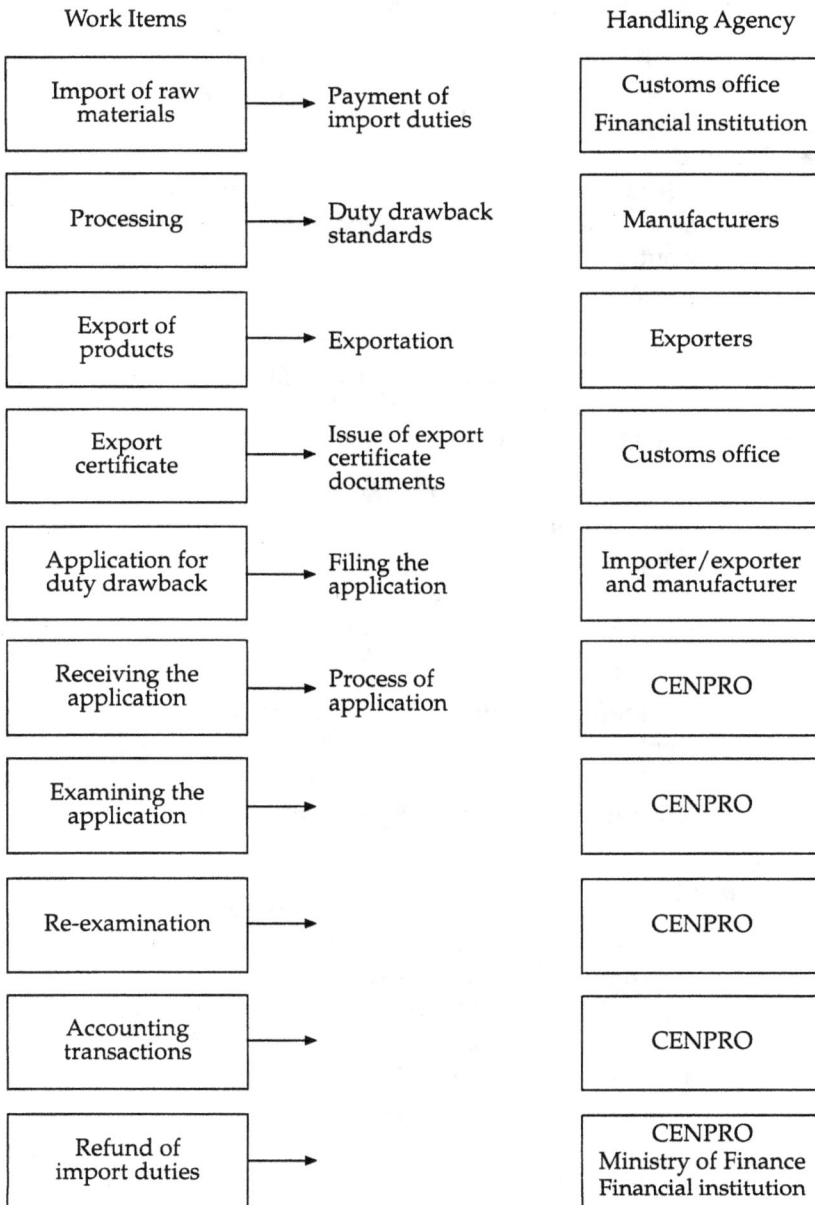

Work Items		Handling Agency
Import of raw materials	→ Payment of import duties	Customs office Financial institution
Processing	→ Duty drawback standards	Manufacturers
Export of products	→ Exportation	Exporters
Export certificate	→ Issue of export certificate documents	Customs office
Application for duty drawback	→ Filing the application	Importer/exporter and manufacturer
Receiving the application	→ Process of application	CENPRO
Examining the application	→	CENPRO
Re-examination	→	CENPRO
Accounting transactions	→	CENPRO
Refund of import duties	→	CENPRO Ministry of Finance Financial institution

Application Procedures

Firms would have to submit the following documents:

- Application for offsetting or drawback of import duties on raw materials for export products (in preestablished form).
- Import declaration (copy).
- Export declaration (original).
- Consent form of other firm involved if product was produced in stages by different firms, where the final exporter is not the direct importer of the inputs.
- Other relevant documents.

Application for duty offsetting or drawback must be filed within eighteen months from the date of customs release of imported raw materials. An application filed beyond that period would be rejected.

CENPRO would be responsible for the following:

- Examining and approving duty drawback applications.
- Processing relevant accounting transactions.
- Establishing raw materials duty refund coefficients and the rates of fixed amount/fixed percentage duty refund.
- Completing necessary computerized operation systems.

The Ministry of Finance would be responsible for appropriating the approved amount of refundable duties. Customs offices would be responsible for customs clearance of imported and exported goods and issuance of customs certificates. Banking institutions would be responsible for guaranteeing activities, accounting transfers, and payment of refundable duties.

Coverage and Timing

Application for duty drawback may be filed for products processed or manufactured for export. Importers, exporters, or processing and manufacturing factories may apply. The duty refund process should be completed within thirty days from the filing date of the application. If the duty refund process cannot be completed within the foregoing period, the duty will be refunded together with interest accrued for the delayed period.

Benefits

From the point of view of government, management control under the duty drawback system is easier than under the export contract system. Follow-up control by government after import of raw materials can be omitted and tax evasion avoided. Computerized operation and management of a duty drawback system would contribute to the reform of the entire national administrative system and improve administrative efficiency, and therefore expedite further development of foreign trade activities.

From the point of view of the private sector, a duty drawback system would be simpler than the export contract system. Manufacturers and firms would have greater flexibility. Furthermore, the duty drawback operation is more direct and faster. In a duty drawback system, importers, exporters, and processing and manufacturing factories would all be eligible to apply for duty drawback. Indirect exporters that supply raw materials would also be entitled to indirect duty drawback. Therefore, this system provides more tax benefits to manufacturers and firms than the export contract system. Manufacturers would be able to reduce significantly their operation and management expenses and lessen their production cost burden. This cost reduction would enhance competitiveness of export products without encountering international retaliation, because the duty drawback system would conform to GATT and World Trade Organization (WTO) regulations.

Tax Deferment

Under a drawback system, with payment of duty upon importation of inputs and drawback of duty after export, manufacturers will face a heavier financial burden. This financial burden could be reduced by adopting an import duty deferment system that provides manufacturers with a three- to six-month grace period for payment of import duties on imported raw materials. To protect national tax revenue and simplify customs operations, a manufacturer would be required to first obtain a bank guarantee for the promissory note issued by it to the customs office for payment of import duty. Upon maturity of the promissory note, the customs office would transfer the promissory note into the exchequer's account. If the promissory note is not cashable, the guaranteeing financial institution would be liable for payment of the import duty due.

Implementation of a duty deferment system would require the policy support of the Ministry of Finance because it involves issues of revenue and expenditures. To implement such a system, financial institutions must establish effective guarantee operation procedures. Establishing a computerized operation system would simplify operation procedures and convenience of administration.

Import Duty Credit

A second way to relieve the financial burden on firms of payment of import duties would be to adopt an import duty credit system to allow raw materials importers to credit import duties against the guarantee provided by financial institutions for payment of the import duties upon exportation of the finished goods. Manufacturers would obtain a guarantee from a financial institution before applying for import duty credit. Import duty credit guarantee would be provided only by the banks approved by the Ministry of Finance. Outstanding import duties not yet offset upon expiration of the time limit for applying for drawback would be paid by the importing firm. If an importer fails to pay the outstanding import duty, the guaranteeing financial institution would be liable for the payment.

Bank Transfer System

To relieve the cost burden on manufacturers, import duties must be refunded to manufacturers in a rapid and direct manner. The most effective, safe, and prompt method of refunding import duties, once the amount is decided by the duty-refunding authority, is to deposit the refunds into the bank accounts of manufacturers by bank transfers. The Ministry of Finance would have to provide support to the implementation of a bank transfer system and designate the banks responsible for handling such transactions. Manufacturers would have to open their respective deposit accounts with the designated banks to transfer the refunded import duty into their accounts.

Bonded Factory Control System

Under a bonded factory control system, manufacturers that meet certain conditions and export a substantial proportion of their products may be registered as bonded factories with the approval of customs authorities. Raw materials and semifinished products used by bonded factories to manufacture export products are exempted from import duties. Manufacturers are given flexibility to select locations for bonded factories.

Under such a system, imported raw materials are exempted from import duties and import duty drawback is not necessary. Bonded factories must maintain a sound accounting and bookkeeping system and they are subject to nonperiodic inspection and constant monitoring by customs authorities. The bonded factory control system and the export products duty drawback system are both intended to encourage export activities; these two systems are complementary to each other and can be implemented in parallel.

The bonded factory control system used in Taiwan (China) allows any export-oriented factory with capital stock of more than NT$20 million, verified by the customs authority, to register as a bonded factory. Up to 50 percent of the products manufactured by a bonded factory may be sold on the domestic market, provided that supplementary payment of the import duties leviable on the raw materials used in the products for domestic sale are made by the bonded factory. A bonded factory controls and accounts for its own operations but is subject to nonperiodic inspections conducted by customs authorities.

Planning and Establishing Criteria

Planning and establishing duty drawback criteria are very important in the implementation of a duty drawback system similar to that used in Taiwan (China). It involves technical considerations, and requires personnel with professional know-how in various scientific fields such as textiles, plastics, chemicals, mechanical, and electrical industries to examine production processes, determine the raw material duty drawback standards, and establish the quantity or ratio of raw materials (consumption rate) eligible for duty drawback.

An ad hoc team could be formed to establish fixed amount and fixed percentage duty drawback rates. These rates have the following advantages:

- Convenience in calculation: manufacturers and customs authorities can easily calculate the amount of refundable import duties based on the duty drawback rates.
- Manufacturers have better control of costs because they can calculate in advance the amount of refundable import duty.
- Both the duty-assessing authorities and the duty payers will benefit from simplified operational procedures and a shorter examination process.

Computerized Operations

A computerized operation system would keep track of raw material import duty payment data, control the amount of refundable import duties, simplify examination procedures, establish a supplementary duty collection function for upgrading administrative efficiency, and establish a duty drawback file to provide data for analysis in policymaking.

Implementing Conversion

To perfect the system, in the initial stage of implementation a pilot project could be launched for selected industries, and either the fixed amount or the fixed percentage method could be adopted to simplify the duty refund procedures. To promote a smooth and steady conversion from the old system to the new system, the law could entitle the authority concerned to select industries (or export products) for a pilot implementation of the new system pending development of a system for general implementation. To simplify the duty drawback operation procedures, save manpower, and accelerate the duty-refunding process, it would be advisable to make a study for adoption of either the fixed amount (specific duty) or fixed percentage (*ad valorem*) duty drawback method.

An interministerial "Export Products Duty Drawback Commission" could be organized to take charge of the planning and management of matters relating to development and implementation of the duty drawback system. Planning and execution of a duty drawback system involves a number of government agencies, including Ministry of Finance, Ministry of Foreign Trade, and MOEA, and also involves the enactment and revision of relevant laws and regulations. It has a great impact on the rights and interests of export-oriented manufacturers. An interministerial organization would enhance communication and coordination among all agencies concerned and take charge of the planning and management of matters relating to proper implementation of the new system. This commission would review and decide issues involving major policies. The agencies in charge of duty drawback operations may be authorized to handle the relevant administrative and staff activities.

7

Safeguard Mechanisms: Their Design and Operation

J. Michael Finger
with the assistance of Rebecca Hardy

All dogs have fleas; therefore, all dogs have legs with which to scratch. Likewise, any government that maintains a liberal trade policy must have ways to deal with constituent pressures for exceptions—pressures for "exceptional protection" of particular domestic sectors.

To create a safeguard mechanism is, however, to play with fire. From the perspective of import-competing industries, a safeguard mechanism will be a "trade remedy" process, an instrument that is there, from import-competing industries' perspective, to provide "import relief" for domestic industries beset by import competition.

Of course, if the government is to maintain a generally open or liberal trade policy, the safeguard system cannot be calibrated to relieve every instance of import competition. It must be calibrated so that protectionist actions will be the exception, not the rule. The trick then with a safeguard mechanism is to create a device through which the government can placate protectionist interests without allowing protectionist interests to dominate the trade policy process.

The objective of this paper is to distill practical guidelines from past experience on the economic dimensions of safeguards, as well as their political and administrative dimensions. The following section reviews the various safeguard processes sanctioned by the General Agreement on Tariffs and Trade (GATT), and examines the history of their usage for lessons. The next section reviews the treatment of safeguards in analyses conducted under the auspices of the Trade Expansion Program (TEP), and draws from these experiences lessons that relate directly to developing country experiences.

Safeguards in GATT

GATT is one of the key instruments with which the international community has created and maintained an open international trading system, yet it provides many avenues for imposing new trade restrictions. Table 7.1 lists these GATT "exceptions" and tabulates the frequency of their use. In

Table 7.1. Frequency of Use of GATT Provisions that Allow Trade Restrictions

Instrument	Frequency of use
1. *Provisions for renegotiating previous concessions and commitments*	
• Periodic (three-year) renegotiations (at the initiative of the country wanting to increase a bound rate), Article XXVII.1 and Article XXVIII.5.	January 1955–March 1994: 206 renegotiation procedures, 128 of these under Article XXVIII.5.[a]
• Special circumstance renegotiations (requires GATT authorization), Article XXVIII.4.	Sixty-four renegotiations since 1948.[b]
• Increase of a duty with regard to formation of a customs union, Article XXIV.6.	Follows procedures of Article XXVIII, hence included in totals.
• Withdrawal of a concession in order to provide infant industry protection, Article XVIII.A.	Nine withdrawals through March 1994.[c]
2. *Restrictions that require specific GATT approval*	
• Waivers, Article XXV.	Through March 1994, 113 waivers granted, 44 still in force.[d]
• Retaliation authorized under dispute settlement, Article XXIII.	Once.[e]
• Exceptions specified in accession agreement, Article XXXIII.	Not tabulated.[f]
• Releases from bindings to pursue infant industry protection, Article XVIII.C.	Nine countries in 47 years.[g]
• Releases from bindings by a "more developed" country to pursue infant industry protection, Article XVIII.D.	Never.[h]
3. *Restrictions that can be imposed unilaterally*	
• General Exceptions, Article XX Article XX allows trade restrictions: to protect public morals; to protect human, animal or plant life, or health; on the importation or exportation of gold or silver; to secure compliance with other regulations; on the products of prison labor; to protect items of historic, artistic, or archeological value; to conserve exhaustible natural resources;	Notification not required. Between 1974 and 1987, six developing countries notified quantitative restrictions under Article XX, covering 131 products.[i]

(table continues on following page)

212

(Table 7.1 continued)

Instrument	Frequency of use
to comply with an intergovernmental commodity agreement; to manage items in short supply [also covered by Article XI.2(a)].	Notification not required. Between 1974 and 1987, eight developing countries notified quantitative restrictions under Article XI.[j]
• Restrictions to apply standards, to classify, Article XI.2.b.	Notification not required. No information available.
• Restrictions on agricultural or fisheries products, Article XI.2.c.	One developing country, Thailand, notified under Article XXI between 1974 and 1987. Further information not available.[k]
• National security exception, Article XXI.	
• Withdrawal of a concession initially negotiated with a government that fails to join GATT, or withdraws, Article XXVII.	As of 1994, Article XXVII has been used by 15 countries with regard to: (a) withdrawals by China, Syria, Lebanon, and Liberia; (b) Colombia, who participated in the Annecy Round (1949) but did not accede then; and (c) the Republic of Korea and the Philippines, who participated in the Torquay Round (1951) but did not accede then.[l]
• Nonapplication at the time of accession, Article XXXV.	As of 1994, this article had been invoked (a) against Japan by 53 countries, invocations since withdrawn by 50; (b) by 16 other countries against 21 countries. Only 10 Article XXXV invocations are presently operative.[m]
• Restrictions to safeguard the balance of payments, general; Article VII.	Three countries had such restrictions in place at least one time during the period 1974–86.[n]
• Restrictions to safeguard the balance of payments, developing countries; Article XVIII:B.	Twenty-four countries had such restrictions in place at least one time during the period 1974–86.[o]
• Emergency actions, Article XIX.	1950–84: 124 actions (3.6 a year). 1985–94: 26 actions (3.25 a year).[p]
• Countervailing duties, Article VI.	July 1985–June 1992: 187 investigations (27 per year): 106 by the United States, 38 by Australia.[q]
• Antidumping duties, Article VI.	July 1985–June 1992: 1,148 investigations (164 per year): 300 by the United States, 282 by Australia, 242 by the European Union, 124 by Canada, 84 by Mexico.[r]

(table continues on following page)

(Table 7.1 continued)

a. GATT 1994a, pp. 892–910.
b. GATT 1994a, pp. 892–910.
c. GATT 1994a, p. 465. These were made by Benelux on behalf of Suriname (1958), Greece (1956, 65), Indonesia (1983), Korea (1958), and Sri Lanka (1955 [2], 56, 57).
d. GATT 1994a, pp. 828–839.
e. GATT 1994a, p. 630.
f. GATT 1994a, p. 948, lists five countries whose protocols of accession included provisions allowing specific measures which were otherwise GATT-illegal to remain in place for a limited time.
g. Anjaria 1987, p. 670. These countries are Côte d'Ivoire, Indonesia, Malaysia, Thailand, Zimbabwe, Cuba, Haiti, India, and Sri Lanka.
h. GATT 1994a, p. 465.
i. OECD, 1992, p. 100. Information relating to Articles XX, XI, and XXI is generally not available, since notification is not required. The OECD source cited provides information on developing-country notification of these articles for the period noted.
j. OECD, 1992, p. 100.
k. OECD, 1992, p. 100.
l. GATT 1994a, pp. 861–62.
m. GATT 1994a, pp. 958–960.
n. Anjaria 1987, p. 675.
o. Anjaria 1987, p. 675.
p. GATT 1994a, pp. 500–516.
q. GATT various years.
r. GATT 1993, Appendix Table 1.

the remainder of this section I will list and explain several lessons that can be drawn from this GATT experience.

GATT Exceptions

Lesson: GATT's exceptions do not make economic sense. The origin of these exceptions suggests no reason to expect that they would make economic, as opposed to political, sense.

Origins. GATT's provisions for restrictions were not developed as guidelines for economic policy, to isolate circumstances in which an import restriction would serve the national economic interest of the country that imposed it. Including such provisions was part of the price the governments that created GATT had to pay their internal protectionist interests to prevent them from blocking the liberalization program that GATT included, hence they mark the free traders' losses, not their victories, in the GATT negotiations. Beyond the provisions for restrictions explicit in GATT, the agreement came into effect through a "protocol of provisional application" that "grandfathered" all national trade law that might otherwise have been inconsistent with its constraints. These parts of the GATT authorize as GATT-legal national actions that are, as economics, ordinary protection.

Economics. In table 7.1, I have sorted into three categories GATT's provisions for imposing restrictions: (a) provisions for renegotiating previous concessions, (b) restrictions that require specific GATT approval, and (c) provisions that allow unilateral action.

Renegotiations. In the first category, GATT provides an explicit framework for changing the concessions made at the more familiar rounds of negotiations of concessions. At regular intervals, a contracting party may withdraw previous tariff concessions. If the contracting parties who "own" these concessions do not agree to the withdrawal and are not bought off by compensating concessions, they may make reciprocal withdrawals (in other words, retaliate) so as to maintain a balance of concessions.[1]

The only constraint on such withdrawals is the risk of retaliation by exporting countries. There is no "conditionality" that would limit the right to withdraw a concession to those instances in which doing so would advance the country's national economic interest.

---

1. From January 1967 through March 1994 there were 151 such withdrawals (renegotiations). Australia, New Zealand, South Africa, and the European Union have been the most frequent users of these provisions.

Waivers. Through GATT's waiver provision, Article XXV, the Contracting Parties[2] can, by two thirds majority vote, allow an individual country to take action that would otherwise be in violation.[3] Through February 1994, 113 such "waivers" had been granted, and 44 of these remained in effect (Davey 1994). Perhaps the example most often noted is the waiver the Contracting Parties granted in 1955 for U.S. import quotas on agricultural goods. This waiver included no time limit, and one could argue that GATT's lack of discipline concerning agricultural policies generally derives from it. A number of waivers have been granted for what one might describe as minor matters and for a limited period of time, for example, to allow a country to impose special tariff surcharges because of balance of payments difficulties (Jackson 1969).

The third category in table 7.1 comprises provisions that allow unilateral action to restrict trade: the action does not require consent of Contracting Parties, nor even of exporting countries. GATT discipline concerning such restrictions is imposed by the conditions GATT specifies that must apply before such a restriction may be applied.[4]

Perhaps the most open group of such exceptions are those listed in Article XX, titled "General Exceptions," and Article XXI, providing for national security exceptions. Generally speaking, these exceptions allow import restrictions for "noneconomic" reasons, as listed in the top half of the third section of table 7.1.

The remainder of the list of exceptions is as follows: restrictions to safeguard the balance of payments, emergency actions under Article XIX, antidumping duties, and countervailing duties. These cannot be excused as "noneconomic" reasons for import restrictions; rather, they are bad economic reasons. Although their conditionality is economic, the conditions in which such restrictions may be imposed are not those in which an import restriction advances the national economic interest of the country that imposes it.

When GATT was first agreed, the provisions allowing trade restrictions to protect the balance of payments were included primarily to cover World War II restrictions still in place in Europe. In 1955, Article XVIII, dealing with governmental assistance to economic development, was amended to include a balance of payments provision specifically for developing countries.

---

2. All references to *Articles* in this chapter are to GATT Articles.

3. As specified in Article XXV, whenever reference is made in the Agreement to the contracting parties acting jointly, they are designated as the Contracting Parties.

4. Action under Article XIX is also constrained by the possibility that the Contracting Parties will authorize retaliation by exporting countries, and action under Article XVIII:B is constrained by the requirement that countries having such measures in place must consult periodically with the Contracting Parties.

By the mid-1960s, most of the European balance of payments restrictions had been negotiated away, but Article XVIII:B, allowing developing countries to impose import restrictions for balance of payments purposes, was increasingly used and defended. According to the then-reigning import substitution view of trade policy for development, developing countries' commodity earnings would inexorably decline and development (synonymous with industrialization) would require vast imports of capital goods. Thus developing countries would have an unyielding tendency towards balance of payments problems, and trade measures would be needed to deal with them. But the Asian model of export-led development, in which realistic exchange rates has been an important element, has discredited this rationale for import restrictions.

Injury-based import relief. The economics of antidumping, countervailing duties, and emergency actions under Article XIX is the economics of "injury" to domestic producers of import-competing goods. The first sentence of Article XIX states:

> If, as a result of unforeseen developments and of the effect of the obligations incurred…under this Agreement, including tariff concessions, any product is being imported…as to cause or threaten serious injury to domestic producers…of like or directly competitive products…the contracting party shall be free…to suspend the obligation…or to withdraw or modify the concession.

In short, if imports displace domestic production, imports may be restricted. Article XIX takes into account only the benefits of import restrictions to import-competing interests. It does not take into account the costs to *users* of imports. Hence, Article XIX does not identify the circumstances in which the national economic interest will be advanced by an import restriction.

GATT allows antidumping duties only when there is both dumping and injury. But dumping, defined in GATT as charging a lower price on exports than on domestic sales, makes no more economic sense than injury.[5] Dumping and injury do not—individually or together—provide a sound basis for determining when it is and when it is not in the national economic interest to restrict imports.

A similar point can be made for countervailing duties. The gains from trade depend on foreign prices being different from domestic costs. It does

---

5. Advocates of antidumping action sometimes suggest that antidumping is an extension of competition law, a way to deal with predatory pricing that takes place across national borders. The parallel, however, is entirely inappropriate. The definitions of dumping and of predatory pricing do not overlap. The standards of evidence and proof needed to justify antidumping action are not those that competition law requires. See Finger (1993a, chapter 2) for elaboration.

not matter if those foreign prices are not equal to foreign costs. The simple economics of "if you can buy it for less than you can build it, then you are better off to buy it" makes sense for a country as for an individual. Hence, the presence of a foreign subsidy does not identify the circumstances in which the imposition of an import restriction will advance the national economic interest.

Protection Instruments

Lesson: Protection instruments are fungible. GATT provides a long list of special purpose instruments: emergency actions, actions to offset dumping, and restrictions to safeguard the balance of payments or to secure compliance with other regulations, and so on. But protection protects, whatever it is labeled. No matter how closely drawn the rules for determining when a particular instrument may be used, interests seeking protection will fit their needs to its standards and, when the mechanism is amended, fit its standards to their needs.

Article XIX actions and renegotiations. Experience has shown that which instrument will be used is a matter of administrative or political convenience. The constraint on use of Article XIX emergency measures and on renegotiation of previous concessions is the same: threat of retaliation if exporting countries are not adequately compensated. Nine of the fifteen pre-1962 Article XIX actions recorded by GATT that were large enough that the exporter insisted on compensation or threatened retaliation were resolved as Article XXVIII renegotiations. Article XXVIII renegotiations, in turn, were often folded into regular tariff negotiations. From 1947 through 1961, five negotiating rounds were completed, and through the last of these, the Dillon Round of 1960–61, the format of a "regular" GATT tariff round and of a renegotiation were virtually the same. Each importer negotiated bilaterally with the "principal suppliers" of each product it imported, in other words, with the same suppliers that would be involved in a renegotiation.

Restrictions to safeguard the balance of payments. Another example of the fungibility of instruments is the concentration of developing countries' notifications on Article XVIII:B. An Organisation for Economic Co-operation and Development (OECD) tabulation found greater than 3,000 developing-country restrictions notified under Article XVIII:B (restrictions to safeguard the balance of payments), but fewer than 100 notified under other parts of Article XVIII that provide for restrictions for industrial development or infant industry protection (OECD 1992). If the restrictions declared under Article

XVIII:B were truly to safeguard the balance of payments, they would cover all import categories. In fact, in almost three-fourths of the countries, they covered less than half of the categories.[6]

Antidumping. Among industrial countries, antidumping has become the all-purpose form of import restriction. The conditions that can be legally labeled "dumping" have been expanded in national regulations (and this expansion sanctioned by GATT) until any incident of troublesome imports can be taken up as dumping. The only effective restraint on antidumping action is the parallel necessity to demonstrate injury to domestic producers. When a U.S. antidumping investigation ends with a nonrestrictive outcome—which is the outcome about one-third of the time—it is almost always because the injury test was negative. During 1990–94, the U.S. government found "no dumping" in less than 2 percent of its investigations.[7]

Conditionality and Reciprocity

Lesson: Conditionality does not discipline, but reciprocity does. GATT history provides many examples of this point, two of which will be discussed below.

Article XIX emergency actions, according to GATT, are disciplined both by specification of conditions that must exist (unforeseen developments and injury) and by the necessity to provide compensation. The intent of conditioning import relief on "unforeseen developments" is obvious: without this qualification relief would be available each time a liberalization had its probable effect (to increase imports) and the emergency action provision would provide for the undoing of all the liberalization negotiated. But in the hatters' fur case of 1950, a GATT working party interpreted "unforeseen developments" in a way that eliminated it as a constraint on emergency actions, As Gary Sampson concludes:

> What this [interpretation] meant in practical terms was that any increase in imports, even if through normal changes in international competitiveness, could therefore be considered actionable under Article XIX (Sampson 1987, p. 143).

Near the same time, another working party concluded that a determination of serious injury from imports did not require even that imports be *increasing* before injury could be determined, leaving specification of the

---

6. Anjaria 1987.
7. Dates are from U.S. International Trade Commission 1990, 1991, 1992, 1993, and 1994. The United States is the only country that publishes separately the outcome of the dumping and of the injury determination in an antidumping case.

conditions in which trade restriction action can be taken with an insignificant constraint on such actions (Sampson 1987).

While Article XIX's specification of "conditionality" did not restrain its use, discipline was provided by another dimension: reciprocity, or the maintenance of the balance of concessions (for example, tariff cuts) that contracting parties had negotiated. The government taking emergency action must compensate exporting countries or, if adequate compensation is not made, the exporting countries can retaliate by withdrawing equivalent concessions.[8] As reviewed in the previous section, this constraint has proven during GATT's history to be binding. Countries that have sought to reinstitute restrictions through Article XIX have been required to provide compensation, although in many situations the compensation was provided through renegotiations under Article XXVIII or as regular tariff negotiations rather than as a formal action under Article XIX.

Customs unions and GATT. GATT has basically three rules for a customs union or free trade area: (a) the agreement must cover substantially all internal trade, (b) all internal restrictions must be removed, not just reduced, and (c) the customs union or free trade area must not on the whole increase restrictions against outsiders.

The European Common Market largely satisfied these requirements. According to GATT rules, outside countries were owed no compensation for the diversion of trade that would obviously result from leaving external duties fixed while removing internal ones.[9] The idea that GATT was about reciprocity proved, however, to be stronger than the idea that GATT was about rules. Though the rules said that they were not entitled to it, the Common Market's trading partners insisted on compensation. Article XVIII renegotiations were the first vehicle to be tried, but again these renegotiations blended into regular negotiations at the Dillon and Kennedy Rounds (Finger 1993b).

Safeguard Mechanisms

Lesson: A safeguard mechanism is in form a mechanism for changing trade policy, but in function a political basis for not changing it. Using the policymaking process of the United States as an example, passage in 1934 of the Reciprocal Trade Agreements Act created the mechanics of negotiating reductions of trade restrictions with trading partners. These mechanics replaced the previous mechanics of

---

8. Article XIX explicitly calls for consultations with exporters and provides for retaliation: suspension of "substantially equivalent concessions or other obligations." Compensation (to buy off retaliation) is implicit in these provisions. The frequent use of GATT's renegotiation provisions was another expression of the acceptance by the Contracting Parties that restoring protection on some product required compensating adjustments elsewhere.

9. Finger (1993b) compares the Common Market and GATT's rules.

Congress periodically adjusting tariff rates in response to domestic constituent pressures, a process in which protectionist pressures were dominant. Creation of GATT in 1948 expanded the mechanics of negotiating from bilateral to multilateral and secured the dominance of international negotiations over direct congressional tariff writing in the U.S. trade policy process.

How do "safeguards" fit into the policymaking process? In I. M. Destler's informative phrase, they provide "protection for Congress" from the wrath of special interests that would press a member of Congress who was sympathetic to the generally liberal thrust of U.S. trade policy (Destler 1992). A protection-seeking interest could be directed to the safeguard procedures, and, so long as these procedures were calibrated to generate trade restrictions at a lower rate than the trade negotiations process was removing them, the overall momentum on the policy process was toward openness to international competition.[10]

But what kept the pace of the safeguard or trade remedies process below that of the trade liberalization process? In other words, what prevented interests seeking protection from using the safeguard process to dominate policymaking? First of all, there were legal limits on what the government could do. Under the U.S. Constitution, Congress has authority over trade restrictions and the government can take only those actions expressly delegated to it by Congress. Beyond the conditions specified in the trade remedy law, the government had no authority to take trade-restricting action. The government having no authority to act (at least, the government having convinced the petitioner that it had no authority to act), the petitioner's next recourse would be to convince Congress to vote explicitly for protection for that industry. But Congress, haunted by the effects of the Smoot-Hawley tariff of 1930, its last attempt to do this, would be reluctant to act. The political campaign necessary to convince Congress to vote protection directly would be expensive and time consuming.[11]

In legal fact, the conditionality implicit in the trade remedy laws (all based on injury to domestic interests from import competition) was quite permissive, and minimizing the number of trade-restricting actions depended on other factors. For one, the government was not sympathetic to such actions. Many of the government officials responsible for administration of the trade remedies were the persons who had negotiated the GATT and otherwise participated in creation of the post–World War II international institutions. They were quite willing to exploit the loopholes and ambiguities in the trade remedy laws to

---

10. The generic term "trade remedy" is used more often in the United States than "safeguards." U.S. trade law provides several different trade remedies: the escape clause (under GATT Article XIX), antidumping, and countervailing duties are the most familiar.

11. In time, protection-seeking interests would develop a new technique: to have a trade remedy law amended so that its conditionality covered that interest's situation.

find reasons not to restrict.[12] Reminders of the Smoot-Hawley tariff debacle were an important part of the politics of Congress not taking a direct hand to protect powerful constituencies.

In addition, the 1950s and 1960s were generally prosperous times in which the United States enjoyed substantial trade surpluses. Directing a protection-seeking industry into a maze of administrative procedures bought time, and before the industry came to realize that there was no prize at the end of the maze it saw that business was good, and so it pressed the case no further. Besides, the system satisfied the American sense of fairness. There was a place to complain; they listened; they investigated; they held hearings. One had one's day in court. To complain further would be un-American, maybe even pro-Communist, if closing the U.S. market tipped a country to the Soviet side in the Cold War.

In sum, the U.S. safeguard process was effective. It said "no" most of the time, and the process itself helped to convince an unsuccessful petitioner to press the matter no further. The reader should be aware, however, of the particular historical and constitutional circumstances in which the U.S. safeguard process helped limit rather than promote import restrictions. As will be argued below, those critical circumstances are not present in the developing countries that have adopted similar instruments.[13]

Safeguards in TEP Country Reports

In this section I will review the trade policy instruments in use in countries that have been the subject of TEP reports. The section covers five countries: Costa Rica, Czechoslovakia, Morocco, Peru, and Romania; these being the only TEP countries in which a safeguard measure was addressed in the TEP report.

Costa Rica

By the early 1980s the Costa Rican economy had exhausted its options in the easy stages of its import substitution strategy. In the 1980s, the antiexport

---

12. Examples abound. To cite just one, in the late 1950s and early 1960s, the U.S. cotton textile industry attempted to use Section 22 of the Agricultural Adjustment Act to gain protection. The section gives the president authority to restrict imports of agricultural commodities or products thereof if these imports interfere with a U.S. agricultural program. Both President Eisenhower and President Kennedy exploited the same trick to avoid acting. They took advantage of their authority over terms of reference to direct the investigation to the impact of imports on the U.S. export enhancement program rather than on the U.S. price support program. Finger and Harrison (1994) provide details, and other examples from the textiles industry.

13. One might argue that those circumstances have been significantly eroded in the United States. Much has been written about the expansion of U.S. trade remedies. My own view is presented in Finger (1992).

bias in Costa Rica's trade policies, combined with several external shocks, led to declining Gross National Product (GNP) and to large fiscal and external deficits. Achieving the present government's goals of macroeconomic stability and trade policy reform has been hindered by the persistence of deficits. Though the customs tariff has been reformed and its rates reduced, import surcharges and deposit requirements have retarded reduction of the antiexport bias implicit in high protection and an overvalued exchange rate. Despite tariff reform, Costa Rica has fallen behind other countries of Latin America in the pace and depth of its trade liberalization.

Authority over trade policy. The structure of trade policy in Costa Rica is typical of many developing countries that have not been able to escape from highly restrictive import substitution regimes. Tariff rates (before the Uruguay Round) were mostly unbound. The government and various ministries hold legal authority to use various instruments of protection. Customs administration is poor and is a significant barrier to importation.

Trade policy instruments. The tariff is the basic mechanism of import regulation. The tariff introduced in 1986 reduced the average tariff rate from 523 percent to 26 percent while cutting tariff dispersion in half. Reforms since then have reduced the average rate to about 17 percent, from reductions mostly on the higher rates that protected local manufacturers of consumer goods.

There are, however, a number of other instruments used to restrict imports (see table 7.2). The only instrument over which the government does not have discretionary control is the import tax, and this is a minor instrument. A new antidumping regulation was promulgated in 1989, in large part to placate interests disturbed about the reduction of tariff rates that had begun in 1986.

Lesson: It never hurts to have one more way to restrict imports. The government of Costa Rica has discretionary control over several instruments to restrict imports. In this legal environment, creating another instrument (antidumping) will not provide the government a basis to refuse to provide protection to a petitioner who cannot demonstrate that dumping is the cause of his problem. But it does add to the conditions in which the government is expressly committed to providing protection. Form and function here work in the same direction, not the opposite. In the Costa Rican situation, antidumping is no more than another way to restrict imports.

Czechoslovakia

The Czechoslovakian economy was heavily centralized during the Communist period, its private sector being far smaller than those of Poland and Hungary.

Table 7.2. Costa Rica: Procedures for Adjusting the Level of Protection

Instrument [a]	Agency that implements	Authority through which the instrument was created	Indicators of frequency of use
Customs tariff (85)	Government	Government decree	The tariff introduced in 1986 reduced the highest rate from 220 to 100 percent, the average from 53 to 26 percent.
Import tax (88)	Change requires legislative approval		Was 3 percent until 1988, now 1 percent.
Import surcharge (88)	Central Bank		Surcharges represented 29 percent of import taxes in May 1991; they expired in August 1991.
Import deposit requirements (89)	Government imposes, deposits made at the Central Bank		From 1986 to 1991, the rate has varied from 100 to 1 percent, up again to 50 percent, down again to 30 percent. Date of deposit is up to 2 months before foreign exchange is delivered.
Tariff concessions (reductions and exemptions) (89)		Some are required by the CACM treaty	1988: 56 percent of total imports (by value) were exempted from customs duties, reducing duty collections by about half.

(table continues on following page)

(Table 7.2 continued)

Instrument [a]	Agency that implements	Authority through which the instrument was created	Indicators of frequency of use
Import licensing (93)	Many products, particularly agricultural products, require licenses from one or more ministries; for example, most wood products require a license from the Director General of Forestry		
AD (96) Import prohibition is a possible remedy.	Manufactured goods: Ministry of the Economy; Agricultural products: Ministry of Agriculture	Law 7134 of 1989, amending Law 2426 of 1959	As of July 1993, Costa Rica had notified no AD investigations to GATT.[b]

Note: AD = antidumping, and CACM = Central American Common Market.
a. Numbers in parentheses refer to page number in TEP–CostaRica.
b. GATT 1993.
Source: TEP 1992–Costa Rica.

Industrial production was concentrated on capital equipment and other energy-
or resource-intensive goods. A large portion of exports of these goods went to
what was then the U.S.S.R. in exchange for low-cost raw materials. Collapse of
the Communist economic system brought two challenges to Czechoslovakian
trade policy: to reorient its trade from the U.S.S.R. to the West, and to lead the
existing structure of technologically backward production to develop the commodity specialization and quality of production necessary to compete in Western markets (World Bank 1992b). At the time of the preparation of the TEP report, most Czechoslovakian internal prices were still controlled by the
government, and privatization had hardly begun.

Trade policy instruments. The Czechoslovakian tariff in 1992, carried over
from the Communist government, was low, averaging just above 5 percent
ad valorem. Nearly all customs duties (4,922 tariff lines out of 5,090) are bound
under GATT. In December 1990, a 20 percent temporary import surcharge,
covering mostly foodstuffs and consumer goods, was introduced for balance
of payments purposes, and so notified to GATT (under GATT Article XII).
(See table 7.3.)

The association treaty with the European Community, in place since January 1, 1992, "calls for complete liberalization of most trade—perhaps more
than 80 percent—within five years."[14] (World Bank 1992b, p. iv).

Lesson: GATT cover is always available. A safeguard mechanism is a relatively sophisticated policy apparatus. An economy that has such extensive
controls in place must look for the means to implement extensive reforms. A
safeguard mechanism is not such an instrument.

Table 7.3. *Czechoslovakia: Procedures for Adjusting the Level of Protection*

Instrument	Indicator of frequency of use
Tariff rates	4,992 of 5,090 tariff lines are bound under GATT.
Import surcharges	December 1990: a 20 percent temporary import surcharge was imposed on most foodstuffs and consumer goods. It was notified under GATT Article XII, allowing restrictions to safeguard the balance of payments.

Source: TEP 1992, Czechoslovakia.

---

14. The TEP report does not clarify if this liberalization applies only to trade with the
European Community, or if the liberalization will be extended on a most favored nation
(MFN) basis to trade with all countries.

Perhaps the only lesson one can draw from the Czechoslovakian experience (as reported in the TEP report) is the familiar one: a country that needs GATT cover for import restrictions can always find it in one or another of GATT's provisions.

Morocco

The liberalization of foreign trade is one of the basic elements of the Moroccan structural adjustment. The adjustment strategy has three major parts: (a) microeconomic reform, including trade liberalization to make the economy more outward-oriented, flexible, and competitive; (b) a flexible management of the exchange rate to further reduce antiexport bias, and (c) a gradual reduction of the budget deficit.

Authority over trade policy. Morocco is a constitutional monarchy. The Ministry of Foreign Affairs, the Ministry of Trade and Industry, and the Ministry of Finance all have responsibility for trade-related matters. The Ministry of Trade and Industry has chief control over planning and implementing Morocco's foreign trade policy, which is based on five-year plans. An interministerial committee under its chairmanship and composed of representatives from other ministerial departments formulates import policy. Industry representatives play a part in the policymaking process through annual surveys designed to evaluate the implementation of trade programs and bring out suggested changes.

Trade policy instruments. With trade liberalization has come a move away from volume-restricting measures toward price-related measures (see table 7.4). The basis of the import regime is the General Import Program, consisting of List A, comprising goods that can be freely imported, and List B, comprising products subject to prior authorization. List C, products for which importation was prohibited, was abolished in February 1986.

Import licensing requirements apply to goods on List B and are the chief instrument of quantitative import control. While no import quotas are in place licensed goods may be heavily restricted.

The Foreign Trade Law of 1989 contained provisions on antidumping and countervailing duty measures but did not include emergency safeguard measures as had its predecessor. Instead, the newer draft authorized a temporary licensing system for imports that cause or threaten injury to domestic production.

The Moroccan government relies on occasional use of reference or official minimum prices intended to act as "antidumping" or safeguard measures. According to the government, this system was established to address

Table 7.4. Morocco: Procedures for Adjusting the Level of Protection

Instrument	Agency that implements	Authority through which the instrument was created	Indicator of frequency of use
Tariff concessions	—	Customs Code, Title V and the relevant implementing decree	Temporary admissions (covering 25 percent of merchandise imports), temporary import and drawback regimes are designed to aid exporters.
Tariff quotas	—	—	Some quotas have been agreed on a reciprocal basis with Tunisia for trade in certain sensitive industrial goods.
Fiscal levies	—	—	In addition to the customs duty, a fiscal levy of 12.5 percent is levied on imports.
Reference prices	—	—	Applied to 367 tariff positions. Explained as protection against dumping.
Import licenses	Foreign Trade Directorate of the MTI and endorsed by the Foreign Exchange Office	General Import Program	Required for imports of List B goods; less than 13 percent of imports fall under this category.
AD and CVD	CSI	Article 8-12 of the Customs Code	Have never been applied.
Safeguards	—	—	Formal mechanism eliminated from 1989 Foreign Trade Law.

— Not available.
Note: AD = antidumping, CSI = *Comité de Suivi des Importations*, and CVD = countervailing duties.
Source: GATT-TPRM, Morocco.

industrialists' fears regarding the effect of lower protection on their competitiveness. Just as the law's standard of "dumping" is not spelled out, it
provides no definitive standards for injury or "prejudice" to domestic industry from imports.[15]

Lesson: There are many ways to provide "exceptional" protection. The government of Morocco can respond to pressures for protection from particular industries by adjusting reference prices or by tightening import licenses. It does
not need an antidumping or a GATT Article XIX safeguards process to deal
with such issues.

Peru

Since 1990, Peru has undertaken major programs of macroeconomic stabilization and industrial deregulation, including the opening of its market to
foreign trade. The average level of tariffs has been reduced, from 66 percent
in 1989 to about 16 percent in June 1993. Foreign trade regulations and institutions that have not been abolished have been simplified.

Authority over trade policy. Under Peru's constitution, the legislature, the
executive, and the judiciary are separate and independent. The legal system
is based on laws or legislative decrees passed by Congress and promulgated
by the president. Congress can pass laws authorizing the executive to legis-
late by decree on specified matters. Under the current (1993) constitution,
the executive has power to regulate tariff levels.

Responsibility for trade policy is shared by the Ministry of Economy
and Finance (MEF), the Ministry of Industry, Tourism, Integration, and International Trade Negotiations (MITINCI), and the National Institute for
the Defense of Competition and the Protection of Intellectual Property
(INDECOPI). The first is responsible for trade policy formulation and tariff
policy implementation, while the latter two are concerned with trade policy
implementation. Trade regulations may be implemented through laws, legislative and supreme decrees, decree laws, or resolutions issued by government institutions or agencies.

Trade policy instruments. The trade policy priorities of the Peruvian government since 1990 have been tariff reductions, the dismantling of trade barriers such as import and price controls, and deregulation of the economy (see
table 7.5). Between April 1990 and March 1991, the number of tariff rates was

---

15. Through June 1993, the government of Morocco had notified no antidumping or
countervailing duty investigations to GATT.

Table 7.5. *Peru: Procedures for Adjusting the Level of Protection*

Instrument	Agency that implements	Authority through which the instrument was created	Indicators of frequency of use
Customs tariff	President	Constitutional authority	Between April 1990 and March 1991, the number of tariff rates was reduced from 39 to 2, 25 and 15 percent.
Tariff concessions (reductions and exemptions for particular importers)	MEF	Legislative decrees, Supreme decrees	Concessional entry allowed for imports covered under preferential agreements (Andean Group) as well as those entering under the temporary admission, stock replacement, temporary import, and free zone regimes. Between 10 and 15 percent of total imports fall under these categories.
Variable import levies and import surcharges	Law decrees, Supreme decrees		As of January 1993, variable levies and import surcharges were applied to 20 agricultural items. During 1991–93, *ad valorem* equivalents ranged from 2 percent to 80 percent.
Reference prices	Ministry of Economy and Finance, the Central Bank and Peruvian Customs	Supreme decree	In the first quarter of 1992, 23 tariff items other than those subject to variable import levies were subject to reference prices.
Official minimum prices	Peruvian Customs	Legislative decree	Minimum import prices apply on iron and steel products.
Import prohibitions: for specified reasons	MITINCI and MEF	Legislative decrees, Supreme decrees, Law decrees	Related to public health or security. Applied to radioactive substances, residues or waste, certain fireworks, certain pesticides, and secondhand clothing and footwear.

(table continues on following page)

(Table 7.5 continued)

Instrument	Agency that implements	Authority through which the instrument was created	Indicators of frequency of use
Import surveillance: for specified reasons	Authorizations provided by various agencies under the Ministry of Fisheries, MITINCI, the Ministry of the Interior and the Ministry of Transport and Communications	Ministerial resolutions, registrations and permits	Prior authorizations are required for industrial fishing boats, explosives, arms and ammunition, ammonium nitrate, chemicals involved in processing cocaine, and radio communication equipment.
AD and CVD	Dumping and Subsidies Surveillance Commission, chaired by the MEF and supported by a Technical Secretariat	Supreme decree	Enacted legislation in 1991. Between July 1991–September 1992, 22 complaints were received; definitive action was taken in only one case.
Safeguards actions: to avert serious injury to domestic producers (may be quotas or surcharges)	MITINCI	Chapter IX of the Cartagena Agreement or Resolution 70 of the Committee of Representatives of the LAIA	No actions under GATT Article XIX since 1963. At the regional level, safeguards measures against 11 agricultural products covered by LAIA agreements, amounting to a 50 percent reduction of the preferential margin.
Import quotas for balance of payments reasons			Since disinvoking GATT Article XVIII:B in February 1991, no import restrictions have been applied for balance of payments purposes.

Note: AD = antidumping, CVD = countervailing duties, MEF = Ministry of Economy and Finance, and MITINCI = Ministry of Industry, Tourism, Integration, and International Trade Negotiations.

Source: GATT, TPRM, Peru.

reduced from thirty-nine to only two rates of 25 percent and 15 percent. The government hopes to reach its goal of a uniform 15 percent rate.

The government has eliminated most exemptions from import surcharges and duties. Import and export prohibitions have been reduced to cover only health and security concerns and foreign exchange restrictions have been lifted.

Peru has had antidumping and countervailing duty provisions in place since 1991. Government authorities have stated that these rules were based on those found in the General Agreement and the Multilateral Trade Negotiations (MTN) Antidumping and Subsidy Codes. Petitions may be presented by threatened or affected domestic producers or sectoral associations. In exceptional circumstances, when national interests are involved but no action is requested by producers, the Dumping and Subsidies Surveillance Commission (responsible for implementing the legislation) can initiate an investigation of its own accord on the basis of "sufficient proof" (GATT 1994b, p. 93).

Peru continues to use reference or official minimum prices formerly used to respond to threats from outside, even though formal safeguards mechanisms are in place. The potential for abuse of this trade-distorting instrument is obvious, with reference prices currently being applied to several agricultural and industrial imports.

Requests for safeguard action are addressed to MITINCI, along with production and import data of the applicants. Peru invoked Article XIX of the General Agreement in February 1993, pending completion of an Article XXVIII:4 renegotiation of duties covering several products.

Peru also has at its disposal safeguards mechanisms administered at the regional level. Such safeguard action has taken the form of suspension of preferential tariff treatment or the introduction of specific duties or quotas on imports covered by the Latin American Integration Association (LAIA) or Andean Group agreements and the Peruvian-Colombian Customs Cooperation Agreement. Some safeguard measures have been extended several times (GATT 1994b).

Lesson: The real test will come over time. Can the government resist pressure to extend special instruments to additional products? So far, the Peruvian government has limited application of each of the nontariff means for restricting imports to a short list of products. Some of the instruments were created specifically to buy off interests that might otherwise have successfully opposed wider liberalization measures. For example, the variable levy system has been applied only to products previously subject to special import regimes or import monopoly (GATT 1994b).

The government of Peru should take warning from the expansion in the industrial countries of antidumping into an all-purpose instrument for restricting imports. And that warning applies to all of the presently limited-purpose instruments. Antidumping was "different" from other instruments in the industrial countries only in that it was available.

Romania

The regime in power in Romania until 1989 sought to transform an essentially agrarian and mining economy into an industrial nation. Romania developed heavy industries and mineral processing activities, but by market standards efficiency was low. These industries were dependent on trading with other members of the Council for Mutual Economic Assistance (CMEA) for their economic viability. Since December 1989, the new government has taken measures to shift toward a market economy, but the transition has been hindered by supply disruptions and macroeconomic imbalances.[16]

Authority over trade policy. The Parliament is the sole legislative authority but, at least through March 1993, Romania did not have an operative foreign trade law (GATT 1992). Trade policy has been made in large part through governmental decision or ministerial order.

Trade policy instruments. Though information on its incidence is not available, delay in obtaining foreign exchange seems to be a significant obstacle for importers (World Bank 1994). Apart from the foreign exchange allocation mechanism, the customs tariff is the major instrument for regulating imports. Romania's current customs tariff was introduced by government decision on January 1, 1992. The tariff schedule's first column provides the statutory rate. The second column provides the generally applied rate, which can differ from the statutory rate because of changes introduced through various procedures that are listed in table 7.6.[17]

Lesson: Protection is flexible and fungible. The instruments to adjust protection, like the basic instrument of import restriction, the customs tariff, were created by government decision and are implemented by government decision or ministerial order.[18] Because the legal authority behind use of these instruments is the same as that behind their creation, the fact that each may be used only when certain conditions apply provides little leverage for the

---

16. The 1991 constitution declares Romania a free market economy.

17. Third and fourth columns indicate preferential reductions on imports from developing countries under each of two preference schemes to which Romania is party.

18. Most of the departures from "base" or statutory tariff rates have been reductions. GATT calculates the simple average of statutory rates at 17.8 percent, of applied rates as of January 1992 at 12.3 percent.

Table 7.6. *Romania: Procedures for Adjusting the Level of Protection*

Instrument	Agency that implements	Authority through which the instrument was created	Indicator of frequency of use
Tariff concessions (reductions and exemptions for particular importers)	Government decision, based on joint proposals of the Ministry of Finance and MTT	Government decision	Tariff reductions and exemptions covered about 2,250 of a total of 5,018 HS tariff lines in the Romanian Customs tariff.
Tariff quotas (used to implement some reductions and exemptions)	Government decision, based on joint proposals of the Ministry of Finance and MTT	Government decision	1992: tariff quotas with zero in-quota rates were applied to 45 tariff lines.
Import prohibitions: for specified reasons	MTT order	Government decision	Since 1990, trade embargoes have been maintained only to comply with UN resolutions against Iraq and the former Yugoslavia.
Import licensing: for specified reasons	MTT order	Government decision	Currently applied to weapons, explosives, toxic products, drugs and narcotics, waste of any kind.

(table continues on following page)

(Table 7.6 continued)

Instrument	Agency that implements	Authority through which the instrument was created	Indicator of frequency of use
AD and CVD	MTT, after investigation by in-house Commission. According to the Romanian government, the AD, CVD and safeguard regulations are GATT-consistent [1]	Government decision, elaborated by MTT order	No actions notified to GATT through March 1993. A 1992 AD investigation was terminated when the government increased the tariff from 5 to 15 percent. Petitions received have not specified the grounds for the requested relief—dumping, subsidy, etc.[2]
Safeguard actions: to avert serious injury to domestic producers (may be quotas or surcharges)	MTT may impose quotas; Government, on joint proposal of the MEF, may impose surcharges	Government decision, elaborated by a joint MTT-MEF order	Temporary import surcharges of 30 percent imposed on 23 tariff lines, May 1, 1992; no safeguard quotas through March 1993.
Import quotas for balance of payments reasons	MTT, at the request of the National Bank	Government decision	No actions through March1993.

Note: AD = antidumping, CVD = countervailing duties, MEF = Ministry of Economy and Finance, and MTT = Ministry of Trade and Tourism.
1. GATT-TPR, p. 71.
2. TEP, pp. 33f.
Source: GATT-TPRM, Romania.

government not to protect an industry that finds itself in a different situation. Furthermore, the list of instruments includes two of GATT's "injury-based" mechanisms for import relief, and the scope of these has proven to be quite broad. GATT experience also affirms that a multiplicity of instruments is, in effect, a list of alternatives a protection-seeking interest can use to press the government for protection.

The flexibility of the trade policy system is further corroborated by the frequency of change of the regulations: the TEP report on Romania lists nineteen changes of regulations and six changes of applied rates of protection. Not all of these changes were applications of the various regulations. Some were direct governmental decisions, at the same constitutional level as the creation of a rule about the applied rate of protection.

Conclusion

A safeguard mechanism, to do what a free trader wants from it, must be a sham, a bright flame that keeps protection-seekers circling about it but delivers little protection. From a private perspective, a safeguard suggests that it will "safeguard" industries from import competition; but from a social perspective, its purpose is to "safeguard" the openness of the economy to import competition from these protection-seeking interests.

It is perhaps obvious, but bears explicit mention, that a safeguard process to be effective must not be the dominant trade policy process. In the U.S. case described above, the trade negotiations process, at first bilateral and later through GATT, was the dominant trade policy process. Trade remedies were a monster but, in the 1950s and 1960s, a small monster, chained to the service of an internationalist master.

To be effective a safeguard procedure must provide a basis to limit trade-restricting actions, and it must help to convince protection-seekers that the government's refusal was reasonable. The cases reviewed bring forward two possible bases for limiting and convincing: conditionality and reciprocity.

Conditionality

Safeguard processes are frequently of a form that conditions protection on the existence of specified criteria or conditions: injury to domestic enterprises resulting from import competition, subsidies to exports, balance of payments difficulties, or some combination of such conditions. For such conditions to be limiting they must incorporate several properties:

- They must logically exclude some circumstances in which an interest would be motivated to seek protection.

- The government, in some constitutional or otherwise compelling way, must be constrained to act only in those circumstances.
- There must be few alternative safeguard instruments.

If a government enjoys broad discretionary authority to act against imports, then a dedicated trade remedy (one assigned to remedy a specific situation, such as dumping) provides no political leverage against requests for protection for other politically attractive reasons.

Worse, in this situation, the criteria of a specific instrument provide the protection-seeking interest leverage to force the government to act when those criteria are met; but, they provide the government no leverage for saying no to a politically attractive reason that happens not to enjoy a dedicated trade remedy.

The TEP Countries

In the developing countries reviewed here, the governments have blanket discretionary authority to adjust tariffs and other forms of trade restrictions. Furthermore, the legal authority to make rules about trade restrictions lies no deeper than the legal authority to make restrictions. In several of the countries reviewed, even the process of making rules is the same as the process of imposing restrictions. In such circumstances, the criteria of any one or of all the instruments are neither limiting nor convincing. As politically attractive new reasons come forward, the government can act.[19]

The conclusion then is that the safeguard mechanisms in place in these countries will not help to defend the countries' liberalization programs against pressures for protection from particular industries. These safeguards do not ensure that protection will not be provided in the circumstances not covered. They only ensure that the government will provide protection in the circumstances specified.

Reciprocity

During GATT's history, reciprocity has been the motivating instinct behind the rounds of negotiations that have created a truly liberal international system. Furthermore, reciprocity has been the effective control over use of the various safeguards or trade remedies that GATT allows. While one should not discount the threat of tit for tat, the power of reciprocity has been more than this threat. GATT's history shows that the contracting parties in many

---

19. As to the requirement that there be few alternative safeguard instruments, no matter how tightly criteria are written, protection-seeking interests have demonstrated that they can present their situation as the one for which the criteria guarantee protection. The more instruments there are, the more such opportunities.

instances have respected their obligation to compensate when domestic politics have forced them to protect a particular sector.

It follows that among the alternatives GATT offers, the best safeguard a developing-country government can create against domestic pressures to reverse a liberalization is to bind that liberalization through the GATT negotiations.

A "National Economic Interest" Safeguard Instrument

Four of the five TEP reports reviewed suggest that a safeguard process should take into account not only the possible benefits of protection to domestic producers who compete with imports but, also, the potential costs to users of these goods. The costs of protection and the citizens who bear these costs should have the same standing in law and in administrative procedures as the gains and the gainers, including the opportunity to petition for removal of a trade restriction already in place. Injury-based standards give expression only to those who would enjoy the benefits of protection.

A national economic interest–based safeguard process is a proposal I have often supported, so I will not go into details here.[20] Because the process of investigation that would flesh out this suggestion would help to publicize the costs of protection, and to rally the interests that would bear these costs, it offers the possibility of both limiting and convincing; in other words, its politics are as attractive as its economics.[21]

Other Recommendations in the TEP Reports

The recommendations of the reviewed TEP reports are summarized in table 7.7. As noted above, four of the five TEP reports reviewed recommend a national economic interest safeguard process, or that a national economic interest test be the basis for granting antidumping relief.

The one report that does not recommend a national economic interest safeguard, the Peru report, recommends an antidumping regulation that follows the GATT code. Following the code would, the report asserts, "avoid antidumping being used for protectionist purposes" (World Bank 1992c).

I disagree with both the recommendation and the reasoning behind it. The criteria of an antidumping action do not make economic sense. They do not identify situations in which an import restriction augments the national economic interest. Furthermore, the criteria of an antidumping action do not

---

20. I do go into some detail in Finger (1993a, chapter 4).

21. It is obvious that such a safeguard mechanism would have to be the only one at the disposal of protection-seekers. If they had the alternative of an injury (only)–based safeguard, they would never petition through the national economic interest process.

Table 7.7. Safeguard Mechanisms in Place in TEP Countries, TEP Recommendations for Modification

Country	Safeguards in place	Recommendations for removal	Recommended additions	Recommended characteristics	Antidumping
Costa Rica	AD, import surcharge, import deposit requirement, import licensing	Eliminate and renounce prior import deposits and surcharges. Costa Rica might be better off with no AD regulations at all.[1]	"The appropriate instrument to provide breathing space to import-competing industries is a safeguard mechanism, not an AD mechanism." Adopt a safeguard mechanism consistent with GATT, that would allow the costs and benefits to society as a whole—consumers as well as producers—to be weighed before action is taken.		Bring AD regulations into accord with the GATT code. Detailed suggestions are provided, allowing for voluntary price actions that allow "the exporter to resolve the problem and avoid … AD duties."[1]
Czechoslovakia	Twenty percent temporary import surcharge on food and consumer goods, notified under GATT Article XII as a restriction to safeguard the balance of payments.	The import surcharge should be removed.	Establish an independent commission to evaluate requests for temporary protection, with transparent procedures to discourage requests for QRs. The commission should take into account both the costs and benefits to the economy as a whole of the proposed import restriction.	Consumer and user interests should be given full weight in evaluating requests for temporary protection. Tariffs to be preferred over QRs. Sunset clause, protection for no more than one year.	AD actions should be avoided in favor of safeguard measures. AD measures, even if GATT-consistent, are criticized for favoring those seeking protection, not taking into account the interests of user industries.

(table continues on following page)

(Table 7.7 continued)

Country	Safeguards in place	Recommendations for removal	Recommended additions	Recommended characteristics	Antidumping
Morocco	AD and CVD laws on the books, but safeguards provisions were removed (1989). Temporary licensing system operating as safeguard mechanism. Reference prices are used by authorities to allay the concerns of producers anxious about the liberalization of QRs, rationalized as protection against dumping.	Replace QRs (the licensing system) with tariffs. A limited list of goods prohibited from importation, on moral and ecological grounds. Revise the tariff to a uniform 20 percent.	Reassess Article XIX as an alternative to difficulties of establishing dumping margins under AD, or establish a specific body to review AD and CVD cases and determine dumping margins or levels of subsidy.	Safeguard mechanism would include guidelines for determining injury and causality (GATT-consistency implied) and "must balance the calculation of injury to producers with calculations of costs of protection to consumers and other users." AD and CVD regulations would include definitions of injury or prejudice, use more reliable data.	AD laws in Morocco were criticized as weak and biased toward protectionist interests. No definitions of dumping, subsidy, or injury. AD and CVD is used to deal with cases that are more appropriately addressed through safeguard provisions.

(table continues on following page)

(Table 7.7 continued)

Country	Safeguards in place	Recommendations for removal	Recommended additions	Recommended characteristics	Antidumping
Peru	Many (see table 7.5), Import surcharges, variable levies, reference prices, official minimum prices, import prohibitions, import surveillance	Resist all measures to re-institute import licensing, even for "statistical" purposes. "The appropriate way to deal with dumping is through transparent investigative procedures that are consistent with the GATT antidumping code."[2]	Measures to make liberalization irreversible: • disciplined macro policy. • realistic exchange rate. • reference prices, other "traditional" NTBs consolidate their legal basis to control discretionary use. • international commitment through the Uruguay Round. Establish formal AD legislation based on the GATT AD code. (i) Transparency is a virtue. (ii) Follow the code closely so as to avoid AD being used for protectionist purposes. (iii) Include clear definitions and time limits on application.		No mechanism in place at the time of the study.

(table continues on following page)

241

(Table 7.7 continued)

Country	Safeguards in place	Recommendations for removal	Recommended additions	Recommended characteristics	Antidumping
Romania	AD, CVD, and safeguard regulations since 1992. Under the safeguard regulation, a 30 percent import surcharge was imposed, mid-1992, on alcoholic beverages, perfumes, electrical appliances, and motor vehicles.	Eliminate the export price office that could easily be corrupted into a minimum import price office or an initiator of AD investigations.	Redraft AD and CVD and safeguard regulations • follow GATT more closely. • sunset clause - 3 or 5 years. • "interest of the national economy" standard. Generally, discourage safeguard, AD and CVD measures (even if GATT conditions are met) when the cost to the national economy exceeds the gain.		Various inconsistencies between GATT and Romanian AD, CVD, and safeguard regulations are listed; for example, AD includes no injury determination, safeguard action is not conditioned on "concessions" nor "unforeseen developments."

Note: AD = antidumping, CVD = countervailing duties, NTB = nontariff barrier, and QR = quantitative restriction.
1. TEP, p. 97.
2. TEP, p. 74.
Source: TEP Reports.

limit. Hence even on the basis of "fewer restrictions rather than more," anti-dumping criteria have no value.

"GATT-consistency" is generally recommended, without distinguishing between GATT's procedural standards (public notice, participation guarantees for interested parties, evidentiary requirements, and so on) and its economic standards. A more detailed analysis by each TEP team would surely have pointed out that the procedural standards are worthy and the economic standards not worthy. But the treatment in the reports is typical of a tendency to put GATT-consistency in the category with milk and apple pie. Had the TEP teams been aware of the depth of procedural detail that is required by the "case law" that is evolving from GATT panel examinations of antidumping investigations, or even of the procedural requirements specified in the Uruguay Round Antidumping Agreement, they might have been less casual about recommending GATT-consistency. Why undertake such an onerous burden to operate a process that makes no economic sense? [22]

The Costa Rica TEP report goes into some detail on changes that should be made to improve GATT-consistency of Costa Rica's antidumping regulations. The recommendation goes perhaps too far in urging Costa Rica to provide for voluntary price undertakings that allow "the exporter to resolve the problem and avoid...antidumping duties" (World Bank 1992a). The economics of that sounds like giving away the rents, something that would not serve the national economic interest.

A final comment on GATT-consistency: I have sometimes advised government officials that if forced by domestic politics to take protectionist action, they should find a GATT-illegal way to do it. That way their trading partners would yell, maybe threaten retaliation, and the government officials would have a basis in domestic politics to resist, at least the next time. The officials' reactions suggested that the reality of trade politics, both domestic and international, had brought them to this strategy more quickly than my intellectual exercises had brought me.

---

22. A national economic interest safeguard process would provide less incentive to develop procedural detail. The detail in the antidumping process comes from protection-seekers adding details that expand the coverage of the instrument. As a national economic interest investigation would be essentially the same investigation done on each of two sides of the ledger—injury to domestic producers from not imposing the restriction, or injury to domestic users if the restriction is imposed—any new trick invented to expand the coverage on one side of the ledger would also be applied on the other.

Bibliography

Anjaria, Shailendra J. 1987. "Balance of Payments and Related Issues in the Uruguay Round of Trade Negotiations." *The World Bank Economic Review* 1 (4): 669–88.

Davey, William J. 1994. "Escape Clauses and Exceptions." Presented at the seminar The Uruguay Round Agreements from an Asia-Pacific Perspective, George Washington University, Washington, D.C., August 1–3.

Destler, I. M. 1992. *American Trade Politics*, 2nd ed. Washington, D.C.: Institute for International Economics; and New York: The Twentieth Century Fund.

Ferguson, Tim W. 1994. "She Changed Customs at a Trade Body." *Wall Street Journal*, March 8: A17

Finger, J. Michael. 1981. "The Industry-Country Incidence of 'Less than Fair Value' Cases in U.S. Import Trade." In Werner Baer and Malcolm Gillis, eds., *Export Diversification and the New Protectionism*. Boston: National Bureau of Economic Research; and Champaign, IL: Bureau of Business and Economic Research, University of Illinois.

_____. 1991. "Development Economics and the General Agreement on Tariffs and Trade." In Jaime de Melo and Andre Sapir, eds., *Trade and Economic Reform*.. Cambridge, MA: Blackwell.

_____. 1992. "The Meaning of 'Unfair' in United States Import Policy." *Minnesota Journal of Global Trade* 1(1): 35–56.

_____. 1993a. *Antidumping: How It Works and Who Gets Hurt*. Ann Arbor: University of Michigan Press.

_____. 1993b. "GATT's Influence on Regional Arrangements." In Jaime de Melo and Arvind Panagariya, eds., *New Dimensions in Regional Integration*, Cambridge, U.K.: Cambridge University Press.

_____. 1994. "Subsidies and Countervailing Measures and Antidumping Agreements." In *The New World Trading System: Readings*. Paris: Organisation for Economic Co-operation and Development.

Finger, J. Michael, and Sumana Dahr. 1994. "Do Rules Control Power? GATT Articles and Agreements in the Uruguay Round." In Alan V. Deardorff and Robert M. Stern, eds., *Analytical and Negotiating Issues in the Global Trading System*. Ann Arbor: University of Michigan Press.

Finger, J. Michael, and K. C. Fong. 1993. "Will GATT Enforcement Control Antidumping?" Policy Research Working Paper 1232. World Bank, Washington, D.C.

Finger, J. Michael, and Ann Harrison. 1994. "The MFA Paradox: More Protection and More Trade?" Working Paper 4751, National Bureau of Economic Research, Cambridge, MA.

GATT. 1958. *Antidumping and Countervailing Duties*. Geneva.

_____. 1970. *Analytical Index: Notes on the Drafting, Interpretation, and Application of the Articles of the General Agreement*, 3rd rev. March. Geneva.

_____. 1990. *Trade Policy Review: Morocco*. Geneva.

_____. 1992. *Trade Policy Review: Romania*. Geneva.

_____. 1993. *International Trade and the Trading System: Report by the Director General 1992–1993*. Geneva.

_____. 1994a. *Analytical Index: Guide to GATT Law and Practice*. 6th ed. Geneva.

_____. 1994b. *Trade Policy Review: Peru*. Geneva.

———. Various years. "Summary of Antidumping Actions." *Basic Instruments and Selected Documents*. Vols. 1985–86 through 1991–92. Geneva.

Horlick, Gary N., and Geoffrey D. Oliver. 1989. "Antidumping and Countervailing Duty Law Provisions for the Omnibus Trade and Competitiveness Act of 1988." *Journal of World Trade*, 5–49.

Hudec, Robert E. 1975. *The GATT Legal System and World Trade Diplomacy*. New York: Praeger.

_____. 1987. *Developing Countries in the GATT Legal System*. London: Gower, for the Trade Policy Research Center.

_____. 1993. *Enforcing International Trade Law: the Evolution of the Modern GATT Legal System*. Salem, NH: Butterworth.

Hufbauer, Gary C. 1981. *Analyzing the Effects of U.S. Trade Policy Instruments*. Washington, D.C.: National Science Foundation.

Jackson, John H. 1969. *World Trade and the Law of GATT*. Charlottesville, VA: Michie.

Jackson, John H., and Edwin A. Vermulst. 1989. *Antidumping Law and Practice: A Comparative Study*. Ann Arbor: University of Michigan Press.

Littan, Robert E., and Richard Boltuck, eds. 1991. *Down in the Dumps: Administration of the Unfair Trade Laws*. Washington, D.C.: Brookings.

Little, Ian M. D. 1982. *Economic Development: Theory, Policy and International Relations*. New York: Basic Books.

McDiarmid, O. J. 1946. *Commercial Policy in the Canadian Economy*. Cambridge, MA: Harvard University Press.

Messerlin, Patrick. 1986. "Public Subsidies to Industry and Agriculture and Countervailing Duties." Paper prepared for the European Meeting on the Position of the European Community in the New GATT Round. The TPRC and the Spanish Ministry of Finance and Economic Affairs, Madrid, Spain, October 2–4.

Organisation for Economic Co-operation and Development (OECD). 1992. *Integration of Developing Countries into the International Trading System*. Paris.

Sampson, Gary. 1987. "Safeguards." In J. Michael Finger and Andrzej Olechowski, eds., *The Uruguay Round: A Handbook for the Multilateral Trade Negotiations*. Washington, D.C.: World Bank.

Staiger, Robert W., and Frank Wolak. 1994. "The Trade Effects of Antidumping Investigations: Theory and Evidence." In Alan V. Deardorff and Robert M. Stern, eds., *Analytical and Negotiating Issues in the Global Trading System*. Ann Arbor: University of Michigan Press.

Stegemann, Klaus. 1992. *Price Undertakings to Settle Antidumping Cases*. Ottawa: The Institute for Research on Public Policy.

Stern, Robert M., John H. Jackson, and Bernard Hoekman. 1986. "An Assessment of the Implementation and Operation of the Tokyo Round Codes." Research Seminar in International Economics, University of Michigan, Ann Arbor, February 19.

Stewart, Terence P., ed. 1993. *The GATT Uruguay Round: A Negotiating History*, vol II. Deventer, Netherlands: Kluwer Law and Taxation Publishers.

United Nations Conference on Trade and Development. 1994. "The Outcome of the Uruguay Round: An Initial Assessment." Supporting papers to the *Trade and Development Report, 1994*. United Nations. New York.

United States International Trade Commission. Various years. *The Year in Trade: Operation of the Trade Agreements Program*. United States International Trade Commission. Washington, D.C.

United States Tariff Commission. 1919. *Information Concerning Dumping and Unfair Foreign Competition in the United States and Canada's Antidumping Law*. Washington, D.C.: Government Printing Office.

World Bank. 1990. *Morocco 2000: An Open and Competitive Economy*. UNDP/World Bank Trade Expansion Program Country Report 7. World Bank, Trade Policy Division, Washington, D.C.

_____. 1992a. *Costa Rica: Strengthening Links to the World Economy*. UNDP/World Bank Trade Expansion Program Country Report 9. World Bank, Trade Policy Division, Washington, D.C.

_____. 1992b. *Czechoslovakia: Integrating into the Global Economy, a Transition Strategy*. UNDP/World Bank Trade Expansion Program Country Report 8. World Bank, Trade Policy Division, Washington, D.C.

_____. 1992c. *Peru: Toward a More Open Economy*. UNDP/World Bank Trade Expansion Program Country Report 10. World Bank, Trade Policy Division, Washington, D.C.

_____. 1994. *Romania: Restructuring to Face the World Economy*. UNDP/World Bank Trade Expansion Program Country Report. World Bank, Trade Policy Division, Washington, D.C.

8

Labor Markets, Foreign Investment, and Trade Policy Reform

Ann Harrison and Ana Revenga

The World Bank and other multilateral institutions have long advocated the removal of tariffs and other barriers to trade as an important step in structural adjustment. Although the benefits from trade reform are well understood, there is no consensus regarding the short-run costs of adjustment. Few studies actually measure the unemployment or wage effects of trade reform in developing countries. One major problem is that it is difficult to disentangle the effects of stabilization and trade reform on employment. Many trade reform episodes are undertaken concurrently with macroeconomic stabilization policies (such as fiscal and monetary restraint), so it is difficult to measure the impact of trade measures on unemployment.

Labor markets are important for two reasons. First, painful spells of unemployment, rising poverty, and rapid real wage declines clearly cannot be ignored. Rising poverty and high unemployment are likely to threaten the very sustainability of the reforms. Second, changes in labor market institutions or regulations may be critical to the success of a proposed reform. Nowhere is this more evident than in the transitional economies of Eastern Europe and the former Soviet Union (FSU), where the lack of labor mobility and the large size of the public sector is a significant impediment to trade reform.

One partial solution has been to encourage foreign direct investment (FDI). The issue is twofold. First, what is the effect of trade reform on foreign investment? Does opening up to trade lead investment to leave the country, or does liberalization attract new investment? Second, how can policymakers alleviate the short-run costs of adjustment by encouraging foreign investment?

This chapter reviews the available evidence on the linkages between trade reform, labor markets, and FDI. We begin by drawing on studies of sixteen countries

The authors would like to thank Wendy Takacs, John Nash, and conference participants for very helpful comments, and Nese Erbil and Francis Ng for valuable assistance in preparing the data used in this chapter.

that underwent trade reforms in the 1980s and 1990s. These sixteen countries were chosen because of their inclusion in the United Nations Development Programme (UNDP)-World Bank Trade Expansion Program (TEP). Wherever possible, we supplement these studies with additional studies and empirical evidence.

The evidence suggests that the employment and wage effects of trade reforms are generally small. The only exceptions are in the transitional economies, such as Czechoslovakia, Mongolia, Poland, and Romania, where trade reforms were accompanied by a restructuring of the entire economy. In these countries, however, it is difficult to distinguish the effects of trade reform from the overall transformation of the economy.

In general, the employment effects of trade reforms were fairly small for a number of reasons. First, a number of studies suggest that real wages in developing countries are very flexible. As a result, wages are allowed to adjust instead of employment. The flexibility of real wages is consistent with minimum wages that are either very low or not enforced.

Second, many other labor market policies that in principle could have affected adjustment to trade reform were also not enforced. In many countries, hiring and firing laws, employer payroll taxes to finance social security and unemployment, and minimum wages are widespread; however, empirical evidence suggests that compliance with these labor market restrictions is poor. In some countries, such as Morocco, implementation of labor laws is highly inadequate. In other countries, labor market regulations are redundant; for example, minimum wages are often set at levels that are not binding to the employer.

Other factors cushioned the impact of trade reform on the labor force. Trade reforms are often implemented in conjunction with exchange rate devaluation, which cushions the effect of the reforms. Finally, many firms responded to greater international competition by cutting profit margins and raising productivity.

One factor that does impede adjustment is the presence of a large and inflexible public sector. In countries like Poland, the lack of public sector adjustment endangers trade reform for two reasons. First, maintaining a large public sector reduces the pool of available labor for private sector growth, and also makes wage adjustment difficult if the public sector acts as a wage leader. Second, the significant fiscal costs of paying public sector employees have significantly hampered efforts to achieve fiscal and monetary restraint.

In all the countries with available data, trade reform was accompanied by significant increases in foreign investment inflows. This appears to be largely because trade reforms were generally accompanied by a liberalization of the foreign investment code and a more positive attitude toward foreign investors in general. There is no evidence that trade reform led foreign investors to leave formerly protected markets.

The remainder of the chapter is organized as follows. *Wage and employment responses to trade reform* describes the impact of trade reform on these areas; *Labor market regulations* discusses the role of the public sector in impeding response to reform; and *Trade Reform and Foreign Direct Investment* discusses the foreign investment response to liberalizing trade.

Wage and Employment Responses to Trade Reform

The debate on the labor market effect of trade reform is not new. Anne Krueger's book on trade and employment in developing countries appeared in the early 1980s. Yet we actually know very little about the short-run impact of trade policy reforms on the labor market. Krueger's book, while illuminating, provides no actual country experience; it merely hypothesizes that trade reform should lead to employment increases because the labor force shifts toward labor-intensive tradables (Krueger 1983).

Aggregate Wages and Unemployment

In a general equilibrium framework provided by the trade models of Ricardo and Heckscher-Ohlin, moving toward international prices via trade reform should have no effect on employment because full employment is generally assumed. In a world where labor mobility is not perfect, however, trade reform could lead to short-run adjustment costs. Heckscher-Ohlin models provide more explicit predictions regarding the impact of changes in international prices on wages: to the extent that industrializing countries have a comparative advantage in labor-intensive goods, trade reform will lead to more production of those goods. The shift toward greater production of labor-intensive goods will in turn increase the demand for labor and raise wages. Although higher wages will lead to a reduction in the capital-labor ratio across all sectors, there will be a reallocation of output toward labor-intensive goods. This implies that trade reform would lead to higher wages, a reduction in the relative returns to capital, and demand shifts to more labor-intensive sectors. However, only data on manufacturing wages are available, so we cannot look at the relative returns to capital and labor.

Figure 8.1 shows a time series of total employment for those TEP countries with available data, before and after each trade reform. Each trade reform was dated based on the year when standard trade reforms were first introduced in a country, such as the conversion of quotas to tariffs, tariff reduction, elimination of state trading agencies, or the relaxation of foreign exchange rationing for import purchases. Information dating these reforms was taken from World Bank and TEP reports. In many cases, the dates of the trade reforms do not coincide with the dates of structural adjustment loans

Figure 8.1. *Trends in Employment*
(thousands of workers)

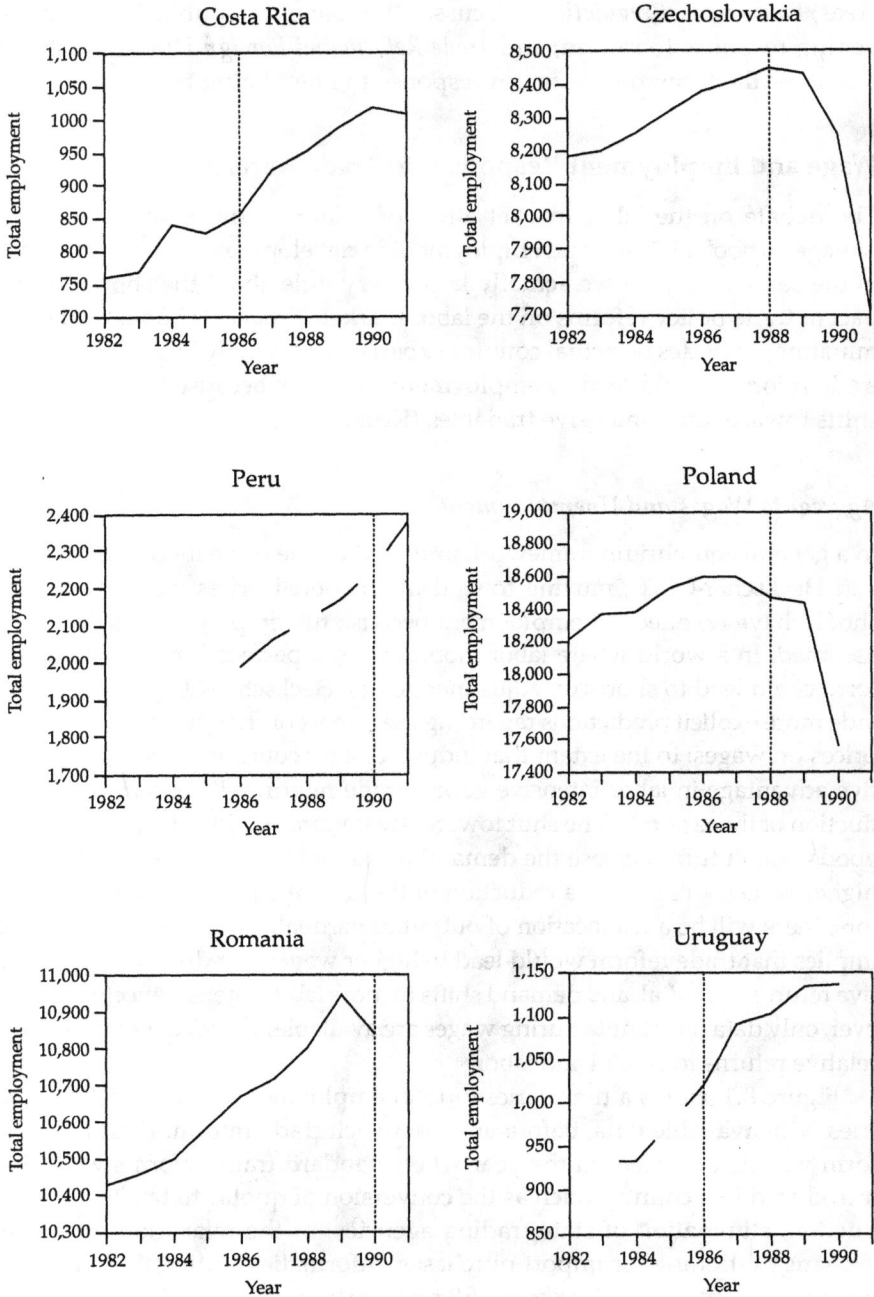

Note: Dotted lines represent years of trade reforms.

(SALs) initiated by the World Bank. SALs were often initiated before or after actual trade policy reforms.

According to figure 8.1, aggregate employment increased after trade reform in all countries except those economies in transition. In Costa Rica, for example, trade reforms were accompanied by strong aggregate Gross Domestic Product (GDP) growth, employment expansion, and increasing wages. In Czechoslovakia, Poland, and Romania, the onset of trade reforms was accompanied by sharp declines in total employment. However, in the transitional economies one could easily argue that the employment decline was not due to the trade reform component of the adjustment package. The transitional economies did not experience the usual expansion in trade that is expected to accompany trade reforms and provide the mechanism that could expand employment. Instead, the collapse of the Council for Mutual Economic Assistance (CMEA) and the conversion of a barter to a hard currency system led to trade decline, disruption, and reorientation. Figure 8.2 shows that exports and imports as a share of Gross National Product (GNP) declined in almost all the CMEA countries with available data in the late 1980s, when trade reforms were also introduced. In Bulgaria and Mongolia, where the declining share of trade in the GNP was less severe, stable trade shares mask a significant decline in the volume of trade (see figure 8.3). Stable or increasing trade shares can be explained in the context of declining trade volumes by the fact that GNP declined even more quickly than trade.

Figure 8.2. *Trade Shares (X+M/GNP) for CMEA Countries, 1980–93*
(percent)

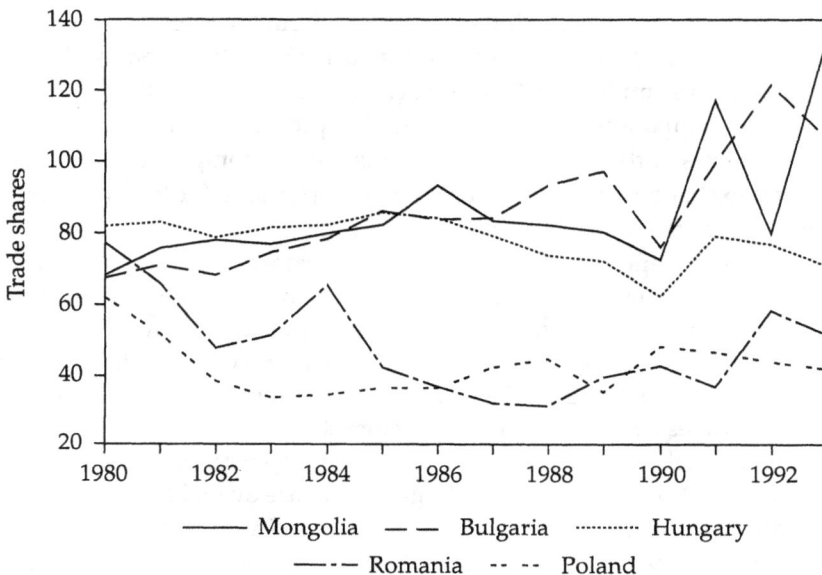

Figure 8.3. *Trade Volumes (X+M), 1980–93*
(thousands of U.S. dollars)

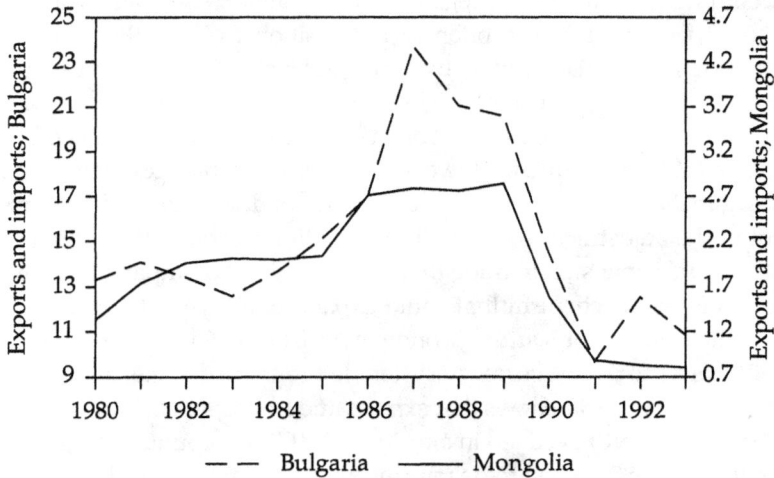

— — Bulgaria   ——— Mongolia

Another explanation for the very different experiences of the transitional and nontransitional economies under adjustment emphasizes the definition of employment. In countries like Kenya, where the social safety net is not well developed, many workers simply cannot afford to become unemployed. Instead, underemployment may rise and wages may fall, but total employment may remain fairly stable. We explore the role played by a well-developed social safety net in fostering employment reallocation later in this chapter.

The trends in manufacturing wages, taken from the International Labour Organisation (ILO), are reported in figure 8.4. The data generally show the same pattern as employment. Wages are reported in U.S. dollars in order to make them comparable across countries. One problem with reporting wages in dollar terms is that many trade reforms were accompanied by devaluation, and exchange rate changes are partly responsible for the observed decline in wages for some countries.

In Costa Rica and Mauritius, trade reforms were accompanied by a rise in manufacturing wages. In the transitional economies, as well as Kenya and Zimbabwe, however, the onset of trade reform coincided with sharp declines in manufacturing wages. Sharp wage declines during the 1980s and early 1990s were not confined to the transitional economies; between 1981 and 1991, real wages in Kenya (across all sectors) fell by 31 percent.

Unfortunately, almost no countries in the sample report unemployment figures. Even those unemployment figures that are available are likely to be underestimated or unreliable. However, for those five countries with unemployment data from the ILO (figure 8.5), the pattern remains the same. Costa

Figure 8.4. *Trends in Real Wages in Manufacturing*
(U.S. dollars)

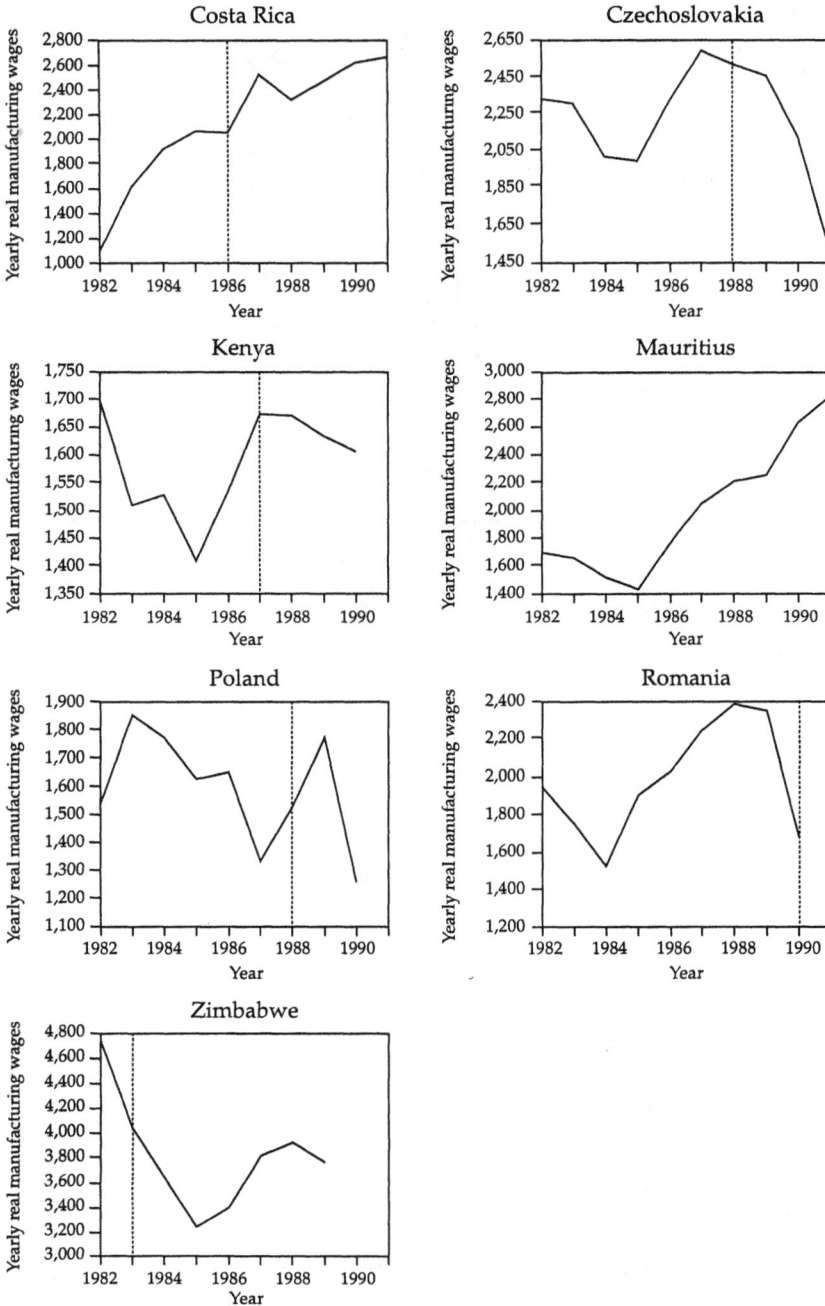

Note: Dotted lines represent years of trade reforms.

Figure 8.5. *Trends in Unemployment*
(percent)

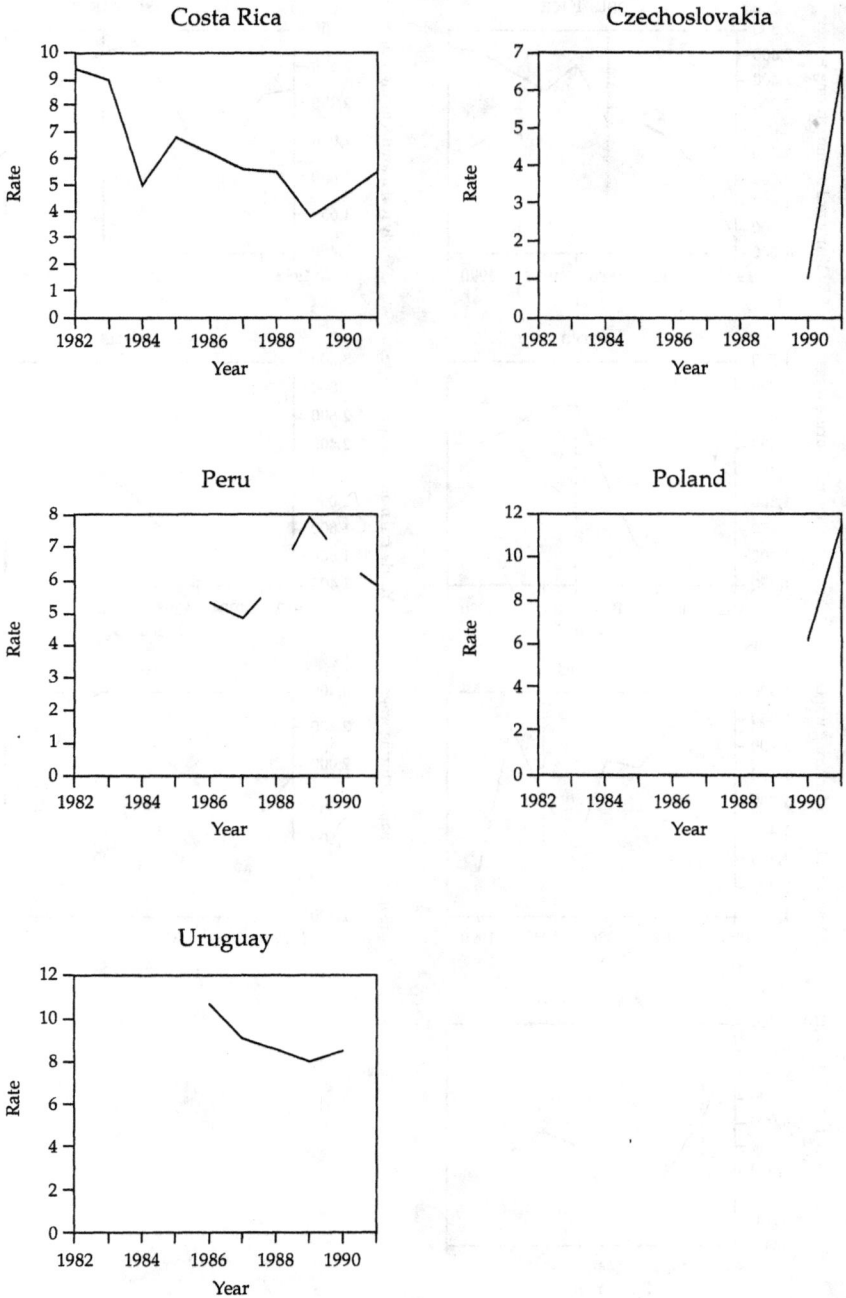

Costa Rica

Czechoslovakia

Peru

Poland

Uruguay

Rica, Peru, and Uruguay report declines in unemployment postreform, while Czechoslovakia and Poland report very large increases in unemployment with the introduction of trade reform.

The evidence presented in figures 8.1 through 8.5 is drawn from a small sample. But more detailed cases for other TEP countries not included in these figures, such as Guatemala, Morocco, Mongolia, Uganda, and Vietnam, reveal the same general pattern. In Guatemala, where trade reforms were introduced in 1987 and 1990, the drop in real wages during the first half of the 1980s was reversed in 1987. Unemployment also declined, from 14 percent in 1987, to 7.8 percent in 1989. In Morocco and Uganda, trade reforms in the mid-1980s were accompanied by rising employment and stable or rising wages, as well as a reduction in poverty. Trade reforms were introduced in Uganda in 1987 as part of the government's Economic Recovery Program. In both rural and urban areas, real GDP per capita growth recovered. However, the economy was also recovering from the political chaos of the Obote II regime, which makes it difficult to disentangle the benefits from the "peace dividend" from the benefits of structural adjustment per se. Nevertheless, a combination of exchange rate adjustment, elimination of import and export licenses, removal of price controls, export monopolies, and trade taxes has encouraged the monetization of the agricultural sector. Despite an overall decline in the terms of trade for agriculture, farmers have shifted resources toward tradables and higher-paying export crops. Real wages of agricultural labor, including both casual and permanent agricultural labor, a good measure of the welfare of the poor, rose steadily during the 1980s.

Trade reforms in Morocco were introduced in 1984, with elimination of quotas and reduction of tariffs continuing throughout the 1980s. Between 1984 and 1991, poverty declined in Morocco, a conclusion that is robust for the types of poverty measures used for the analysis. The reduction in poverty can be traced to the growth of employment opportunities, particularly in export-oriented manufacturing. Although employment growth was accompanied by a decline in the real manufacturing wage of about 0.4 percent per year between 1985 and 1990, increased employment opportunities appear to have offset the wage declines and led to an overall reduction in the incidence of poverty.

In Mongolia, as in the other transitional economies, reforms were accompanied by sharp declines in employment and real wages. Real wages dropped 50 percent between 1990 and 1992, with an estimated further decline of 33 percent in 1993. With a growing rate of unemployment, the percentage of the population living below the poverty line was estimated to have increased from essentially zero before 1990 to 27 percent in 1994. However, it is difficult to estimate how much, if any, of the unemployment and wage declines were due to trade reform, because structural adjustment encompassed every aspect of the economy. The increase in poverty in Mongolia is more likely to be due to several other factors, including termination of financial support from the FSU, fiscal contraction, inflation, privatization, the closure of nonviable enterprises, and reductions in such services as basic education, health care, and social assistance. In fact, it could be argued that price and trade liberalization are bringing benefits to Mongolia that offset the contractionary effects of other policies. The growth of employment in tradables such as garment industries, meat, meat products, and skins and hides has been significant.

Vietnam, which shares many of the characteristics of the transitional economies, has nevertheless managed to avoid many of the large adjustment costs shared by these other economies. Although unemployment did increase following the trade and other reforms introduced in 1988, it was only at 6 percent in 1991. In part this reflects the country's rapid growth rate (9.3 percent in 1992), yet it also reflects the fact that Vietnam began the transition away from Central Planning with a significantly lower percentage of the labor force in public sector employment. Nevertheless, it is difficult to attribute the lower adjustment costs purely to the smaller public sector share. The small public sector share could simply reflect the largely agricultural nature of the economy, which in turn implied that a relatively small fraction of the labor force was "misallocated" to nonviable sectors. Yet the relative ease of the transition does provide some insights into the conditions that could sustain a less costly reform process.

Vietnam was and continues to be a heavily rural, agricultural society, and the vast majority of Vietnamese families are not dependent on enterprises for income and subsistence. Total public sector employment in Vietnam accounted for only 15 percent of the labor force in 1987, in contrast to the 77 percent of the labor force in state-owned enterprises (SOEs) in the FSU. In addition, other social services such as health care, education, and social safety nets were provided in transitional economies through the SOEs; whereas in Vietnam they play no role in the provision of social services. Vietnam has a tradition of community-based systems of social safety nets, which were also provided through the central command mechanism in the transitional economies.

At the aggregate level, trade reform seems to have been accompanied by employment expansion and relative wage stability in all the countries under TEP except for the transitional economies and some of the African countries. The evidence also suggests significant wage flexibility across countries. For economies in transition, it easy to argue that the significant declines in wages and employment are more likely to arise from the difficulties in moving from a centrally planned economy dominated by public sector enterprises, than from trade reforms alone. This certainly seems to be the case when we compare countries such as Mongolia and Vietnam. Nevertheless, trade reforms are likely to have uneven effects across sectors because protection is reduced more in some sectors than in others. The evidence on sectoral responses to trade reform is discussed below.

Sector-Level Effects of Trade Reform: Testing for Employment Reallocation

Although it is difficult to establish statistical linkages between changes in the trade regime and employment or wage effects at the aggregate economywide level, it is easier to measure the differential effect of trade reforms across subsectors. This so-called partial equilibrium approach is possible because changes in the trade regime typically are uneven across goods. In a well-functioning labor market, one would expect small wage changes and larger employment shifts between sectors because wages for similar occupations should equalize across sectors. But changes in output prices should lead to reallocation of labor toward the higher-priced goods. The United States, for example, which by most standards has a very flexible labor market, clearly shows small wage responses to changes in relative prices across sectors and big employment effects.

One of the first attempts to measure the partial equilibrium effects of import competition was by Grossman (1986, 1987). Grossman analyzed the effect of tariff protection in the United States, finding that wages are fairly unresponsive to (tariff-inclusive) import prices but that employment responses in some sectors have been quite significant. Grossman concludes from the low wage elasticities and higher employment elasticities that there is fairly high intersectoral labor mobility within the United States. Other cross-industry studies of the United States and Canada include Freeman and Katz (1991), Revenga (1992), and Gaston and Trefler (1994). These studies also find significant effects of changes in import competition on intersectoral changes in employment, but smaller effects on wages. In the United States and Canada, it appears that trade policy changes lead to employment reallocation across industries, with very little effect on wages.

Evidence on trade and employment linkages is much weaker for developing countries. Krueger (1983) describes a project sponsored by the National Bureau of Economic Research (NBER) that analyzed the linkages between trade policies and employment in ten industrializing countries. The NBER studies focused on (a) measuring the relative labor intensity of exportables against import-substituting production, and (b) measuring the extent to which greater protection encourages a shift toward more capital-intensive means of production. Krueger and her colleagues hypothesized that moving toward a more neutral trade regime led to greater labor intensity in production. However, none of the case studies directly measured the actual impact of trade reforms on the labor market.

One study that does explicitly examine the relationship between trade reform and employment is the work on Chile produced by de la Cuadra and Hachette (1989). Yet their study also leaves many questions unanswered. They argue that the 16 percent unemployment rate in Chile during the 1976–81 episode cannot be ascribed solely to trade reform, given the deteriorating terms of trade and severe recession (beginning in 1975) during that period. De la Cuadra and Hachette attempt to disentangle the relative effects of other factors and trade reform on employment. Using a simulation model, they argue that the effects of trade reform were in fact quite small. They argue that, overall, the effect on employment in manufacturing and mining was negative, but that it was more than compensated for by an increase in agricultural employment. They also find very different effects across manufacturing. For example, they find that employment went up by 50 percent in some exportable sectors such as wood products, and declined by essentially the same amount in import-competing sectors such as electrical and non-electrical machinery.

Partial equilibrium approaches, similar in spirit to the U.S. studies, have recently been completed for Mexico, Morocco, and Uruguay. For Uruguay, which introduced trade reforms in 1979 and again in 1985, Rama (1994) used four-digit industry data between 1978 and 1986 to measure the effect of trade liberalization on employment reallocation and real wages in the manufacturing sector. The results show that trade reforms had a significant impact on the level of employment across manufacturing subsectors, but almost no effect on real wages. Reducing the protection rate within a sector by 1 percent led to an employment reduction of between 0.4 and 0.5 percent within the same year. These results suggest that during those years the labor market in Uruguay was fairly competitive, with significant employment reallocation between sectors after the reforms.

Currie and Harrison (1997) find small wage and employment responses to trade reform, using plant-level data for Morocco between 1984 (when the trade reform began) and 1990. Although employment in most manufacturing firms was unaffected by the tariff reductions and the elimination of quotas, there was a significant employment response for firms most highly affected by the reforms. The 21-point decline in tariff protection for firms in the textiles, beverages, and apparel sectors was associated with a 6 percent decline in employment.

Puzzled by the small employment response to seemingly large reductions in tariffs and quotas, Currie and Harrison explore several possibilities. They present evidence on the fluidity of the market and argue that labor market rigidities cannot account for the small response. Instead, their explanation centers on the ability of capital to share the cost of adjustment. Instead of adjusting employment, most firms reduced their profit margins.

Currie and Harrison also examine the employment response for exporting firms, which were generally located in the sectors that experienced the largest reductions in protection (such as textiles and apparel). Exporting firms were able to adjust to a 24 percentage point decline in tariff protection by reducing employment by less than 2 percent. Faced with a contraction in domestic demand, export-oriented firms were able to adjust by reorienting themselves toward export markets, at very little cost to employment or wages.

Revenga (1997) examines the impact on wages and employment of Mexico's trade reform, which began in 1985. Revenga also finds a small effect of the reform on employment. Unlike Currie and Harrison, who attribute the small employment response to product market imperfections, Revenga addresses imperfections in factor markets. In contrast to Morocco, where unions are few and organizers are sometimes jailed, organized labor is important in Mexico. Around 30 percent of the labor force is unionized, which is high by developing-country standards.

Revenga finds that most of the adjustment to trade reform in Mexico occurred through wage reductions. Prior to the trade reform, rent-sharing agreements allowed workers to earn higher wages. Revenga estimates that on average real wages declined by 3 to 4 percent as a consequence of the trade reform, with more-affected sectors experiencing a 10 to 14 percent decline. In firms in which rent-sharing had previously allowed workers to benefit from industrywide protection, the fall in real wages was even greater.

These partial equilibrium studies, combined with the more aggregate evidence discussed above, present a general picture of well-functioning labor markets (except in the transitional economies) that respond smoothly to trade reforms. At the aggregate level, aggregate employment generally rose. At the subsector level, employment was reallocated away from formerly protected sectors. Real wages rose in some economies and fell in others; the fall in real wages in countries such as Kenya, Morocco, and Zimbabwe suggests that real wages were certainly not rigid downwards. As expected in a labor market in which employment adjusts to output shocks, wages equalized across sectors, generating no observable wage effects at the subsector level. One surprising result is that in some countries the extent of employment reallocation in responding to trade reforms seemed too low. In Morocco, employment in most sectors was unaffected by trade reforms, and even in highly affected sectors the employment effects were not large. These relatively small effects have been estimated for both industrial (United States, Canada) and industrializing (Mexico and Morocco) countries.

There are several explanations for the small response of employment to trade reforms. If firms simply respond to increased international competition by raising productivity of the existing labor force, efficiency gains can be achieved without shedding labor. Currie and Harrison (1997), Haddad (1993), and Tybout and Westbrook (1995) show an increase in firm-level productivity in both Morocco and Mexico following the trade reforms. Although trade reforms were often far reaching, protection levels still remained high in comparison to the industrial countries. In Morocco, despite the elimination of quotas and tariff reduction, average tariffs remained above 30 percent throughout the 1980s. In both Morocco and Mexico, the real exchange rate (RER) also depreciated significantly with the onset of trade reform. Figure 8.6 [using the International Monetary Fund's

Figure 8.6. *Real Exchange Rates in Mexico and Morocco, 1979–93*

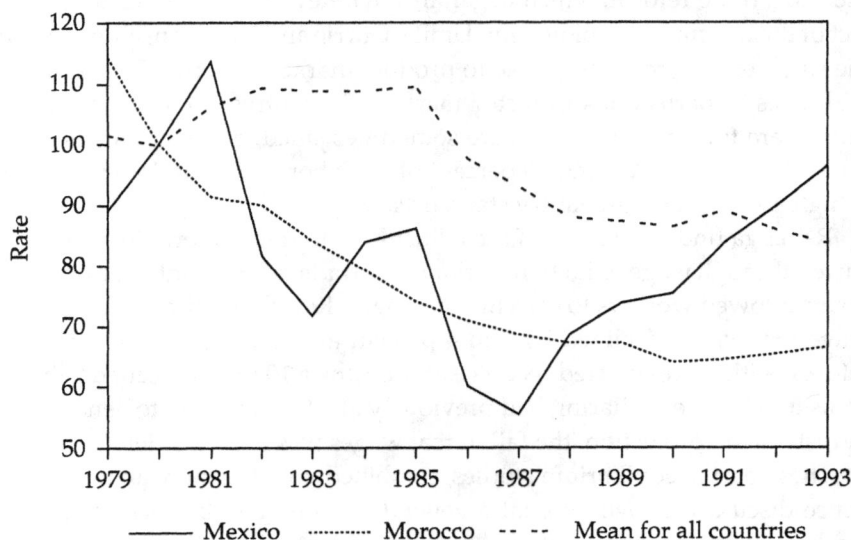

(IMF's) RER series] shows that, compared with other developing countries during this period, the RER in Mexico and Morocco depreciated significantly in the mid-1980s, when trade reforms were introduced in both countries. (In Mexico, however, the RER began to appreciate beginning in 1988). Consequently, the exchange rate changes partially offset the greater competition due to lower tariffs, and firms were able to avoid dramatic changes in their labor force. Evidence consistent with this hypothesis is the sluggish output response to tariff and quota reforms in both Mexico and Morocco. In very poor countries, it is likely that employment adjustment is lower due to the lack of a social safety net.

Labor Market Regulations

One puzzling aspect of trade reform in Mexico and Morocco is that it has had almost no impact on employment or wages. Trade reforms have not led to a significant reallocation of labor. One popular explanation is that labor market policies such as hiring and firing costs or minimum wage policies inhibit the response to reform. Inability to fire may prevent employers from reallocating production to more profitable areas of production. Evidence for both India and Venezuela suggests that this may be the case. Minimum wage laws may inhibit wage flexibility and undermine international competitiveness, leading to the observed lack of wage declines in most TEP countries. Lack of downward wage flexibility could also be important if rapid expansion of the private sector labor force is necessary to absorb workers released from public sector enterprises. Other labor market regulations that could affect labor market flexibility include payroll taxes imposed on employers, large tax burdens that discourage labor demand, and large or sluggish public sectors. A large and inflexible public sector is likely to be particularly problematic in transitional economies, where the development of the private sector is dependent on a labor force drawn from downsizing public enterprises.

We argue below that labor market regulations have not been a significant impediment to trade reforms in most TEP countries. Minimum wages are often set too low to be binding for the majority of enterprises. Even in countries where the minimum wage is set high enough to be binding, as in Morocco, stringent labor laws conceal the fact that implementation of labor laws is almost nonexistent. Payroll taxes, although sometimes high, can generally be passed on to employees in the form of lower wages. The only real impediments seem to be (a) the difficulty in firing labor, which is significant in countries such as India, and (b) a large public sector, typical of most transitional economies.

Payroll Taxes

Mandated payroll taxes, shared between the employer and employee, vary from as low as 15 percent of the payroll in Mauritius to as high as 58 percent in Costa Rica. To what extent do these high payroll taxes inhibit wage responses to trade reform and affect the competitiveness of enterprises? Due to paucity of research in this area, the answer is somewhat unclear. Payroll taxes will only affect labor costs and employment if the cost of these taxes cannot be passed on to workers in the form of lower wages. In fact, if there is full shifting to wages, employers will see no net rise in their compensation costs, and there will be no resulting disemployment. However, if wages were rigid downwards, possibly due to minimum wage laws, employers would be unable to shift the tax burden to employees in the form of lower wages. The only evidence to date on the incidence of payroll taxes in developing countries are two studies, by Gruber (1997) and MacIsaac and Rama (1997).

Gruber examines the effect on employment of reducing payroll taxes in Chile. In 1981, Chile shifted from a social security system paid through taxes on employers to a privately funded system, which led to a reduction in the employer's share from 30 to 5 percent. Gruber finds that the payroll decline was fully offset by an increase in wages, with no effect on employment. MacIsaac and Rama examine the incidence of nonwage costs in Ecuador, where these account for 75 percent of take-home pay in some cases. Like Gruber, MacIsaac and Rama conclude that a large fraction of the mandated nonwage costs imposed on employers are shouldered by workers in the form of lower wages.

If evidence for Chile and Ecuador is transferable to other countries, this would suggest that payroll taxes per se are unlikely to affect the relationship between trade reform, wages, and employment. The only exceptions would be where taxes are unusually high or wages are rigid downwards due to binding minimum wages. However, minimum wages are not binding in most TEP countries.

Minimum Wages

Minimum wages, or other price-setting mechanisms such as tripartite agreements to regulate wages, exist in quite a few of the TEP countries, including Costa Rica, Kenya, Mauritius, Morocco, and Uruguay. Despite their widespread use, however, the evidence suggests that most minimum wage laws are not binding. In Costa Rica, which has eighty or so different minimum wages defined by occupation, the minimum wages are nevertheless not directly binding in determining wages in most sectors (World Bank 1992). One possible reason is that minimum wage increases in Costa Rica during the second half of the 1980s generally kept pace with inflation, but rarely exceeded it. In Kenya, another country with an elaborate system of seventy-eight minimum wages specified by sector, occupation, location, and age group, the minimum is also not binding (World Bank 1993). During the entire decade of the 1990s, the minimum wage for adults declined more quickly (3.1 percent per year) than average wages (2.1 percent per year), which suggests a steady deterioration in the real value of the minimum wage.

Bell (1997) and Harrison and Islam (1993) analyzed plant-level and household data for Morocco and Mexico to measure compliance with minimum wages. In both countries, the evidence suggests that a large percentage of individuals receive earnings below the statutory minimum wage. Further evidence for Mexico also suggests that the minimum wages had no impact on overall labor demand. In the Moroccan case, such behavior has been legitimized by recent laws allowing firms to legally ignore labor legislation when hiring new entrants into the labor force. This law, which was passed in an effort to address the high rates of unemployment for youth, suggests that in the cases in which minimum wages do inhibit employment growth, the government is likely to find politically acceptable means to remove the minimum wage constraint.

Although there is insufficient evidence to suggest any effect of minimum wage laws on employment in the TEP countries, in part due to their nonbinding nature and in part to poor compliance, minimum wages should not be ignored. Case studies of countries with relatively high minimum wages, as in Puerto Rico and Colombia, do show that high minimums have contributed to unemployment rates and reduced overall labor demand. Castillo-Freeman and Freeman (1991) show that in Puerto Rico, imposition of the U.S. minimum wage raised average earnings on the island, lowered the aggregate employment-population ratio by a significant amount, and shifted employment away from low-wage sectors. Bell (1997) found that increases in minimum wages in the Colombian manufacturing sector led to a significant reduction in employment. Even in countries where the minimum wage does not appear to be a binding constraint, as in Costa Rica and Morocco, it appears that the minimum wage has contributed to an overall compression in the structure of wages. In addition, minimum wages may reduce incentives for firms to provide on-the-job training, because firms often provide this type of training only if workers are able to "pay" for it through lower wages. Thus, minimum wages may limit on-the-job training by eventually becoming binding for apprentices or trainees.

Minimum wages, often readjusted with great fanfare at the start of a new year, provide a visible means for governments to respond to the welfare of poorer segments of the population. From this perspective, eliminating minimum wages would be a politically volatile solution, and in many cases not even possible. Instead, developing-country governments appear to be coping with the issue by allowing the real value of the minimum wage to deteriorate. As described by Freeman (1993), increases in minimum wages did not keep pace with inflation during the 1980s, leading to real minimum wage declines that exceeded 50 percent between 1980 and 1989 in Mexico. Yet even in cases in which the legislated minimum increased substantially in real terms, as in Morocco, firms appear to have implemented the legislation selectively.

Hiring and Firing Laws

Many industrializing countries have highly restrictive labor codes that make it both difficult and costly to fire employees. In Kenya, Mauritius, Morocco, and Uruguay, private firms must first obtain permission from government bodies to fire permanent employees, and must then pay a severance payment to dismissed employees ranging from two weeks' to one month's pay per year employed. For public sector firms, restrictions on dismissals are typically even more severe. These restrictions can make it extremely difficult for firms to restructure or for economies to reallocate labor following a trade reform.

In practice, it is unclear how important role restrictions on dismissals actually play in allowing private sector enterprises to respond to trade reform. Restrictions on dismissals typically only apply to the largest formal sector enterprises. In Kenya, Mexico, and Morocco, many enterprises have responded to restrictions on firing permanent workers by hiring temporary employees, who can be easily dismissed. In Morocco, the share of temporary workers in manufacturing rose by nearly 20 percentage points between 1984 and 1990.

Econometric evidence on the extent to which job security regulations affect the speed of labor market adjustment is available for India, Morocco, and Zimbabwe. For India and Zimbabwe, Fallon and Lucas (1991) estimated the effect of tighter job security legislation on adjustment in employment levels. For Morocco, Currie and Harrison (1997) examined the extent to which a sluggish adjustment of the labor force could explain the low elasticities of employment and wage responses to trade reform.

Fallon and Lucas find no evidence that the introduction of job security legislation in India or Zimbabwe affected the speed of labor market adjustment to demand shocks. This suggests that labor market regulations affecting hiring and firing cannot provide the explanation for lack of a labor market response to reforms, at least in these two countries. However, Fallon and Lucas do find that these laws reduced the level of total employment. One interpretation for these somewhat puzzling results is that total formal sector employment in India and Zimbabwe was replaced by temporary labor when stricter job security regulations were enforced, allowing employers to maintain flexibility of the labor force but leading to an observed decline in the formal sector labor force.

Currie and Harrison used a lagged adjustment model of labor demand to test the speed of adjustment in Morocco. They find that with the exception of parastatals, employment adjustment takes place within the year. Their econometric estimates are in the same range as most of the industrial country estimates surveyed by Hammermesh (1993). In terms of the speed of adjustment, private sector firms in Morocco are more like North American firms than European firms. The latter typically adjust employment more slowly. These comparisons support the contention that in Morocco, despite legislation that on paper appears to be quite restrictive, labor mobility is comparable to the United States, where there are essentially no restrictions on hiring or firing. However, the evidence for Morocco does suggest that parastatals adjust much more slowly.

Despite this evidence that hiring and firing laws do not appear to pose a significant problem for adjusting firms, there are important exceptions. In Mauritius, regulations on dismissal in the sugar sector have prevented it from downsizing and also deprived the rest of the economy of additional labor. This is particularly problematic because employment shortages have led to rising wages, which in turn threaten the competitiveness of export-oriented sectors. The sugar sector employs approximately 40,000 workers, or almost 15 percent of the labor force employed in large firms. Under the Sugar Industry Efficiency Act, plantations with more than ten hectares are required to provide job security to all workers hired before 1988, even during the intercrop season. These plantations are not allowed to reduce their labor force through attrition either, because they are obliged to hire additional workers to make up any difference between their current employment and their 1988 labor force.

Estimates of labor redundancy in the Mauritius sugar industry range from 25 to 50 percent of total employment in that sector. If those workers could be released to other sectors, yielding a 3 to 7 percent increase in employment in the rest of the economy, GDP could increase by several percentage points.

Restrictions on dismissals and the resulting overstaffing problems are most severe in the public sector. This is the case for countries as diverse as Mauritius, Morocco, and Vietnam. The need to reduce the size of the public sector labor force is particularly important for two reasons. First, the release of workers into the private sector acts as a mechanism to lower wages elsewhere in the economy and provides a growing employment pool for the expanding private sector. Second, public sector layoffs are particularly important as a means of reducing public sector deficits, improving fiscal constraints, and attaining macroeconomic stability. These issues are critical in the transitional economies, which have a large public sector component.

Easing the Costs of Adjustment

Adjusting to trade policy reform almost always involves some social costs in the short run. These costs can be substantial if reform comes in the midst of deep economic crisis, as in the case of the transitional economies. The combination of aggregate drops in demand and sectoral shocks can lead to sharp drops in employment. For the individuals involved, and for their families, displacement can entail substantial welfare losses. The affected family may lose a portion or even all of its income, sometimes for a long period of time. Moreover, displaced workers often face a loss of specific human capital tied to firm- or sector-specific skills, and such a loss can be permanent. Research from the United States indicates that, even in dynamic labor markets in industrial countries, long-term losses for reemployed displaced workers can be as high as 30 percent of previous earnings (see Carrington and Zaman 1994).

The welfare costs of reform raise some key questions regarding the role of government policy. In particular, can government policy facilitate adjustment and alleviate the social costs? Can it do so without disrupting the process of sectoral reallocation necessary for a resumption of growth?

The main issue in designing a safety net is resolving the conflict between economic efficiency and equity. Policy needs to satisfy two sometimes conflicting objectives: providing flexibility to the labor market, and helping those individuals adversely affected. This potential conflict is well exemplified by the use of severance payments. On the one hand, they represent a safety mechanism for displaced workers; on the other, they may reduce labor mobility. In designing a safety net, governments must find an acceptable balance between the necessity of ensuring flexible labor markets and the concern about providing income security.

In most cases, resolving the dual objectives of flexibility and income security will require a combination of measures. Policies aimed at increasing labor mobility—geographical, as well as occupational—will be crucial to accelerating adjustment. These policies may include removal of rules and regulations that impede job mobility, measures to encourage retraining of workers, and, particularly in the case of transitional economies, reform of the housing market.

Policies aimed at increasing flexibility should be combined with mechanisms that support the standards of living of those adversely affected by reform. How much protection governments should grant depends to a great extent on what they can afford. The priority should be to protect the most vulnerable groups from falling below a poverty line. Yet more ambitious programs may be needed on political economy grounds, to ensure support for the reforms.

The experience of different countries illustrates that the degree of government involvement and the types of policies it uses varies greatly according to a country's structure, administrative capacity, and income level. The challenge is to design mechanisms that are rational, provide the right incentives, and are comprehensive and easy to administer. In general, simplicity and transparency should be a guiding principle. There are examples of effective and sophisticated assistance to workers of collapsing enterprises in many Organisation for Economic Co-operation and Development (OECD) countries, but it is unlikely that these administratively intensive schemes would work in economies characterized by much lower administrative capacity.

In developing countries, much simpler schemes would be preferable. For example, in economies with relatively large formal sectors, simple severance pay mechanisms jointly financed by firms and workers may be more appropriate than complex unemployment insurance schemes. Ideally, the precise amount of the payment should be negotiated between workers and employers, with some government oversight to ensure equity. Costs would be partially paid by workers benefiting from the insurance, either directly (as in Chile) or through lower wages.

Where public sector retrenchment is an important element of reform, it may be preferable to offer retrenched workers a menu of options combining severance payments, early retirement, and possibly funds for retraining. This may help reduce the burden on the budget and, if designed appropriately, could reduce some of the selection problems involved in reducing employment in the public sector, namely, the loss of those workers with better outside opportunities. The menu approach has been followed in a number of developing and industrial countries with some success. Chile and Spain are two examples. In other countries, however, public sector adjustment to reforms has been more sluggish, in large part because of obstacles to dismissing redundant labor. India and Zambia are two such examples.

In low-income countries, or in countries with a large informal sector, programs involving low-paid public works are most often the only effective mechanism for providing a safety net. Low wages act as a self-selection mechanism because only the truly needy will accept the jobs. These schemes are particularly appropriate during economic downturns, when other job opportunities are unavailable. They are also well suited for rural areas during the slack season, and can have a secondary benefit of building or maintaining important infrastructure assets.

Public works programs have been used extensively in many developing countries. The Food for Work program in Bangladesh and the Emergency Social Fund in Bolivia provide a basic level of employment and consumption for some of the poor. The Employment Guarantee Scheme in Maharashtra, India uses taxes to redistribute income from the wealthier urban areas, particularly Bombay, to the poor who work in rural parts of the state. Chile introduced large government-financed urban public works programs during the recessions of the mid-1970s and early 1980s. Like the Indian scheme, the Chilean program's main objective was to create employment. At the bottom of the recession of the early 1980s they absorbed more than 10 percent of the labor force. By December 1988, a year after Chile's vigorous economic recovery, that share had fallen to less than 0.1 percent.

Public works programs tend to have a greater chance of success where labor is more mobile and where there is a tradition of community work. When workers are able to move, the location of the program can be determined mainly by the quality of the projects. Poor laborers looking for public jobs are usually willing to relocate, at least temporarily, to obtain them. In addition, community participation greatly enhances the probability of success. Studies from Niger and Senegal indicate that communities with strong employment pooling traditions can assist in the mobilization of workers and facilitate the production of public goods, such as local production on common fields for common stockholding or simple neighborhood assistance schemes.

The level of wages in such programs is important in determining their success at targeting the needy. High wages may attract better-off workers and, given limited budgets, lead to fewer jobs created for the truly destitute. The importance of appropriate wage setting is illustrated by the Maharashtra program in India, which seeks to guarantee employment on demand. In its initial fifteen years, the program maintained wages at the level of market wages for unskilled casual agricultural labor. But in 1988 wages were sharply increasing, in line with a doubling of the statutory minimum wage. The higher wage, combined with budgetary pressures, eliminated the employment guarantee a year after the wage increase.

Most public works programs have two objectives: providing relief to laborers in distress and creating a public asset. To achieve both objectives, programs must be flexibly managed with the capacity to expand employment rapidly during a crisis. This suggests focusing on high-return public works programs during normal times but expanding public investments that generate employment, to include lower priority projects, during crises. Nevertheless, designing effective programs is always difficult. Such programs may become permanent fixtures if politicians are reluctant to dismantle them after economic recovery.

Trade Reform and Foreign Direct Investment

Many of the TEP reports point to FDI as an important source of capital that could help reforming countries acquire valuable technology and at the same time ease the transition to a more open economy. We begin by analyzing the trends in foreign investment in the TEP countries before and after the trade reforms. We then briefly discuss the role that foreign investment has played to ease the transition process, and conclude with policy recommendations for countries wishing to maximize the benefits from FDI.

The Impact of Trade Reform on Foreign Investment

Until recently, a significant share of foreign investment in industrializing countries was drawn by the prospect of highly protected home markets. Multinationals producing automobiles in Mexico and Venezuela were able to benefit from high tariff walls and weak domestic competition. With the movement toward more open markets, some feared that "tariff-jumping" FDI would leave these countries. Other factors, however, were expected to offset the expected loss of this kind of FDI. Trade reforms were often accompanied by liberalization of the foreign investment code (see, for example, India, Morocco, Poland, Venezuela, and Vietnam). In addition, the trade reforms conveyed reassuring messages to investors about the future strength of the economy.

Figure 8.7 plots the annual share of net foreign investment in GDP for each TEP country with available World Bank data. The time series, available before and after each trade reform, allows us to quickly summarize the relationship between foreign investment inflows and trade reform. In most countries, net foreign investment inflows increased substantially following trade reforms. In some countries, the magnitudes are quite large. In Costa Rica, foreign investment nearly tripled, amounting to an inflow of more than 3 percent of GNP by 1992. In all three transitional economies, foreign investment surged in 1990, although as a share of GNP it was very small in Poland and Romania. Other TEP countries not shown in figure 8.7, such as Vietnam, also experienced a surge in foreign investment.

The combination of freer trade and more generous policies on foreign investment, both of which boost investor confidence, appears to have led to significant increases in foreign investment inflows. Despite the overall positive trend, however, two points are worth noting. First, the magnitude of the foreign investment inflows was often small. Foreign investment inflows into Romania, for example, were a very small fraction of GDP. Second, at least one TEP country did lose foreign investors after reform. In Kenya, foreign investment inflows declined following trade reforms in 1980 and 1987. One reason may be that foreign investment has traditionally been attracted to the protected manufacturing sector. According to the TEP study on Kenya, most of this investment was actually welfare-worsening, because the after-tax repatriable earnings to foreign investment actually exceeded the value added of these investments when measured using world prices (World Bank TEP report).

One important policy question is the extent to which these postreform surges in foreign investment in the TEP countries reflect the impact of the trade reforms, more liberal foreign investment regulations, or an improved macroeconomic environment. Case studies of the individual TEP countries suggest that more liberal foreign investment codes, as well as an improved macroeconomic climate, are important factors. Trade reforms did not appear to play any independent role in encouraging foreign investment inflows. However, trade reform is critical for ensuring that foreign investment is not "immiserizing," as in Kenya. In addition, when foreign investment flows to more open economies it is much more likely to be oriented toward export markets than domestic markets. A joint program of trade reform and liberalization of foreign investment codes will ensure that increased foreign investment inflows lead to welfare gains, not losses, for the host country.

Individual case studies help to shed light on the importance of policy and macroeconomic climate in promoting foreign investment inflows. In Guatemala, although the surge in foreign investment coincided with the trade reform in 1987, the increase in FDI probably reflects the sharp increase in *maquila* assembly and investment related to the Caribbean Basin Initiative (CBI). Guatemalan investment policy, one of the most liberal in Central America, has not been a deterrent to foreign investment. The only detrimental aspects are the treatment of foreigners under the tax code and the processing delays associated with informal approval procedures that can take up to three years. Under the tax code, dividend income to resident investors is exempt from income tax, whereas dividends to foreign shareholders are subject to a 12.5 percent withholding tax. An even more important deterrent to FDI in Guatemala is the perception that the country is unstable economically and politically. This perception is exacerbated by the fact that foreign exchange is frequently unavailable and exchange rate policy is often erratic.

Figure 8.7. *Trends in Foreign Investment*
(net FDI flows as share of GDP)

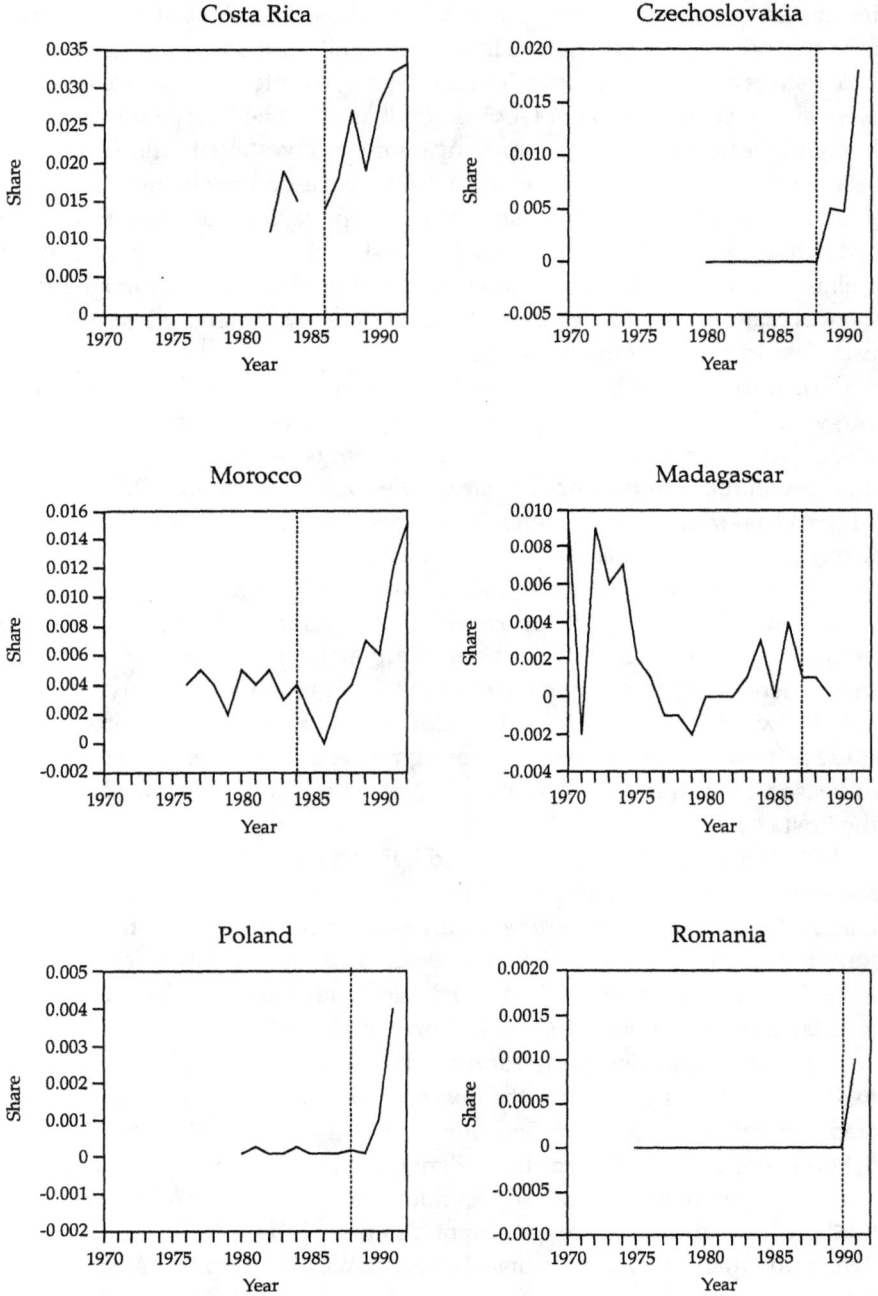

(figure continues on following page)

(Figure 8.7 continued)

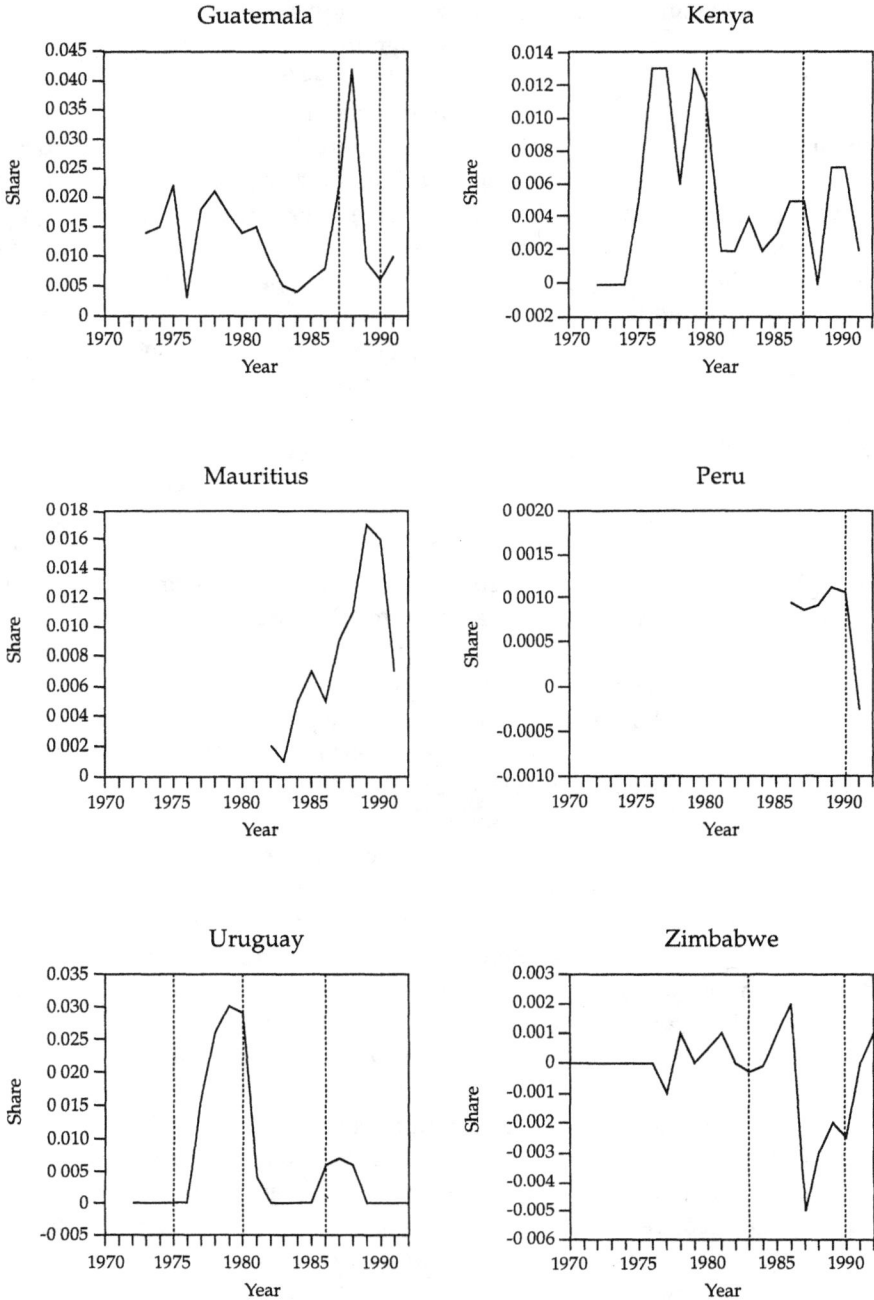

Note: Dotted lines represent years of trade reforms.

In Vietnam, FDI has been increasing since a foreign investment law was introduced in 1987 and the country began to encourage foreign investors. Following a 1990 revision that clarified several provisions to the law, reviewing authorities approved twice as much foreign investment as the previous year. The increasing trend continued in 1992 and 1993 as further reforms were introduced. Yet the actual share of foreign investment in the country remains quite small. In large part, this reflects continuing uncertainty about the macroeconomic climate. Nevertheless, regulatory constraints in three areas do remain a problem for foreign investors, and efforts to remove those impediments could help to increase foreign investment inflows. First, the current screening process for foreign investment should be streamlined by abolishing the list of priority industries, which is too broad to be useful. Second, the requirement for feasibility studies by small- and medium-scale foreign investors should be eliminated. Third, the issue of overlapping authority for approving foreign investment between local and central governments, and among multiple agencies within the central government, needs to be resolved.

The role played by trade reforms, policies, and the macroeconomic climate is well illustrated by the varying degrees of success experienced by the Czech Republic, Poland, and Romania in attracting foreign investment. Although all three countries introduced trade and other reforms at about the same time, the Czech Republic has been much more successful than either Poland or Romania in attracting foreign investment (see figure 8.7). Romania has been the least successful of the three countries. Yet all three countries had similar transitional programs, and offered close proximity to European markets, low wages, and a relatively skilled labor force. What accounts for the differential response of foreign investors?

The success of the Czech Republic in attracting more foreign investment stems from the combination of a better macroeconomic outlook and a more liberal investment regime. In contrast, Romania's poor performance in attracting foreign investment has been caused by a weaker macroeconomic environment, distortions in the investment regime, and a binding limitation on profit repatriation that was not removed until July 1993. Although promotional incentives such as tax holidays and tariff exemptions on imports have been very generous in Romania, particularly in relation to the other economies, these types of incentives are clearly not critical to attracting new investment.

Instead, the customs duty exemptions, tax holidays for foreign investors, and joint ventures in Romania have generated distortions and abuse. Because the types of goods eligible for customs duty exemptions have been vaguely defined, customs officials have been granted considerable discretion. Consequently, importers have attempted to bribe officials to qualify for these exemptions, and even exporters have found it more attractive to register as a joint venture than to apply for duty drawback treatment. The exemptions have also raised the effective rate of protection for foreign companies, contributed to the economy's antiexport bias, and provided an unfair advantage to foreign firms in relation to domestic firms and SOEs.

In response to these types of problems, other countries in the region have reformed their policies to limit both the range and duration of customs exemptions. The Czech Republic has revoked all custom exemptions. In Hungary and Poland, only in-kind contributions of imported capital goods remain exempt; however, special incentives promised to existing investors were not withdrawn.

Romania also provides all new firms with an automatic two- to five-year holiday from taxation on profits. It appears that this incentive has also done little to promote foreign investment and has contributed to additional distortions. The differing lengths of tax holidays tend to distort the allocation of capital. Investors have taken advantage of the tax holiday by registering as a new joint venture when the firm's tax holiday expires. This problem of multiple registrations for the purpose of tax evasion is particularly acute because the government is deprived of the fastest growing component of the tax base. This is likely to lead the government to raise taxes elsewhere or adopt inflationary finance to bridge the revenue gap. In response to these problems, countries elsewhere in the region, including the Czech Republic, Hungary, Poland, and the Slovak Republic, have now taken steps to eliminate or restrict tax holidays.

Romania's restriction on the repatriation of profits earned in lei acted to offset the incentives to foreign investors provided by the tax holidays and customs duty exemptions. Limits on profit repatriation have served as a major deterrent to foreign investment in many countries. Another TEP country, Zimbabwe, experienced significant declines in foreign investment inflows when repatriation of profits was eliminated in 1984 (see figure 8.7). Foreign investment inflows increased with a relaxation of the law in 1986, but subsequently declined in 1987 when profit repatriation was again restricted (see figure 8.7). Romania, however, removed its restriction on profit repatriation in 1993. In removing the restriction on repatriation of profits, Romania joins the rest of the region in moving toward a policy that allows full, unrestricted repatriation of profits, dividends, and proceeds from the liquidation of assets, after the payment of taxes and at the official rate of exchange.

Easing the Transition under Trade Reform: The Role of Foreign Investment

Foreign capital is an important component of domestic accumulation, accounting for as much as one-third of the capital stock in countries like Morocco. In Mauritius, foreign investors played an important role in the development of textile exports. Nevertheless, the fraction of foreign investment as a share of GDP, as indicated by figure 8.7, remains low. Most of the foreign investment in developing countries is concentrated in a few high-performing countries such as China. Although FDI currently accounts for the largest single source of capital inflows to developing countries, only a small fraction of global foreign investment flows are attracted to industrializing countries.

In light of the recent peso crisis in Mexico, one question that arises is the extent to which these flows are a sustainable source of capital for promoting growth, rising wages, and a better work force. Although FDI is a more stable source of capital than portfolio investment, many foreign firms are in footloose industries such as garments, where exit costs are low.

Although foreign investment may be more unstable than domestic sources of capital, the alternative route is even more unattractive: foregoing the new job opportunities created by the entrance of multinational firms. The Mexican case is more a lesson in managing exchange rates than in the costs of financing a trade reform with foreign investment. The government's delay in adjusting the exchange rate magnified the inevitable devaluation and exacerbated the effects of the policy failure. A more realistic exchange rate policy could have prevented the current crisis.

Formulating Policy Guidelines

Country experience suggests the following policy guidelines for maximizing both the magnitude of foreign investment inflows and the benefits derived from foreign investors:

- *Promote policies for a stable macroeconomic environment and long-run growth.* Empirical evidence on the determinants of foreign investment suggest that the most important factors in attracting FDI are large markets, high growth, and a stable political and macroeconomic climate. Consequently, adjustment policies (including trade reforms) are likely to be the most powerful tools for attracting foreign investment in the longer term, as countries resume higher growth and attain macroeconomic stability.
- *Avoid targeting sectors in the approval process.* Screening for the financial soundness of investment proposals (Romania, Vietnam) is not warranted. In general it is unlikely to be successful because government staff often do not have the time, expertise, or access to accurate data for the task. Recognizing this, the Czech Republic and Hungary recently dismantled their mandatory screening and approval process for investment. If government officials wish to control investment in some sensitive sectors, such as defense, a short negative list should be used (as in Poland).
- *Eliminate restrictions on profit repatriation.* Evidence drawn from country case studies in Romania, Zimbabwe, and elsewhere suggests

that imposing limits on profit repatriation is likely to act as a major deterrent to foreign investment.

- *Eliminate special incentives for foreign investors.* Providing attractive packages for foreign investors in the form of tax holidays, duty-free inputs, and subsidies for infrastructure should be eliminated. Evidence suggests that such incentives are not effective in attracting foreign investors. In addition, it is not clear why regulations should favor the foreign investor over the domestic firm, as in Vietnam, or formerly in Czechoslovakia, where profits were taxed at a higher rate for state enterprises (50 percent) than joint ventures (40 percent).

Recent experience suggests that countries are sometimes forced to give higher concessions to outside investors in order to compete with other countries that are doing the same thing. These kinds of bidding wars (see, for example, the CMEA experience) suggest the need for a more coordinated policy toward foreign investors across countries. One possibility would be for multilateral institutions such as the World Bank, the IMF, or the World Trade Organization to take a more active role, in an effort to both minimize destructive bidding and to encourage foreign investment inflows to developing countries through more uniform, transparent, and stable policies.

Tax and tariff concessions disrupt the uniformity of trade reform packages and lead to an erosion in the tax base. The need to minimize special treatment for foreign investors is particularly important because there is no clear rationale for subsidizing these investors. There is no evidence to date that foreign investment per se generates externalities in the form of technology transfer to domestic competitors.

Bibliography

Bell, L. 1997, "The Impact of Minimum Wages in Mexico and Colombia." *Journal of Labor Economics* 15(3), Part 2 (July).

Carrington, William J., and Asad Zaman. 1994. "Interindustry Variation in the Costs of Job Displacement." *Journal of Labor Economics* 12 (April): 243–75.

Castillo-Freeman, Alida, and Richard B. Freeman. 1991. "When the Minimum Wage Really Bites: The Effect of the United States–Level Minimum on Puerto Rico." Proceedings of the Industrial and Labor Relations Association, Madison, Wisconsin.

Currie, J., and Ann Harrison. 1997. "Sharing the Costs: The Impact of Trade Reform on Capital and Labor in Morocco." *Journal of Labor Economics* 15(3), Part 2 (July).

de la Cuadra, Sergio, and Dominique Hachette. 1989. "Chile." In Michael Michaely, Armeane M. Choksi, and Demetrios Papageorgiou, eds., *Liberalizing Foreign Trade*, vol. 1. New York: Basil Blackwell.

Fallon, Peter R., and Robert E. B. Lucas. 1991. "The Impact of Changes in Job Security Regulations in India and Zimbabwe." *The World Bank Economic Review* 5 (3): 395–413.

Freeman, Richard B. 1993. "Labor Market Institutions and Policies: Help or Hindrance to Economic Development?" Proceedings of the World Bank Annual Conference on Development Economics 1992, Washington, D.C.

Freeman, Richard B., and L. Katz. 1991. "Industrial Wage and Employment Determination in an Open Economy." In John M. Abowd and Richard B. Freeman, eds., *Immigration, Trade and the Labor Market.* Chicago: University of Chicago Press.

Gaston, Noel, and Daniel Trefler. 1994. "The Role of International Trade and Trade Policy in the Labour Markets of Canada and the United States." *World Economy* 17: 45–62.

Grossman, Gene. 1986. "Imports as a Cause of Injury: The Case of the U.S. Steel Industry." *Journal of International Economics* (20): 201–23.

_____. 1987. "The Employment and Wage Effects on Import Competition in the United States." *Journal of International Economic Integration* (2): 1–23.

Gruber, J. 1997. "The Incidence of Payroll Taxation: Evidence from Chile." *Journal of Labor Economics* 17 (July): S72–S101.

Haddad, Mona. 1993. "How Trade Liberalization Affected Productivity in Morocco." Policy Research Working Paper 1096. World Bank Policy Research Department, Washington, D.C.

Hammermesh, Daniel. 1993. *Labor Demand.* Princeton, N.J.: Princeton University Press.

Harrison, Ann, and Roumeen Islam. 1993. "Morocco Private Sector Assessment: The Labor Market." Washington, D.C.: World Bank. Photocopy.

Krueger, Anne O. 1983. *Trade and Employment in Development Countries.* Chicago: University of Chicago Press.

MacIsaac, Donna, and Martin Rama. 1997. "Determinants of Hourly Earnings in Ecuador: the Role of Labor Market Regulations." *Journal of Labor Economics* 15(3), Part 2 (July): 136–65.

Rama, Martin. 1994. "The Labor Market and Trade Reform in Manufacturing." In Michael Connolly and Jaime de Melo, eds., *The Effects of Protectionism on a Small Country.* Washington, D.C.: World Bank.

Revenga, Ana. 1992. "Exporting Jobs? The Impact of Import Competition on Employment and Wages in U.S. Manufacturing." *Quarterly Journal of Economics* 107 (February): 255–84.

_____. 1997. "Employment and Wage Effects of Trade Liberalization: the Case of Mexican Manufacturing." *Journal of Labor Economics* 15(3), Part 2 (July): 20–43.

Tybout, James, and M. Daniel Westbrook. 1995. "Trade Liberalization and the Dimensions of Efficiency Change in Mexican Manufacturing Industries." *Journal of International Economics* 39: 53–78.

World Bank. Various TEP reports. See appendix A in this volume for a detailed listing.

9

Trade Policy Reform and Agriculture

Alberto Valdés

The purpose of the United Nations Development Programme (UNDP)/World Bank Trade Expansion Program (TEP) country studies for seventeen developing countries was to evaluate their trade reform programs at an early stage, and make recommendations as to further policy adjustments to ensure that trade policies were kept on track. In order to make this early assessment, the UNDP/World Bank studies for most countries were done only two or three years after the initiation of the reform process (see table 9.1). Overall, it seems that the TEP missions arrived at an opportune time and contributed to the trade reform process. However, conclusions as to how far trade policy reforms have progressed and how successful they have been cannot be derived from the country reports. However, a brief ex post analysis of the effect of these reforms on agricultural growth and overall growth is presented in the section *Sectoral and overall growth.*

Based on the TEP reports, which cover 1988 to 1993, this commentary examines the implications of this early phase of the trade reforms for agriculture in ten of the TEP countries.[1] Was the reform package conducive to promoting an efficient and dynamic agricultural sector? Were there issues regarding the mix and sequencing of reforms that could jeopardize the effectiveness of reform efforts? What can we learn from this experience for future reform efforts?

Having a larger tradable component than most sectors in most of these countries, the structure of incentives for agriculture is strongly affected by developments in trade and exchange rate policies. The evidence for eighteen developing countries during the period from 1965 to 1985 clearly shows that the trade and exchange rate regime discriminated heavily against agriculture, directly, by taxation of the sector, and indirectly, by protecting industry and real exchange rate (RER) misalignment (Schiff and Valdés 1992). Moreover, the study showed that indirect taxation of the sector was twice as important as direct taxation. As agriculture was a relatively large sector of the economy in several of the countries sampled, the consequence of

The author is most grateful to Lia Venezian for her excellent research assistance and useful comments, and to John Nash for his comments on an earlier version.

1. These ten were the TEP countries in which agriculture issues were most important.

Table 9.1. *Evaluation of Trade Reforms at Time of TEP Missions*

Country (period of liberalization program)	Mission	Quantitative restrictions (QRs) on imports	Tariffs	Export policy
Low-income:				
Kenya (1978–80, 1987–91, and 1992)	Jan. 1993	All QRs had been eliminated by mid-1991; later some were reimposed.	34 percent (nominal average), maximum 70 percent.	Export licensing eliminated; duty drawback schemes work poorly.
Madagascar (1986–89)	Jan. 1990	Import bans are only 2 percent of import lines.	46 percent (average nominal tariff).	Industrial free export zones, imported inputs are exempt of tariffs.
Mali (1986–88)	July 1988	All imports require licenses, but authorized import volumes are not binding.	Tariffs of 0 to 100 percent, depending on the product and based on posted prices instead of real import values. Customs duty of 5 percent, and a special tax of French franc zone (CFA) francs 5/kg.	All exporters require licenses; however, a large part of agricultural exports passes through parallel channels. Export tax of 5 to 10 percent and an anticyclical tax on profits (mostly agricultural products).
Uganda (1987–90)	May 1990	100 percent of imports subject to QRs; 85 percent of total are with government allocated foreign exchange.	10 to 50 percent. Previously exempted raw materials and capital goods now subject to 10 percent tariff.	Only coffee (97 percent of total exports) has a residual export tax. All non-coffee exporters require export licenses, but are allowed to retain foreign exchange earnings for input imports.

(table continues on following page)

(Table 9.1 continued)

Country (period of liberalization program)	Mission	Quantitative restrictions (QRs) on imports	Tariffs	Export policy
Middle-income:				
Costa Rica (1986–91)	Aug. 1991	No QRs, but agricultural imports face nontariff barriers (NTBs).	17 percent (nominal average). Temporary and ad hoc tariff surcharges; exemptions for imported inputs of nonexporting activities.	Significant promotion of nontraditional exports, taxation of traditional agricultural exports.
Guatemala (1986–89)	Jan. 1989	None.	21 percent (average nominal tariff).	QRs on exports of basic grains. Temporary tax of 40 to 80 percent on exports to collect devaluation and higher world price revenues. No duty drawback scheme for exporters.
Mauritius (1980–)	Feb. 1992	None.	30 percent (average nominal tariff). Fiscal duties (0 percent to 600 percent), import levies and more than 400 tariff exemptions.	Export tax on sugar. Preferential treatment for export processing zones.
Peru (1990–91)	Mar. 1991	All QRs eliminated by Sep. 1990.	17 percent (average nominal tariff). Temporary tariff surcharges for fiscal reasons.	Import duty exemption is now extended to all exporters. Export tax of 5 percent on traditional exports, except for a 10 percent tax on mining exports.

(table continues on following page)

(*Table 9.1 continued*)

Country (period of liberalization program)	Mission	Quantitative restrictions (QRs) on imports	Tariffs	Export policy
Transition: Romania (1990–92)	Dec. 1992	State monopolies and QRs have been eliminated. Important restrictions in acquiring foreign exchange for importers.	12 percent early 1993, scheduled to increase to 18 (average nominal tariff).	Export quotas and licenses on raw material and foods that are subsidized for the domestic market. New duty drawback scheme.
Vietnam (1987–88 and 1991–92)	Oct. 1992	Import licenses for all importers. Only raw material for cigarettes subject to quotas. Controlled imports of fertilizers, automobile and television parts.	11 percent (nominal average tariff).	All exporters require licenses. Only rice is subject to export quotas. Export bans only on logs, sawn timber, and rattan. Exports of crude oil and rice still controlled by government. Export taxes from 0 to 45 percent of free-on-board (FOB) values.

Note: Most export controls are imposed on agricultural commodities. Few countries restrict manufactured exports.
Source: Central America Country Department, World Bank, based on UNDP/World Bank Trade Expansion Program country reports.

trade reforms on the economic performance of agriculture was important for overall growth in these countries.

The structure of this commentary is as follows: The section *What kind of changes?* examines what types of reforms directly affect agricultural trade (tariffs, quantitative restrictions, and subsidies). The following section, *Macroeconomic variables*, examines the interface between some key macroeconomic considerations and incentives for agriculture. *Reducing antiexport bias* attempts to examine the extent to which the reforms succeeded in reducing or removing the antiexport bias usually found in developing countries toward their agriculture.[2] The section *Sectoral and overall growth* comments on the effect of agricultural sector reforms on growth, both within that sector and more broadly. *Reform in other sectors* discusses how reforms in other sectors could enhance agriculture's performance. The last section presents concluding comments.

What Kind of Changes?

Most of the TEP countries tried to reduce quantitative restrictions and lower tariffs, as well as reduce export taxes; however, in some countries (Mali, Uganda, Vietnam, and to some extent Costa Rica and Kenya), quantitative restrictions were still far too influential at the time the reports were written. This is an important distortion. As shown in Michaely, Choksi, and Papageorgiou (1990), liberalization programs that do not decisively remove quantitative restrictions and other nontariff barriers (NTBs) have usually failed.

The country sample can be roughly grouped into three sets based on differences in initial conditions. These are four low-income African countries; four middle-income countries; and two transitional economies. Table 9.1 presents quantitative restrictions, tariff levels, and export policy for each country at the time when evaluation of reforms was undertaken by the TEP studies.

As a group, the four low-income African countries were the least advanced in their trade reforms. Their trade reforms decreased import restrictions, but postreform tariffs in the four countries were high, import policies lacked transparency, and the countries still taxed or required export licenses, or both, for their agricultural exports (table 9.2). In Kenya, Mali, and Uganda, most imports were subject to license requirements. Mali and Uganda taxed their exports. Although Kenya did not directly tax exports, duty drawback schemes functioned poorly and exporters faced substantial bureaucratic procedures.

Middle-income countries showed better progress in the opening up of their economies (table 9.2). Their average nominal tariffs were lower than those of

---

2. Attempts, because this issue was not addressed explicitly in most reports.

Table 9.2. Macroeconomic Policy and Trade Reform

Country (period of liberalization program)	Consistency with trade reform	Exchange rate (ER) policy	Fiscal policy	Government revenues and tax reform
Costa Rica (1986–91)	Currently inconsistent, although trade reform has so far been successful	Periodic devaluations of the nominal ER have led to a modest depreciation of the RER. Tight monetary policy has not curbed inflationary pressures from the fiscal sector, and this has tended to appreciate the RER.	Fiscal deficit of 5.1 percent in 1990 is expected to fall in 1991 due to increased revenues, but current expenditure level is high.	Temporary tax surcharges on imports and increase in the sales tax.
Guatemala (1986–88)	Consistent	In 1986 the foreign exchange market was simplified to three: "official" ER for before-reforms debt service (fixed ER), "regulated" market for trade operations (fixed ER), and "banking" market with floating ER for other operations.	Reduction of the fiscal deficit to 2.7 percent of GDP in 1986.	A temporary tax surcharge of 40 to 80 percent on traditional exports (to be phased out by 1990); 4 percent tax on nontraditional exports, and two-year suspension of fiscal incentives to exports.
Kenya (1978–80), (1987–91), and (1992)	Inconsistent	Crawling peg for nominal ER, adjusts less than domestic inflation and has led to RER appreciation over the 1980s. A new foreign exchange market based on retention of export earnings will allow for more ER flexibility.	Money financing of the fiscal deficit; increase of current expenditures; reduced public investment.	Import taxes represent 23 percent of total revenues in 1989; revenues from export taxes are not significant.
Madagascar (1986–89)	Consistent	Madagascar franc tied to a basket of currencies. Since foreign exchange operations for importers have been liberalized in 1987, RER has remained stable.	Fiscal deficit has stabilized in 1987–88 at 4 percent of GDP, from 18 percent of GDP in 1981.	Trade taxes represent 62 percent of government revenues in 1988. Most export taxes have been removed except for three traditional exports.

(table continues on following page)

(Table 9.2 continued)

Country (period of liberalization program)	Consistency with trade reform	Exchange rate (ER) policy	Fiscal policy	Government revenues and tax reform
Mali (1986–88)	Apparently consistent	Belongs to West African Monetary Union, cannot unilaterally modify nominal ER. RER depreciated in the 1980s.	Budget deficit of 10 percent in 1988, financed mainly by foreign aid and not by money creation.	Tax/GDP ratio 12 percent in 1988; 40 percent of indirect taxes from foreign trade.
Mauritius (1980–)	Consistent	Nominal ER pegged to a basket of currencies. RER has remained stable, appreciating slightly in the late 1980s.	Fiscal deficits have been controlled and were below 2 percent of GDP in 1990–91.	Taxes on international transactions account for 50 percent of total revenues.
Peru (1990–91)	Consistent	Nominal ER unified and devalued. RER by early 1991 had appreciated, as effect of price liberalization on price of nontradables was greater than effect of QR and tariff reductions.	Money financing of fiscal deficit reduced, lower current expenditures. Total public sector deficit fell from 10 percent of GDP in 1989 to 6.6 percent in 1990.	Revenues were increased by raising taxes, eliminating subsidies, increasing prices of public goods, and freezing public sector wages.
Romania (1990–92)	Inconsistent	Appreciation of the RER in 1991–92. Inefficient official auctions of foreign exchange and overvalued nominal ER. Black market premium of 30 percent in December 1992. High inflation rates have led to appreciation of the RER.	Money financing of the fiscal deficit (estimated at 6 percent of GDP in 1992), and of quasi-fiscal expenses such as debts of state enterprises and capitalization of state-owned banks.	Basic structure of subsidies remains, and consumer subsidies are 3 percent of GDP in 1991. Elimination proposed in 1993, together with price controls.

(table continues on following page)

(Table 9.2. continued)

Country (period of liberalization program)	Consistency with trade reform	Exchange rate (ER) policy	Fiscal policy	Government revenues and tax reform
Uganda (1987–90)	Inconsistent	ER regime based on non-transparent, administrative allocation of foreign exchange. Over-valued fixed official ER for government imports, coffee exports, and debt service; parallel rate for others. Unstable and appreciated RER in the 1980s.	Money financing of the public deficit led to high inflation rates.	Tax/GDP of 5.6 percent in 1988. Half of all tax revenues are from international trade.
Vietnam (1987–88) and (1991–92)	Consistent	ER unified and devalued in 1989, RER has appreciated 1991–92, due in part to strong capital inflows.	Money financing of the fiscal deficit was reduced in 1991 and tight fiscal policy led to a decline in the fiscal deficit from 7.9 percent of GDP in 1990 to 2.5 percent in 1991, due to lower current and investment expenditures.	Reforms contribution to revenues of state enterprises has fallen, but is still 60 percent of total. Agriculture and trade taxes' shares have increased, while revenues from the private sector have remained stable.

Note: ER = exchange rate, GDP = gross domestic product, and RER = real exchange. For mission dates, see table 9.1.
Source: UNDP/World Bank Trade Expansion Program country reports.

the first group. However, we assume due to fiscal revenue considerations, some countries still taxed their traditional exports (mostly agricultural) and applied temporary surcharges on some imports.

Three of these countries had explicit export promotion policies at the time of the studies, but import duty drawback schemes did not work very efficiently (in Guatemala they had not yet been implemented). Mauritius had increased its exports significantly by implementing export promotion zones and by taking full advantage of its special access to European Union (EU) markets for its sugar and textiles and apparel exports. (Mauritius has the largest sugar import quota to the European Union). This also meant that export diversification was not high, and 90 percent of Mauritius' exports were concentrated on six products. Costa Rica also promoted nontraditional exports by duty-free imports, direct subsidies, and three export promotion institutions.

In Peru the average nominal tariff fell from 45 percent to 17 percent in less than a year. Tariff exemptions, which had covered about 50 percent of imports, were eliminated in order to increase government revenues. By March 1991 most NTBs had been eliminated, including quantitative restrictions, quality certifications, and state monopolies on imports of some agricultural products. However, agricultural imports were still covered by a special regime (specific duties on border prices) as a mechanism to support prices for domestic producers of milk products, corn, wheat, sugar, and food pastes.

The two transitional economies (Romania and Vietnam) had made considerable progress in liberalizing trade. Quantitative restrictions on imports were converted to tariffs. Previously the trading system consisted of state trading monopolies and quotas and trade bans on almost all products. However, to fully benefit from trade liberalization these countries still had to make major changes on other fronts, such as foreign exchange markets, property rights legislation, and domestic price deregulation.

In the case of Romania, direct quantitative restrictions on imports had been removed but imports were still limited by an inefficient foreign exchange market. Some exports were still restricted by a rigid regime of nontransferable licenses that linked future quota allocations to current quota fulfillments. Trade promotion institutions had been introduced, but these were still relatively inefficient. The duty drawback scheme for exporters needed strengthening and free trade zones had been proposed.

In Vietnam by 1993, there were few quantitative restrictions left, average tariffs were low, and decisionmaking on production and pricing had been decentralized to the enterprise level. However, licensing was widespread and there was still strict government control concerning who could trade, and in what products, through the system.

This progress in the TEP countries can be compared with the experience in agricultural trade liberalization of other reformers. Latin America appears to be the region showing greatest progress. A study of agricultural price and trade policies for selected Latin American countries, for the period 1985–94 analyzed the results of trade reforms and the current status of tariffs and quantitative restrictions for agricultural tradables (Valdés 1995).[3] It found that, although quantitative restrictions remain in the region, there has been substantial progress toward reducing restrictions in the last few years compared with the 1980s. Quantitative restrictions on agricultural products have declined significantly in most countries, while tariffs for the most part are under 20 percent (the exceptions are Colombia, with a maximum tariff of 30 percent on some products, and Uruguay, with 36 percent).

Although progress and completeness of liberalization varies widely across countries, developing countries in other regions still have a considerable way to go in opening up their economies and agricultural trade (Valdés and McCalla 1996). In the former Soviet Union and Eastern Europe, Estonia is an exception. It has carried out significant liberalization. Since 1992, Estonia has had zero tariffs for most products, with some exceptions in agriculture and automobiles. Import quotas and licensing requirements are not restrictive, and state trading enterprises have neither exclusive rights nor special privileges in purchases or sales related to imports and exports. Indonesia, which started reforms in 1986, lowered tariffs to a range of 5 to 30 percent on agricultural products, but many quantitative restrictions remain, and a parastatal enterprise has a legal monopoly on imports of wheat, rice, soybean, and sugar. India started economic reforms in 1991 and reduced trade barriers for manufactured goods but not for agricultural trade. In addition to very high tariff bindings, parastatals have a legal monopoly on imports of most food products and import licenses are required for most agricultural products.

Macroeconomic Variables

There is evidence from previous studies that one of the main causes of the reversal or discontinuation of trade reform programs is incompatible macroeconomic policies (see, for example, Michaely, Choksi, and Papageorgiou 1990). This policy inconsistency affects the output response of agriculture to the trade reforms implemented (Schiff and Valdés 1992).

We suggest a simple framework to examine the general direction of long-term profitability of the tradable sector in agriculture. Because agriculture has a large tradable component, the RER, defined as the ratio of the price of tradable to nontradables, is the most important price for both agricultural exports and import-competing products. In trade reform programs that succeeded,

---

3. Argentina, Brazil, Chile, Colombia, Dominican Republic, Ecuador, Paraguay, and Uruguay.

that is, in which RERs depreciated (implying an increase in the relative price of tradables) or were stable, the agricultural sector grew faster and increased its share in the gross domestic product (GDP).

Expansionary fiscal policies cause a deterioration in the trade balance and put upward pressure on prices of nontradables, leading to an appreciation of the RER. Restrictive or neutral fiscal and monetary policies that keep inflation low, and thus sustain an RER depreciation, are critical to successful trade reforms.

Another important factor in sustained trade reform is an initial RER depreciation. It increases the price of tradables, helping exports and at the same time raising the domestic price of import-competing activities for which protection has usually been reduced as a result of liberalization. Initial depreciation of the RER and stable RERs in the medium term help reduce pressure for trade reform reversals by promoting export growth and overall economic growth.

Also important for agriculture is the link between macroeconomic policies and real interest rates. In countries where capital markets are more developed, tight monetary policy tends to control inflationary pressures caused by high public expenditure. Real interest rates are higher than they would be with lower fiscal deficits, and they reduce investment and credit to the agricultural sector. In countries with access to world capital markets, high domestic interest rates also attract capital inflows, inducing further appreciation of the RER, which harms the tradable sector of the economy.

What do we find? In order to assess consistency with trade reform, a brief analysis of the evolution of the RER and related macroeconomic policies in the TEP countries was carried out. (Table 9.2 gives more details of macroeconomic policies in each country.) Out of ten countries examined, three (Kenya, Romania, and Uganda) had macroeconomic policies inconsistent with sustained trade reform; that is, they had persistent money-financed fiscal deficits that led to inflation and RER appreciation, which in turn undermined the reform effort. The rest had consistent macroeconomic policies, although in some countries there were certain elements in policy that could lead to future inconsistencies (particularly, a failure to reduce further their fiscal deficits).

Of the four low-income countries, Kenya had one trade reversal in 1980 and another, partial reversal in 1991. The main reason seemed to be money-financed fiscal deficits and RER appreciation, with subsequent attempts to achieve external balance by reestablishing import restrictions instead of devaluing the exchange rate. Uganda also had money-financed deficits that led to high inflation, exchange rate appreciation, and unsustainable current account deficits, all factors which impeded further liberalization efforts. Both Madagascar and Mali had apparently stable RERs and managed either to control their fiscal deficits or finance them without money creation, helped by substantial foreign aid.

Most middle-income countries had implemented macroeconomic policies consistent with trade reforms. The most important factor was reduction of fiscal deficits, by both increasing revenues (tax reforms) and decreasing expenditures.

Costa Rica, which up to 1991 had a successful liberalization effort, with export growth and diversification, faced the possibility of partial trade reversal. Although fiscal deficits declined, current expenditures in 1991 were high and fueling inflation in spite of tight monetary policy. Appreciation of the RER and high real interest rates threatened both production and export growth, and therefore there was pressure to reverse reforms. Costa Rica's import licensing system was not fully dismantled in the reform process, and NTBs were easily renewable. Credibility of reforms hinged on reduction of public expenditures—mainly by lowering public sector wages and employment—and removal of import licenses.

In the two transitional economies, consistency of macroeconomic policies and trade reform is clearly related to fiscal deficit and RER management. In the case of Romania, money financing of the fiscal deficit, together with price liberalizations, led to high inflation rates and RER appreciation, which discouraged export growth. The foreign exchange market regime was also one of the most serious restrictions to trade growth because inefficient auctions of foreign exchange at an overvalued nominal exchange rate caused exporters to retain foreign exchange earnings and importers to encounter long delays in obtaining foreign exchange, thus posing a further strain to productive sectors.

In Vietnam, the exchange rate was unified in 1989 and, after a failed stabilization effort in 1990–91, inflation was slowed in 1992 by tight monetary and fiscal policies. In 1993 strong capital inflows led to exchange rate appreciation pressures. Because the monetary authority did not have the financial instruments to support the exchange rate by sterilizing capital inflows, further liberalization of imports as a means of increasing demand for foreign exchange and restraining the real appreciation was proposed in the report.

Reducing Antiexport Bias

In the previous section, the evolution of an aggregate measure of the RER was used in order to present a general direction of long-term profitability of the tradable sector in relation to home goods. However, in analyzing the effect of trade policy in agriculture, which in most developing countries is characterized by a large tradable component, it is also important to distinguish between exportables and import-competing goods.

The antiexport bias present in many countries before trade reforms was the result of trade and macroeconomic policies that protected the industrial or import-competing sectors of the economy at the expense of other sectors, especially agriculture. A policy that protects industry raises the cost of importable inputs such as fertilizers, machinery, and other materials used by farmers. Domestic import prices increase in response to import restrictions, and this eventually leads to an increase in wages and the price of home goods, which all rise in relation to the prices of exportables (including agricultural exportables) determined by world markets.

Trade policy thus alters the relative price between importables and exportables, and between these and home goods. Several indicators are available to measure the effect of trade interventions on production incentives (table 9.3). Two indicators commonly used in the literature are the nominal

Table 9.3. Measurement Concepts of Agricultural Protection

Concept	Policy coverage	Definition
Nominal rate of protection (NRP)	Support policy on output markets	$NRP = 100 (Pi-Pw)/Pw$ Pi = domestic price Pw = world price
Producer subsidy equivalents	Various direct agricultural policies	Aggregate measure for the impact of agricultural policy (trade and budgetary outlays) on producer earnings.
Effective rate of protection (ERP)	Output and input market policies for one sector	$ERP = 100 (VAi-VAw)/VAw$ VAi = value added with protection VAw = value added under free trade conditions
True protection	Implications of trade policies in one sector on relative prices between sectors of the economy	True tariff: True subsidy: $t^* = \Delta(Pm/Pnt)$ $s^* = \Delta(Px/Pnt)$ Pm, Px, Pnt are prices of importables, exportables and nontradables. Δ denotes change in the variable
Nominal rate of protection of the price ratio between agriculture and nonagriculture	Measures impact of direct (agricultural) and indirect (economywide) policies on agricultural relative price	Total agricultural protection: $NRPt = \{(Pa/Pna)/(Pa^*/Pna^*)\}-1$ Pa is the domestic producer price of agricultural product at the official exchange rate; Pna is the price index of nonagricultural goods and services (tradable and nontradable); Pa^* is the border price at the equilibrium exchange rate and Pna^* is Pna without interventions in the nonagricultural sector, at the equilibrium exchange rate.

Source: Adapted from table 1, p. 7, in Wiebelt and others (1992).

and effective rates of protection (NRP and ERP, respectively); and more recently the producer subsidy equivalent (PSE) has been added for farm activities. When ERPs (that is, protection to value added) are available for all tradable sectors, this measure is useful to examine the resource pull between agriculture and other sectors. Similarly, in most countries we find a wide dispersion in NRPs and ERPs *within* agriculture, the incentives almost always being higher for importables.

Evidence from the agriculture surveillance study cited above (Valdés 1995) shows that in eight Latin American countries there has been strong import substitution and antiexport bias in the past. Most countries had a high dispersion of NRPs and ERPs among the various agricultural products. Importables were protected (regional average NRP ranging from 11 to 28 percent between 1985 and 1992) and exportables were taxed (regional average NRP ranging from -6.6 to -2.3 percent in that same period). Since the initiation of trade reforms, the average regional level of direct taxation of exportables has declined from -6.6 percent in the mid-1980s, to -0.7 percent post-1992. However, protection of importables continues, although a reduction is observed in Brazil, Chile, and Colombia.

However, these measures (NRPs, ERPs, and PSEs) do not capture the consequences of industrial protection on the price of home goods, and thus on *true protection* of agricultural production ("omega" in Sjaastad 1980). Using this approach, evidence for several developing countries showed a strong bias against agriculture (Valdés 1986). The concept of direct, indirect, and total agricultural (nominal) protection was used to measure the effect of sectoral and economywide policies on agricultural relative prices (Schiff and Valdés 1992). The results for eighteen countries for the period 1960–85 showed that the indirect tax on agriculture from industrial protection and macroeconomic policies (mainly RER misalignment) was 22 percent on average, with 8 percent direct tax from agricultural pricing policies. Thus, the total tax on the sector was 30 percent on average for this period.

The focus of the TEP country studies was not only agriculture, so the degree of agricultural taxation is touched on only indirectly in the reports. Detailed estimates of agricultural protection were beyond the terms of reference of these studies, and lack of appropriate data for some of the countries would have made estimates difficult.

However, agricultural exports represent a high share of overall exports in all the countries studied except Romania, so the reports provide substantial information to capture a sense of the extent of antiexport bias in these countries before and after the trade reform. Table 9.4 presents a summary of the structure of exports, and of direct and indirect taxation on agricultural exports for the ten countries.

Table 9.4. Bias against Agricultural Exports

Country (period of liberalization program)	Structure of exports	Direct taxation	Indirect taxation
Costa Rica (1986–91)	Traditional exports (coffee, bananas, beef, and sugar) 45 percent of total in 1990, compared to 62 percent in 1986.	Direct taxation of coffee with *ad valorem* tax that varied according to world prices. The coffee pricing and marketing system was heavily regulated by the government.	Nominal protection of nondurable consumption imports was 30 percent, of raw materials for agriculture 11 percent, and 15 percent for agricultural capital goods. There were domestic price controls and/or maximum profit margins for most agricultural importables at the wholesale and retail level. A potential source of anti-export bias was the antidumping code, which could be used to protect certain activities.
Guatemala (1986–89)	Exports of coffee, sugar, and beef over 70 percent of total exports.	Direct temporary taxation of primary exports, and QRs on the exports of some grains.	Effective protection of manufacturing sector was 48 percent in 1987; expected to decline to 37 percent by 1990. Guatemala has potential for expanding agricultural frontier.
Kenya (1978–80), (1987–91), and (1992)	1985–89 fuel 19 percent manufactures 15 percent traditional primary 55 percent horticulture 11 percent	No direct taxation of agricultural exports.	Average (tariff-based) effective protection rates for manufacturing as a whole had fallen slightly but still 45 percent in 1992. Numerous government regulations were a barrier for small and medium-size firms in the formal export sector. Horticulture appeared to be the only sector with lower taxation.

(table continues on following page)

(Table 9.4 continued)

Country (period of liberalization program)	Structure of exports	Direct taxation	Indirect taxation
Madagascar (1986–89)	Primary commodities over 70 percent of total exports.	Direct taxation of coffee, vanilla, and cloves, depending on level of world prices. Although marketing boards for coffee, cloves, and pepper had been eliminated, the government still intervened in price determination.	Effective protection in several industrial subsectors was reduced by the reform, and that of agriculture increased from 12 percent in 1984 to 57 percent in 1989. Industrial free trade zones introduced. Although duty drawback schemes existed for exporters, they had not been used so far.
Mali (1986–88)	1982–86 cotton 40 percent cattle 33 percent	Cotton subsector was directly taxed; producers received about half of the export price. Government oversaw all production and marketing processes.	Little refunding of taxes on imports used in export goods production. Extensive smuggling of imports undermined protection for state-produced goods and protected industries and reduced government revenues.
Mauritius (1980–)	sugar 30 percent, and textiles and apparel 50 percent of total exports.	Export tax on sugar was 9 percent. Sugar is marketed by the government, and producers receive a price that is a weighted average of prices in three markets: EC (80 percent of total), domestic (6 percent), and world market (14 percent). Local sales were below world price; EC price above world prices.	Preferential treatment of export-processing zones (EPZs) led to negative protection of exports from non EPZs. Indirect tax on exports from tariffs was estimated in the range of 30 to 42 percent.

(table continues on following page)

(Table 9.4 continued)

Country (period of liberalization program)	Structure of exports	Direct taxation	Indirect taxation
Peru (1990–91)	Traditional exports (mining, fish meal, and coffee) were 70 percent of total exports in 1990.	In Feb. 1991 direct taxes were 5 percent on traditional exports.	Indirect taxation of traditional exportable crops (coffee and sugar) was 15 to 50 percent from protection of importables and 15 percent due to no refunding of tariffs on agricultural inputs. Subsidies for nontraditional exports were temporarily suspended by the reform.
Romania (1990–92)	Over 75 percent of exports were industrial goods; only 8 percent were primary commodities in 1991.	Direct price controls still remained for agricultural products, due to policy of low food prices for consumers. Export bans for many agricultural products, such as major grains, dairy products, and oils.	Indirect price controls as purchasing, storage, and distribution of grains still managed by state-owned enterprises. Romania has a comparative advantage in agriculture if distortions are eliminated.
Uganda (1987–90)	1988 coffee 97 percent non-coffee (cotton, tea, tobacco) 3 percent	Only coffee was subject to a residual tax that varied depending on world prices and was 3 percent in 1989 (has been as high as 37 percent). Producer prices and margins of coffee set by government who also monopolized marketing.	Exchange rate–based implicit tax, since coffee exports were subject to the over-valued official ER. Eight industrial sub-sectors producing consumer goods had access to import subsidies. All private exports still restrained de facto by parastatal monopolies.

(table continues on following page)

(Table 9.4 continued)

Country (period of liberalization program)	Structure of exports	Direct taxation	Indirect taxation
Vietnam (1987–88) and (1991–92)	Agricultural exports were 40 percent of exports to convertible currency area in 1990. Oil was the main export, followed by rice.	Rice exports subject to minimum export prices set by the government. Only rice and rubber subject to export taxes. Government retained control over rice exports in order to ensure adequate domestic consumption and also allocated markets and quantities. Agricultural land tax and various taxes at the marketing level.	Although average tariff was low, there was high dispersion. NTBs also contributed to indirect taxation of some activities, favoring production for the domestic market.

Note: For mission dates, see table 9.1.
Source: UNDP/World Bank Trade Expansion Program country reports.

In general, it seems that trade reforms led to a reduction in the antiexport bias of agricultural products by reducing direct and indirect taxation of agricultural production and exports. This was accomplished by lowering export taxes and quantitative restrictions, by reduced effective protection of manufacturing, and, in some countries, by maintaining a stable or depreciated RER. Nevertheless, in many cases the main agricultural export was still taxed (relative to other agricultural exportables and to nonagricultural exports) because countries tried to promote nontraditional exports but maintained some taxation of traditional exports.

In all four low-income economies agricultural exports represent from two-thirds to all of exports; and in all except Kenya there was direct taxation of primary exports. The number of taxed products and average export tax rates, however, fell. As in other studies (see, for example, World Bank 1994), the continuing domination of traditional export sectors in Africa by parastatal monopolies imposes large direct and indirect costs on producers and impedes the supply response to trade reforms.

In Kenya, indirect taxation of agriculture was still high. Effective protection of industry was 45 percent in 1992, although it fell slightly in later years. Exports stagnated during the 1980s with the exception of horticultural products, which grew without any explicit export promotion policy. (Their share in total exports rose from 5 percent in 1970 to 13 percent in 1989.) In fact, no government intervention existed in the horticulture sector and exporters were taking advantage of direct air routes to the EC market.

In Mali and Uganda, the principal exports (cotton and coffee, respectively) were heavily regulated, and the government oversaw or controlled production and marketing of these products. In Uganda, non-coffee exports were allowed to retain their foreign exchange earnings for input imports, and thus theoretically bypass the exchange rate tax, because they could sell inputs in the domestic market at the parallel exchange rate. In practice all private exporters were indirectly restricted by government agencies. In Mali, a large informal sector and extensive smuggling made trade barriers more ineffective. Although there was, officially, effective protection of certain industries, in practice this protection was undermined by smuggling and fraud.

In Madagascar, effective protection of industry was reduced by the reform, and export taxes became more closely linked to variations in world prices. Effective protection of several industrial subsectors was reduced by reforms, and that of agriculture increased. Principal agricultural exports were constrained by parastatal monopoly control of marketing and pricing.

In the middle-income countries primary exports were still taxed, although at a lower rate than previous to reforms. At the time of the reports in Guatemala and Peru, which were at early stages of trade reform, primary commodities were the bulk of exports and indirect taxation of agriculture was still high. These taxes were later removed.

Costa Rica and Mauritius, which had initiated reforms at least five years previously and had diversified their exports significantly, nevertheless still taxed their main agricultural products relative to other exportables. In spite of this, trade reforms promoted overall export growth and agricultural production. Costa Rica's traditional exports (mainly bananas, beef, and coffee) fell from 62 percent of total exports in 1986, to 45 percent in 1990. In Mauritius, the share of sugar exports fell from 61 percent in 1982, to 28 percent in 1991. Although their share in total exports fell, traditional exports still grew at substantial rates in the 1980s (more than 10 percent for coffee and bananas in Costa Rica for 1986–90, and 12 percent for sugar exports in Mauritius). Beef exports fell in Costa Rica as a result of decline in productivity and export controls on joint products such as milk and leather.

In Romania and Vietnam, several direct controls on agricultural exports remained. In Romania, there were direct price controls and export bans for many products in order to keep food prices low and satisfy domestic demand, although it appeared that producers would be able to export them competitively. The most important indirect taxation came from an overvalued exchange rate and restrictions in use of foreign exchange. There was still high protection of industry relative to agriculture at the time of the TEP report; but it has been substantially dismantled since reforms began.

In Vietnam, agricultural products were taxed at various levels. A land tax for annual crops varied depending on the type of land. For perennial crops, the agricultural tax depended on the average yield and on the life span of the plantation; the rate varied from 10 to 16 percent. The burden of the tax also varied depending on the region. Agricultural exports were also subject to a sales tax at the marketing level (paid by wholesalers, which come immediately before exporters in the marketing channel). Rice was the only product still subject to an export tax. The most important restriction to export growth was the export-licensing system, which was discretionary and a weakness in the banking system.

Sectoral and Overall Growth

Analysis of the effects of trade policy on overall economic growth, agricultural growth, and distribution of income was beyond the scope of the TEP studies. Trade reforms were generally in the initial stages, and it was difficult to evaluate this aspect of liberalization in these countries from the reports. However, a brief ex post examination of overall economic and agricultural growth in the years following the main trade policy reform efforts provides some interesting evidence on the positive effects of liberalization on agricultural growth.

The link between trade liberalization and growth has been extensively studied. A World Bank comparative study of thirty-six liberalization episodes in eighteen countries found that sustained trade reforms led to higher economic growth, even in the short term (Michaely, Choksi, and Papageorgiou 1990). For successful trade reform episodes, the average real GDP growth rate was 4.7 percent in the year before liberalization and 6.0 percent for the four years after reforms (including the first year of the program).

In particular, most prereform trade regimes had discriminated against agriculture, so this sector grew faster after reforms. In sustained episodes, the average agricultural growth rate was 2.8 percent in the year previous to reforms, and 5.7 percent for the four years following reforms. For collapsed episodes, the rates for agricultural growth were 2.8 percent and 2.3 percent for the same periods. Growth in the manufacturing sector in general slowed the first year after reforms and then recovered.

Regarding the effects of reforms on the distribution of income, the empirical evidence of the above-mentioned study does not allow a definite conclusion on whether reforms benefited the poor or not. A priori, in developing countries, where the export sector is usually agriculture and relatively labor-intensive, reforms should tend to increase growth, employment, and eventually real wages in that sector. Because wages are usually low in agriculture, the distribution of income would improve.

In Krueger, Schiff, and Valdés (1990), the hypothesis that agricultural GDP growth is related to overall GDP growth and to price incentives was tested for four Latin American countries. The model tested, which used total protection rates (direct and indirect protection of agricultural products) as a proxy for price incentives, showed that both global economic growth and total price intervention were important variables in the determination of agricultural GDP.

The extensive World Bank comparative study cited above (Schiff and Valdés 1992) on agricultural pricing policy for eighteen developing countries provided evidence on the effects of antiexport bias on agricultural growth. It showed that high taxation of agriculture (in other words, reducing price incentives) was associated with lower growth of both agricultural GDP and the overall economy. The GDP growth rate for the least interventionist group (the least protectionist) was 6.5 percent during 1960–85, compared with 3.3 percent for the most interventionist (extreme taxers).

Further evidence from a recent World Bank report on Sub-Saharan Africa that examined economic reforms in twenty-nine countries found that, when overall macroeconomic policies are considered, the group of countries that had a "large improvement" had a weighted average agricultural growth rate of 3.5 percent per year between 1986 and 1993, in contrast to a 2.5 percent per year growth rate in those countries with "small improvement," and 0.3 percent per year for the same period for countries that had a "deterioration" in overall macroeconomic policies (World Bank 1994).

In the TEP countries where trade reforms have apparently been sustained for at least four years, the results of reforms appear to be positive. When the trade reform efforts are classified in two groups as above, of those countries that have sustained reforms compared with those in which reforms have been reversed, partially reversed, or have not advanced enough, there is a significant divergence in growth rates, both in overall GDP and in agriculture in the successful compared with the collapsed episodes (table 9.5). When trade reforms were successful, GDP growth rates in the first four years of reforms (including the year of reforms) were 5.2 percent per year, in contrast to -1.5 in the collapsed episodes.

Agriculture shows an important rate of recovery, even in the year when reforms were implemented, and an average growth rate of 5.7 percent in the four years following reforms (including the year of reforms). In collapsed or partially sustained episodes, although agriculture still grew at a higher rate than overall GDP (1.1 percent), it was a substantially lower growth rate than in the successful episodes.

In Costa Rica, where the liberalization effort covered by the reform started in 1986, the average GDP growth rate for 1986–90 was 4.6 percent, after very low growth in the early 1980s. Exports grew 7 percent in dollar terms for the same period, and nontraditional exports grew at a 15 percent average rate (30 percent of these exports are agricultural). Although on average growth in traditional export value was low, export volumes for the two main traditional exports, coffee and bananas, grew 3 and 10 percent respectively during 1986–90. Minimum wages for agriculture (which are binding in the sector) increased 2 percent in real terms during 1986–91, but there is no additional information on income distribution effects.

In Mauritius, real GDP growth was 6 percent on average for 1981–90, and exports grew 15 percent in dollar terms in that same period, mostly as a result of sugar and textile and apparel exports. Real wages have grown at an average of 4.4 percent in agriculture and 7 percent in manufacturing in the period 1984–90.

Reforms seem to be successful also in Guatemala, Peru, and Vietnam, and are beginning to show results in Mali and Uganda. There seems to be little progress so far in Kenya and Madagascar. In Romania, although agricultural growth recovered during 1993–94, stabilization has not yet been achieved and further structural reforms need to be implemented.

Reform in Other Sectors

The impact of trade reform on agricultural growth can be greatly influenced by developments in several sectors such as roads, credit, and land markets. Some of the TEP reports include information on these sectors,

Table 9.5. *Trade Policy Reforms, Overall GDP Growth, and Agricultural GDP Growth*
(percent per year)

Item	Year before trade reforms	Year of reforms 1	Years after reforms 2	3	4	Average rate for years 1–4	Average rate for years 2–4
Real annual growth of GDP							
All episodes	-1.0	3.1	3.6	3.4	5.5	3.9	4.2
Sustained episodes	0.0	5.6	4.3	3.8	7.0	5.2	5.0
Costa Rica 1986	0.8	5.5	4.8	3.4	5.7	4.9	4.6
Guatemala 1986	1.7	0.1	3.5	3.9	3.9	2.9	3.8
Kenya 1987	7.1	5.9	6.2	4.7	4.2	5.2	5.0
Mali 1986	2.4	13.8	1.2	-1.9	11.8	6.2	3.7
Mauritius 1981[a]	-10.4	5.4	5.8	0.3	4.8	4.1	3.6
Peru 1991	-5.4	2.8	-2.5	6.5	12.9	4.9	5.6
Uganda 1987	-1.4	5.5	6.8	5.5	4.4	5.5	5.6
Vietnam 1991	5.1	6.0	8.3	8.1	8.5	7.7	8.3
Partially sustained episodes	-3.6	-3.7	1.8	2.5	-6.7	-1.5	-0.8
Kenya 1992[b]	1.5	0.4	0.1	2.8		1.1	1.5
Madagascar 1988	1.2	3.4	4.1	3.1	-6.7	1.0	0.2
Romania 1992	-13.4	-14.9	1.3	1.5		-4.0	1.4
Real annual growth of agriculture							
All episodes	-3.7	4.9	5.2	2.3	6.3	4.7	4.6
Sustained episodes	-5.1	8.1	5.5	2.1	7.0	5.7	4.9
Costa Rica 1986	-5.5	4.8	4.2	4.6	7.4	5.3	5.4
Guatemala 1986	0.3	-0.8	5.0	3.4	3.1	2.7	3.8

(table continues on following page)

(Table 9.5 continued)

Item	Year before trade reforms	Year of reforms 1	Years after reforms			Average rate for years 1–4	Average rate for years 2–4
			2	3	4		
Kenya 1987	4.9	4.2	4.5	4.1	3.5	4.1	4.0
Mali 1986	-2.1	25.3	4.3	1.6	20.7	13.0	8.9
Mauritius 1981	-34.2	21.9	19.8	-13.0	0.8	7.4	2.5
Peru 1991	-5.7	1.8	-7.3	6.2	13.2	3.5	4.0
Uganda 1987	0.1	3.9	7.1	6.3	3.6	5.2	5.6
Vietnam 1991	1.1	3.4	6.1	3.8	4.0	5.2	4.6
Partially sustained episodes	0.1	-3.4	4.5	2.7	0.5	4.3	2.6
Kenya 1992	-0.7	-3.7	-4.1	2.0		1.1	-1.1
Madagascar 1988	2.5	2.2	5.2	2.1	0.5	-1.9	2.6
Romania 1992	-1.5	-8.7	12.4	4.0		2.5	8.2

Note: Trade policy reforms in ten World Bank/UNDP Trade Expansion Program countries are covered in this table.

a. In Mauritius, where liberalization of the economy has been successful, the most significant trade policy reforms began in 1980–82. The TEP report is from 1992, and is dedicated to deepening of trade reforms and to reforms in other sectors of the economy.

b. In Kenya, reforms that began in 1987 were sustained until 1991, when they were partially reversed. Although here the reform episode begun in late 1992 is classified under "partially sustained" (based on GDP data), there is recent evidence that the reform effort is strengthening.

Source: LATAD, based on World Bank Data Tables. Where applicable, growth data for 1994 are Economist Intelligence Unit estimates based on official government projections.

chosen according to the authors' judgment on their relevance. A synthesis of the actual proposed reforms for related sectors in the ten countries is presented in table 9.6.

In countries where trade reforms were not very advanced when reports were written (such as Kenya, Mali, Romania, Uganda, and Vietnam), the most important sector mentioned related to agriculture is the financial sector. In these countries the financial sector is still dominated by state banks or institutional credit, and government-fixed interest rates abound.

In Uganda, for example, where the main export crop is coffee, coffee crop financing represented more than 80 percent of all crop finance requirements. The Bank of Uganda lent directly to the coffee board about 75 percent of total requirements at a subsidized rate (30 percent) and the rest was channeled through the Uganda Commercial Bank to cooperative unions and private processors at higher rates of 40 to 50 percent (with the ceiling set by the central bank). The coffee board had an unlimited overdraft facility, which caused inefficient use and excess expansion of credit and the money supply, fueling domestic inflation. In Kenya, exporters and producers had difficulties obtaining credit because export production was considered risky as a result of the unpredictable incentive structure, and financial institutions, bound by interest rate ceilings, could not adequately cover risks.

In countries where trade reforms were more advanced and there had already been important export growth, reforms in other sectors were more relevant, such as greater flexibility in the labor market. Mauritius, which had full employment, needed to increase flexibility in employment policies in the regulated sugar sector, in order to raise labor productivity.[4] In Costa Rica, minimum wage adjustments in the formal agricultural sector influenced wage adjustments throughout the formal sector.

The Peru and Romania reports mention land market reforms as being essential in making agricultural property more tradable, and therefore leading to investment in the sector. In Mauritius, land legislation favored allocation of land to sugar production in particular, and proposed reforms for a more market-determined use of land.

In Costa Rica and Peru the state of infrastructure (particularly roads and ports) was insufficient for current and expected export volumes. In most countries more public and private investment in infrastructure was needed for trade expansion.

---

4. Labor regulations in Mauritius' sugar industry (which employs 15 percent of total labor force) establish that all workers hired before 1967 cannot be fired during the intercrop season, and the employer is forced to hire additional workers to make up for natural attrition of the labor force, which means employment in sugar production cannot fall below 1967 levels.

Table 9.6. *Summary of Conditions and Reforms in Other Sectors of the Economy (proposed or effective)*

Country (period of liberalization program)	Land market and property rights legislation	Labor market legislation	Access to credit	Other
Costa Rica (1986–91)	n.m.	Minimum wage adjustments in agriculture tend to accelerate wage adjustments throughout the formal sector. Labor taxes are high.	Tight monetary policy to compensate for expansive fiscal policy has led to real lending rates of 20–23 percent in 1991 to the private sector. High spreads reflect an inefficient financial market, which is dominated by monopolistic state banks.	Current infrastructure insufficient for efficient handling of export volume. Banana production is the most affected sector. Also proposed is greater technical assistance for promoting nontraditional exports.
Guatemala (1986–89)	n.m.	Removal of wage indexation recommended.	n.m.	n.m.
Kenya (1978–80), (1987–91), and (1992)	n.m.	n.m.	Most private exporting firms cannot obtain financing mainly because export risk is not covered by government fixed interest rates.	Modernization of transportation and telecommunications is proposed, as is promotion of foreign investment.
Madagascar (1986–89)	Firmer legislation of property rights in general is required.	n.m.	Banking system favors export operations rather than loans to producers of tradables. Small farmers have no access to credit.	Increased investment in infrastructure is required.

(table continues on following page)

(Table 9.6 continued)

Country (period of liberalization program)	Land market and property rights legislation	Labor market legislation	Access to credit	Other
Mali (1986–88)	n.m.	n.m.	BCEAO has means for distributing credit to productive activities (export and import substitution).	A reliable consumer price index is needed, as is improvement of customs system, and elimination of state control period regulations.
Mauritius (1980–)	Current legislation favors use of land for agriculture and encourages production of relatively land-intensive sugar.	Restrictive regulations in the sugar sector (employs 15 percent of labor) have led to overemployment in this industry.	Controlled interest rates and maximum amounts of credit per bank make the financial market biased against small firms. Subsidized rates for EPZ modernization, agricultural diversification.	Full employment of resources and increasing real wages are reducing competitiveness of exports. Investment in human capital and technology is required to enhance competitiveness.
Peru (1990–91)	Land market liberalized in 1991, by making agricultural property more secure and freely tradable.	Labor stability law is an obstacle to trade reforms. Ports are still under worker monopolies.	Financial reforms have been introduced in order to promote formation of capital markets.	Transportation and communications infrastructure in poor condition, so there are heavy investment requirements in this sector.

(table continues on following page)

303

(Table 9.6 continued)

Country (period of liberalization program)	Land market and property rights legislation	Labor market legislation	Access to credit	Other
Romania (1990–92)	Process of privatization of collective farms continues, and preliminary land certificates have been issued for more than 90 percent of area returned to private ownership.	n.m.	Agrobank is the main source of financing for agricultural firms: 90 percent of its loans are to agriculture and 60 percent are to state trading companies. Some subsidized loans are available for agricultural inputs.	n.m.
Uganda (1987–90)	n.m.	n.m.	Coffee crop financing is dependent on inefficient institutional credit.	Proposed removal of monopoly of parastatal marketing agents and administrative impediments to exports.
Vietnam (1987–88) and (1991–92)	n.m.	n.m.	Barter trade is falling, but the banking system is still weak, and needs to develop in order to promote trade to non-CMEA countries.	Export processing zones are proposed to attract foreign investment.

n.m. Not mentioned in the report.
Note: BCEAO is the West African Central Bank. CMEA is the Council for Mutual Economic Assistance. For mission dates, see table 9.1.
Source: UNDP/World Bank Trade Expansion Program country reports.

It would seem that related reforms are very important for agricultural growth once the main structural reforms are in place. Even in low-income countries, reforms in infrastructure (roads, communications, and ports) and further deregulation of markets quickly become relevant for the sector to continue growing.

These findings are largely consistent with those of other studies. One such study on economywide and agricultural reforms for two early reformers, Chile and New Zealand, examined in detail the issue of related reforms (Valdés 1993). In Chile, apart from trade, exchange rate, and fiscal reforms, reforms crucial to agriculture were labor markets (removing wage indexation), land markets (legal security of property rights), water rights, and reform of the financial sector. In New Zealand, liberalization of financial markets and regulatory reform in agriculture (removal of government interventions) were important reforms.

The case of another transitional economy, Poland, also illustrates the importance of related reforms (Valdés and Gnaegy 1995). Poland liberalized prices and reduced tariffs for agricultural and food products, and the agricultural sector grew rapidly in the early years of reform. This has improved marketing and processing efficiency, the land market, and extension services available to farmers. One of the most important obstacles in the agricultural sector, however, is the continued presence of large monopolistic agricultural marketing and processing enterprises that intervene in pricing, distribution, and procurement. As noted above, this has also been a major obstacle to agricultural growth in several of the TEP countries, especially those in Africa.

Conclusion

Obviously this commentary could not hope to answer all the specific questions that emerge about the various liberalization episodes as they affected agriculture in the TEP countries. But could one offer some broad guidelines for reformers? Are there some basic economic conditions (per capita income and others) and initial circumstances that help or hinder the adjustment of agriculture to a more open trade regime?

Tariffs, Quantitative Restrictions, and Export Taxes

For the low-income group of TEP countries, tariffication (replacing quantitative restrictions with tariffs) moved slower and average statutory tariffs remained higher than in middle-income countries. On the other hand, due to the prevalence of unofficial trade, tariffs and quantitative restrictions were less binding in these countries. One might hypothesize that the administrative aspects of tariffication, such as customs administration, are still too demanding for this set of countries.

At the time of the TEP analysis, the explicit export tax on the traditional agricultural exports in low-income countries was still high. This is due to a thin tax base, in which export taxes, including the profits of state agencies active in exports, were the single most important source of government revenue. Thus, for such countries, lowering the export taxes should be accompanied by fiscal reform (broadening tax base, increasing compliance, expenditure reduction).

Macroeconomic Policy

The key seems to be control of the fiscal deficit. Those countries that could not do this experienced inflationary pressures and an RER appreciation. The need for fiscal reform early in the reform process seems important. An underdeveloped foreign exchange market, still based on a foreign exchange allocation system, was a considerable constraint for the trade liberalization program. The macroeconomic policies in the four middle-income countries were more consistent with the trade reform than those in the low-income and transitional economies. The latter group still rely on money financing of the fiscal deficit.

Bias against Agricultural Exports

The focus on import barriers in the design of the TEP studies did not force them to emphasize enough the analysis of the implicit antiexport bias as it affected agriculture. This antiexport effect was not documented in most cases. The one exception is Costa Rica, but the analysis was limited to removal of sectoral interventions (on coffee and banana exports).

However, the general reduction in tariffs on imports and the reduction in quantitative restrictions should have reduced the bias against traditional agricultural exports, aside from the RER issue in some countries mentioned above. Agricultural exports generally should have expanded, and in fact they did.

Trade Liberalization

There seems to be substantial evidence that trade liberalization, when sustained over a period of time, leads to higher GDP and agricultural growth. The response of the agricultural sector to reforms is almost immediate. Once the main structural reforms are in place, sustained growth in agriculture later depends on related reforms in other sectors.

Most TEP missions took place fairly soon after the initiation of the trade reform program, and hence no conclusion could be drawn on the consequences for rural employment and income distribution. However, in those countries where reforms had started earlier (Costa Rica and Mauritius in particular) the studies report a significant growth of labor-intensive exports.

Related Reforms

The TEP reports paid considerable attention to the importance of adjustments in credit and infrastructure for agriculture, and specific recommendations were outlined for Costa Rica, Mauritius, and Peru.

Related reforms is another area in which the reports show a contrast between the low-income and the middle-income countries. It is in the middle-income countries that the bottlenecks in infrastructure and financial markets emerge more vividly in the TEP reports. This was in part, I believe, because the reform process was more advanced among the middle-income countries. For the low-income and transitional countries, the concern was how to facilitate the "creation" of factor markets. For the middle-income countries it was more a question of how to make them more efficient. Furthermore, in middle-income countries, where the agricultural sector represents a low share of the economy (10 percent of GDP, for example), one would expect a more elastic factor supply compared with lower-income countries.

In order to either "create" factor markets or make them more efficient, certain reforms in the agricultural sector are particularly important. Privatization of land and security of property rights are central to ensuring that private farming is the main component of the farming system. Land markets should facilitate entry and exit from farming. Food distribution, agroprocessing, and input supply should be privatized and de-monopolized by allowing the emergence of new and restructured private firms in processing, input supply, and services. Finally, financial institutions that serve the agricultural sector must be developed.

To conclude, can trade reform work anywhere? I have no doubt that this conference will identify the critical factors that will make a well-designed trade reform succeed in middle-income countries. The broad guidelines on the trade and macroeconomic components of the reforms in low-income countries will also be well advanced. But how broad the reforms should be, and the implications for the mix and sequencing of the related reforms for the low-income and transitional economies is an extraordinarily complex issue that deserves further analysis. One implication is that this set of countries would benefit from a larger technical assistance component to deal with administrative aspects of the reform package.

Bibliography

Cleaver, Kevin M., and W. Graeme Donovan. 1995. *Agriculture, Poverty and Economic Reform in Sub-Saharan Africa.* World Bank Discussion Paper 280. Washington, D.C.

Krueger, Ann, Maurice Schiff, and Alberto Valdés. 1990. "Economía Política de la Intervenciones de Precios Agrícolas en América Latina." San Francisco: Centro Internacional para el Desarrollo Económico (Center for International Development) for the World Bank.

Michaely, Michael, Armeane Choksi, and Demetrios Papageorgiou. 1990. *Liberalizing Foreign Trade in Developing Countries: The Lessons of Experience.* Washington, D.C.: World Bank.

Schiff, Maurice, and Alberto Valdés. 1992. *The Political Economy of Agricultural Pricing Policy Vol. 4: A Synthesis of the Economics in Developing Countries.* Baltimore: Johns Hopkins University Press.

Sjaastad, L. 1980. "Commercial Policy, True Tariffs, and Relative Prices." In J. Black and Brian Hindley, eds., *Current Issues in Commercial Policy and Diplomacy.* New York: St Martin's Press.

Valdés, Alberto. 1986. "Exchange Rates and Trade Policy: Help or Hindrance to Agricultural Growth?" In Allen Maunder and Ulf Renborg, eds., *Agriculture in a Turbulent World Economy.* Proceedings of XIX International Conference of Agricultural Economists. Brookfield, Vermont: Gower.

_____. 1993. "Mix and Sequencing of Economywide and Agricultural Reforms: Chile and New Zealand." *Agricultural Economics* (Netherlands) 8:295–311.

_____. 1995. "Surveillance of Agricultural Price and Trade Policy: A Synthesis For Selected Latin American Countries."LATAD Report 14809. World Bank, Central American Country Department, Washington, D.C.

Valdés, Alberto, and S. Gnaegy. 1995. "Economywide Reform and Agricultural Recovery: Observations of Economic Darwinism among Transition Economies." Presented at the Conference on Agriculture and Trade in Transition Economies: Policy Design and Implementation, CERGE-EI, USAID.

Valdés, Alberto, and A. McCalla. 1996. "The Uruguay Round (GATT) Agreement on Agriculture and LDCs." *Food Policy* (U.K.) 21(4–5): 419–31.

Wiebelt, M., and others. 1992. "Discrimination against Agriculture in Developing Countries?" Kieler Studien 243, Tübingen.

World Bank. 1994. *Adjustment in Africa: Reforms, Results, and the Road Ahead.* New York: Oxford University Press.

10

Technical Assistance for Policy Reform: Lessons from the Trade Expansion Program

Elliot Berg

The Trade Expansion Program (TEP) is probably the largest technical assistance effort ever launched in trade policy reform. Under TEP, teams of economists were sent to seventeen developing countries. In each case this resulted in publication of a detailed report analyzing trade policy issues and setting out recommendations for reform. The program also financed follow-up studies and generated numerous background research papers, several books, and two regional trade policy seminars. Since TEP's inception in 1987, these activities have absorbed more than $5 million provided by the United Nations Development Programme (UNDP), its principal financier, and the World Bank, the implementing agency.

The ultimate objective of TEP was faster and more sustainable growth via comparative advantage-based trade expansion. This goal was to be achieved by three general means:

- Provision of high-quality technical assistance to countries wishing to undertake trade policy reforms. This was principally in the form of policy assessment missions (short-term visits by teams of trade policy specialists).
- Strengthening of developing-country policymaking capacity by local participation in the country assessments, by one-on-one dialogue between nationals and the visiting trade specialists, and by local participation in seminars and conferences associated with the TEP presence.
- Production of assessment reports and background research by TEP missions and TEP-sponsored research, which will lead to greater knowledge about trade policy reform through wider dissemination of this knowledge to academics, officials, and policymakers in the developing countries.

This chapter is concerned primarily with the direct technical assistance aspects of TEP—those indicated in the first two points above. The research and dissemination dimension could be regarded as indirect technical assistance and included in our scope; after all, the more that is known about national reform experiences and the better the analytic grasp of the policy issues involved, the greater the prospects for effective reform everywhere. But there is no space here to consider in any detail the research and dissemination aspects.

This chapter has three parts: *Objectives, instruments, and outcomes; Lessons;* and *Conclusions and recommendations for the future.* It draws heavily from the January 1995 evaluation of the program (see Berg 1995).

Objectives, Instruments, and Outcomes

Four major objectives of TEP are set out in the initiating project papers: accelerate the pace and improve the quality of trade policy reform in the assisted countries; produce research (in addition to the country policy assessment reports) that will clarify trade policy issues and country reform experiences; disseminate the results of this research in assisted countries and elsewhere; and increase local capacity in trade policy analysis.

Instruments are also specified in project documents. These are the activities intended to realize the project's objectives—country policy assessment missions, research, and so forth.

Outcomes are of two kinds: outputs and impacts. *Outputs* are indicators of performance in meeting project targets. Did the project do what it was supposed to do, that is, produce country assessments of the specified number and quality, do follow-ups, and generate research papers as anticipated? These are proximate outcomes. *Impacts* are ultimate outcomes. Did the assessment missions accelerate or improve the quality of trade policy reform in client countries? Did they strengthen local capacity in policy analysis? Have the research outputs added meaningfully to the stock of intellectual capital?

More and Better Reform

This was the prime objective, the main rationale for the program. Three related instruments were used. Country policy assessments were the centerpiece. Teams of trade policy analysts (usually eight to ten in number and led by an independent consultant) visited client countries for two to four weeks to gather data and do interviews. A country assessment report was put together in the ensuing months.

The initial target was to dispatch two such missions each year—fourteen during the seven-year life of the program. The country assessment reports were to be "prepared in close association with local counterpart teams...(and were to) contain a comprehensive review of the country's trade policies, its plans for a reform of those policies, as well as a series of issues and options for the implementation of the reforms" (UNDP/World Bank 1991).

The second instrument was dialogue with local officials and academics at different stages: during the initial data gathering, when the draft report was ready for discussion, and, if possible, after the final report was submitted. The seminars and workshops were aimed at engaging high-level policymakers in policy debate.

The third instrument was follow-up. Country assessments should not be one-shot affairs but rather part of a continuing relationship with host countries. Thus, implementation of TEP recommendations were to be monitored by TEP staff, and specific and more in-depth activities were to supplement the general assessments. Also, TEP missions were to try to identify potential fundable projects in the trade sector.

Performance on the preparation of country policy assessments was excellent. During the seven-year effective life of the program, seventeen country assessments were produced. The mix and level of assessment team members was also excellent. Independent consultants headed most of the missions, and members included many well-known academic specialists in trade policy as well as experienced staff from the World Bank and elsewhere. Few countries outside the TEP countries have been able to benefit from the insights and analyses of such distinguished teams of economists.

Seminars and workshops followed almost all country assessment reports.[1] Follow-up activities, however, were few. Many implementation reviews were intended, including field trips; but, it proved possible to do only six desk study reviews of limited scope. The "gap-bridging" follow-up studies were scaled back mainly for budget reasons; the TEP budget was cut substantially, by $300,000 in midstream, and follow-up studies were asked to bear the brunt of the cutback. Of the originally targeted ten follow-ups, only four were done: two in Costa Rica, one in Mauritius, and one in Uganda. The mandate to identify potential fundable trade projects was not exercised.

What can be said about the program's impact on the pace and quality of trade policy reform? Such impact could come in various ways. The presence of TEP missions presumably provided better analysis to local policymakers than they could otherwise enjoy. The availability of better-defined and argued policy options, plus the process fallout (interviews and informal discussions of the assessment team members, local reading and response to draft and final reports, debate in seminars, and face-to-face argument) would lead host governments to adopt some specific TEP recommendations. A variant of this proposition is that the quality of reform programs would be higher and would be adopted faster than without TEP.

---

1. In several countries, seminars were not held—in Madagascar for reasons of political instability, and in Kenya because of deterioration in World Bank–government of Kenya relations.

Moreover, reforms would be more sustainable because the "independent" analysis supplied by TEP would deepen local ownership and hence commitment. It was possible that no changes would be induced directly and in the short run by the TEP presence in a country; but, the force of analysis, its independent origin, and the ensuing debate and argument might change the minds of some policymakers, officials, and intellectuals, and help shift the balance of opinion toward more or faster reform.

There can be no doubt that TEP has had some positive effects via all these routes. It would be extraordinary if this were not true. The program made available to participating countries analysts of superior quality in much greater number than would otherwise have been possible. The presence of the missions in most cases stimulated thinking and debate among local people and rarely failed to provide fresh insights to the analysts themselves.

Moreover, there are numerous instances in which there seem to be direct links between TEP missions and policy changes. One set of such cases is due to fortuitous timing: a ministerial change or a policy shift coinciding with the arrival of a TEP mission whose ideas find a ready audience.[2] Much more frequently, the recommendations of the TEP mission have found their way into trade sector projects or policy loans.[3] In other cases TEP reports served to focus policy attention on critical issues.[4]

---

2. The classic case is Peru, where the TEP mission arrived in February 1991, when a new Finance Minister was contemplating a major trade reform. The mission reoriented its tasks and provided intensive policy advice to the Minister, leaving a detailed memorandum behind. Several of the recommendations were included in the sweeping liberalization that soon followed. Much the same happened in Uganda. A follow-up mission to the country assessment arrived in January 1993 to study tax and tariff reform. The timing could not have been more propitious: the government, faced with a crisis of declining tax receipts, was urgently reviewing its tax and customs policies. The advice of the mission was incorporated in the budget program introduced later that year.

3. Thus in Kenya, some of the draft TEP report recommendations were included in a World Bank export development project: reduction of maximum tariff rate, raising of minimum rates, and exempting indirect exports from the value added tax. In Uganda, the TEP report served as the basis of a World Bank–financed export development project and helped shape other donor programs in trade promotion. In Mali, a structural adjustment loan borrowed TEP policy proposals to reduce tariff rates from 28 to 3, eliminate most import licenses, simplify export procedures, and replace export taxes by a profits tax. The Moroccan report was similarly used. And TEP recommendations are the basis for trade conditionality in Georgia's Rehabilitation and Structural Adjustment Credit.

4. In Uruguay, for example, the report identified the antidumping arrangements as a major source of excessive import protection. Soon after the report appeared, some of its recommended improvements were adopted; for example, putting the burden of proof of dumping and of damage on the local producer; converting "minimum export prices" into reference prices, which reduced their protective effects; and reducing the level of some reference prices and minimum export prices. In Mongolia, the TEP mission focused attention on tax and price policy issues regarding cashmere, and in Romania energy pricing was highlighted.

Despite these seemingly unambiguous instances of TEP's impact on policy reform, in most cases it is difficult to identify, and especially to quantify, the effects. This is one of the lessons of the program and is discussed below.

Research

Research on trade policy was an integral part of TEP. The reports of the country assessment teams were one research element. Eight analytic background papers were also to be produced. In fact, nineteen such papers appeared.

Evaluation of the intellectual capital–creating aspects of the program presents formidable difficulties. Many of these effects are intangible, hence hard to seize. Global judgments about the program's written outputs are rendered difficult because of its large volume and diversity, and also because it cannot be measured by the usual academic criteria; these are policy papers, not journal articles.[5]

One generalization is warranted, however: the analysis is of superior quality in most cases. This is what we should expect, a priori. Many of the authors are well-known specialists, some of them leaders in international economics. All are experienced, and brought comparative perspectives to their analyses. It is no surprise then that most of this writing is technically sure.[6] Nor is it surprising that TEP books, country reports, and occasional papers are finding their way into the international economics literature (see, among many examples, Harrison and Revenga 1995).

TEP outputs were aimed at audiences wider than those of professional economists. Their prose was to be clear and little encumbered with jargon. Also, the project designers specified that the reports should lay out policy options for local decision.

On the whole there was admirable adherence to the guideline to write clearly and avoid unnecessary jargon. There was less adherence to the guideline that a range of options be presented in country assessments. Issues are discussed in these documents and sometimes the pros and cons of alternative policies are presented, but most commonly the country assessments set out recommendations and present analytic arguments for particular lines of policy.

Dissemination

Widespread distribution of research findings was a central concern. Dissemination was to be promoted by making reports readable by nonspecialists,

---

5. Much of what they contain, however, has found or will find its way into refereed publications.
6. Some client readers, however, assert that the report on their country was too academic, or too long and general, or not sufficiently targeted on institutional issues.

preparing summary versions of country reports and publishing these in local languages, seeking publication of selected TEP country assessments, organizing three regional workshops, holding a synthesis conference at the end
of the project, and publishing the papers.

Actual outcomes show mixed performance on dissemination. Only three
summaries were prepared, all during the pilot phase (pre-1991) and all in
English. Six country assessments were published in local languages (Costa
Rica in Spanish, Georgia in Georgian, Mali, Madagascar, and Morocco in
French, and Vietnam in Vietnamese). Only two of the nineteen other papers
were translated: one to Ukrainian, the other to Spanish.

Three factors seem to explain the failure to produce the other reports in local
languages: the relevant audiences were judged to read English; costs of translation are very high; and even English versions of reports appeared after long
delays, and time-consuming translation would have exacerbated this problem.

Capacity Building

Capacity building, which had not been among the objectives of TEP's initial phase (1987–90), became a significant concern after 1991. Thus the
TEP Phase II project paper called for "Formation of core units of officials
within the governments concerned with trade policy matters, initially
through the establishment of counterpart teams to work with the international experts provided by the TEP." The theme recurs: "The participating country is expected to establish a strong counterpart team of officials
to work with TEP experts, thereby helping to ensure greater 'ownership'..." In preparing analytic papers, TEP was supposed to collaborate
with key developing-country institutions.

Capacity building has two main aspects: training of people and strengthening institutions (organizations and procedures). In some cases both occurred. Training was often indirect. Efforts were made to make use of regional consultants. The participation of Argentinean and Uruguayan trade
economists in the Uruguay mission was a notable success. In Mongolia, a
local institution was linked to the TEP assessment. In many cases, local
officials participated in mission interviews. Much informal discussion took
place between mission members and local specialists and officials. Team
members also gave formal lectures to local audiences. But training efforts
received little or no systematic attention. It is hard to find evidence of efforts to associate local academics or researchers with the country assessment teams or follow-up missions, so training impacts have to be regarded
as incidental and marginal.

Similarly, gearing of TEP work with local institutions was not extensive.
The suggestion in the Phase II project paper calling for the establishment of

local working groups to collaborate with the visiting TEP mission proved almost entirely a dead letter. One must conclude that capacity-building activities were marginal and that TEP did little to strengthen local capacity in trade policy analysis.

Lessons

The lessons considered here refer only marginally to substantive generalizations and analytic insights that emerged from TEP country studies and research papers, which are taken up elsewhere in this volume.[7] The findings here refer to the experience of TEP as a vehicle for technical assistance-induced policy change and capacity building.

Finding Consensus

Lesson: Despite unsettled issues in trade strategy and ideological differences among analysts, the TEP experience shows that in operational terms a broad technical agreement exists about good and bad policies. The policy orientations in the country reports confirm the view of TEP sponsors that in real world situations trade policy analysts tend to share perspectives about what is wrong with trade policy and how to fix it. This seems to be true even for analysts coming from widely different points on the ideological spectrum.

The consensus that arose in the mid-1980s was based on a few general propositions. Almost all analysts agreed that a persistent imbalance in external accounts, and the administrative allocation of foreign exchange that flows from it, is devastating for growth and harmful to the powerless and the poor. Reestablishment of external equilibrium via appropriate trade and exchange rate policies is an essential element in any policy posture aimed at macroeconomic stability, which in turn is a precondition of sustainable growth.

Trade liberalization reduces rents that benefit mainly the rich and well-placed. It gives exporters greater access to imports and improves incentives, and should spur efficiency in production. Open economies tend to be more attractive to foreign investment and more likely to gain quick access to new technologies and new ideas. Poor countries and poor people tend to benefit from expansion of exports, which are often unskilled labor-intensive.

---

7. We ignore also other indirect technical assistance-type aspects. For example, involvement of World Bank staff in the implementation of TEP broadened and deepened their knowledge of trade policy issues, with spillover effects into their other World Bank work and among other Bank staff, and the findings of TEP country assessment missions often directly informed structural adjustment loan design.

The policy reform packages prescribed in the TEP country reports all reflect this paradigm. Policymakers are urged to achieve macroeconomic stability, get the exchange rate right and move away from administrative allocations of foreign exchange, get rid of quantitative restrictions and replace them with tariff structures that are low and neutral in their incentive effects, and give priority to assuring exporters untrammeled access to imports. On the institutional side, policymakers are urged to get rid of export-marketing monopolies and use private sector institutions for export promotion.

The uniformity of the reform packages proposed in the country assessments might have come about because they are the product of a single trade policy cookie cutter fabricated on 19th Street in Washington. TEP was, after all, a World Bank-executed project.

This is certainly a factor, but probably a minor one. First, the content of country reports varies considerably depending on the particular policy issues posed in each country. In Romania, for example, the TEP mission addressed problems of state trading, made recommendations on how to do it better, and put energy policy at the center of its industrial policy concerns. In Zimbabwe, TEP considered regional trade potential and the role of marketing boards.

More generally, the country teams cast widely for high-quality trade policy specialists. Academics dominated, and many policy perspectives were represented. Moreover, country team leaders were almost all from outside the World Bank. The similarity in diagnosis and prescription is mainly a reflection of the broad convergence of views that has come to dominate thinking about trade policy in its practical aspects.[8]

Challenges to the dominant policy paradigm certainly exist. In some respects they have grown more insistent in recent years. The East Asian experience, which is said to be characterized by emphasis on export growth and gradual import liberalization, and by extensive government intervention, is widely cited as evidence that the standard Bretton Woods reform package is flawed. But not everybody interprets what happened in East Asia in the same way. And the "standard package" is not necessarily inconsistent with going slowly on import liberalization while accenting export promotion (World Bank 1994). In any case, without a competent state capable of effective intervention, the East Asian model is not importable.

---

8. This on-the-ground consensus exists despite the weak theoretical base for trade liberalization and the sparsity of strong empirical demonstrations of its effectiveness. For a recent illustration of the academic skepticism about the case for trade liberalization and strategies of openness, see Rodrik (1993). The Mexican peso depreciation in 1995 spawned a number of requiems for trade policy reform. See Krugman (1995), and Taylor and Schlefer (1995).

Most important in understanding the consensus issue is that these cosmic issues of development strategy enter only marginally and indirectly into the hurly-burly of real world policymaking. The common tone and policy orientation found in the country assessments reflect the fact that the configuration of prereform trade policy deficiencies analysts confront on the ground does not usually differ much from country to country: exchange rates are overvalued and macroeconomic policies are awry, quantitative restrictions are too widely used, tariff levels are too high and rates too dispersed, internal regulatory systems block quick supply responses, exports incentives are inadequate, and so forth. In practice, protectionism usually retains deep roots, and more antiexport bias persists than is good for most countries. It is not surprising that the general diagnosis and policy prescriptions are highly similar and consistently in favor of liberalization.

The real issues about the appropriateness of TEP advice are those relating to timing and sequencing and to tradeoffs between policy options. The problem is not that the reformers are all reading from the same choir book, but that their songs may not have varied enough from country to country.[9]

Independent Advice

Lesson: Local ownership of policy reforms is unlikely to be much increased by externally planned, financed, and executed policy analyses along the lines of TEP country studies. TEP's initiators believed that policy reform progress was often being held back, particularly in the low-income countries, by insufficient access to the technical skills required. Local capacities to prescribe well-grounded reform measures and overcome implementation blockages were believed to be unavailable in many parts of the world. It did not seem feasible, moreover, for reforming governments to find on world markets, among private consultants, the highly specialized kinds of technical competence they needed.

As a result, reform programs were usually crafted by World Bank or other external agency staff, almost always to be inserted as conditionalities in policy

---

9. Some Ugandan officials, for example, complain that the TEP report for that country had the sequencing all wrong. They see three types of obstacles to growth in the Ugandan economy: those internal to the firm (bad management, government intervention in state enterprise decisions, and so on); domestic problems (such as high-priced inputs, labor market rigidities, and infrastructure gaps); and trade policy biases and institutional deficiencies. They say the reform program should have given more attention to the first two, attacking them first. Since this was not done, industry could not face up to external competition. They also argue that the pacing was wrong. Exposure to external competition (deprotection), removal of exemptions, and so on should be done gradually and in recognition of second-best conditions, for example, the fact that Kenya subsidizes its industries, that taxes in Uganda are higher than in Kenya, and that input costs are also higher.

loans. Technical dialogue was sparse and locally supplied technical inputs in most cases limited. Donor agencies, and especially the World Bank, defined the policy reform agendas, their components, priority, speed, and sequencing. The local role was largely reactive.

It followed that local officials, economic interest groups, and political classes saw these policy reform programs as an outside imposition, a perception reinforced of course by the dominance of conditionality in the dialogue, and by the limited extent of genuine bureaucratic and political participation in the process. Therefore, adoption of reforms was slow and local commitment to them lukewarm. The frequent backsliding apparent by the late 1980s was attributable to a significant degree to this lack of local ownership.

Access to independent technical assistance would, according to this line of argument, increase ownership of trade reforms. TEP would be the vehicle for provision of that independent technical assistance. But things did not work out as anticipated. A fundamental assumption in the design of the program was that TEP could be run by World Bank staff and follow World Bank operational procedures, yet retain a separate identity. This never really worked even within the World Bank, where TEP gradually lost its distinctive character and became substitutable for other vehicles drawn on to finance economic and sector work.

More basically, TEP was rarely seen by client countries as something truly separate from the World Bank. This is so despite the program's success in staffing missions with independent consultants and in most cases naming independent outsiders as mission leaders or co-leaders. In none of the countries visited during TEP evaluation did local participants or others clearly understand that the TEP mission was not a World Bank mission and its report not a World Bank report.

This means that some of the underlying assumptions of the program's design proved inoperative: that its product would be differentiated, that it would be regarded as containing analysis independent from the World Bank and unrelated to conditionality in policy loans, and that ownership of the recommended policies would be enhanced.

The association of TEP with the World Bank was extremely advantageous in many ways: it made access to policymakers much easier, it facilitated recruitment of first class consultants and eased access to World Bank staff, and its ideas circulated quickly within the World Bank and led to better policy dialogue during structural adjustment loan (SAL) processes. And many of its recommendations found their way into policy loans. But it was not readily compatible with independence, and hence could not bring about the desired growth in local ownership and commitment.

Measuring Results

Lesson: Convincing quantification of the economic impact of policy advice is impossible. Intuition suggests that economic advisors and advice can bring substantial economic benefits. They do so by putting good ideas on the table or, more often, by shooting down bad ideas.[10] If, in growth accounting, one attributes the residual (growth unaccounted for by increases in factor inputs) to better policy, and further attributes even a little of this policy-determined residual to economic advisors, extremely favorable benefit-cost ratios result.

There are a lot of problems with these and similar efforts. One is the counterfactual. The countries that had TEP missions have almost all moved forward with trade liberalization. In many cases broader changes intervened after the TEP mission (Poland, for example). More generally, the theory of the program was that TEP missions would be sent only to countries already committed to reform. So it is essentially the differential contribution to the reform effort that would have to be measured, the difference between progress under a TEP-assisted reform program and one without TEP. Arbitrary judgments would be necessary.

Most important, it is extremely difficult to establish unambiguous links between TEP activities and ensuing reforms. In all cases, the forces making for (or obstructing) reform are so numerous that disentangling the influence of any one event or activity involves delicate and necessarily highly subjective estimates.

The attribution problem mentioned earlier is especially thorny, and makes problematic all efforts to derive systematic measures of TEP's impact on policy change. In addition to the matter of disentangling program effects from powerful political and economic forces in the general environment, there is the more banal problem of separating the effects of one mission or report from all others.

Most developing countries are visited by a large number of donor missions from which reports crowd shelves in government offices. In the more heavily aided, lower-income countries, there will be scores of such missions and such reports every year. Many of these will be concerned with policy reform issues. So the TEP contribution has to be assessed in this context: that it is usually one stream feeding into a great river of reports, seminars, policy loans, and consultative group meetings, all aimed at inducing client governments to adopt trade liberalization or related reforms.

---

10. Ronald Coase somewhere estimated that an economist in the United States could save society twice his lifetime salary by delaying for one week adoption of a policy that would decrease the Gross National Product (GNP) by $100 million.

Few policy reports are so focused and few study missions so substantial, competent, and well prepared as the TEP missions. But the problem of distinguishing TEP from related reform interventions, including those of other World Bank and UNDP programs, is nonetheless overwhelming. One of the striking findings of the field visits done for the evaluation was that few of the economists and officials interviewed in the Ministries of Finance or Economy and Commerce, or in bilateral agencies, could identify the TEP report even when it was only a year or two old. Fewer still could distinguish the mission that produced it from other World Bank missions. Often, this was due to changes of government, or to turnover of bilateral aid staff. But it is part of a general phenomenon: donor-sponsored reports descend in such numbers in these countries that even the best quickly lose their identity.

Flexibility

Lesson: Policy assessment missions of relatively large size and composed of busy experts or academics tend to be insufficiently flexible, and take too long to produce reports. Smaller mission teams making several visits would be a better vehicle for timely assistance. The dispatch of large teams (usually eight to twelve members) allows depth and breadth of analysis, brings benefits of synergy, and allows wider impact via face-to-face discussion with local analysts and decisionmakers. But, aside from high cost, it presents some disadvantages. The process of putting together these heavy assessment teams, writing first drafts, discussing these with governments, and then issuing final drafts has proved to be extremely lengthy in many cases. Table 10.1 shows that in six of the sixteen countries more than two years passed between the initial request for a country assessment and the completion of the final report. Most others took about eighteen months. Usually six months elapsed between the assessment mission and first draft.

In the reform process of most countries these are very long periods. It is likely that governments will be changed and the local cast of characters transformed as ministers are replaced and with them key senior officials. The macroeconomic environment is likely to be different. Many of the officials with whom the reconnaissance missions or the assessment teams discussed problems and priorities are likely to have changed jobs. Impact is reduced.

Timing entered in another way. In many countries, arranging the arrival of a study mission is a delicate matter. Those who organize it must pick a time when other activities competing for official attention will not be too numerous. But change is constant and missions must often be rescheduled.

The TEP missions were not easy to reschedule. They were set up with difficulty, usually many months in advance, because they assembled a

Table 10.1. Timeliness

Country	The number of months between formal request and formal response	The number of months between formal response and reconnaissance mission	The number of months between reconnaissance mission and full mission	The number of months between full mission and first draft	The number of months between first draft and follow-up mission	The number of months between follow-up mission and final report
Costa Rica	7 days		4	5	8	0
Czechoslovakia	No lapse			9	2	3
Guatemala		8	17 days	3	26	15
Kenya	4 days				4	
Madagascar		4				
Mali		1	6	6		
Mauritius			6	8	5	4
Mongolia	1	2	2	2	5	17
Morocco	1	1	1	2	1	5
Peru		4	3		20	
Poland		5	7	3	4	4
Romania	1	5	2	4	6	1
Uganda	1	1	7	8		
Uruguay	1		2	2		
Vietnam	25 days	8	1		4	
Zimbabwe	15 days	2	3	7	9	6

sizable number of busy people (usually eight to ten), each with many commitments. In some instances the missions could not be rescheduled despite
unpromising local conditions, and so they took place at inopportune times.
In Romania, for example, a change in government created big problems for
the long-planned country assessment mission. The World Bank representa-
tive urged that it be rescheduled; but the difficulties of finding an alternative date acceptable to all team members were so great that it was decided
to go ahead anyway. The effectiveness of the mission was significantly reduced as a result.

Practicality

*Lesson: Organizations that put high value on analytic work and are good at it tend to
be weak on implementation and bad at capacity building. They tend also to give preference to analytic issues when compared with institutional questions.* The World Bank
has had the reputation of being such an organization (Buyck 1991), and performance on TEP confirms it. The country assessments and the other research or
analytic exercises were generally excellent. And indirect capacity building was
intensive during time spent in the field. But the program fell short in meeting
its targets in capacity building, monitoring of implementation, follow-up studies, and identification of fundable projects. Problems related to timeliness also
were experienced, as previously noted. And most of the country reports concentrate on analytic as opposed to institutional problems.

One possible reason for performance lags on these matters is that the activities in question are highly management-intensive, and time available for
TEP management was absorbed in putting together country assessment teams,
editing and publishing assessment reports, arranging post-report workshops
with decisionmakers, and organizing the preparation of analytic background
papers and regional seminars. Another reason is that process-related activities and implementation are less challenging intellectually and less attractive
to TEP managers than substantive and analytic problems.

Similar factors explain the neglect of training and institution building and
hence the lack of impact on local capabilities in trade policy analysis and
implementation. As in many projects, whatever the project paper says, host
country and executing agency priorities prevail. What everybody wanted
from TEP was sound analysis useful in the design or implementation of trade
liberalization programs. That was priority number one.

Incorporating local collaborators in country assessment teams would have
been difficult, might have been fruitless in some cases, and would have required in all cases a willingness to risk a product that was perhaps not quite
top of the line technically. It would have required also a change in standard
World Bank methods for policy work. These factors are hardly unique to TEP.

They have been prevalent in most aid donor programs of the past decade, particularly in low-income countries. They underpin the frequent inadequacy of capacity building efforts in technical assistance generally.

Organizational inclinations seem to account for a bias in the content of assessment reports in favor of analytic issues and against institutional problems. This should not be exaggerated. The reports contain a great deal on trade institutions; nonetheless, some client country officials complained that institutional matters were inadequately treated. Local officials are often concerned mainly with such issues as drawback schemes, export incentives, and revenue maintenance while reforming tariff structures. Many of the reports focus on the structure of protection, exchange rate policies, and related macroeconomic and microeconomic issues.

Conclusions and Recommendations for the Future

TEP has been highly effective in meeting its major objective: provision of high-level technical assistance to countries engaged in trade policy reform. It has mobilized world class economists who have produced high-quality reports, analytic papers, and books on major problems of trade policy and liberalization. It has thus made valuable contributions to knowledge in this vitally important area of development policy. The lessons and insights generated from TEP work have been circulated widely in TEP-assisted countries and many others. Because of the overlap between World Bank trade policy lending and TEP activities, these lessons have directly and indirectly informed and shaped the trade policy work of the World Bank.

The country assessment missions and ensuing reports, and the dialogue surrounding them, undoubtedly had positive effects on policy reform. There is considerable anecdotal evidence to this effect; but it is difficult to assess how significant this impact was. It was clearly greater in some TEP countries than in others—more in Costa Rica, Peru, and Uganda, for example, than in Kenya, Poland, and Vietnam. In any event, the notion that the dispatch of independent assessment teams would increase local ownership of reform ideas proved largely illusory. And the reports seem to have left few footprints in local memory. As noted above, they were a long time in gestation.[11] And they seem to have had short shelf lives: few local people remember them only a year or two after they appeared, and very few could distinguish the TEP report from others.

---

11. The draft reports were made available much more quickly than the final documents, however, and this augmented the impact of the missions. Some TEP staff argue that much of the value of the country missions came from the mission's presence on the ground, its face-to-face dialogue, and the discussions of the first draft.

The program was weak in meeting nonresearch objectives. Follow-up activities such as translating reports and papers, monitoring reform implementation, undertaking specific follow-up studies, and generating trade-related projects were fewer than expected.[12] And, most important, local capabilities in trade policy formulation and implementation were strengthened very little if at all.

The original need identified by UNDP and World Bank staff a decade ago still exists, although in reduced and modified form. Trade liberalization has made huge strides everywhere. Exchange rate misalignments are less dramatic, quantitative restrictions are fewer, and levels of protection lower. Export promotion is the order of the day, and most governments are doing it much better than even a few years ago.

Yet protectionist propensities are hardly absent and most governments still have a long way to go to get incentives right and export-enhancing institutions working well. Access to state-of-the-art ideas and techniques is still not easy for many countries. Local policymaking capacity in the trade sector remains thin, especially in low-income developing countries, and sources of high-quality technical assistance for design and implementation of policy reforms and institutional restructuring remain limited.

Skill deficiencies, therefore, still hinder better performance in trade-related policymaking and programming. Few countries, especially in Sub-Saharan Africa (SSA), are adequately supplied with analysts who can inform and shape policies on macroeconomic issues (balance of payments and exchange rate problems) and on such matters as antidumping actions, duty drawbacks, foreign investment incentives, export promotion institutions, negotiating postures in international forums, and commodity economics.

Some training and capacity building needs are being addressed. The TRAINFORTRADE program of the United Nations Conference on Trade and Development (UNCTAD), for example, is strengthening national training institutions and developing training material on trade-related matters. Its focus is primarily institutional, and it is aimed at nuts-and-bolts type problems. Its priorities are to improve the trading capacity of developing countries in commodity exporting, explore diversification possibilities, and strengthen developing-country negotiating capacities in the trade area. The World Trade Organization (WTO) offers training courses to developing-country officials [the former General Agreement on Tariffs and Trade (GATT) courses]. These are highly focused on international trade regulatory and legal issues. And transitional economies have access to training at European Development Bank (EBRD) programs in Prague, Czech Republic.

---

12. The decision to cut funding in midstream bears much of the responsibility for the cutback in follow-up activities.

Needs for development of local analytic skills are much less attended to. It is hard to identify any programs at all that focus on the training of skilled analysts, people who can, for example, do studies of trade policy measures, analyze exchange rate issues, and implement and interpret effective protection studies.[13] Particularly needed are analysts who can work at the policy-making levels: producers of readable, technically sound qualitative analyses who can tell ministers in plain language what the effect of a given policy change is likely to be, and can base their argument on basic quantitative and theoretical tools. Few analysts with this kind of competence can be found in low-income developing countries. They are particularly scarce in SSA; but they are not plentiful even in the more advanced developing countries.

On the substantive side, some of the issues that will require analytic attention are readily apparent. Exchange rate management problems will persist, as will questions of protection and appropriate forms and degrees of government intervention. The trade policy debate in most countries will increasingly unfold in the context of antidumping policy. Nobody is a protectionist in principle anymore, but plenty of people see dumping in every port. Effective administration of export incentives is almost as ubiquitous a concern. The widespread search for workable duty drawback systems is symptomatic. And the aftermath of the Uruguay Round preoccupies policymakers in many countries.

Any new effort has to give highest priority to capacity building. Any TEP-like assessment reviews would have to engage a much larger proportion of local analysts and entail much more systematic collaboration with local research institutions or government policy units. The role of the World Bank or other executing agency would be to organize these largely locally implemented efforts at policy analysis, participate in them by providing staff or consultants good at "coaching," and review the technical quality of the work.

---

13. It appears that no such courses now exist. The UNCTAD TRAINFORTRADE program does much with institutional issues but little on the analytic side. The United Nations (UNDDSMS) and UNCTAD organized in 1992 the Coordinated African Program of Assistance Services (CAPAS), with financing from the French Government, the International Development Research Centre (IDRC) in Canada, and the Carnegie Corporation. It is described in its "Phase II Work Program" as "a capacity-building program of technical assistance to African countries focusing on services. Its main goal is to develop an analytic and decisionmaking capacity at the country level in areas of domestic service sector policy, regional integration in services and multilateral negotiations on trade in services." CAPAS in its first phase sponsored ten national studies of the "services sector." These were essentially descriptive, and given the vast scope of the sector, could not deal in depth with many problems or issues. Its second phase (after 1994) is intended to be more analytical, working through national research teams and so-called interinstitutional working groups. Although national capacity can be strengthened by this program, it relies on consultants for much of the analytic bush clearing, including definition of methodologies, and on local academics. It does not seem to entail any direct training-up of policy analysts.

Appropriate structures can provide some protection against tendencies to erode capacity building objectives that emerge in all policy- or research-related technical assistance. The most obvious is not only to utilize local participants more intensively, but also to stress coaching models—use of a small number of expatriate consultants who would make repeat visits of short duration and contribute to the analytic work by retaining electronic contact with local analysts between visits.

A number of additional strategies might be pursued to strengthen local capacity in trade policy analysis and implementation:

- According to officials interviewed in Costa Rica, Kenya, Romania, and Uganda, the priority training need is for intensive short courses (four to eight weeks, for example) that would combine down-to-earth economic analysis of trade issues with consideration of institutional problems such as export promotion arrangements.
- Financing (limited) could be made available to regional institutions that could organize special training in trade policy; for example, the Economic Commission for Africa, the African Economic Research Consortium, or the EBRD-financed facilities in Prague, Czech Republic, that now provide training in foreign trade administration.
- A special small grants facility could be financed (managed, say, by the Canadian IDRC) to encourage graduate students in North America and Europe to undertake thesis research in the trade area. Present thesis research by African graduate students in the United States, for example, shows little attachment to trade-related subjects.

The most fundamental conclusion that emerges from the TEP experience is that reform will be truly sustainable only when there is genuine local ownership. But without greater local capacity to design and implement trade policy reforms, ownership is elusive and fragile. So the priority task in this field even more than in others is to help create this capacity.

Bibliography

Berg, Elliot. 1995. *UNDP/World Bank Trade Expansion Program: Evaluation Report.* Bethesda, MD: Development Alternatives Inc.

Buyck, Beatrice. 1991. "The Bank's Use of Technical Assistance for Institutional Development." Policy Research Working Paper Series 578, World Bank, Policy Research Department, Washington, D.C.

Coordinated African Program of Assistance Services (CAPAS). "Phase II Work Program."

Harrison, Ann, and Ana Revenga. 1995. "The Effects of Trade Policy Reform: What Do We Really Know?" Prepared for the Economics Department, Columbia University Conference on Economic Reform in Developing and Transitional Economies, May 12.

Krugman, Paul. 1995. "Dutch Tulips and Emerging Markets." *Foreign Affairs* (July–August) 74: 28–44.

Rodrik, Dani. 1993. "Trade and Industrial Policy Reform in Developing Countries: A Review of Recent Theory and Evidence." In J. Behrman and T. M. Srinivasan, eds., *Handbook of Development Economics*, rev. ed., vol. III. Amsterdam: North-Holland.

Taylor, Lance, and Jonathan Schlefer. 1995. "Mexico's Made-in-USA Mess; the Consensus That Spawned Failure." *The Washington Post.* (October 1).

UNDP/World Bank. 1991. "Trade Expansion Program, Phase II, 1991–1994, Project Document." World Bank. Washington, D.C.

World Bank. 1994. *Adjustment in Africa: Reforms, Results, and the Road Ahead.* New York: Oxford University Press.

Appendix A

UNDP/World Bank Trade Expansion
Program Output

Table A.1. UNDP/World Bank Trade Expansion Program—Country Reports

Number	Author(s)	Title	Date	Language
1	Havrylyshyn, Oleh, et al.	Poland: Policies for Promotion	01/89	English
2	Cavallo, Domingo, et al.	Guatemala: An Evaluation of a Recent Tariff Reform Proposal	01/89	English
3	Guillaumont, Patrick, et al.	Mali: Economic Policy and International Trade	05/89	English
		Mali: politique économique et commerce extérieur	06/89	French
4	Guillaumont, Patrick, et al.	Madagascar: politique économique, commerce extérieur et développement	05/90	French
5	Connolly, Michael, et al.	Uruguay: Trade Reforms and Economic Efficiency	06/90	English
6	Matin, Kazi, et al.	Uganda: An Agenda for Liberalization	05/90	English
7	Havrylyshyn, Oleh, et al.	Morocco 2000: An Open and Competitive Economy	07/90	English
		Maroc 2000: une économie ouverte, une économie compétitive	07/90	French
8	Havrylyshyn, Oleh, et al.	Czechoslovakia: Integrating into the Global Economy: A Transition Strategy	12/92	English
9	Nash, John, et al.	Costa Rica: Strengthening Links to the World Economy	07/92	English
		Costa Rica: fortaleciendo los vínculos con la economía mundial	07/92	Spanish
10	Hachette, Dominique, et al.	Peru: Toward a More Open Economy	10/92	English
11	Matin, Kazi, et al.	Kenya: The Challenge of Promoting Exports	11/93	English
12	Hachette, Dominique, et al.	Mauritius: Toward the 21st Century	12/93	English
13	Guillaumont, Patrick, et al.	Vietnam: Policies for Transition to an Open Economy	02/94	English and Vietnamese
14	Winters, L. Alan, et al.	Romania: Restructuring to Face the World Economy	12/94	English
15	Takacs, Wendy, et al.	Mongolia: Toward a Stable, Open Market Economy	12/94	English
16	Takacs, Wendy, et al.	Zimbabwe: Consolidating the Trade Liberalization	06/95	English
17	Nash, John, et al.	Georgia: Trade Policy for a Successful Transition	02/96	English and Georgian

Note: For additional copies of these reports, contact John Nash at the World Bank; UNDP/World Bank Trade Expansion Program; International Trade Division; 1818 H Street, N.W.; Washington, D.C. 20433; tel. (202) 473-7947, fax (202) 522-1159; e-mail Trade@worldbank.org.

Table A.2. *UNDP/World Bank Trade Expansion Program—Country Summaries*

Number	Author(s)	Title	Date	Language
1	Connolly, Michael, et al.	Uruguay: Trade Reform and Economic Efficiency	06/90	English
2	Havrylyshyn, Oleh, et al.	Morocco 2000: An Open and Competitive Economy	07/90	English
3	Havrylyshyn, Oleh, et al.	Poland: Policies for Trade Promotion	01/89	English

Table A.3. UNDP/World Bank Trade Expansion Program—Occasional Papers

Number	Author(s)	Title	Date	Language
1	Lopez, Ramon, and Vinod Thomas	Growth in Imports and Income: Considerations for Africa	08/88	English
2	Keesing, Donald B.	The Four Successful Exceptions: Official Export Promotions and Support for Export Marketing in Korea, Hong Kong, Singapore, and Taiwan, China	09/88	English
3	Takacs, Wendy	Alternative Transitional Measures to Liberalize Quantitative Trade Restrictions: Implications for Developing Countries	04/89	English
4	Halevi, Nadav	Trade Restrictions and Reforms by Developing Countries in the 1990s	04/89	English
5	Winters, Alan	How Developing Countries Might Influence the Talks on Agriculture in the GATT's Uruguay Round	12/89	English
6	Guillaumont, Patrick, and Sylviane Guillaumont	Why and How to Stabilize Producer Prices for Export Crops in Developing Countries	05/90	English
7	Langhammer, Rolf J., and Ulrich Hiemenz	Regional Integration Among Developing Countries: Survey of Past Performance and Agenda for Future Policy Action	12/91	English
8	Corden, W. Max	Integration and Trade Policy in the Former Soviet Union	06/92	English
9	Greenaway, David, and Chris Milner	The Fiscal Implications of Trade Policy Reform: Theory and Evidence	11/93	English
10	Gisselquist, David	Import Barriers for Agricultural Inputs	12/94	English
11	Gisselquist, David, and Charles Benbrook	Technology Transfer, Competition and Trade Liberalization for Low-Risk Pest Management	11/96	English

332

Table A.4. *UNDP/World Bank Trade Expansion Program—Other Products*

Number	Author(s)	Title	Date	Language
1	Horlick, Gary	Comments on Costa Rica's Antidumping Countervailing Duties Law (report to the Government of Costa Rica)	1992	English
2	Mahler, Walter, and Kazi Matin, et al.	Uganda: Tariff and Tax Policy and Administration (report to Government of Uganda prepared by joint TEP-IMF mission)	2/93	English
3	Chuang, Shui-Chi	Duty Drawback System/Practice—The Republic of China (report to the Government of Costa Rica)	8/93	English
4	Chuang, Shui-Chi	Propuesta de reforma a los incentivos a la exportación (report to the Government of Costa Rica)	8/93	Spanish
5	Havrylyshyn, Oleh	Integrating Ukraine in the World Economy: World Experience in Trade Liberalization (conference volume)	1993	Russian and Ukrainian
6	Connolly, Michael, and Jaime de Melo, eds.	The Effects of Protectionism on a Small Country: The Case of Uruguay (World Bank Regional and Sectoral Studies)	1994	English
7	Gupta, Shyama, Garry Pursell, and John Nash, eds.	Trade Policy Reforms (published by Macmillan India Ltd. for Indian Council for Research on International Economic Relations)	1994	English
8	Michalopoulos, Constantine, and David Tarr, eds.	Trade in the New Independent States. Studies of Economies in Transformation (jointly with Europe and Central Asia Regional Vice Presidency of World Bank)	1994	English and Russian
9	Foroutan, Faezeh, and John Nash, eds.	Trade Policy and Exchange Rate Reform in Sub-Saharan Africa: What Went Right? What Went Wrong? What Lessons for the Future? (mimeo)	forthcoming	English
10	Carr, Peter	Republic of Georgia: Draft Law on Foreign Investment (Amendments) and Law on Free Zones	6/96	English
11	Fisker, Jeppe, Claus Nielsen, and Kim Bak	UNDP/World Bank Trade Expansion Program for Georgia (Technical Assistance on Customs Issues)	4/96	English and Russian

Table A.5. *UNDP/World Bank Trade Expansion Program Country Reports by Title and Subject*

Country report title	Mission date	FP	ER	TR	EP	FI	CP	IN	AG	RA	Other	Language
1. Poland: Policies for Trade Promotion	05/88	X	X		X						X[a]	E
2. Guatemala: An Evaluation of a Recent Tariff Reform Proposal	06/87		X	X	X			X	X		X[b]	E
3. Mali: Economic Policy and International Trade	07/88	X		X	X[c]		X	X	X		X[d]	E,F
4. Madagascar: politique économique, commerce extérieur et développement	02/90	X	X	X	X		X		X		X[e]	F
5. Uruguay: Trade Reforms and Economic Efficiency	12/89	X	X	X	X			X[f]		X	X[g]	E
6. Uganda: An Agenda for Trade Liberalization	09/89	X	X	X	X			X	X			E
7. Morocco 2000: An Open and Competitive Economy	09/89			X	X	X		X		X		E,F
8. Czechoslovakia: Integrating into the Global Economy: A Transition Strategy	02/91			X	X		X	X[h]			X[i]	E
9. Costa Rica: Strengthening Links to the World Economy	08/91	X	X	X	X						X[j]	E,S
10. Peru: Toward a More Open Economy	03/91	X[k]	X	X	X			X	X	X		E
11. Kenya: The Challenge of Promoting Exports	11/90	X	X		X			X	X		X[l]	E
12. Mauritius: Toward the 21st Century	02/92	X	X		X[m]			X			X[n]	E
13. Vietnam: Policies for Transition to an Open Economy	09/92	X	X	X	X	X			X[o]		X[p]	E, V

(table continues on following page)

(Table A.5 continued)

Country report title	Mission date	FP	ER	TR	EP	FI	CP	IN	AG	RA	Other	Language
14. Romania: Restructuring to Face the World Economy	12/92		X	X	X	X	X	X	X	X	X[q]	E
15. Mongolia: Toward a Stable, Open Market Economy	08/92	X	X	X	X[c]				X		X[s]	E
16. Zimbabwe: Consolidating the Trade Liberalization	02/94	X		X	X		X[c]	X	X	X		E
17. Georgia: Trade Policy for a Successful Transition	10/94		X		X	X	X		X		X[a]	E

Key to topics and languages
AG: Agricultural Sector
CP: Credit Policy
EP: Export Promotion and Removal of Export Taxes
ER: Exchange Rate and Foreign Exchange Policy
FI: Foreign Investment and Capital Movement Liberalization
FP: Fiscal Policy or Tax Structure
IN: Industrial and Manufacturing Sectors
RA: Regional Arrangement
TR: Tariff Reform/Import Liberalization
Languages: E (English), F (French), S (Spanish), V (Vietnamese), G (Georgian)
Note: Other issues were addressed in the following notes:

a. Poland: monetary imbalance and excess demand, price and wage reforms and competition, investment and materials allocations.
b. Guatemala: nominal and effective rates of protection, equilibrium real exchange rate.
c. Mali: price policy for agricultural exports (cotton).
d. Mali: impact of macroeconomic policy on competitiveness.
e. Madagascar: restrictive monetary policy, transparency and credibility of different policies.
f. Uruguay: automobile sector protection.

(table notes continue on following page)

(Table A.5 notes continued)

g. Uruguay: labor market, role of the private sector, reference prices.
h. Czechoslovakia: concentration on heavy industry, energy, and resource-intensive exports.
i. Czechoslovakia: reorientation of trade after the collapse of CMEA market, support services for exports.
j. Costa Rica: trade facilitation and transportation infrastructure.
k. Peru: fiscal deficit, interest rates, money, and inflation.
l. Kenya: consistency of import liberalization, macroeconomic environment and promotion of private investment.
m. Mauritius: export processing zones.
n. Mauritius: sugar sector, textiles and apparel sectors, factor market policies and incentives (land, financial markets, investment incentives, labor markets).
o. Vietnam: taxation of agricultural exports.
p. Vietnam: export-import licensing system.
q. Romania: energy policy.
r. Mongolia: free trade and special processing zones.
s. Mongolia: reform of domestic distribution and state order systems.
t. Zimbabwe: financial liberalization, credit, and investment.
u. Georgia: trade finance, state order finance.

Index

Acta de Buenos Aires *(1990)*, 137–38

"Adding-up problem," agriculture and, 10–11; Africa *versus* Southeast Asia and, 11; traditional export crops, optimal taxes and, 11

Adjustment loans: strong *versus* weak reform and, 1–2

Africa. *See also* SubSaharan Africa; *specific countries:* convertible currency, major financial centers and, 80–81; own funds liberalization and, 72–73; trade liberalization credibility in, 69–70

Agriculture, trade reform and, 10–12, 277–308; antiexport bias reduction, 288–96, 306; changes affecting, 281–86; export promotion policies and, 285; growth and, 296–98, 299–301; low-income African countries, 281; macroeconomic policy and, 282–84; macroeconomic variables, 286–88; measuring protection concepts of, 289–90; middle-income countries, 281, 285, 288; related reforms and, 298–305, 307; related reforms summary, 302–4; total tax on, 290; transitional economies, 285

Allende, Salvador, 175–76

Antidumping measures: CEE European Agreements and, 117; competition law and, 217n; European Union and, 24; exemption from, foreign aid and, 26; GATT provisions for, 216, 219; injury-based import relief and, 217; Morocco, 227, 229; NAFTA policies on, 24, 112n; Peru, 232–33; trade policy debate and, 325; trade reform and, 13–14

Antiexport bias: macroeconomic disequilibrium and, 34, 35; measurement difficulties and, 35–36; reducing, 288–96, 306

Argentina: *versus* Chile trade reform, 178–79; MERCOSUR and, 137–38; trade reform in, 177–78

Auction(s): exchange rate mechanisms reform and, 73–75; foreign exchange markets and, 5; institutional transitions and, 70; in Nigeria, 83; participating agents in, 75; in Poland, 84; in Romania, 84; sales agents in, 5, 75; source of money for, 73–74; transparency of, *versus* interbank markets, 77; in Uganda, 84

Authoritarian regimes, political economies of, 44, 45, 57–58

"Bad start" countries, macroeconomic disequilibrium and, 34; internal or terms-of-trade shocks and, 35

Balance of payments exceptions, GATT, 216; restrictions to safeguard, 218–19

Bangladesh: Food for Work program, 267; trade and tax reform in, 183

Banks, commercial. *See also* Central bank; Interbank markets: foreign exchange auction and, 5, 82–85; interbank markets and, 76–77

Bauer, P. T., 44n

Bell, L., 262, 263

Berg, Elliot, 26, 27

Bhagwati, Jagdish, 22, 87, 108n, 109, 119

"Big bang" approach, trade reform, 3

"Big shock" countries, macroeconomic disequilibrium and, 34

Bolivia, Emergency Social Fund program, 267

Bonded factory control system, 16, 208–9; Taiwan (China), 189

Borrowing, temporary public, exchange rate overshoot and, 66

Bosworth, P., 113n

Brada, Josef C., 88